Companies Act 2006: A Guide for Private Companies

Second edition

Companies Act 2006: A Guide for Private Companies

Second edition

Peter Van Duzer LLB
Solicitor

Company Secretary

JORDANS

Published by
Jordan Publishing Limited
21 St Thomas Street
Bristol BS1 6JS

British Library Cataloguing-in-Publication Data

A catalogue record for this book is available from the British Library.

ISBN 978 1 84661 133 9

Typeset by Letterpart Ltd, Reigate, Surrey

Printed in Great Britain by Antony Rowe, Chippenham, Wilts

PREFACE

This book states law as set out in the Companies Act 2006. It seeks to cover the main items that are likely to be encountered by a private company. However, please note that this law has been implemented in stages from 6 November 2006 and at the time of writing is still not all in force. The final provisions are due to come into force on 1 October 2009. Appendix 3 sets out a commencement table giving the date of commencement and relevant implementing statutory instrument for sections of the Act.

The staged implementation of the new law has resulted in extensive detailed transitional provisions that apply to existing companies. Chapter 12 gives further information about the coming into force of the Act and many of the transitional provisions that apply to existing companies. Readers should refer to the website dealing with the Act that is maintained by the Department for Business Enterprise and Regulatory Reform (known as 'BERR') for up-to-date information about commencement and supporting statutory instruments (see Appendix 5 for website details).

Each relevant Chapter has a separate section at the end setting out the major changes made by the Act to previous law regarding the matters covered by that Chapter and also giving brief details regarding the commencement dates. This indicates the relevant sections of the Act and can be used for quick reference.

I should like to express thanks to Mary Kenny of Jordan Publishing for her help with the second edition.

Peter Van Duzer
15 October 2008

CONTENTS

Chapter 4
Legal Capacity, the Articles and the Company's Constitution – What can the Company do and how?   **39**

Chapter 8
Annual Compliance – Registers, Records, Annual Return and Accounts **135**

TABLE OF STATUTES

References are to paragraph numbers.

TABLE OF STATUTORY INSTRUMENTS

References are to paragraph numbers.

Chapter 1

INTRODUCTION AND BACKGROUND TO THE 2006 ACT

IMPLEMENTATION

1.1   At the time of publication of this edition the Companies Act 2006 is still in the process of being brought into force. This implementation has been a staged process. It started in November 2006, when the Act received Royal Assent, and is forecast to complete on 1 October 2009, when the final parts of the Act are to be activated. Implementation has involved eight separate commencement orders, each of which has its own transitional provisions. The commencement orders are listed in **Appendix 3**, which gives further information. The transitional provisions are referred to in the text where relevant. **Appendix 3** also lists the commencement dates for the different sections in the Act and **Chapter 12** covers the more important transitional provisions that are likely to be encountered in practice by a private company.

BACKGROUND

1.2   The Act is the culmination of a comprehensive review of company law that started in 1998. The review was launched with a consultation document entitled *Modern Company Law for a Competitive Economy*. The original aim of the review was to make the UK a good place to do business by bringing company law up to date to meet modern business needs.

1.3   There was much discussion about how to make law more relevant to small businesses, given that much of the law was still based on nineteenth century concepts designed for investment in railway companies. The consultation document suggested (perhaps rightly) that the development of company law in the twentieth century had come mostly from a series of reactions to 'scandals and mischiefs' resulting in a 'patchwork of legislation that is immensely complex and seriously out of date'. The consultation document further pointed out that the existing company law suffered from over-formal language, excessive detail and over-regulation. So simplification and rationalisation of company law were themes of the review from the beginning. Extensive consultation and a series of additional consultative documents followed, looking at particular areas of company law.

1.4   The possibility of a separate small companies' statute was briefly considered, but was rejected early on as so many of the provisions of company law can apply equally to small and large companies. However, there was recognition that the regulatory burden for small companies needed to be simplified. This has resulted in a 'think small first' approach (see below).

1.5   During the company law review, events such as the collapse of Enron in the USA, with massive loss of shareholder value, focused attention on public confidence in company financial statements and the audit process. Consequently parts of the review looked more closely at questions in connection with the audit of accounts, the accountability of companies with publicly traded shares to their shareholders and related questions of corporate governance. Once again company law reform reacted to a perceived 'scandal and mischief'.

1.6   The twin themes of reducing the burden for small companies and ensuring that companies with publicly traded shares are properly accountable has resulted in a further divergence of the compliance requirements applying to private companies on the one hand and public and quoted companies on the other.

1.7   The original Bill as introduced to Parliament (then known as 'The Company Law Reform Bill') repealed large parts of the Companies Act 1985 which were replaced by new provisions in the 2006 Act, but also left some of the old provisions of the 1985 Act in place. This would have resulted in a 'patchwork' of two Acts and the need to cross refer between the two pieces of legislation. As the Bill progressed through Parliament it was recognised that this was likely to make company law more inaccessible and difficult to apply in practice. So the name of the Bill was changed to 'The Companies Bill' and Government agreed to add a large number of clauses to the original Bill, restating much of the law previously contained in the Companies Act 1985. This resulted in the consolidation of the majority of company law provisions into the 2006 Act and it becoming the longest ever considered by Parliament! The few parts of the Companies Acts 1985 and 1989 that remain include provisions dealing with investigations into companies, provisions about the Financial Reporting Council and the law applicable to community interest companies.

1.8   However, despite the consolidation, quite a lot of the detail of the law applicable to companies remains outside the 2006 Act. This is because in many specific areas the Act gives power to make regulations regarding the detail of the relevant provisions. These include items such as the disclosure requirements on company documentation and websites and at business locations, the requirements relating to registration and disclosure by branches of foreign companies, the details of company accounts requirements and penalties for the late filing of accounts. These statutory instruments are referred to in the text where considered relevant. This means that there is still a lot of company law and regulation from different sources to assimilate, for private companies as well as public ones.

MAIN THEMES OF THE COMPANIES ACT 2006

1.9   The Act has four main themes:

1   **A 'think small first approach'** – so that the basic law applies to private companies and additional requirements apply to public, quoted and traded companies. This is a reversal of the previous approach, which applied the law to all companies, but permitted certain exemptions in some circumstances for smaller companies or if all shareholders agreed. As well as building from the base requirements up, depending on the type of company, the Act provides an 'opt in' approach for private companies, rather than 'opt out'. So the default position for a private company is that it has the minimum amount of regulation applicable to it. This will result in an easier life for private companies in relation to annual compliance. However private companies are still subject to a large amount of detailed regulation that is applicable to all companies.

2   **Making it easier to set up and run a company** – this stems from the desire to make the UK a more attractive place for business. It means some changes of process and some simplifications of areas of company law that were seen as difficult or impeding business flexibility. However, in its final form, the Act still contains a mass of detail.

3   **Enhancing shareholder engagement and a long term investment culture** – these changes are aimed mainly at listed companies. They stem mainly from a desire to make directors of these companies more accountable to shareholders and enhance the abilities of shareholders in this respect. These are beyond the remit of this book, but they do illustrate the increasing gulf between the law applicable to private companies and that applicable to public companies with traded shares.

4   **Flexibility for the future** – the Government originally intended to take power to alter company law for the future by way of statutory instrument. The aim was to make company law more responsive to changing business needs. The argument in support of this was that a review of company law has resulted in changes to the law that will finally come into force fully over 11 years after commencement of the review. This is too slow for the needs of modern business. The argument against this power was that government may change the law without proper scrutiny. In the event the general power to amend company law by regulation faced stiff opposition and was removed from the Bill. However, many specific parts of the Act still empower the Government to supplement the Act by regulations, which may of course be changed much more easily than the main Act.

The difference is that it is only in these specific areas that change may be easily implemented. So in the end certainty and restraint on unfettered Government power won over the aim of flexibility.

1.10 The provisions of the Act extend to the whole of the United Kingdom, including Northern Ireland. This is a departure from previous practice. Previously, company law provisions applicable to Northern Ireland were contained in an Ordinance, which tended to follow the provisions applicable to the rest of the UK but with differing clause numbers.

1.11 In this book the Companies Act 2006 is referred to as 'the Act'. After much thought I have also chosen to refer to 'the Registrar' rather than use the term 'Companies House' by which most of us now know the Companies Registry in Cardiff, in deference to the fact that the Act also covers the Registries in Scotland and Northern Ireland.

Chapter 2

COMPANY FORMATION AND TYPES OF COMPANY

INTRODUCTION TO COMPANY FORMATION

2.1 The procedures for forming a company are simplified by the Act. Provisions have been included specifically to remove any remaining obstacles to the efficient formation of companies wholly by electronic means on-line. The 2006 Act law relating to company formation, the company's constitution and related matters is mostly due to come into force on 1 October 2009 and the first companies will be formed under the Act on 5 October 2009 (see **12.43**). This chapter sets out the law as it will be from 1 October 2009. Please see the summary at the end of this chapter for the commencement dates of specific changes introduced by the Act.

2.2 Companies are formed by delivering the required information in the required format to the Registrar in the correct jurisdiction (England and Wales, Scotland or Northern Ireland). The correct jurisdiction depends on the intended location of the registered office of the new company. If what is submitted is correct, the Registrar will issue a certificate of incorporation. The certificate is conclusive evidence that the company is duly registered.

2.3 The Act provides that all companies can be formed by a single subscriber. A company may not be formed for an unlawful purpose.

2.4 The incorporation documents required by the Act to be delivered to the Registrar are:

- the memorandum of association (in the prescribed form and authenticated by each subscriber, see below)

- the application for registration (which must state and contain required information, including, for a company with share capital, a statement of initial shareholdings and a statement of capital)

- articles of association (to the extent that the standard prescribed form of articles for that type of company are not adopted), and

- a statement of compliance.

2.5   The memorandum of association has been reduced to a prescribed form that evidences the intention and consent of the subscribers to form a company and become members of it on incorporation.

2.6   The 'documents' may either be delivered in paper form or by using one of the electronic methods to form a company that have been approved by the Registrar. Increasing numbers of companies are formed electronically due to the advantages of speed and simplicity. Normally companies in England, Wales and Scotland formed by the submission of information electronically are incorporated within 24 hours without the payment of any additional fee. The Government announced some time ago that the Registrar will seek to offer a web incorporation facility, so that specialist software will not be needed, but currently there are no details on this and it has not yet been implemented. Up-to-date information can be obtained from the Companies House website.

2.7   The prescribed fee must be paid to the Registrar by one of the methods provided. Currently there are fee differentials depending on whether a company is formed by submitting information electronically or in paper format and whether a 'same-day' formation is required. Electronic submission results in cheaper fees. A same-day formation incurs a slightly increased fee. Up-to-date information about fee levels and current methods of electronic incorporation can be obtained from the Companies House website.

2.8   A large proportion of companies are in practice formed by specialist 'formation agent' companies that provide articles of association, are very familiar with the requirements of Companies House in Cardiff and have appropriate electronic links to provide a speedy service.

OVERVIEW OF COMPANY STRUCTURE AND TYPES OF COMPANY

2.9   A company is a separate legal entity that can only be formed if the provisions of the Act (and regulations made under the Act) are fully complied with. Every company will have at least one member (described in a company limited by shares as a shareholder) and at least one director. A public company must have at least two directors and a company secretary. Every company must have at least one director who is a natural person, but otherwise corporate directors are permitted. It is not possible to appoint a person under 16 as a director. Further details about directors are contained in **Chapter 5**.

2.10   In brief summary, member(s) are the owner(s) of a company and the director(s) control and manage the affairs and activities of the company on behalf of the members. So a company is a flexible entity that can encompass separation of the ownership and management of the entity. This flexibility combined with separate legal personality and the possibility for limited liability of the members is the reason for the success of a company as an entity. If separation of ownership and management is not required at any stage the member(s) and director(s) can be the same people. So a private company can be formed, owned and managed by one person.

2.11 The first person(s) that agree in the formation documents to become members of the company and, in the case of a company that has share capital, to take at least one share each in the company on its incorporation are generally known as 'subscribers'. As stated above, all companies can now be formed by one subscriber.

2.12 It is possible for a private company to have a company secretary, responsible for such matters as the directors may decide, but the Act does not require it. A public company must have a company secretary with the required qualifications/experience.

2.13 It is possible to form the following types of company.

* a company limited by shares

* a company limited by guarantee

* an unlimited company.

2.14 A company may be a private company or a public company. The Act defines a 'private company' as any company that is not a public company. A 'public company' is a limited company with shares that has complied with the requirements to be a public company and whose certificate of incorporation states that it is a public company. The principle reason for forming a public company is that private companies cannot offer shares (or other securities) to the public or allot or agree to allot shares (or other securities) with a view to their being offered to the public. 'Offer to the public' has a wide meaning, as described briefly in **Chapter 9**. A company or company promoter that is considering offering to allot shares to others should take legal advice. Note that a public company does not necessarily have to be listed or allow its shares to be publicly traded. Many public companies are formed for the kudos of the 'plc' name and many are privately owned. Public companies are not covered by this book, but note that before a public company is permitted to commence trading it must comply with minimum issued share capital requirements and obtain a trading certificate from the Registrar.

2.15 It is also possible to form Community Interest Companies (CICs) in accordance with Part 2 of the Companies (Audit, Investigations and Community Enterprise) Act 2004. A CIC is a specific type of company, designed for social enterprises that want to use their profits and assets for the public good. CICs are also outside the remit of this book.

COMPANY LIMITED BY SHARES

2.16 This is the most common form of company and is the type with which most people are familiar. It is used for most forms of business and commercial enterprise. Normally the proportion of ownership rights will be the proportion of shares owned (subject to any special share rights). So that a person owning 70 per cent of the shares will have the right to receive 70 per cent of the profits distributed, be entitled to cast 70 per cent of the votes of shareholders and be entitled to receive 70 per cent of surplus assets on a winding up of the company.

2.17 A person becomes a member of a company limited by shares by subscribing for new shares issued by the company, or by the transfer of shares to him by a person who is already an existing shareholder, and in addition in each case by entry of his name in the register of members. If you cease to hold shares (e g because you have transferred them) you cease to be a member of the company. Members are referred to as 'shareholders'. When a share is first issued by a company it will have a nominal or 'par' value, which must be paid to the company. Sometimes a share may be issued by a company for a 'premium', which requires payment to the company of not only the nominal value, but also an additional sum of money. Usually full payment is made to the company for the share by the recipient when the share is issued. However, this is not always the case, so that a share may be issued as an 'unpaid share' in respect of which no payment has been made to the company; or a 'partly paid share', in respect of which some money is still owing to the company. See **Chapter 9** for further explanation.

2.18 A 'company limited by shares' is a company that has the liability of its members limited to the amount (if any) unpaid on the company's shares. So if the amount due on the shares (whether nominal value or nominal value and premium) is paid to the company at the time that the shares are issued, then no further payment is required from the members even if the company becomes insolvent and is wound up. On the other hand, if money is still owing to the company under the terms on which the share was issued, then the shareholder can be required to pay the unpaid amount towards the company's debts if it is wound up and further monies are required.

2.19 A company limited by shares may be formed as either a private company or a public company (subject to the requirements of the Act).

COMPANY LIMITED BY GUARANTEE

2.20 This form of company is used by many different types of non-profit making organisations. It is no longer possible to form a company limited by guarantee with share capital (and has not been possible in Great Britain since 1980 nor in Northern Ireland since 1983), although some rare examples are still on the register of companies.

2.21　A person becomes a member of a company limited by guarantee in accordance with the provisions of its articles of association. These may, for instance, provide that the directors shall decide whether to admit a person to membership, or provide that only persons satisfying a requirement (such as ownership of a unit on an estate managed by the company, or membership of a club) can become members. A person must also agree to become a member and be entered in the register of members. Normally the articles provide that a person ceases to be a member by resignation, but the articles may contain different provisions providing that a person automatically ceases to be a member on the happening of a certain event (eg on ceasing to be an owner of a unit on an estate owned by the company or ceasing to be a member of a club). Membership of a guarantee company is not transferable and in normal circumstances each member has one vote. So companies limited by guarantee are attractive to organisations that do not wish any one party to build up a stake which will give a decisive influence (eg golf clubs that are concerned about a controlling party attempting to sell their land for development).

2.22　The liability of the members of a company limited by guarantee is limited to such amount as the members undertake to contribute to the assets of the company in the event of its being wound up. The amount of the guarantee can be any amount, but in practice is almost invariably £1 for each member. The amount of the guarantee is set out in the 'statement of guarantee' filed with the incorporation documents (see below).

UNLIMITED COMPANY

2.23　An unlimited company is a company that does not have any limit on the liability of its members. So if the company becomes insolvent and is wound up, the members can be required to contribute money to pay the debts of the company without any limit on the amount. Such a company provides the advantages of corporate personality and the possibility to separate ownership and management between shareholders and directors, but it will not provide the advantage of limited liability. So unlimited companies are relatively uncommon. They have been used in the past to take advantage of the possibility of not filing accounts at the Registrar (as some unlimited companies are not required to publicly file accounts) or to take advantage of simpler provisions regarding reduction of issued share capital. However, the tightening of provisions over the years regarding the requirement to deliver accounts to the Registrar where an unlimited company is owned by limited liability entities has made them less attractive. The simplified provisions in the Act regarding reduction of issued share capital by a company may mean that unlimited companies are also used less often where a reduction of capital is required. So they may be used less, except in specific situations where they are deemed suitable and the disadvantage of unlimited liability is deemed to be an acceptable risk. It is usual for an unlimited company to have share capital.

MEMORANDUM OF ASSOCIATION

2.24   Prior to the Act, the memorandum of association used to be a document which set out the objects for which the company was formed (with accompanying powers) together with other information such as the name, jurisdiction of registered office, limited liability and authorised share capital of the company. It was required to be signed by the subscribers.

2.25   The Act almost completely changes the nature of the memorandum of association, but does not do away with it altogether. Under the provisions of the Act, it is now used only to evidence the intention of the subscribers to form a company and become members of it on its incorporation. The other information previously contained in the 'old style' memorandum is now either contained in the 'new style' application for registration or the requirement for it has been abolished.

2.26   The memorandum of association must now be in the form prescribed (whether paper or electronic) and is a memorandum stating that the subscribers wish to form a company under the Act, and agree to become members of the company and, in the case of a company that is to have share capital, to take at least one share each. So it is no longer part of the company's constitution and it is not capable of later alteration. The memorandum must be authenticated by each subscriber; either by signature on a paper form or by an approved form of electronic assent if it is submitted electronically.

2.27   For a discussion of the effect of the new provisions on companies formed before the provisions of the Act took effect, please refer to **Chapter 4**. In brief summary, other provisions in the 'old style' memorandum of such companies are now treated as provisions of the company's articles.

APPLICATION FOR REGISTRATION OF THE COMPANY – INTRODUCTION

2.28   The application for registration must state:

1   the company's proposed name

2   whether the company's registered office is to be in England and Wales (or in Wales), in Scotland or in Northern Ireland

3   whether the liability of the members is to be limited and if so whether it is to be limited by shares or guarantee

4   whether the company is to be a private or a public company, and

5   the name and address of the agent for the subscribers that is delivering the application on behalf of the subscribers (if there is one).

2.29   The application must also contain:

1   a statement of the company's proposed officers (see below), and

2   a statement of the intended address of the registered office, and

3   a copy of any proposed articles of association (to the extent that these are not supplied by the default application of model articles prescribed under the Act), and

4   in the case of a company that is to have share capital a statement of capital and initial shareholdings, or

5   in the case of a company that is to be limited by guarantee, a statement of guarantee.

STATEMENT OF THE COMPANY'S PROPOSED OFFICERS

2.30   This must contain the required particulars of the person(s) who is/are to be the first directors of the company. For a private company that proposes to appoint a secretary on incorporation (which is optional for a private company but compulsory for a public company) it is also necessary for it to contain the required particulars of the person(s) who is/are to be the first secretary(ies) of the company.

2.31   The 'required particulars' for an individual who is to be a director are:

- name and any former name (see below for detail)

- a service address (see below and **5.14**)

- the country or state (or part of the UK) in which he is usually resident

- nationality

- business occupation (if any)

- date of birth.

2.32   In this context '**name**' means a person's Christian name (or other forename) and surname, except that in the case of a peer, or an individual usually known by a title, the title may be stated instead of his/her Christian name (or other forename) and surname or in addition to either or both of them. Note that '**former name**' means a name by which an individual was formerly known for business purposes and that where a person was formerly known by more than one such name, each of them must be stated. It is not necessary to include a former name: in the case of a peer or an individual normally known by a British title, where the former name is one by which the person was known previous to the adoption of or succession to the title; or in the case of any person, where the former name was changed or disused before that person attained the age of 16 years or has been changed or disused for 20 years or more. This is a change from the previous law, which did not refer to 'a name by which the individual was formerly known for business purposes' and which provided that in the case of a married woman, the name by which she was known previous to marriage did not have to be stated. So the Act requires that a married woman who has changed her name on marriage would have to state her former name if it was a name by which she was formerly known for business purposes.

2.33 See **5.14** for a fuller discussion regarding service addresses. A service address may be stated to be 'The company's registered office'. Again, this is a modification to the previous law. Previously directors were required to give their residential address unless a 'confidentiality order' had been granted on the basis that the disclosure of the director's address would create a risk that the director or a person living with the director would be subjected to violence or intimidation. Under the Act, all directors will use a service address. Only the service address is put on the public record after the certificate is granted and the residential address of the director is a 'protected address' to which only certain specified public authorities and credit reference agencies have access. The major problem with the practical effectiveness of this is that there is no provision requiring the Registrar to 'weed' previous documents from the public record which contain the director's address from when it was previously disclosed under requirements of the old legislation. Therefore for directors that have previously notified their residential address in respect of another company (for instance a company in the same group) a service address is not completely effective.

2.34 If the director is a body corporate (eg another UK company, a UK LLP, or a foreign company) or a firm that is a legal person under the law by which it is governed (eg a partnership governed by Scottish law) then the 'required particulars' are different. However, if a body corporate or firm that is a legal person is to be a director, it is important to remember that every company must have at least one director who is a natural person. The 'required particulars' for a corporate body (or a firm that is a legal person) that is to be a director are:

- corporate or firm name

- registered or principal office

- in the case of a company governed by the law of a state in the European Economic Area to which the First Company Law Directive applies, particulars of: (i) the register in which the company public file is kept (including details of the relevant state), and (ii) the registration number in that register

- in any other case, particulars of: (i) the legal form of the company or firm and the law by which it is governed; and (ii) if applicable, the register in which it is entered (including details of the state) and its registration number in that register.

2.35 If the private company is to have a secretary on incorporation, the required details in the case of an individual who is to be secretary are:

- name and any former name

- address.

The address required to be stated in the register is a service address and may be stated to be: 'The company's registered office'.

2.36 It is quite common to appoint a company as secretary. In the case of a body corporate or a firm that is a legal person under the law by which it is governed, the required particulars of the secretary are the same details as those required of a corporate director.

2.37 The statement must also contain consent by each of the persons named as director or secretary to act in the relevant capacity.

STATEMENT OF REGISTERED OFFICE

2.38 This is important. The registered office of the company is its official address to which all communications and notices may be addressed. The location of the address of the registered office (ie whether it is in England and Wales, Scotland or Northern Ireland) dictates the jurisdiction in which the company is registered and therefore the official registry to which the incorporation information must be delivered.

2.39 A company must at all times have a registered office. It must be a physical location and a PO Box is not acceptable. Service of a document on a company is effective if it is sent by post to, or left at, a company's registered office. Court papers and official notices of all types will go to the registered office. So it is important that the company ensures that there are proper procedures in place to deal promptly with documents and post received at the registered office.

2.40 A company may change its registered office by giving notice in the prescribed form to the Registrar. The change takes effect upon the change being registered by the Registrar, but until the end of the period of 14 days beginning with the date on which it is registered a person may validly serve any document on the company at the address previously registered. Many companies run into problems through failing to notify changes of registered office to the Registrar promptly. So it is important, during the ongoing life of the company, to ensure that any change of registered office is notified promptly and that appropriate arrangements are put in place to ensure that items received at, or addressed to, the old registered office will be promptly received by the company for a period of at least 14 days after registration of the change (and in practice probably for a longer period).

2.41   There are special rules applicable to companies with their registered office in Wales, which provide that a company with its registered office in Wales may state that its registered office is in Wales (rather than 'England and Wales').

2.42   During consultation about company law reform, there was some discussion about the possibility of allowing companies to change their registered office between Scotland and England and Wales, and vice versa. This has not been provided for. So currently a company with its registered office in Scotland (or England and Wales) cannot change its registered office to the other jurisdiction.

ARTICLES OF ASSOCIATION

2.43   The articles of association are the constitution of the company. It is possible to form a limited company without delivering articles of association to the Registrar. The Act provides for model forms of articles to be prescribed for companies of different types. It further provides that in the case of a limited company, if articles are not registered, or if articles are registered, then in so far as they do not exclude or modify the relevant model articles, the relevant model articles will form part of the company's constitution as if articles in that form had been duly registered.

2.44   So some companies may choose not to register articles and instead to rely wholly on the model form of articles prescribed under the Act. However, these are likely to be a minority.

2.45   Most companies will wish to ensure that their constitution fully meets their needs and instead of relying totally on the model form articles will choose to deliver articles to the Registrar that are specifically designed for a company with their specific circumstances in mind (eg a single person company, a wholly owned subsidiary etc).

2.46   For a fuller discussion of articles of association, the model articles and the company's constitution, please refer to **Chapter 4**.

STATEMENT OF CAPITAL AND INITIAL SHAREHOLDINGS

2.47 This is required for a company that is to have share capital. It contains information that would previously have been contained in the memorandum of association under the old legislation and is also a snapshot of the company's share capital at a particular point in time. It must be delivered to the Registrar on the formation of the company and, as outlined in **Chapter 9**, notification to the Registrar is also required by a statement of capital when a company makes an alteration to its share capital. For incorporation, the statement of capital and initial shareholdings must state:

- the total number of shares of the company to be taken on formation by the subscribers to the memorandum of association

- the aggregate nominal value of those shares

- for each class of shares – (i) prescribed particulars of the rights attached to those shares; (ii) the total number of shares of that class, and (iii) the aggregate nominal value of the shares of that class, and

- the amount paid up and the amount (if any) to be unpaid on each share (whether on account of the nominal value of the share or by way of premium).

2.48 The statement of capital and initial shareholdings required on formation must contain such information as may be prescribed to identify the subscribers to the memorandum of association and it must state with respect to each subscriber:

- the number, nominal value (of each share) and class of shares to be taken by him on formation, and

- the amount paid up and the amount (if any) to be unpaid on each share (whether on account of the nominal value of the share or by way of premium).

2.49 The statement of capital should enable information about a company's share capital position to be easily understood from a search of the public record.

STATEMENT OF GUARANTEE

2.50 This is required for a company that is to be limited by guarantee. It is the equivalent of the statement that used to appear in the 'old style' memorandum.

2.51 It must contain such information as may be prescribed for the purpose of identifying the subscribers to the memorandum of association. It must state that each member undertakes that, if the company is wound up while he is a member, or within one year after he ceases to be a member, he will contribute to the assets of the company such amount as may be required for: (i) payment of the debts and liabilities of the company contracted before he ceases to be a member, (ii) payment of the costs, charges and expenses of winding up, and (iii) adjustment of the rights of contributories amongst themselves, not exceeding a 'specified amount'. In practice the 'specified amount' is almost invariably £1, so that no member of the company limited by guarantee should be required to contribute more than £1 by reason of membership.

STATEMENT OF COMPLIANCE

2.52 The statement of compliance is a statement that the requirements of the Act as to registration have been complied with. This statement does not need to be witnessed and may be in paper or electronic form. Rules will be made to specify who should make this statement. It is to be expected that the persons eligible will include a proposed director named in the statement of proposed officers and a solicitor engaged in the formation of the company.

CERTIFICATE OF INCORPORATION

2.53 If the Registrar is satisfied that the requirements of the Act as to registration have been complied with, the information filed will be placed on the public record and the Registrar will give a certificate that the company is incorporated.

2.54 The certificate of incorporation will state:

* the name and registered number of the company

* the date of its incorporation

* whether it is a limited or unlimited company, and if it is limited whether it is limited by shares or guarantee

* whether it is a private or a public company, and

* whether the company's registered office is in England and Wales (or in Wales), in Scotland or in Northern Ireland.

2.55 The certificate is conclusive evidence that the requirements of the Act as to registration have been complied with and that the company: (i) is duly registered under the Act, and (ii) where relevant, is duly registered as a limited company or public company.

REGISTERED NUMBER

2.56 It is important to note that the registered number is unique to the company and will not change. It is possible for a company to change its name (including a name that was previously used by a different company) but it is not possible for it to change its number. For this reason it is often helpful to include reference to the company number in legal documents, so that the company may be more easily identified in later years when it may have changed its name. For this reason the Registrar also uses the company number as the main identifier in the Registrar's public records.

EFFECT OF REGISTRATION OF A COMPANY

2.57 The registration of the company has the following effects as from the date of registration:

- the subscribers to the memorandum, together with such other persons as may from time to time become members of the company, are a body corporate by the name stated in the certificate of incorporation

- that body corporate is capable of exercising all the functions of an incorporated company

- the status and registered office are as stated in, or in connection with, the application for registration

- the persons named in the statement of proposed officers as director or secretary are deemed to have been appointed to that office

- the subscribers to the memorandum become members of the company and must be entered as such in its register of members and in the case of a company having share capital, the subscribers to the memorandum become holders of the shares specified in the statement of capital and initial shareholdings.

2.58 During the life of the company, every other person who agrees to become a member of the company, and whose name is entered in its register of members, is a member of the company (s 112).

SUMMARY OF MAJOR CHANGES INTRODUCED BY THE ACT

1   Any company may be formed by one subscriber (previously a public company or an unlimited company was required to be formed by two subscribers and have two members) (see s 7). *To be brought into force on 1 October 2009 by Commencement Order 8.*

2   Every company must have at least one director who is a natural person. A person under the age of 16 cannot be appointed a director. There is no longer any upper age limit for directors (see ss 155–159). *Brought into force on 1 October 2008 by Commencement Order 5, subject to transitional provisions for some companies in existence on 8 November 2006* (see **12.31**).

3   All individual directors (and proposed individual directors) will have a service address, to keep their residential address off the public record and in a protected register with restricted access. However old records maintained by the Registrar will not be removed (see ss 163–166 and 244–246). *To be brought into force on 1 October 2009 by Commencement Order 8.*

4   It is now optional whether to have a company secretary for a private company. So a private company may be formed, owned and managed by one person. If a private company does have a company secretary, his details must be entered on the public record (including a service address) (see ss 270 and 275–279). *Brought into force on 6 April 2008 by Commencement Order 5.*

5   The memorandum of association has been reduced to a prescribed form that evidences the intention and consent of the subscribers to form a company and become members of it on incorporation (see s 8). *To be brought into force on 1 October 2009 by Commencement Order 8.*

6   Companies with share capital will no longer have an 'authorised share capital' but instead just have an 'issued share capital'. Shares in a limited company still have a fixed nominal value (sometimes called 'par value') (see ss 10 and 540–548). *To be brought into force on 1 October 2009 by Commencement Order 8.*

7   The new 'application for registration' will state or contain much of the information that previously was submitted in the memorandum of association or form 10. There have been some changes to the detail of information required about directors (and any company secretary) that must be provided, including provision for service addresses (see ss 9–12, 162–166 and 277–279). *To be brought into force on 1 October 2009 by Commencement Order 8.*

8   The application for registration will also contain, in the case of a company that is to have share capital, a 'statement of capital and initial shareholdings'. In the case of a company that is to be limited by guarantee it must instead contain a 'statement of guarantee' (see ss 10 and 11). *To be brought into force on 1 October 2009 by Commencement Order 8.*

9   New model forms of articles are to be prescribed for limited companies that will apply to the extent that they are not excluded or modified by the company's own articles (see ss 19 and 20). *To be brought into force on 1 October 2009. Drafts of the model forms are available via the BERR website* (see **Appendix 5** for the website address) and the final form is expected to be available for reference from the beginning of 2009.

10 There is now no need for a statutory declaration on formation of a company. The old statutory declaration and electronic statement to confirm compliance with requirements of the Act as to registration of a company have been replaced with a 'statement of compliance' that does not need to be witnessed and may be made in paper or electronic form (see s 13). *To be brought into force on 1 October 2009 by Commencement Order 8.*

Chapter 3

COMPANY NAMES

INTRODUCTION TO COMPANY NAMES

3.1   The Act deals with company names (in Part 5) and the use of business trading names (in Part 41). These provisions cover:

- company names registration and restrictions on the words and characters etc in company names – due to come into force on 1 October 2009

- issues connected with similarities between company names – some of which came into force on 1 October 2008

- how a company may change its name – due to come into force on 1 October 2009

- requirements to disclose a company's name (so that customers, suppliers and others know who they are dealing with) – which came into force on 1 October 2008

- restrictions on the use of inappropriate or misleading business names – due to come into force on 1 October 2009

- requirements to disclose the name(s) of the individual or partners carrying on a business under a business name and an address for service of documents on that business – due to come into force on 1 October 2009.

3.2   Anyone dealing with company names must also have due regard to the common law rules regarding the use of business names and possible trade mark rights. The registration of a company name may be just one part of the work required in connection with a new name. If it is to have value, additional checks and registrations are often appropriate (see below).

3.3   Company names are an area where disputes often can arise. There are many cases where a name is registered (or used in business) which inadvertently (or in some cases deliberately) infringes or is alleged to infringe the goodwill owned by others, because it is confusingly similar to a name used by another business. Many cases of this type are pursued through the courts and there is a large body of case law in connection with such matters. This infringement is generally referred to as 'passing off' and the common law established by the courts is intended to prevent traders misrepresenting themselves in such a way that they injure the business or goodwill of another business. Specialist legal advice is recommended in such cases.

3.4   Due regard must also be taken of the trade and service marks registration system, that provides for the registration of names, logos and some other recognisable items used in connection with certain types of goods and services. Registration of a trade or service mark provides a greater degree of protection for this intellectual property. Again specialist advice is required in this area.

3.5   There have in the past been well documented cases of attempts to register a company name with the intention of using the goodwill of others, suggesting association with another business or person, or stopping the legitimate owner of a name registering a company. Perhaps because of these issues, the Act has introduced 'company names adjudicators' who are empowered to receive applications objecting to company names and in appropriate cases require a company to change its name. This enlarges the potential impact of company law on company name disputes and is covered in further detail below.

NAME CHECKS, TRADE/SERVICE MARKS, DOMAIN NAMES AND NAME PROTECTION

3.6   It is important to check whether anyone else has prior rights in a proposed name and to consider whether additional enquiries and registrations are appropriate. Checks and registrations carried out at the start of the process of choosing a name can often save additional expense and trouble later on, when a name is already in use. Initially, information can often be found by using the internet. More formal searches can be carried out on existing company names and trade/service marks at the appropriate registries (for trade marks it is normally appropriate to use trade mark agents or other professionals). You can also conduct searches on domain name registrations.

3.7   The extent of searches and enquiry required will depend upon the name being registered (eg is it a 'made-up' name that is to be widely marketed and intrinsic to recognition of the business/product(s)/service(s)?) It is obviously worth taking some care to ensure that (1) it is not already in use by others, and (2) that the rights connected with it are protected as necessary by appropriate registrations. If the name is to be used internationally, then consider whether searches and/or registrations are appropriate in other jurisdictions.

RESTRICTIONS ON COMPANY NAMES

3.8   The Act's rules in this area have been designed mainly with the intention that third parties are not misled by the use of certain words or descriptions in a company's name. Some names are prohibited, some words require permission for their use in a company name, the range of characters and symbols allowed is restricted and there are also restrictions on the inappropriate use of words etc that indicate the legal form of an entity. The powers of the Secretary of State in respect of the approval of names are likely to be exercised by the Registrar. Similar provisions already exist under the Companies Act 1985 and many of the 2006 Act provisions (which in some respects are closely similar) are due to come into force on 1 October 2009.

PROHIBITED NAMES

3.9　A company cannot be registered by a name if, in the opinion of the Secretary of State:

- its use by the company would constitute an offence; or

- it is offensive.

3.10　There are various statutes which may make it an offence to use specific words in a company name (normally where their use would be misleading unless used by a certain type of entity).

NAMES SUGGESTING CONNECTION WITH GOVERNMENT OR PUBLIC AUTHORITY

3.11　The approval of the Secretary of State is required for a company to be registered by a name that would be likely to give the impression that the company is connected with:

- Her Majesty's Government, or any part of the Scottish administration or Her Majesty's Government in Northern Ireland

- a local authority, or

- any public authority specified for the purpose by regulations made by the Secretary of State.

For these purposes, 'local authority' means: a local authority within the meaning of the Local Government Act 1972, the Common Council of the City of London or the Council of the Isles of Scilly, a council constituted under s 2 of the Local Government etc (Scotland) Act 1994, or a district council in Northern Ireland; and 'public authority' includes any person or body having functions of a public nature. Any regulations made may require that an applicant for registration must seek the view of a specified Government department or other body. See **3.14** for the required procedure in such cases.

OTHER SENSITIVE WORDS OR EXPRESSIONS

3.12   The Act empowers the Secretary of State to make regulations specifying words or expressions for which approval is required for inclusion in a company name. This follows the same course as in previous legislation, which specified various types of words, such as:

- words implying national or international pre-eminence, eg 'International' or 'British'

- words implying business pre-eminence or representative or authoritative status, eg 'Institute', 'Society' or 'Association'

- words implying specific objects or functions, eg 'Holding', 'Group', 'Trust' or 'Chemist'.

3.13   Again, the regulations may require that an applicant for registration of a company name must seek the view of a Government department or other body. Examples where this applied under previous legislation included use of the words: 'Royal' (where agreement had to be obtained from the Department of Constitutional Affairs); 'Dental' and 'Dentistry' (where agreement had to be obtained from the General Dental Council); and 'Charity' and 'Charitable' (which required agreement from the Charity Commission). Companies House website provides up-to-date guidance regarding sensitive words and expressions and the names and addresses of the bodies from who to seek views where relevant.

REQUIREMENT TO SEEK THE VIEW OF A GOVERNMENT DEPARTMENT OR OTHER BODY

3.14   The Act specifically requires that if a requirement to seek the view of a specified Government department or other body applies, the applicant must request the specified department or other body (in writing) to indicate whether (and if so why) it has any objections to the proposed name. Where such a request has been made, the application for registration of the company must include a statement that the request has been made and be accompanied by a copy of any response received. Similarly, where such a request has been made in connection with a change of a company's name, the notice of the change of name sent to Company's House for registration must be accompanied by a statement by a director or secretary of the company that such a request has been made and a copy of any response received.

PROVISION OF MISLEADING INFORMATION – POWERS OF SECRETARY OF STATE

3.15 The Secretary of State has power, within five years of registration of a company name, to direct a company to change its name if it appears to him that (i) misleading information has been given for the purposes of the company name registration, or (ii) that an undertaking or assurance given for that purpose has not been fulfilled. The direction will be in writing and will specify a time for compliance. Failure to comply is an offence.

3.16 There is a new additional power for the Secretary of State to direct a change of name later than five years from the company name registration. This applies if in his opinion the registered company name 'gives so misleading an indication of the nature of its activities as to be likely to cause harm to the public'. The direction must be complied with within six weeks or such longer period as the Secretary of State may allow. Failure to comply is an offence. It is possible for a company to apply to the court within three weeks of the date of the direction for the direction to be set aside.

PERMITTED CHARACTERS, ACCENTS, SYMBOLS ETC

3.17 In the past, the Registrar has sometimes faced problems regarding signs, symbols and punctuation that have been requested in a company name. The Act deals with this by providing that the Secretary of State may make provision by regulations as to the letters or other characters, signs or symbols (including accents and other diacritical marks) and punctuation that may be used in the name of a company. The regulations may also specify a standard style or format for the name of a company for the purposes of registration and may prohibit the use of specified characters, signs or symbols when appearing in a specified position (in particular, at the beginning of a name). At the time of writing a draft of the Company and Business Names (Miscellaneous Provisions) Regulations is available via the BERR website (see **Appendix 5**). The permitted characters roughly accord with those available on an English language keyboard and provide that a company name must not consist of more than 160 permitted characters.

INDICATIONS OF COMPANY TYPE OR LEGAL FORM

3.18 The Act contains restrictions designed to ensure that the correct indication of company type or legal form is used by the correct entity in the correct place in the name. The restrictions are:

- the name of a limited company that is a public company must end with 'public limited company' or 'plc' (or in the case of a Welsh company 'cwmni cyfyngedig cyhoeddus' or 'ccc')

- the name of a limited company that is a private company must end with 'limited' or'ltd' (or in the case of a Welsh company 'cyfyngedig' or 'cyf').

The above provisions do not apply to community interest companies.

3.19 The Secretary of State may also make regulations prohibiting the use in a company name of 'specified words, expressions or other indications' that are associated with a particular type of company or form of organisation or that are similar to words, expressions or other indications that are associated with a particular type of company or form of organisation. The regulations may prohibit the use of words, expressions or other indications in a specified part (or otherwise than in a specified part) of a company's name or in conjunction with (or otherwise than in conjunction with) such other words, expressions or indications as may be specified. Again, please see the draft (or perhaps final) Company and Business Names (Miscellaneous Provisions) Regulations for the details specified in the Regulations (referred to in **3.17**).

EXEMPTION FROM THE REQUIREMENT TO USE THE WORD 'LIMITED'

3.20 A private limited company is exempt from the requirement to have a name ending in 'limited' if:

- it is a charity

- it is exempted from the requirement by regulations made by the Secretary of State, or

- it meets the required conditions for continuation of an existing exemption in place prior to the implementation of the Act.

The draft of the Company and Business Names (Miscellaneous Provisions) Regulations that is available at the time of writing (see **3.17**) provides that a private company limited by guarantee is exempt from the requirement to have a name ending with 'limited' (or permitted alternative) so long as it meets the following two conditions:

(1) that the objects of that company are the promotion or regulation of commerce, art, science, education, religion, charity or any profession, and anything incidental or conducive to any of those objects, and

(2) that the company's articles:
  - require its income to be applied in promoting its objects
  - prohibit the payment of dividends, or any return of capital, to its members, and
  - require all the assets that would otherwise be available to its members generally to be transferred on its winding up either:

- to another body with objects similar to its own, or
- to another body the objects of which are the promotion of charity, and
- anything incidental or conducive thereto

whether or not the body is a member of the company.

3.21 The exact conditions for continuation of a previously existing exemption under older legislation (and the circumstances in which such exemptions will be lost) are set out in ss 61 and 62 of the Act. They are different for a company limited by shares and a company limited by guarantee. It is now very rare for a company limited by shares to have the exemption. For a company limited by guarantee, it will continue to have the exemption if it does not change its name and (in basic terms) continues to comply with the provisions previously set out in the Companies Act 1985, which have been reproduced in s 62. See the sections for full details.

3.22 A company with an existing exemption under previous legislation that does not use 'limited' in its name must not amend its articles so that it ceases to comply with the conditions for exemption; contravention of this is an offence.

3.23 The Secretary of State is empowered to direct a company whose name does not include 'limited' to change its name if it has ceased to be entitled to the exemption or has acted inconsistently with the relevant provisions for the exemption.

SIMILARITY TO OTHER NAMES ON THE INDEX OF COMPANY NAMES

Same name on the index

3.24 A company cannot be registered by a name that is the same as another name already on the index of company names. The Secretary of State may make regulations providing what matters are to be disregarded and as to words, expressions, signs or symbols that are, or are not, to be regarded as the same. The draft of the Company and Business Names (Miscellaneous Provisions) Regulations (see **3.17**) includes currency symbols and their written equivalents (eg '£' and 'pound'), '%' and 'per cent' and numerals and their written equivalents (eg '1' and 'one') amongst the items that are to be treated as the same. The draft regulations also list other words and symbols to be disregarded (many of which are connected with internet addresses) for the purposes of determining whether a name is treated as the same. The draft regulations also provide that a name that might otherwise be prohibited for this reason is permitted if the company which would be treated as having the same name is a member of the same group and gives its consent to the use of the name.

Power to direct change of similar name

3.25 The Secretary of State may, within 12 months of registration of a company name, direct a company to change its name if it has been registered with a name that is the same as or, in the opinion of the Secretary of State, too like a name appearing on the index (or that should have appeared on the index) at the time of registration. The direction must specify the period in which the name must be changed (this period can be extended). Failure to comply with such a direction is an offence. In practice, the powers are likely to be exercised by the Registrar. There is also provision for the Secretary of State to make regulations supplementing these provisions.

3.26 This power to order a change of name is similar to that contained in previous legislation. Experience with that legislation was that the issue of such orders by the Registrar was not frequent and depended on objection being made and the names being found to be closely similar. Consequently, in most cases it was more common to pursue a remedy through the courts if it was felt that goodwill attached to a name was being unlawfully used by another party. New procedures are introduced by the Act in relation to names in which a person has goodwill (see below). So it may be that the power of the Secretary of State to direct a change of name due to similarity will be used even less often.

SIMILARITY TO ANOTHER NAME IN WHICH A PERSON HAS GOODWILL

3.27 There are new provisions in ss 69–74 of the Act that came into force on 1 October 2008. These allow a person to apply for a company to be directed to change its name on the grounds that it is the same as a name in which the applicant has goodwill or that it is so similar that its use in the UK would be likely to mislead by suggesting a connection with the applicant. The case of the person making the application is even stronger if the applicant can show that the name was chosen with the principal intention of seeking monies from him or preventing him using the name where it is one in which he has previously acquired reputation or goodwill. In this context 'goodwill' includes reputation of any description. These new provisions are designed to address problems that have arisen in the past regarding registration of company names to 'squat' on the name.

3.28 The Act provides for the Secretary of State to appoint 'company names adjudicators' (and a 'Chief Adjudicator') and make rules about proceedings before a company names adjudicator. Adjudicators may make rulings on such applications and in appropriate cases order that a company name be changed. Such disputes are now to be put on a formal footing without necessitating a full court application. The Company Names Adjudicator Rules 2008 (SI 2008/ 1738), which came into force on 1 October 2008, set out rules regarding such proceedings. These cover such matters as fees, rules for a statement and counter statement, evidence rounds, provision for oral hearings, powers of the adjudicator, the award of costs etc. The office of the company names adjudicator is based at the Intellectual Property Office (previously the Patent Office) (see **Appendix 5** for the address). Further detail on the Act's provisions is set out below.

3.29 A person (which includes both individuals and corporate bodies) may object to a company's registered name on the ground:

- that it is the same as a name associated with the applicant in which he has goodwill, or

- that it is sufficiently similar to such a name that its use in the UK would be likely to mislead by suggesting a connection between the company and the applicant.

3.30 The objection is made by application to a company names adjudicator. The company concerned is the primary respondent to the application, but any of its members or directors may be joined as additional respondents. If the ground specified above is established, the burden automatically passes to the respondents to show to show that one of a list of circumstances applies. If the respondent cannot establish one of these grounds, the objection will be upheld. The list of circumstances upon which the respondent may rely are that:

- the name was registered before the commencement of the activities on which the applicant relies to show goodwill, or

- the company:
  - is operating under the name, or
  - is proposing to do so and has incurred substantial start-up costs in preparation, or
  - was formerly operating under the name and is now dormant, or

- the name was registered in the ordinary course of a company formation business and the company is available for sale to the applicant on the standard terms of that business, or

- the name was adopted in good faith, or

- the interests of the applicant are not affected to any significant extent.

If the facts set out in one of the first three bullet points above are established, the objection must still be upheld if the applicant shows that the main purpose of the respondents (or any of them) in registering the name was to obtain money (or other consideration) from the applicant or prevent him from registering the name. If the objection is not upheld under the grounds set out, it will be dismissed.

3.31 If an application is upheld, the adjudicator will make an order requiring the respondent company to change its name by a specified date and requiring all the respondents to take all such steps as are within their power to facilitate the change and not to register another company with a similarly offending name. Such an order may be enforced through the courts and also if there is default the adjudicator may determine a new name for the company.

3.32 It is possible to appeal to the court in respect of any decision of a company names adjudicator to uphold or dismiss an application. If notice of appeal is given, the effect of the adjudicator's order is suspended.

CHANGE OF COMPANY NAME

3.33 Section 77 (which is due to come into force on 1 October 2009) provides that a company may change its name by special resolution of the members or by other means provided for in the company's articles. There are also special circumstance provisions for (i) a change of name by resolution of the directors acting under a direction by the Secretary of State where a company has ceased to be entitled to the exemption from using 'limited' or (ii) by an order of a company names adjudicator. In any case a change of a company's name has effect on the date on which a new certificate is issued by the Registrar (see below).

3.34 Where a change of name has been agreed to by special resolution, the company must give notice to the Registrar. This is in addition to the requirement to forward a copy of the resolution to the Registrar. Where a change of name has been made by other means provided by a company's articles, the company must again give notice to the Registrar and this notice must be accompanied by a statement that the change of name has been made by means provided for in the company's articles. The Registrar may rely on this statement.

Conditional change of name resolutions

3.35 Where a change of name by special resolution is conditional on the occurrence of an event, the notice given to the Registrar must specify that the change is conditional and state whether the event has occurred. If the notice states that the event has not occurred, the Registrar is not required to register the change of name and issue a certificate until further notice, and when the event occurs, the company must give notice to the Registrar that it has occurred. The Registrar should then rely on that statement and register the change of name.

Effective date of change of name

3.36 Although the company's name will change from the date on which the new certificate is issued by the Registrar, the company number will not change.

The change of name does not affect any rights or obligations of the company or render defective any legal proceedings by or against it. Any legal proceedings that might have been continued or commenced against it by its former name, may be continued or commenced against it by its new name.

REQUIREMENTS TO DISCLOSE COMPANY NAME AND DISCLOSE COMPANY DETAILS

3.37 It has always been a matter of concern to legislators that those dealing with companies and other businesses should know who they are dealing with and at what address legal documents (such as claims) can be served on the company or business. Previously some inflexible requirements were contained in legislation which contained some areas of uncertainty as to the details of compliance. In some cases real difficulties were caused for companies without any material assistance resulting for those dealing with the company. Perhaps in recognition of past problems, the Act lays down a skeleton structure for these requirements to be supplemented by regulations. The Companies (Trading Disclosures) Regulations 2008 (SI 2008/495) came into force on 1 October 2008, setting out the detailed requirements regarding such disclosures.

3.38 The Companies (Trading Disclosures) Regulations 2008 contain requirements regarding:

- the display of a company's registered name

- particulars of the company that must appear in business letters, order forms and websites, and

- the disclosure on request of the address of a company's registered office, the address of any inspection place and the type of company records kept there.

For these purposes an 'inspection place' is any location, other than the company's registered office, at which a company keeps available for inspection any company record which it is required under the Companies Acts to keep available for public inspection. Also for these purposes, 'company record' means:

- any register, index, accounting records, memorandum, minutes or other document required by the Companies Acts to be kept by a company, and

- any register kept by a company of its debenture holders.

'Document' includes hard copy, electronic or any other form.

3.39 The Regulations require a company (unless it has been dormant since incorporation) to display its registered name at:

- its registered office

- any inspection place, and

- any location at which it carries on business (unless the location is primarily used for living accommodation).

The registered name must be displayed so that it can be easily seen by a visitor. If the office, place or location is shared by six or more companies, each such company is only required to display its name for at least 15 continuous seconds at least once in every three minutes. This is designed to provide for an electronic rolling display, but does seem to resort to a ridiculous level of detail!

3.40 The draft Companies (Trading Disclosures) (Amendment) Regulations available at the time of writing are proposed to come into effect on 1 October 2009. These will make minor amendments to the disclosure requirements in the following respects:

- the requirement to display the registered name shall not apply to a company where a liquidator, administrator, receiver or manager of the property of the company has been appointed and the registered office or inspection place of that company is also a place of business of that liquidator, administrator, receiver or manager, and

- the requirement to display the registered name at other business locations shall also not apply to any place at which business is carried on by a company of which every director who is an individual is a director who has the benefit of the additional protection under s 243(4) that prevents the Registrar from disclosing a director's residential address to a credit protection agency (see **5.14**).

3.41 The company's registered name must also be disclosed on:

- its business letters, notices and other official publications

- its order forms, bills of exchange, promissory notes and endorsements

- cheques purporting to be signed by or on behalf of the company

- orders for money, goods or services purporting to be signed by or on behalf of the company

- its invoices and other demands for payment, receipts, letters of credit and bills of parcels

- its applications for licences to carry on a trade or activity, and

- all other forms of its business correspondence and documentation.

Every company must also disclose its registered name on its websites.

3.42 The following must also be disclosed on every company's business letters, order forms and websites:

- the part of the UK in which the company is registered (ie England and Wales, Scotland or Northern Ireland)

- its registered number

- its registered office address

- if it is exempt from the use of the word 'limited', the fact that it is a limited company

- in the case of a community interest company that is not a public company, the fact that it is a limited company

- in the case of an investment company within the meaning of s 833 of the Act, the fact that it is such a company.

Any disclosure of the amount of share capital in business letters, order forms or on websites, must be disclosure of paid up share capital. Where a company's business letter includes the name of any director of the company, other than in the text or as a signatory, the letter must disclose the name of every director of the company.

3.43 A company must also disclose:

- the address of its registered office

- any inspection place (as defined in **3.38**), and

- the type of records (as defined in **3.38**) which are kept at that office or place

to any person it deals with in the course of business who makes a written request to the company for that information. The company must send a written response to that person within five working days of the receipt of that request.

3.44 Failure, without reasonable excuse, to comply with any of the requirements set out in the Regulations (as summarised in **3.38–3.43**), is an offence. Section 83 also provides for civil consequences of failure to comply with the Regulations. Section 83 applies to any legal proceedings brought by a company to enforce a right arising out of a contract made in the course of a business in respect of which the company was, at the time the contract was made, in breach of the Regulations. Section 83 provides that such legal proceedings shall be dismissed if the defendant shows:

- that he has a claim against the claimant arising out of the contract that he has been unable to pursue by reason of the latter's breach of the regulations, or

- that he has suffered some financial loss in connection with the contract by reason of the claimant's breach of the Regulations.

For the purposes of these trading disclosure requirements, matters such as:

- whether upper or lower case characters are used

- whether diacritical marks or punctuation are present, and

- whether the name is in the same format or style as used for the purposes of registration

may be ignored, provided that there is no real likelihood of names differing only in those respects being taken to be different names.

RESTRICTIONS ON BUSINESS NAMES

3.45   The Act also contains provisions (similar to those at the time of writing contained in the Business Names Act 1985) regulating the use of business names. These are set out in ss 1192–1208 of the Act and are due to come into force on 1 October 2009. In broad terms they apply to persons (including partnerships) carrying on business under a name other than their own names. They impose on such businesses similar restrictions and disclosure requirements to those applying to companies for names purposes. The provisions apply to any person carrying on business in the United Kingdom. The following paragraphs set out the provisions that will apply from 1 October 2009.

3.46   It is specifically stated that these provisions do not prevent an individual carrying on business under a name consisting of his surname (with nothing added other than his forename or initial) and do not prevent a partnership carrying on business under a name consisting of the surnames of all the partners (with nothing added other than (i) the forenames or initials of individual partners, or (ii) where two or more individual partners have the same surname, the addition of 's' at the end of that surname. The provisions also do not prevent, either for individuals or partnerships, an addition merely indicating that the business is carried on in succession to a former owner of the business.

3.47   It is not intended to cover here the detail of the business names provisions, but in summary they operate in much the same way as for companies, to create a 'level playing field' between the rules for company names and business names. The business names provisions provide for:

- restrictions on names suggesting connection with government or public authority without the approval of the Secretary of State

- restrictions on the use of sensitive words or expressions without the approval of the Secretary of State

- restrictions on misleading names.

However, there is no requirement to register a business name and no register of business names. The comments in **3.3**, **3.4**, **3.6** and **3.7** also apply (in general terms) to business names.

DISCLOSURE REQUIREMENTS FOR AN INDIVIDUAL OR A PARTNERSHIP

3.48 Individuals or partnerships carrying on business in the United Kingdom under a business name are subject to disclosure requirements. These requirements are designed to ensure that people dealing with the business know who they are dealing with. The information required to be disclosed is:

- in the case of an individual, his name

- in the case of a partnership, the name of each member of the partnership

and in relation to each such person, an address in the United Kingdom for service of any document relating to the business. This required information must be stated, in legible characters, on all:

- business letters

- written orders for goods or services to be supplied to the business

- invoices and receipts issued in the course of the business, and

- written demands for payments of debts arising in the course of the business.

3.49 A person with whom anything is done or discussed in the course of the business is entitled to ask for this information and the person carrying on business under the business name must supply it by written notice on receiving such a request. There is also a requirement to display the required information in any premises where the business is carried on and to which customers of the business, or suppliers of goods or services to the business have access. This information must be displayed in a prominent position, so that it may easily be read by such customers or suppliers.

3.50 Failure to comply with the relevant disclosure requirements is an offence and the civil consequences of failure to comply are set out in s 1206. They are in basic terms the same as those which apply to companies in similar circumstances under s 83 as explained in **3.44**.

Disclosure requirements for large partnerships

3.51 A partnership of more than 20 persons is entitled to maintain at its principal place of business a list of the names of all the partners and instead state on the relevant business documents the address of the partnership's principal place of business and that the list of partners' names is open to inspection there.

SUMMARY OF MAJOR CHANGES INTRODUCED BY THE ACT

1   A company may change its name by other means provided for in its articles, as well as by special resolution. In each case notice must be given to the Registrar (in addition to the requirement to file the special resolution) (see ss 77–81). *Due to come into force on 1 October 2009.*

2   There are new provisions covering conditional change of name resolutions that require additional notices to be given to the Registrar (see s 78). *Due to come into force on 1 October 2009.*

3   There are various provisions for new regulations regarding names, including regulations covering the detail of disclosure of company names etc (see ss 54–57, 60, 65–67, 71 and 82). *Section 82 came into force on 1 October 2008 and the provisions of the Companies (Trading Disclosures) Regulations 2008 are explained in 3.37–3.44. The other sections are due to come into force on 1 October 2009.*

4   There are 'company names adjudicators'. If a company name has been registered in which you have goodwill it is possible to make an application to a company names adjudicator to order it to change its name. The burden is on the respondent to show that the name is being used in a bona fide manner. This will clearly cover cases where a company name is registered to 'squat' on the goodwill of another or demand money to release the name (see ss 69–74). *This came into force on 1 October 2008 and is explained in more detail in 3.27–3.32.*

5   More detailed codification of requirements if applying to use a 'sensitive' word in a name where there is the requirement to seek the view of another body prior to registration (see s 56). *Due to come into force on 1 October 2009.*

6   Provision for new regulations to cover the letters, signs, symbols etc that may be used in company names (see s 57). *Due to come into force on 1 October 2009. More detail regarding the draft of the Company and Business Names (Miscellaneous Provisions) Regulations which is available at the time of writing is given at 3.17 onwards.*

7   Changed conditions for exemption from the use of the word 'limited' (with saving provisions for companies with an existing exemption, provided that they do not change their name) (see ss 60–64). *Due to come into force on 1 October 2009. See 3.20.*

8   Business names provisions are consolidated into Part 41 of the Act (see ss 1192–1208). *Due to come into force on 1 October 2009.*

Chapter 4

LEGAL CAPACITY, THE ARTICLES AND THE COMPANY'S CONSTITUTION – WHAT CAN THE COMPANY DO AND HOW?

INTRODUCTION

4.1　The Act substantially changes previous provisions regarding a company's constitution and capacity to carry out actions and enter into contracts. Under the new provisions, unless a company's articles specifically restrict the objects of the company, its objects are deemed to be unrestricted. This is very different from the old law, which relied on the company's constitution setting out what a company could do. When the new provisions come into force the complete reverse will be true and the company will be able to carry out any lawful action unless its constitution imposes restrictions on it. Generally these provisions are mostly contained in ss 17–52 of the Act. Nearly all of the provisions referred to in this chapter are due to come into force on 1 October 2009, apart from ss 29 and 30 which came into force on 1 October 2007 and s 44 which came into force on 6 April 2008.

4.2　The change to allow companies to carry out any lawful action unless restricted by their constitution will be very welcome for commercial companies set up after the new law comes into force, but has the potential to cause confusion and problems for existing companies. There are transitional provisions contained in the Act to ease this situation (see below), but each company will, I suggest, need to review its constitution in the light of the new law to see if its constitution now meets its current needs.

4.3　Companies are now to have articles of association, instead of memorandum and articles. As stated in **2.24–2.27**, the old style memorandum will be replaced by a prescribed form memorandum that is used on the incorporation of a company. This form is authenticated by each subscriber to signify his or her wish to form a company and agreement to form a company (and if it is a company with share capital, to take at least one share each); it has no other purpose. Because of this, the constitutions of older companies will look very different to those of companies formed after this part of the Act has been brought into force. Such new companies will be formed from 5 October 2009 onwards (see **Chapter 12**). The transitional provisions contained in the Act and proposed to be contained in Commencement Order 8 state that items contained in the memorandum of a company formed before 5 October 2009 (other than provisions of the type contained in the new style prescribed form memorandum) will be treated as provisions of the company's articles.

4.4　There are provisions in the Act (in ss 22–24) dealing with the entrenchment of provisions where this is required or is already contained in the constitution of an existing company.

4.5　A company's 'constitution', where referred to in the Act, includes its articles and resolutions or agreements affecting the company's constitution that are covered by s 29 of the Act (see **4.20** for further detail).

4.6　The Act contains provisions regarding the use and effect of a company seal and the execution of documents by companies. The law of Scotland is different in these respects. Scottish companies and those executing documents to which Scottish law may apply should consult a Scottish solicitor regarding exact requirements under Scottish law.

A COMPANY'S CAPACITY – WHAT CAN IT DO?

4.7　The Act states (in s 31) that unless a company's articles specifically restrict the objects of a company, its objects are unrestricted. What does this mean for:

- new companies formed under the Act (from 5 October 2009) that wish to have unrestricted objects

- new companies formed under the Act (from 5 October 2009) that wish to have some form of restriction about what the company may do

- companies formed under older legislation that had a memorandum setting out what the company was entitled to do?

NEW COMPANIES FORMED UNDER THE ACT WITH UNRESTRICTED OBJECTS

4.8　A company formed after implementation of the relevant part of the Act will be able to rely on the statutory provision that the objects of the company are unrestricted. Provided that the company's constitution does not contain any wording that might be construed as 'specifically' restricting its objects, the activities of the company will not be subject to any restriction. Of course, the activities of the company must be lawful and presumably not contrary to public policy, but this new provision is to be welcomed as it gives companies flexibility to engage in activities as they think fit to meet their current circumstances and needs.

NEW COMPANIES FORMED UNDER THE ACT THAT WISH TO HAVE RESTRICTIONS ON WHAT THEY DO

4.9   There will be many cases where those forming a company wish there to be restrictions on what it can do, or where other provisions require there to be some restriction on what the company can do. Examples include:

- **charities** – any company that is, or wishes to register as, a charity, is subject to a large volume of additional legal requirements; one of these is that the objects of the charity must be expressed in its governing document (in the case of a company, its articles) in exclusively charitable terms – so of necessity such companies must have restrictions in their articles on what they can do; the Act also specifically makes some of its provisions in this area subject to charities legislation (see for instance s 31(4) and (5))

- **companies subject to regulatory requirements** – some companies may be required or wish to register with some form of regulatory body; it is possible that one of the requirements for such registration will be having some specified restrictions in the company's constitution

- **clubs and companies formed for specific events or purposes** – in such cases, those involved with the company may well find it appropriate for the company's constitution to contain restrictions on what it can do

- **companies formed to manage the common parts of a property development ('flat management companies')** – such companies are again formed for a specific purpose and normally owned and run by owners of properties in the development; again it is likely to be inappropriate for such companies to have unrestricted objects

- **other companies formed for very specific purposes** – these may include pension trustee companies, or any company formed to hold or administer property on behalf of others.

In each case wording will have to be inserted into the articles of association of the company to specifically restrict the company's objects to the desired extent. However, it is important to understand that even the insertion of restrictions into the company's articles can have a limited effect. In many cases, if the company in fact does something in contravention of restrictions in its articles, it may still be legally bound to a third party by its action.

Validity of acts in contravention of constitution

4.10   The Act (in s 39) provides that (subject to the exceptions noted below) the validity of an act done by a company shall not be called into question on the ground of lack of capacity by reason of anything in the company's constitution. This carries over a provision previously contained in the

Companies Act 1985. It means that as regards outsiders, they do not have to be too concerned whether there are restrictions in the articles of which they are unaware. If the company acts in contravention of a restriction on its capacity contained in its constitution ('constitution' includes its articles and resolutions and agreements affecting it that fall within s 29 of the Act) the validity of the act by the company cannot be challenged on this ground.

4.11 So you may ask, what is the point of a restriction on what the company can do that is contained in the articles? The answer is that the restriction is still effective on the directors and members of the company. The directors are under a statutory duty (set out in s 171 of the Act) to act in accordance with the company's constitution and to only exercise powers for the purposes for which they are conferred. Such a duty is enforceable as a fiduciary duty owed to a company by its directors and the consequences of a breach (or threatened breach) are the same as would apply if the corresponding common law rule or equitable principle applied. So it is possible to restrain the directors from acting in breach of the company's capacity as set out in its constitution by action through the courts in advance of any such act by the company. If the company has already carried out such an act and the directors have acted beyond the company's capacity in breach of the constitution, the act will still be valid (see above) but the directors may be pursued through the courts in respect of damage suffered by the company as a result. The Companies Act 1985 contained specific provisions in old s 35 setting out:

- the right of a member of a company to bring proceedings to restrain an act beyond the company's capacity

- that action beyond the company's capacity may only be ratified by special resolution and that such a resolution does not affect any liability incurred by the directors (or any other person)

- such relief from any such liability must be agreed to separately by special resolution.

These provisions have not been carried over into the Act as the Government regarded it as unnecessary for them to be explicitly stated. Despite the fact that these provisions are no longer set out in statute, common law is likely to maintain the same principles.

4.12 Companies that are charities are subject to different provisions. The normal provision that ignores restrictions in the company's constitution does not apply to the acts of a company that is a charity except in favour of a person who:

- does not know at the time the act is done that the company is a charity, or

- gives full consideration in money or money's worth in relation to the act in question and does not know that the act is beyond the company's constitution.

See s 42 for detail on this.

COMPANIES FORMED UNDER OLDER LEGISLATION

4.13 Companies formed prior to 5 October 2009 will, of necessity, have had an old style memorandum of association setting out what the company could do in the form of objects and powers. This is because, under the previous law, the company could only do what its memorandum empowered it to do. Although, as the law progressed, the external effect of this restriction was largely nullified, the internal effect still survived, in the same way as an internal effect continues to survive under the new law if there is a restriction on a company's objects (see above). Such companies formed under the old law either set out specific objects or made use of a 'general commercial object' stating that the object of the company is 'to carry on business as a general commercial company'. The effect of the general commercial object under the old law was that:

- the object of the company was to carry on any trade or business whatsoever, and

- the company had power to do all such things as were incidental or conducive to the carrying on of a trade or business by it.

Because there were some uncertainties about whether the general commercial object alone sufficiently empowered a commercial company, it was normal to also set out additional clauses with the general commercial object in a company's memorandum. Note that under the old law, the objects and powers set out in a company's memorandum tended to be widely drafted to empower a company to carry out any acts that might be suitable in the context of its intended activities.

4.14 The objects and powers set out in the memorandum of association of an 'old' company, under the new law, form part of the company's articles. The Government's view is that these clauses of existing companies, which were originally drafted as a list of things that the company could do, will in future be read as a restriction on what the company can do. So such companies will not have the benefit of the unrestricted objects provided for by the new legislation. This may be perceived as a benefit by companies that always intended to have restricted objects, but is likely to be seen as a drawback by commercial companies that would prefer to have completely unrestricted objects. It is possible that old companies with a 'general commercial object' will in practice have few (if any) actual restrictions on what they do in practice. But it is important to recognise that they reach this result by a different legal route.

Companies with unrestricted objects will have just that under the Act. For companies with a general commercial object there is always the possibility (perhaps remote) that there may be argument about whether the wording of the clauses in what was once the memorandum (but now is deemed to form part of the articles) poses some restriction on the capacity of the company. See **4.10–4.12** for a discussion about the effect of such restrictions. Also consider that clauses originally drafted to empower the company will now have to be construed in the context that they are imposing a restriction on the company – a purpose for which they were never originally designed.

4.15 Depending on their circumstances, many active companies may choose to redraft their articles in a new format designed with the provisions of the Act in mind, rather than carry on with wording designed to meet the requirements of different law. However, there is no actual requirement to do this and companies can choose to carry on without adopting a new constitution.

ARTICLES OF ASSOCIATION AND MODEL ARTICLES

4.16 A company must have articles of association which set out the rules that govern the internal affairs of the company. The matters that these may cover are likely to include:

- limits on the directors' functions and authority (if any) – most private commercial companies are likely to provide that the directors are responsible for the management of the company's business, for which purpose they may exercise all the powers of the company, which is the provision in the proposed draft model articles for companies limited by shares (see below)

- how directors take decisions – usually by a majority, but see also **Chapter 6**

- how directors may delegate some of their functions to committees and others and any restrictions on delegation

- the appointment and termination of appointment of directors

- share transfers

- dividends

- use of a company seal

- directors' indemnities and authority to take out directors' indemnity insurance

- other matters where it is thought appropriate to supplement the statutory provisions – e g in relation to the conduct of shareholder meetings.

The above list only contains examples. The articles of association may cover any area regarding the internal rules of the company, so long as they do not conflict with applicable law. The articles must be contained in a single document and be divided into paragraphs numbered consecutively.

4.17 The Act gives the Secretary of State power to prescribe model articles of association for companies. At the time of writing it is expected that there will be model articles of association for private companies limited by shares, for private companies limited by guarantee and for public companies. On the formation of a limited company, if articles are not registered, or if articles are registered, in so far as they do not exclude or modify the relevant model articles, the relevant model articles will automatically apply and form a part of the company's articles. A company may adopt all or any of the provisions of model articles. The 'relevant model articles' may of course change from time to time, so the ones that apply to a company are those in force at the time of the company's registration. Any amendment to the model articles does not affect a company registered before the amendment takes effect. If the company is one to which model articles do not apply (ie an unlimited company) then it must register its own articles to be incorporated.

4.18 The concept of model articles follows that used in previous legislation (for instance 'Table A'). Draft model articles to be prescribed under the Act for a private company limited by shares, a private company limited by guarantee and a public company are available at the time of writing in the form of draft regulations on the BERR website (see **Appendix 5**). These use modern language (rather than outdated 'legal speak') and are designed to be short and easily understood. The draft model articles for a private company limited by shares contain 54 clauses, whereas the old 1985 Table A contains 118 clauses. It is true that some items previously contained in Table A are now contained in the Act, which now contains more detailed provisions regarding decision taking by members of a company. However, some of these provisions may be modified by provision in a company's articles. Some other items previously provided for by the old Table A (such as provision for partly paid shares, calls on shares and forfeiture) are now not covered at all. These new model articles are designed for a 'stand-alone' trading company.

4.19 It may be that these 'slim fit' model articles will be a welcome relief for small stand alone businesses that choose to incorporate as a company. However 'slim fit' is unlikely to fit all sizes of private company. For instance subsidiary companies within groups may well wish to have a fuller form of articles. It may be that we see an increasing divergence of different private company articles for private companies formed for different sizes of business – and perhaps this is no bad thing. The model articles for public companies are unlikely to be used as such by many companies, but do provide very useful examples for the wording of some articles which many public (and private) companies may choose to use within their own specially drafted articles.

ARTICLES OF ASSOCIATION AND THE COMPANY'S CONSTITUTION

4.20 The articles of association may be supplemented by special resolutions (see **Chapter 7**) or agreements between all the members of a company or all the members of a class of shareholders. The Act (perhaps confusingly) differentiates between a company's articles and a company's 'constitution'. Section 17 provides that:

> 'Unless the context otherwise requires, references in the Companies Acts to a company's constitution include—
>
> (a)   the company's articles, and
> (b)   any resolutions and agreements to which Chapter 3 of this Part applies (see section 29)'.

If one then looks at s 29 (which is in the said Chapter 3) it states:

> 'This Chapter applies to—
>
> (a)   any special resolution;
> (b)   any resolution or agreement agreed to by all the members of a company that, if not so agreed to, would not have been effective for its purpose unless passed as a special resolution;
> (c)   any resolution or agreement agreed to by all the members of a class of shareholders that, if not so agreed to, would not have been effective for its purpose unless passed by some particular majority or otherwise in some particular manner;
> (d)   any resolution or agreement that effectively binds all members of a class of shareholders though not agreed to by all those members;
> (e)   any other resolution or agreement to which this Chapter applies by virtue of any enactment.'

Items under the last category include a resolution to redenominate share capital in accordance with s 622 and a resolution that a company may send or supply documents etc by making them available on the company's website pursuant to para 10 of Sch 5. Where transitional provisions allow a company to pass an extraordinary resolution, or a resolution pursuant to the Companies Act 1985, s 80 giving authority to allot shares, the transitional provisions also bring these resolutions within the ambit of Chapter 3. Sections 29 and 30 of the Act came into force on 1 October 2007.

4.21 The same list applies in respect of resolutions or agreements required to be forwarded to the Registrar within 15 days after they are passed or made (see **10.17**). Every copy of a company's articles issued by a company must be accompanied by a copy of every resolution or agreement relating to the company to which Chapter 3 applies unless the effect of it has either been incorporated into the articles by amendment or is not for the time being in force (see s 36). Again, failure to comply is an offence.

EFFECT OF THE COMPANY'S CONSTITUTION

4.22 Section 33 provides that the provisions of a company's constitution bind the company and its members to the same extent as if there were covenants on the part of the company and of each member to observe those provisions.

4.23 Money payable by a member to the company under its constitution is a debt due from him to the company. In England and Wales and Northern Ireland it is of the nature of an ordinary contract debt.

ALTERATION OF ARTICLES

4.24 A company can alter its articles by special resolution of its members (see s 21) (see also **Chapter 7** regarding special resolutions). This includes the ability to adopt an entirely new set of articles, which is often the most efficient way to alter a private company's articles or bring them up to date (see **4.27** and **4.33** regarding the requirement to send to the Registrar a copy of the articles as amended and the requirement to provide an up-to-date copy of the articles to a member on request).

4.25 Normally a valid alteration to the articles is binding on all the members. However, there is a protection so that existing members cannot be required to contribute more money to the company unless they agree individually to do this. Unless a member consents in writing, he is not bound by an alteration to a company's articles after he became a member if and so far as the alteration:

- requires him to take or subscribe for more shares than the number held by him at the date on which the alteration is made, or

- in any way increases his liability as at that date to contribute to the company's share capital or otherwise pay money to the company.

4.26 If the company is a charity (or registered in the Scottish Charity Register), the ability for the company to alter its articles is subject to restrictions contained:

- in England and Wales, in s 64 of the Charities Act 1993

- in Northern Ireland, in Art 9 of the Charities (Northern Ireland) Order 1987 (SI 1987/2048 (NI 19))

- in Scotland, in s 112 of the Companies Act 1989 and s 16 of the Charities and Trustee Investment (Scotland) Act 2005.

4.27   If a company does alter its articles, it must send a copy of the articles as amended to the Registrar not later than 15 days after the amendment takes effect. Failure to comply with this is an offence. Note that the Act empowers the Registrar (in s 27) to send notice to a company requiring it to comply with any enactment requiring it to send to the Registrar:

- a document making or evidencing an alteration to the company's articles, or

- a copy of the company's articles as amended.

The notice must state the date on which it is issued and require the company to comply within 28 days. **If the company does not comply with the notice within the specified time, it is liable to a civil penalty of £200.** This civil penalty will apply automatically without the need for further proceedings and may be recovered by the Registrar. It is in addition to any liability to criminal proceedings for the failure to comply. These provisions are due to come into force on 1 October 2009.

4.28   There are also requirements to send notice to the Registrar where a company's constitution is altered by an enactment (other than an enactment amending the general law) or where a company's constitution is altered by an order of a court or other authority. Again, a 15 day time limit applies and failure to comply is a criminal offence.

ENTRENCHED PROVISIONS OF THE ARTICLES (SS 22–24)

4.29   A company's articles may provide that specified provisions within them may be amended or repealed only if conditions are met, or procedures are complied with, that are more restrictive than those of a special resolution. This is referred to in the Act as 'provision for entrenchment'.

4.30   Provision for entrenchment may only be made either in the company's articles on formation of the company or by an amendment to the company's articles agreed to by all the members of the company. Note that in any case, provision for entrenchment does not prevent amendment of the company's articles by agreement of all the members of the company (but also note that some companies, such as charities – see above, may be subject to other statutory restriction on how they may alter their articles).

4.31   Where a company's articles contain a provision for entrenchment the company must give notice to the Registrar (either on formation or on later amendment to include that provision, as appropriate). Thereafter, if the company whose articles contain the provision for entrenchment amends its articles and is required to send a document making or evidencing the amendment to the Registrar as a result, it must send with it a 'statement of compliance'. This is a statement certifying that the amendment has been made in accordance with the company's articles.

4.32 Where a company whose articles contain provision for entrenchment amends its articles so that they no longer contain any such provision, it must give notice of that fact to the Registrar together with a statement of compliance.

CONSTITUTIONAL DOCUMENTS TO BE PROVIDED TO MEMBERS

4.33 A company must, on request by any member, send to him a copy of the company's constitutional documents which are set out in a list in s 32 of the Act. These include:

- an up-to-date copy of the company's articles

- a copy of any resolution or agreement relating to the company to which Chapter 3 of Part 3 applies (see list of documents set out in s 29, referred to at **4.20**) and that is for the time being in force

- copies of other specified documents required to be sent to the Registrar whereby the constitution is altered

- copies of specified court orders

- a copy of the current and any past certificates of incorporation

- in the case of a company that has share capital, a current statement of capital

- in the case of a company limited by guarantee, a copy of the statement of guarantee.

4.34 The 'current statement of capital' required under this provision is a statement of:

- the total number of shares of the company

- the aggregate nominal value of those shares

- for each class of shares
  - prescribed particulars of the rights attached to those shares
  - the total number of shares of that class, and

   – the aggregate nominal value of the shares of that class, and

- the amount paid up and the amount (if any) unpaid on each share (whether paid on account of the nominal value of the share or by way of premium).

Failure to comply with this requirement is an offence.

WHO CAN BIND THE COMPANY TO A LEGAL COMMITMENT?

4.35 A company may have the capacity to do something (for instance because its objects are unrestricted), but who can bind a company to a legal commitment? The Act carries over previous provisions providing safeguards for those dealing with a company, so that they can rely on decisions made by the Board of directors. Section 40 provides that, in favour of a person dealing with a company in good faith, the power of the directors (this means the Board) to bind the company, or authorise others to do so, is deemed to be free of any limitation under the company's constitution. It is for this reason that for a transaction that may involve a high value, a third party dealing with a company will often ask for confirmation of a Board minute recording the decision of the directors to enter into the transaction or to authorise somebody to bind the company. Note that once again modified provisions apply to charities and also there are special provisions that apply to transactions with directors or their associates (see below).

4.36 This provision does not affect the right of a member to bring court proceedings to restrain an action that is beyond the power of the Board of directors, provided that this is done before the company enters into a legal obligation. Once the Board have committed a company to a legal obligation, the company is committed. However, the statutory provisions do not affect any liability incurred by the directors, or any other person, by reason of the directors exceeding their powers. So in appropriate cases directors may still be liable for damages if they exceed their powers. Directors still need to take care that actions of the company are within its capacity and that their exercise of their functions is carried out within the powers given to them by the company's constitution.

4.37 For these purposes, a person 'deals with' a company if he is a party to any transaction or other act to which the company is a party. A person dealing with the company:

- is not bound to enquire as to any limitation on the powers of the directors to bind the company or to authorise others to do so

- is presumed to have acted in good faith unless the contrary is proved

- is not to be regarded as acting in bad faith by reason only of his knowing that an act is beyond the powers of the directors under the company's constitution.

4.38 Note that 'limitations on the directors' powers under the company's constitution' include limitations deriving from a resolution of the company or of any class of shareholders and from any agreement between members of the company or of any class of shareholders.

4.39 These provisions are again modified for charities. The normal provision that ignores restrictions in the company's constitution on the power of the directors to bind the company does not apply to the acts of a company that is a charity except in favour of a person who:

- does not know at the time the act is done that the company is a charity, or

- gives full consideration in money or money's worth in relation to the act in question and does not know that the act is beyond the company's constitution.

See s 42 for detail on this.

TRANSACTIONS INVOLVING DIRECTORS OR THEIR ASSOCIATES

4.40 Under provisions in s 41, where the directors enter into a transaction that contravenes a limitation in the company's constitution and the parties to the transaction include a director of the company or of its holding company, or a person connected with any such director, the transaction is voidable at the instance of the company. This means, in effect, that if it so wishes the company is entitled to disown and extricate itself from the transaction. The transaction ceases to be so voidable if:

- the restitution of any money or other asset which was the subject matter of the transaction is no longer possible, or

- the company is indemnified for any loss or damage resulting from the transaction, or

- rights acquired bona fide for value and without actual notice of the directors' exceeding their powers by a person who is not a party to the transaction would be affected by the avoidance, or

- the transaction is affirmed by the company.

4.41 In addition any such party (and any director of the company that authorised the transaction) is liable to account to the company for any gain that he has made directly or indirectly by the transaction and to indemnify the company for any loss or damage resulting from the transaction. A person other than a director is not so liable if he shows that at the time the transaction was entered into he did not know that the directors were exceeding their powers. The section also gives the court wide powers to make such order as it thinks just on the application of the company or a party to the transaction other than a director of the company (or a director of its holding company) or connected person.

HOW DOES A COMPANY ENTER INTO OR MAKE A CONTRACT?

4.42 Provided that the company has the capacity to enter into or make the contract (for instance because it has unlimited objects – see **4.7–4.15**) the next questions must be (i) whether the company has authorised that it enter into the contract, (ii) who it has authorised to agree and make the contract on its behalf and (iii) whether the formalities required by law in making the contract have been properly complied with.

4.43 As stated above, normally the articles of association of a commercial private company will give full power to the Board of directors to exercise all the powers of the company and the Act provides certain protections to outsiders who rely on decisions of the Board. As a result, ultimate authority for contracts normally comes from the Board of directors. However, only more important contractual matters are likely to be considered by the Board and usually it will delegate authority to others within the company to take decisions and enter into contracts. Those with delegated authority will sometimes have authority to themselves delegate further down to others employed by the company. See also **Chapter 5** regarding directors' duties, which must be taken into account when deciding what and how to delegate.

4.44 Please note that third parties may be able to rely on a person who has 'apparent authority' or 'implied authority' binding the company to a contract. Examples of this include people granted the title of 'director' by a company. Outsiders are in many circumstances entitled to a certain extent to rely on the apparent fact that a company that has given a person the title 'director' has entrusted that person with a certain amount of power to bind the company to matters that may be considered to be within that director's remit. The same principles can apply to others holding apparent positions of authority within a company (either by virtue of their title or by virtue of what the company permits that person to do in practice). In a well regulated company, all officers and employees should be aware of the extent of their authority to bind the company and act within the limits of that authority. It is not intended to enter into any detail about the limits and effects of apparent or implied authority in this book. In cases of doubt, take legal advice.

4.45 A contract may be made by a company:

- in writing using the company's common seal

- in writing using the statutory alternative to the common seal

- by a person acting on behalf of the company under its authority, which may be either express authority or (as mentioned above) implied authority.

4.46 Where a contract is made by a person acting on behalf of a company, it does not have to be in writing, but of course can be, and often will be for larger contracts, or certain types of contract. Any formalities required by law in the case of a contract made by an individual also apply, unless a contrary intention appears, to a contract made by or on behalf of a company.

4.47 It is assumed for the purposes of this discussion that those binding the company to a contract are acting under actual authority granted by the company. So the contract has been authorised and they have been authorised to make it either by a decision of the Board, or more usually, in accordance with delegated (or properly sub-delegated) authority.

PRE-INCORPORATION CONTRACTS

4.48 It is not possible for a company to enter into a contract until it has been incorporated, as until then it does not exist. A contract that purports to be made by or on behalf of a company that has not been formed has effect, subject to any agreement to the contrary, as one made with the person purporting to act for the company as agent for it, and he is personally liable on the contract.

4.49 Given that it is possible to incorporate companies on a 'same day' basis, hopefully the situation of a pre-incorporation contract should not arise. Anyone wishing for a new company to enter into a contract on the same day can deal with this by arranging for a company to be incorporated accordingly on a 'same-day' basis, so that it is in existence on the day the contract is made.

THE COMPANY'S COMMON SEAL

4.50 Some documents may be executed by the company, rather than signed on its behalf. For this purpose a company in England and Wales or Northern Ireland may use its common seal (if it has one) or alternatively it can just be signed in accordance with statutory requirements (see **4.56–4.59**).

4.51 A company may have a common seal, but need not have one unless it chooses to do so. If it does have a seal, this will usually take the form of a die and counterpart with a mechanism capable of making an impression on paper. The company's name (as it appears on the certificate of incorporation or change of name) must be engraved in legible characters on the seal (if the company does have a common seal, failure to comply with this requirement is an offence). This provision regarding a seal does not apply to Scotland, and under the law of Scotland, a document signed or subscribed by or on behalf of the company in accordance with the provisions of the Requirements of Writing (Scotland) Act 1995 has effect as if executed by a company using its common seal.

4.52   The Act is silent about who is required to sign when the seal is applied to a document. Instead it provides that under the law of England and Wales and Northern Ireland a document is executed by a company (as opposed to being signed on its behalf) by affixing the common seal or alternatively by signature in accordance with the statutory provisions (as to which see below). Under previous law there were usually two signatories to attest the use of the seal, comprising the director and the company secretary or two directors. However, it is (and has been) possible for a private company to have one director and under the Act there is no longer any requirement for a private company to have a company secretary (although a private company may choose to have one – see **Chapter 5**). The articles of association of each company will state who must sign when a seal is applied to a document. The draft model articles for a private company limited by shares (see **4.18**) provide that the common seal shall only be used by authority of the directors and that unless otherwise decided by the directors, if the common seal is applied to a document, the document shall be signed by an authorised person in the presence of a witness who attests the signature. For these purposes 'an authorised person' is stated to be:

- any director of the company

- the company secretary (if any), or

- any person authorised by the directors for the purpose of signing documents to which the common seal is applied.

4.53   So, if a seal is used by a company that has adopted the new model articles, the signature of an officer or a person authorised by the directors in the presence of a witness will be required (unless the company's articles have special provisions stating otherwise). This contrasts with the 1985 Table A, which requires signature by either the director and secretary or two directors. So if using the seal. check the articles for signature requirements. Also remember that both the 1985 Table A and the new model regulations make the signature requirements for use of the seal subject to any contrary determination by the directors. So it is always open to the directors to resolve upon some other procedure for counter signature of the seal. Such complications may result in wider use of the statutory procedure for executing documents (see **4.56**).

OFFICIAL SEAL FOR USE ABROAD AND OFFICIAL SEAL FOR SHARE CERTIFICATES ETC

4.54 A company that has a seal may have an official seal for use outside the UK. This must look the same as the common seal, with the addition on its face of the place or places where it is to be used. A company can, by writing under its common seal (or, if a Scottish company, by the appropriate Scottish procedure) authorise any person to affix this seal to any deed or document to which the company is a party. The person affixing this seal must certify in writing on the deed or other document to which the seal is affixed the date on which, and the place at which, it is affixed (see s 49).

4.55 A company that has a common seal may have an official seal for use for sealing securities issued by the company, or sealing documents creating or evidencing the securities so issued. This seal must look the same as the common seal, with the addition on its face of the word 'Securities'. When affixed to the document it has the same effect as the company's common seal (see s 50).

EXECUTION OF DOCUMENTS – STATUTORY PROCEDURE

4.56 Section 44(2) (which came into force on 6 April 2008) sets out the alternative statutory procedure for a company to execute a document. It applies whether or not a company has a common seal and therefore is always available as an alternative method of execution of a document by a company. It states that a document is validly executed by a company if it is signed on behalf of the company:

- by two authorised signatories, or

- by a director of the company in the presence of a witness, who attests the signature.

4.57 For the purposes of this provision 'authorised signatories' means:

- every director of the company, and

- in the case of a private company with a secretary or a public company, the secretary (or any joint secretary) of the company.

4.58 Presumably the provision that a document may be executed by a company by the signature of one director attested by a witness was included to cater for the case of a private company with one director and no company secretary, as the company only has one statutory officer. However, note that this option is not restricted to such a company, so any company (including a public company) can execute a document by the signature of one director attested by a witness.

4.59 In favour of a purchaser in good faith for valuable consideration (including a lessee, mortgagee or other person who for valuable consideration acquires an interest in property), a document is deemed to have been duly executed by a company if it purports to be signed in accordance with the statutory provisions. A document is validly executed by a company as a deed for the purposes of s 1(2)(b) of the Law of Property (Miscellaneous Provisions) Act 1989 and for the purposes of the law in Northern Ireland if, and only if:

- it is duly executed by the company (for which see above), and

- it is delivered as a deed.

For these purposes a document is presumed to be delivered upon its being executed, unless a contrary intention is proved.

COMPANIES APPOINTING AN ATTORNEY TO EXECUTE DEEDS OR OTHER DOCUMENTS

4.60 The Act provides that a company may by an instrument executed as a deed, empower a person, either generally or in respect of specified matters, as its attorney to execute deeds or other documents on its behalf. A deed or document so executed, whether in the UK or elsewhere, has effect as if executed by the company. This provision does not apply under the law of Scotland. Scottish companies should consult a Scottish solicitor.

4.61 It is often useful for a company to appoint an attorney to execute documents relating to a particular arrangement or transaction on its behalf when it is carrying out activities in a foreign jurisdiction. Often this will be combined with other documents as part of a declaration by a Notary for use abroad confirming that the company may enter into the proposed transaction and that the attorney is duly authorised to execute any required documents on behalf of the company.

SUMMARY OF MAJOR CHANGES INTRODUCED BY THE ACT

1　Companies will have unrestricted objects unless the articles specifically restrict them (see s 31). *Due to come into force on 1 October 2009.*

2　Companies will now have just articles of association and the memorandum will be replaced by a prescribed form that is only relevant to the incorporation of the company. Provisions in the old style memorandum of an existing company will generally be treated as provisions of its articles (see ss 8, 18 and 28). *Due to come into force on 1 October 2009.*

3　The company's 'constitution' will include its articles and resolutions or agreements affecting the articles that are covered by s 29 of the Act (see s 17). *Due to come into force on 1 October 2009 (but note that s 29 came into force on 1 October 2007).*

4　There are new rules regarding 'provision for entrenchment' in a company's articles and requirements to give notice to the Registrar about them in certain circumstances (see ss 22–24). *Due to come into force on 1 October 2009.*

5　New model forms of Articles are to be prescribed for (i) private companies limited by shares, (ii) private companies limited by guarantee, and (iii) public companies. The latest draft regulations are available on the BERR website (see **Appendix 5**). *Due to come into force on 1 October 2009, but the final form of regulations may be available for planning, drafting and reference purposes as early as December 2008.*

6　On amendment of a company's articles, if a company fails to send to the Registrar a copy of the company's articles within 15 days after the amendment, the Registrar may give notice to the company to comply. Failure to comply within 28 days results in an automatic civil penalty of £200 (see s 27). *Due to come into force on 1 October 2009.*

7　A document can be executed by a company if it is signed on behalf of the company by a director in the presence of a witness who attests the signature. This applies as an alternative to use of the seal. The new provision applies to any company (see s 44). *Came into force on 6 April 2008.*

Chapter 5

DIRECTORS, THEIR DUTIES, AND THE OPTIONAL COMPANY SECRETARY

INTRODUCTION

5.1   See **Chapter 6** for discussion regarding how directors make decisions and the collective nature of their responsibility for the direction of the company. This Chapter focuses on the company's individual directors and their duties. It also covers the Act's new provisions regarding the company secretary of a private company.

5.2   Directors may be subject to various duties under other legislation (such as taxation provisions or health and safety legislation) which are outside the scope of this book. However, they are also subject to duties owed to the company under company law. In carrying out his duties and responsibilities, each director has in the past been subject to various duties that have evolved through decisions of the courts based on common law rules and equitable principles (which I shall refer to as 'common law duties'). The Act has introduced a potentially far reaching change to the director's duties owed to the company, by attempting to list them in statute as 'statutory duties'. As can be seen in the more detailed comment below, the exact interaction between the statutory duties now introduced and the principles contained in the common law duties they replace is uncertain. It seems likely that following implementation of the Act we may see a 'bedding down' period regarding the new statutory directors' duties where challenges in the courts and the judgments which they elicit establish some further clarity about the exact effect of the Act on this area. Note that the Act's statutory duties introduce some changes to the duties previously established under the common law and equitable principles, but it is quite possible that the courts may regard these changes as minor.

5.3   The Act has also introduced some changes about who may be a director, removing a previously imposed statutory maximum age limit and imposing a new statutory minimum age limit (perhaps a sign of legislation driven by a demographically aging population?). Corporate directors are permitted, but now every company must have at least one director who is a natural person (subject to transitional provisions, see **5.12** below).

5.4   There are (as before) provisions requiring the disclosure of directors' details in a register of directors and on the public record at the Registrar, although there are slight changes to the detail of what is required. These changes are due to be introduced from 1 October 2009. Prior to the Act there was concern about the requirement to disclose a director's residential address. This was in the past partly assuaged by the use of 'confidentiality orders' in cases of serious risk. The Act will deal with this issue by providing for the use of a 'service address' by any director. This provision is also due to come into force on 1 October 2009. So the residential address of a director will no longer have to be publicly available. However, the residential address will still have to be registered and notified, to be kept as 'protected information' which is only open to certain parties.

5.5   The provisions that deal with possible conflicts of interest between directors and their company and the requirement for shareholder's approval in some cases of such possible conflict have been re-written. It is now possible for a private company to make a loan to a director if the requisite members' approval is obtained.

5.6   A public company is required to have a company secretary but there is no longer any statutory requirement for a private company to appoint a company secretary. If a private company does have a company secretary, this must be notified to the Registrar and details entered in a register of secretaries.

WHO CAN BE A DIRECTOR, NUMBER OF DIRECTORS AND WHAT ARE THE EFFECTS OF A BREACH?

Number of directors (s 154)

5.7   A private company need only have one director (and under the Act is not required to have a company secretary, although it can choose to have one – see **5.123**).

5.8   A public company is required to have a minimum of two directors. In practice a public company which has shares held by the public will have more directors to ensure a balanced board, containing sufficient expertise, which operates under principles of good corporate governance.

Minimum age for appointment as director

5.9   A person cannot be appointed to take office as a director unless he is at least 16 years old (subject to any provisions set out in regulations made by the Secretary of State) (see ss 157–158). This provision came into force on 1 October 2008.

5.10   Where a person was appointed a director of a company before this provision came into force, and that person was still 16 when it came into force on 1 October 2008, that person automatically ceased to be a director, the

Registrar will have automatically notified that on the public record and the company should have altered its register of directors (see s 159).

Maximum age for appointment as a director

5.11 There is no longer any restriction on the maximum age of a director.

Corporate directors

5.12 It is possible to appoint a corporate body as a director. However, note that the Act requires that every company must have at least one director who is a natural person (see s 155). This provision came into force on 1 October 2008. However, note that there is a transitional saving for companies that on 8 November 2008:

- had at least one director if a private company (or at least two directors if a public company), and

- none of the directors were natural persons.

In such a case, the requirement under s 155 to have at least one director who is a natural person does not apply until 1 October 2010.

Effect of breach of requirements regarding number of directors or corporate directors

5.13 If it appears to the Secretary of State that a company is in breach of requirements as to number of directors or the requirement to have at least one director that is a natural person, he may give the company a direction under s 156 of the Act. The direction must:

- specify the statutory requirement the company appears to be in breach of

- specify what the company must do in order to comply with the direction

- specify the period in which it must do so (which must be not less than one month or more than three months after the date on which the direction is given), and

- inform the company of the consequences of failing to comply.

The company must comply with the direction by making the necessary appointment(s) and giving notice of them to the Registrar in accordance with statutory requirements (see **Chapter 10**). Failure to comply is an offence.

SERVICE ADDRESSES FOR DIRECTORS

5.14   Every company must keep a register containing details of its directors and notify such details to the Registrar so that they are contained on the public record (see **8.26–8.31** for full requirements). In the past some directors have been concerned about, or suffered problems because of, notifying their residential address in accordance with previous statutory requirements. The law was previously modified to allow for confidentiality orders where availability of a director's residential address might put that director at risk. The Act extends this, and under its provisions (which are due to come into force on 1 October 2009):

- The company's own register of directors (which is open to inspection) will contain a service address for each director who is an individual. A person's service address may be stated to be 'The company's registered office' and it is also possible for a person to use his usual residential address as his service address; there is provision to make regulations regarding conditions with which a service address must comply. The regulations – the Companies Act 2006 (Annual Return and Service Addresses) Regulations, SI 2008/3000 – provide that a service address must not be a PO Box number or a Document Exchange number and that it must be a place where:
  - the service of documents can be effected by physical delivery, and
  - the delivery of documents is capable of being recorded by the obtaining of an acknowledgement of delivery.

- The company must also maintain a separate register of directors' usual residential addresses for directors who are individuals (see **8.34–8.36**); if a director's usual residential address is the same as his service address, this register need only contain an entry to that effect, but this does not apply if the service address is stated to be 'The company's registered office'.

- This information must be provided to the Registrar on incorporation or on any change in the details registered in either register in accordance with statutory requirements (see **2.30–2.37**, **8.27–8.34**, **10.13** and **10.16**).

- The usual residential address of the director that is an individual (or, if applicable, the information that his service address is his usual residential address) is defined by the Act as 'protected information' (and it continues to be such after a person ceases to be a director).

- A company must not use or disclose such protected information except:
  - for communicating with the director concerned
  - in order to comply with any requirement of the Companies Acts as to particulars to be sent to the Registrar, or
  - in accordance with an order of the court for disclosure under s 244.

- The Registrar must omit protected information from the material on the register available for public inspection if it has been provided to the Registrar under these provisions. However, the Registrar is not obliged to check other documents, or other parts of the document providing the information, to ensure the absence of protected information, or to omit from material available for public inspection anything registered before this provision comes into force. This means that the Registrar does not have to (and will not) 'weed' information previously provided, so that if a director's residential address was provided before this comes into force, it will remain on the public record. However, see also **5.15** regarding the possibility of making addresses filed from 1 January 2003 unavailable for public inspection.

- Save as above, the Registrar must not use or disclose protected information except:
  – for communicating with the director
  – to a public authority (which for these purposes includes any person or body having functions of a public nature) specified in regulations (see immediately below)
  – to a credit reference agency (which for this purpose means a person carrying on a business comprising the furnishing of information relevant to the financial standing of individuals, being information collected by the agency for that purpose) (but see also the further detail set out in the regulations referred to immediately below)
  – in accordance with an order of the court for disclosure under s 244.

- The Secretary of State may make regulations covering:
  – conditions for the Registrar disclosing information and fees
  – provisions for applications to the Registrar to refrain from disclosing protected information to a credit reference agency (and related matters).

At the time of writing draft regulations regarding this and to whom the Registrar may disclose protected information are available on BERR's website (see **Appendix 5**) entitled 'The Companies (Disclosure of Address) Regulations'. They detail the specified public authorities to whom the Registrar may disclose this information and also regulate disclosure by the Registrar to credit reference agencies.

Under s 243 and the draft regulations, an individual who is, or proposes to become, a director may make an application to the Registrar to refrain from disclosing his residential address to a credit reference agency. The grounds for such an application will be serious risk of violence or intimidation or that he has been employed by the Government Communications Headquarters, the Secret Intelligence Service, the Security Service or a police force. A s 243 application may also be made by a company on behalf of directors who are individuals on the ground of serious risk of violence or intimidation or by a subscriber to a memorandum on behalf of proposed directors on the same grounds. A director in respect of whom a confidentiality order was in force immediately before 1 October 2009 will automatically be treated as having made a successful s 243 application. Therefore a person with a confidentiality order in force at that date will automatically benefit and his or her residential address will not be disclosed to a credit reference agency.

• The court may make an order for disclosure of protected information under s 244 by the company or by the Registrar if:
  – there is evidence that the service of documents at a service address other than the director's usual residential address is not effective to bring them to the notice of the director, or
  – it is necessary or expedient for the information to be provided in connection with the enforcement of an order or decree of the court
  and the court is otherwise satisfied that it is appropriate to make the order. An order for disclosure by the Registrar may only be made if the company does not have the director's usual residential address, or has been dissolved.

• The Registrar may (under provisions in ss 245 and 246) put a director's usual residential address on the public record if:
  – communications sent by the Registrar to the director and requiring a response within a specified period remain unanswered, or
  – there is evidence that the service of documents at a service address is not effective to bring them to the notice of the director.
  The Registrar must give notice of the proposal to the director and every company of which the Registrar has been notified he is a director. This notice must state the grounds on which it is proposed to put the director's usual residential address on the public record, and specify a period within which representations may be made before that is done.

• If the Registrar does put a director's usual residential address on the public record in accordance with the above provisions, it must give notice that it has done so to the director and to the company. On receipt of that notice, the company must enter the director's usual residential address in its register of directors as his service address and state in its register of directors' residential addresses that his usual residential address is the same as his service address.

• A director whose usual residential address has been put on the public record by the Registrar in accordance with s 246 may not register a service address other than his usual residential address for a period of 5 years (see s 246(7)).

APPLICATION TO THE REGISTRAR TO MAKE ADDRESS UNAVAILABLE FOR PUBLIC INSPECTION

5.15 Under s 1088 the Secretary of State may make regulations requiring the Registrar, on application, to make an address on the register unavailable for public inspection. This could apply to any address, not just a director's address. At the time of writing a draft of 'The Companies (Disclosure of Address) Regulations' is available on BERR's website (see **Appendix 5**). These provide for the circumstances of such an application by an individual and by a company. An application may be made by an individual who is, or proposes to become a director (or who was a director, secretary or permanent representative of a company) whose usual residential address was placed on the register in accordance with statutory requirements from 1 January 2003 onwards. The grounds for the application are those of serious risk of violence or intimidation or that he has been employed by the Government Communications Headquarters, the Secret Intelligence Service, the Security Service or a police force or that he is a person in respect of whom a s 243 application has been granted (or is deemed to be granted) (see above). An application may be made by a company in respect of all of its members and former members whose addresses were contained in an annual return or a return of allotments delivered to the Registrar or in respect of subscribers' addresses where such addresses were on a memorandum delivered to the Registrar on grounds of serious risk of violence or intimidation.

APPOINTMENT OF A DIRECTOR

5.16 On incorporation of a new company, the persons named as directors in the statement of proposed officers automatically are deemed appointed as directors, both under the Companies Act 1985 and under the Act's provisions due to come into force on 1 October 2009 (see s 16(6)). No further action is required apart from entries in the company's register of directors and register of directors' residential addresses.

5.17 After registration, the appointment of directors is governed by the company's articles. The draft regulations prescribing model articles of association for private companies limited by shares (available on BERR's website, see **Appendix 5**) simply provide that:

> 'Any person who is willing to act as a director, and is permitted by law to do so, may be appointed to be a director:
>
> (a) by ordinary resolution of the shareholders; or
> (b) by a decision of the directors.'

The draft model articles also provide that if, as a result of death, a company has no shareholders or directors, the personal representatives of the last shareholder to die have the right to appoint a director.

5.18 It is of course possible for a company to have entirely different provisions in its articles regarding the appointment of directors. For instance a wholly owned subsidiary may have provisions stating that the holding company may simply appoint and remove directors by notice in writing to the company.

5.19 On appointment of directors after incorporation, various event related compliance requirements apply, see **10.12–10.14**.

TERMINATION OF A DIRECTOR'S APPOINTMENT

5.20 Termination of a director's appointment is covered by a mixture of automatic legal provisions and what is contained in the company's articles. For instance a person is prohibited from being a director if he becomes bankrupt or is disqualified from being a director. These are provisions that will apply regardless of a company's articles, but they will only happen in a minority of cases.

5.21 The simplest way to terminate the appointment of a director is for that director to resign by notice in writing to the company stating that he resigns with effect from a specified date (normally the same date as the letter, but it may be a future date). That is what will occur in the majority of cases. On any occasion where the termination of the appointment of the director is involuntary (apart from death) legal advice should be taken prior to the termination to deal with any points connected with the director's contractual, employment or other legal rights and to ensure that the intended actions will be effective.

5.22 It is important to check the provisions contained in the articles. For instance, the draft model articles of association for private companies limited by shares available on the BERR website provide that:

'A person ceases to be a director as soon as:

(a)   that person ceases to be a director by virtue of any provision of the Companies Act 2006, or is prohibited from being a director by law;

(b)   a bankruptcy order is made against that person;

(c)   a composition is made with that person's creditors generally in satisfaction of that person's debts;

(d)   a registered medical practitioner who is treating that person gives a written opinion to the company stating that that person has become physically or mentally incapable of acting as a director and may remain so for more than three months;

(e)   by reason of that person's mental health, a court makes an order which wholly or partly prevents that person from exercising any powers or rights which that person would otherwise have; or

(f)   notification is received by the company from the director that the director is resigning or retiring from office, and such resignation or retirement has taken effect in accordance with its terms.'

5.23 The provisions in the latest draft model articles are very different from an earlier draft, which contained wording attempting to deal with the situation where a director refused or omitted to take part in Board meetings and processes, or simply disappeared. However, the wording previously suggested to deal with this was felt to be too open to abuse, and so does not appear in the current draft.

5.24 On termination of appointment of a director, various event related compliance requirements apply, see **10.15–10.17**.

MEMBERS' RESOLUTION TO REMOVE A DIRECTOR

5.25 Section 168 of the Act provides that a company may by ordinary resolution remove a director from the office of director, notwithstanding anything in any agreement between it and him. However, this section does not deprive the director (or former director) of compensation or damages payable to him in respect of the termination of his appointment as director or of any appointment terminating with that as director.

5.26 Removal of a director in accordance with s 168 is subject to compliance with some special requirements.

1   'Special notice' is required of a resolution to remove a director under s 168 or to appoint somebody instead of a director so removed at the meeting at which he is removed. 'Special notice' is defined by s 312. This provides that where the Companies Acts require special notice of a resolution, **the resolution is not effective unless**:
   –   notice of intention to move it has been given **to the company** at least 28 days before the meeting at which it is moved
   –   the company must, where practicable, give its members notice of any such resolution in the same manner and at the same time as it gives notice of the meeting
   –   where that is not practicable, the company must give its members notice at least 14 days before the meeting either by advertisement in a newspaper having appropriate circulation or by any other manner allowed by the company's articles
   –   if, after notice of intention to move such a resolution has been given to the company, a meeting is called for a date 28 days or less after the notice has been given, the notice is deemed to have been properly given, though not given within the time required. (This is designed to deal with the case where the directors deliberately call a meeting on shorter notice in an attempt to invalidate the special notice.)

2   On receipt of notice of an intended resolution to remove a director under s 168, the company must forthwith send a copy of the notice to the director concerned.

3   The director, whether or not a member of the company, is entitled to be heard on the resolution at the meeting.

4   Where notice is given of an intended resolution to remove a director under s 168, and the director concerned makes with respect to it representations in writing to the company (not exceeding a reasonable length) and requests their notification to members of the company, the company shall (unless the representations are received too late for it to do so):
    –   in any notice of the resolution given to members of the company state the fact of the representations having been made, and
    –   send a copy of the representations to every member of the company to whom notice of the meeting is sent (whether before or after receipt of the representations by the company).

5   If a copy of the representations is not sent as required (whether because they are received too late or because of the company's default) the director may (without prejudice to his right to be heard orally) require that the representations shall be read out at the meeting.

6   Copies of the representations need not be sent out and the representations need not be read out at the meeting if, on the application either of the company or of any other person who claims to be aggrieved, the court is satisfied that the rights conferred by s 169 are being abused (and there is provision for the court to order the director to pay the company's costs).

5.27   It is not possible to use a written resolution to pass a resolution under this section removing a director before the expiration of his period of office. This protects the rights of the director to ensure that his views are received and/or heard and that the matter is considered at a meeting where discussion is possible.

5.28   Because this statutory provision is somewhat tortuous, detailed and lengthy, many companies choose to have an alternative provision in their articles allowing for a director to be removed by simpler means. Section 168 specifically provides that it does not derogate from any power to remove a director that may exist apart from that section. So a simpler provision in the company's articles is perfectly permissible (and perhaps advisable for wholly owned subsidiaries). Once again, such a provision will not affect any rights of any such director to receive compensation or damages.

TYPES OF DIRECTOR

5.29   In the Companies Acts, the word 'director' includes any person occupying the position of director, by whatever name called (see s 250). So, if the articles use a term other than 'directors' for those who are the governing structure of the company, this does not make any difference, they will still be regarded as 'directors' under the Companies Acts.

Executive and non-executive directors

5.30 These are terms in general use, but they are not derived from the Companies Acts. The term 'executive director' is generally used to refer to a director who is an employee taking part in and directing the day-to-day operations of the company. The term non-executive director is generally used to refer to a director who does not take part in the day-to-day activities of the company but whose views, expertise, experience and perhaps also contacts contribute to the planning, deliberations and activities of the Board. Many private companies choose to have a non-executive director or directors to gain a broadening of the perspective taken by the Board. Sometimes outside investors will insist on the appointment of one or more non-executive directors.

Shadow director

5.31 This is a term in the Companies Acts and is defined as 'a person in accordance with whose directions or instructions the directors of a company are accustomed to act' (see s 251). A person is not to be regarded as a shadow director by reason only that the directors act on advice given by him in a professional capacity. A body corporate is not to be regarded as a shadow director of any subsidiary companies for the purposes of the following provisions of the Act:

- Chapter 2 (general duties of directors)

- Chapter 4 (transactions requiring members' approval), or

- Chapter 6 (contract with sole member who is also a director)

by reason only that the directors of the subsidiary are accustomed to act in accordance with its directions or instructions.

5.32 Many provisions in the Act that apply to directors also apply to shadow directors (for instance (i) the general duties of directors owed to the company apply to shadow directors where, and to the extent that, the corresponding common law rules or equitable principles so apply, and (ii) a shadow director is treated as an officer of the company for the purposes of committing the offence of failing to keep a correct register of directors' residential addresses).

5.33 The intention of the shadow director provisions is to 'catch' a person who, although not appointed as a director, stands behind the directors, who are accustomed to act in accordance with what he directs and instructs, so that person is the real directing mind of the company and the actual directors are 'men of straw'. Whether a person is a shadow director in any case will depend on the particular facts of the case. The important point for a person dealing with a Board of directors (and for the Board and company secretary) is not to accidentally create a situation where that person may be a shadow director. Proper records of deliberations and decisions of the Board can help to demonstrate that a person is not a shadow director.

De facto director

5.34 The court can decide that a person who, although not appointed as a director, carries on actions as if a director, is a 'de facto director' and therefore subject to the requirements, duties and sanctions that apply to a normal director. The critical factor here is whether the person is part of the governing structure of the company. A de facto director must participate, or have the right to participate, in corporate decision-making, as opposed to merely advising the company's decision-makers. Do not confuse a 'de facto director' with a 'shadow director' (see above). Whether a person is a de facto director will depend on the particular facts and again, proper records of the deliberations and decisions of the Board can help to demonstrate that a person is not a de facto director.

DIRECTORS' DUTIES OWED TO THE COMPANY – INTRODUCTION

5.35 As stated in the introduction to this chapter, the Act provides for a major change to the law regarding the general duties owed by a director of a company to that company. For the first time, these duties are set out in statute by being listed in the Act to have effect in the place of certain common law rules and equitable principles that have been developed over time by the courts. However, the courts are still given some latitude in the way in which they interpret and apply the new statutory general duties. Sections 170(3) and (4) state:

'(3) The general duties are based on certain common law rules and equitable principles as they apply in relation to directors and have effect in place of those rules and principles as regards the duties owed to a company by a director.

(4) The general duties shall be interpreted and applied in the same way as common law rules or equitable principles, and regard shall be had to the corresponding common law rules and equitable principles in interpreting and applying the general duties.'

5.36 Also note that, although based on the common law rules and equitable principles, the new statutory general duties are not exactly the same as them and in some cases have introduced some very important changes and differences. This means that we may see a period of increased litigation and argument regarding:

•   the exact meaning of some of the new statutory duties

• the way in which such duties should be interpreted and applied.

5.37 See also the comments in **5.71–5.73** regarding derivative actions regarding who may bring a court action in connection with breach of these duties. Any questions connected with directors' duties should be treated with care and if there is any question or doubt, legal advice should be sought.

5.38 Set out below are the general statutory duties contained in Part 10, Chapter 2 (ss 170 to 181) of the Act.

5.39 Where the company's articles contain provisions for dealing with conflicts of interest, the general duties are not infringed by anything done (or omitted) by the directors, or any of them, in accordance with those provisions in the articles (see s 180(4)). This is likely to have particular importance in relation to the duty to avoid conflicts of interest under s 175 (see below). Many companies may be advised to insert provisions into their articles which provide a more practical solution to conflicts of interest than that provided by the statutory provisions. Existing companies that have adopted reg 85 of the 1985 Table A already have provisions that allow a director to be a party to a transaction with the company subject to disclosure safeguards. However, companies may be advised to review their existing articles generally in the light of the new law. Note that charitable companies are restricted by the Act regarding what they put in their articles in this respect.

5.40 The general duties have effect subject to the common law rule that all of the members can, in appropriate cases, unanimously give authority, specifically or generally, for anything to be done (or omitted) by the directors (or any of them) that would otherwise be a breach of duty (see s 180(4)). Companies and directors should take legal advice before seeking to rely on this provision. Note also that under s 239 the members of a company may by resolution of the members ratify conduct by a director amounting to negligence, default, breach of duty or breach of trust in relation to the company. For this purpose, votes of the director (if a member) and any member connected with him are disregarded.

Duty to act within constitution and powers (s 171)

5.41

'A director must:

(a)   act in accordance with the company's constitution, and
(b)   only exercise powers for the purposes for which they are conferred.'

5.42 See also **Chapter 4** regarding legal capacity and a company's constitution. In carrying out or authorising an action by the company, in addition to being satisfied that they and the company are complying with any other applicable legal requirements, the directors should be satisfied that:

- the company has the capacity to do it and this is not restricted by its constitution

- the directors have authority under the company's constitution to exercise the power, and

- the directors are exercising that power for the purpose for which it was conferred by the constitution.

An example of the exercise of a power for a purpose other than that for which it is conferred might arise in relation to the issue of shares. The issue of shares to raise capital for a commercial company would be a proper purpose, but the issue of shares solely to forestall a takeover bid is unlikely to be (even if the directors believe that this is in the best interests of the company).

Duty to promote the success of the company (s 172)

5.43

'A director of a company must act in the way he considers, in good faith, would be most likely to promote the success of the company for the benefit of its members as a whole, and in doing so have regard (amongst other matters) to:

(a) the likely consequences of any decision in the long term,
(b) the interests of the company's employees,
(c) the need to foster the company's business relationships with suppliers, customers and others,
(d) the impact of the company's operations on the community and the environment,
(e) the desirability of the company maintaining a reputation for high standards of business conduct, and
(f) the need to act fairly as between members of the company.'

5.44 Where (or to the extent that) the purposes of the company consist of (or include) purposes other than for the benefit of its members, the above duty has effect as if reference to promoting the success of the company for the benefit of its members were to achieving those purposes. An example where this is likely to apply is a charitable company.

5.45 This is a new duty that has resulted in a lot of discussion about its meaning and practical effects. Note that the duty to promote the success of the company is **for the benefit of the members** (and not necessarily for the benefit of any of the stakeholder groups referred to) and that the director must have regard to the listed items **amongst other matters**.

5.46 This duty does not affect any enactment or rule of law requiring directors, in certain circumstances to consider or act in the interests of creditors. If a company is approaching insolvency (or is insolvent) the directors should take professional advice – for many reasons, and this includes advice on how far they should consider or act in the interests of creditors.

Duty to exercise independent judgement (s 173)

5.47

> '(1) A director of a company must exercise independent judgment.
> (2) This duty is not infringed by his acting –
>   (a) in accordance with an agreement duly entered into by the company that restricts the future exercise of discretion by its directors, or
>   (b) in a way authorised by the company's constitution.'

5.48 The meaning of this is clear, although its application to specific circumstances may sometimes be difficult. The company can enter into an agreement that restricts the future exercise of discretion, but remember that the decision of the directors allowing the company to enter into such an agreement is also subject to the need to comply with directors' duties, including those such as the duty to promote the success of the company and the duty to avoid conflicts of interest.

Duty to exercise reasonable care, skill and diligence (s 174)

5.49

> '(1) A director of a company must exercise reasonable care, skill and diligence.
> (2) This means the care, skill and diligence that would be exercised by a reasonably diligent person with –
>   (a) the general knowledge, skill and experience that may reasonably be expected of a person carrying out the functions carried out by the director in relation to the company, and
>   (b) the general knowledge, skill and experience that the director has.'

5.50 This test is the same as that applies to certain actions of directors under the Insolvency Act 1986. Note that the test is both objective in relation to the position held by the director ('may reasonably be expected of a person carrying out the functions carried out by the director in relation to the company') and subjective in relation to the director's own actual knowledge and experience ('the general knowledge, skill and experience that the director has').

Duty to avoid conflicts of interest (s 175)

5.51 For companies other than a company that is a charity, this duty does not apply to a conflict of interest arising in relation to a transaction or arrangement with the company (see s 175(3)) (but also see other statutory provisions below which may require members' consent in some of such cases). For the special provisions that apply to a charitable company, see below.

5.52   Also note that, as stated in the introduction to the general duties in **5.39**, if a company's articles contain provisions for dealing with conflicts of interest, the general duties of directors are not infringed by anything done (or omitted) by the directors (or any of them) in accordance with those provisions in the articles (see s 184(4)). So check whether there are provisions in the articles for dealing with conflicts of interest and comply with them. The following states the position as set out in the Act only. Also remember that the members can give authority for conflicts (see **5.40**) and in many cases for a private company with few members, this may be the preferred course.

5.53   Section 175(1) provides:

> 'A director of a company must avoid a situation in which he has, or can have, a direct or indirect interest that conflicts, or possibly may conflict, with the interests of the company.'

5.54   This is the starting point for this duty. It includes a conflict of interest and duty and a conflict of duties (see s 175(7)). So far it seems pretty draconian as it includes situations where a director **has or can have** a direct or indirect interest and/or duty **that conflicts or possibly may conflict**. This could cover a wide range of situations. So s 175(4) provides:

> '(4) This duty is not infringed –
>
> (a)   if the situation cannot reasonably be regarded as likely to give rise to a conflict of interest; or
> (b)   if the matter is authorised by the directors.'

5.55   The exception in sub-clause (4)(a) would seem to be of limited effect in protecting directors. The exception in (b) – authorisation of the conflict by the board of directors – is likely to be the preferred course to clear away the possibility of an infringement of this duty. However, note that under sub-section (5) authorisation by the directors of a private company can only be given if nothing in the company's constitution invalidates such authorisation, and the authorisation must be given by the matter being proposed to and authorised by the directors. So if there is argument on whether the Act has been complied with, it will presumably not be enough to say the other directors knew and agreed, unless it is possible to show that the matter was proposed to and authorised by the Board. Note also that for private companies incorporated before 1 October 2008 (when this provision came into force), it is necessary for the members of the company to first resolve that authorisation of conflicts can be given in this way by the directors. An authorisation resolution of this type must be filed at Companies House. For a public company the requirements go further, because its constitution must include a provision enabling the directors to authorise the matter and it must be proposed to and authorised by them in accordance with the constitution.

5.56   Note also that sub-section (6) provides that the authorisation by the directors is only effective if:

'(a)   any requirement as to the quorum at the meeting at which the matter is considered is met without counting the director in question or any other interested director, and

(b)   the matter was agreed to without their voting or would have been agreed to if their votes had not been counted.'

However, there is nothing that says that the proposal and authorisation has to be made at a meeting (see **Chapter 6** on Decisions of the Directors). Similar restrictions should be taken to apply to a directors' decision to give authorisation where that decision is taken by other means.

5.57   The practical effects of complying with this duty where the company's articles do not contain provisions for dealing with conflicts of interest must be thought through by each director and by the company and legal advice may be required.

5.58   Section 175 states that the duty applies in particular to the exploitation of any property, information or opportunity (and it is immaterial whether the company could take advantage of the property, information or opportunity).

5.59   Where any of the statutory provisions in Chapter 4 of Part 10 of the Act apply to a matter (see **5.85** onwards), and

- approval of the members is given in accordance with those provisions, or

- the matter is one as to which it is provided that approval is not needed,

it is not necessary to also comply with this duty, or the duty under s 176 (duty not to accept benefits from third parties).

Duty not to accept benefits from third parties (s 176)

5.60

'(1)   A director of a company must not accept a benefit from a third party conferred by reason of –
(a)   his being a director, or
(b)   his doing (or not doing) anything as a director.'

5.61   A 'third party' means a person other than the company, an associated body corporate (which basically means a body corporate in the same group, see s 256 for precise definition) or a person acting on behalf of the company or an associated body corporate.

5.62   Benefits received by a director from a person by whom his services (as a director or otherwise) are provided to the company are not regarded as conferred by a third party. This might apply, for instance, if the director's services are provided via the medium of another company.

5.63 This duty is not infringed if the acceptance of the benefit cannot reasonably be regarded as likely to give rise to a conflict of interest or duty.

5.64 Where any of the statutory provisions in Chapter 4 of Part 10 of the Act apply to a matter (see **5.85** onwards), and

- approval of the members is given in accordance with those provisions, or

- the matter is one as to which it is provided that approval is not needed,

it is not necessary to also comply with this duty, or the duty under s 175 (duty to avoid conflicts of interest).

Duty to declare interest in proposed transaction or arrangement (s 177)

5.65

'If a director of a company is in any way, directly or indirectly, interested in a proposed transaction or arrangement with the company, he must declare the nature and extent of that interest to the other directors.'

5.66 The declaration may (but need not) be made:

- at a meeting of the directors

- by notice in writing to the other directors (which may be sent in hard copy or, if the recipient has agreed, by electronic means, and which must be retained with the records of the next meeting of the directors after it is given (s 184)), or

- by general notice that the director has an interest (as member, officer, employee or otherwise) in a specified body corporate or firm, or that he is connected with a specified person, and that he is to be regarded as interested in any transaction or arrangement made after the date of the notice with that body corporate or firm or person;
    - the general notice must state the nature and extent of the director's interest in the body corporate or firm or (as the case may be) the nature of his connection with the person
    - the general notice is not effective unless:
        - (a) it is given at a meeting of the directors, or
        - (b) the director takes reasonable steps to secure that it is brought up and read at the next meeting of the directors after it is given.

5.67 Any such declaration must be made before the company enters into the transaction or arrangement. However, the section does not require a declaration of interest of which the director is not aware or where the director is not aware of the transaction or arrangement in question. For this purpose a director is treated as being aware of matters of which he ought reasonably to be aware (see s 177(5)).

5.68 If such a declaration of interest proves to be, or becomes, inaccurate or incomplete, a further declaration must be made (see s 177(3)).

5.69 A director need not declare an interest:

- if it cannot reasonably be regarded as likely to give rise to a conflict of interest

- if, or to the extent that, the other directors are already aware of it (and for this purpose the directors are treated as being aware of anything of which they ought reasonably to be aware), or

- if, or to the extent that, it concerns terms of his service contract that have been or are to be considered:
  – by a meeting of the directors, or
  – by a committee of the directors appointed for the purpose under the company's constitution.

5.70 When considering how to comply with this duty in practice, it is also necessary to consider compliance with the duty to avoid conflicts of interest (see **5.51** onwards). For instance, it may be that a general notice (and also any specific notice) provided in accordance with provisions connected with this duty might be used to obtain director's authorisation for a possible conflict of interest or duty in accordance with the requirements to avoid a conflict of interest. Consider also the statutory provisions **requiring** a director to declare an interest in an **existing** transaction or arrangement (see **5.80** onwards) (as opposed to the **duty** to declare an interest in a **proposed** transaction or arrangement – which is the subject of this section).

DERIVATIVE ACTIONS – WHO CAN ENFORCE THE COMPANY'S RIGHTS?

5.71 If a director is in breach of a duty owed to the company (or all of them are) who can enforce the rights of the company against him or them? Normally the rights of a company will be enforced following a decision of, and/or under the direction of, the directors. They are likely to be unwilling to enforce the company's rights against themselves. Because of this problem, the courts evolved the concept of a 'derivative action', under which in certain circumstances a member of the company could bring a claim in the courts to enforce the company's rights. The Act puts the derivative claim on a statutory footing. There are provisions in the Act for (i) England & Wales or Northern Ireland, and (ii) Scotland, to take account of differences in Scottish law. Only the first of these is summarised below.

5.72 The derivative claims provisions apply to proceedings by a member of a company in respect of a cause of action vested in the company, and seeking relief on behalf of the company – a 'derivative claim'. A derivative claim may only be brought in accordance with the derivative claims provisions contained in the Act (see s 260 onwards) or in pursuance of an order of the court in proceedings for protection of members against unfair prejudice in accordance with s 994 of the Act. A derivative claim may be brought only in respect of a cause of action arising from an actual or proposed act or omission involving negligence, default, breach of duty or breach of trust by a director of the company (which includes a former director and a shadow director). The cause of action may be against the director or another person or both.

5.73 Because of concerns about frivolous derivative actions, the Act imposes conditions that are intended to ensure that such frivolous claims are dismissed early in the process and that the court has power to make any consequential order (whether as to costs or otherwise) that it considers appropriate (see s 261 onwards).

CONSEQUENCES OF BREACH OF GENERAL DUTIES

5.74 All of the duties are regarded as fiduciary duties of directors, save for the duty to exercise reasonable care, skill and diligence. This means that the remedies available for breach of such duties by a director remain:

- damages or compensation for loss suffered by the company

- restoration of the company's property

- an account of profits made

- where the director has failed to disclose an interest in a contract, rescission of the contract.

5.75 If a breach of any of the general duties is suspected, take legal advice. In appropriate cases it may be possible for all the members to unanimously agree to authorise the breach and relieve the directors from any liability to the company in respect of such breach. Note also the provisions of s 239 of the Act that provide for ratification of acts of directors by a mere resolution of members (see **5.40**).

MODIFICATIONS OF PROVISIONS IN RELATION TO CHARITABLE COMPANIES

5.76 For a company that is a charity, s 175 (Duty to avoid conflicts of interest) has effect subject to modifications (see s 181).

5.77   Normally, for other companies, this duty does not apply in relation to a conflict of interest arising in relation to a transaction or arrangement with the company. For a company that is a charity, the duty can only not apply in relation to a transaction or arrangement with the company to the extent that the company's articles allow such disapplication. The articles may only allow this in relation to descriptions of transaction or arrangement specified in the articles.

5.78   Normally, for other companies, the directors can (subject to certain requirements, see above) authorise a conflict of interest, or a potential conflict. For a company that is a charity, such authorisation may only be given by the directors where the company's constitution includes provision enabling them to authorise the matter, by the matter being proposed to and authorised by them in accordance with the company's constitution.

5.79   In addition, some other exemption provisions are modified so that they apply if or to the extent that the company's articles allow the particular duties to be disapplied, which they may only do in relation to descriptions of transactions or arrangement specified in the company's articles (see s 181).

REQUIREMENT FOR A DIRECTOR TO DECLARE AN INTEREST IN AN EXISTING TRANSACTION OR ARRANGEMENT

5.80   Where a director is in any way, directly or indirectly, interested in a transaction or arrangement that has been entered into by the company, he must declare the nature and extent of the interest to the other directors (see s 182).

5.81   Note that this is a different provision from the **duty** to declare an interest in a **proposed** transaction or arrangement (see **5.65**). This provision is not a 'general duty' under the Act. The sanction for failure to comply with this provision requiring a declaration in relation to a transaction **that has been entered into by the company** is that it is an offence to fail to comply. However, failure to disclose may also involve breach of a statutory duty (eg duty to avoid conflicts of interest). Consider also the interaction between the requirement and the duty. This **requirement** to declare the nature and extent of an interest in an **existing** transaction or arrangement of the company does not apply if or to the extent that that the interest has been declared under the separate **duty** to declare this in respect of a **proposed** transaction or arrangement. So the original declaration is sufficient, provided that neither the nature nor the extent of the interest changes.

5.82   If a declaration of interest under this requirement proves to be, or becomes, inaccurate or incomplete, a further declaration must be made. Any declaration required must be made as soon as practicable. No declaration of an interest is required of which the director is not aware or where the director is not aware of the transaction or arrangement in question. For this purpose a director is treated as being aware of matters of which he ought reasonably to be aware.

5.83 The declaration must be made:

- at a meeting of the directors

- by notice in writing to the other directors (which may be sent in hard copy or, if the recipient has agreed, by electronic means, and which must be retained with the records of the next meeting of the directors after it is given (s 184)), or

- by general notice that the director has an interest (as member, officer, employee or otherwise) in a specified body corporate or firm, or that he is connected with a specified person, and that he is to be regarded as interested in any transaction or arrangement made after the date of the notice with that body corporate or firm or person;
  - the general notice must state the nature and extent of the director's interest in the body corporate or firm or (as the case may be) the nature of his connection with the person
  - the general notice is not effective unless:
    (a) it is given at a meeting of the directors, or
    (b) the director takes reasonable steps to secure that it is brought up and read at the next meeting of the directors after it is given.

5.84 A director need not declare an interest under this requirement:

- if it cannot reasonably be regarded as likely to give rise to a conflict of interest

- if, or to the extent that, the other directors are already aware of it (and for this purpose the other directors are treated as aware of anything of which they ought reasonably to be aware), or

- if, or to the extent that, it concerns terms of his service contract that have been or are to be considered:
  - by a meeting of the directors, or
  - by a committee of the directors appointed for the purpose under the company's constitution.

Where a declaration of an interest under s 182 is required of a sole director **of a company that is required to have more than one director** (ie a company other than a private company) then the declaration must be recorded in writing and retained with the minutes of the next Board meeting.

TRANSACTIONS WITH DIRECTORS REQUIRING APPROVAL OF MEMBERS – INTRODUCTION

5.85 The directors are in the position of directing the company on behalf of its members. The Act follows the model of earlier legislation requiring some transactions between the directors and the company to be approved by the members, but has introduced differences to the previous provisions. Usually, no approval is required under the provisions on the part of the members of a body corporate that is not a UK registered company or is a wholly-owned subsidiary. The provisions also apply in respect of a transaction between the company and a person 'connected' with the director. The following is a summary of the items that require members' approval. Note also the new provisions referred to further below regarding loans to directors. This continues to be a complicated area of the law and readers should also refer to the detailed statutory provisions.

5.86 The following is a summary of those who are deemed 'connected' with a director (see ss 252 and 253):

- members of the director's family:
  - spouse or civil partner
  - any other person (whether of a different sex or the same sex) with whom the director lives as partner in an enduring family relationship
  - children or step-children
  - children or step-children of a person in the second sub-paragraph above who live with the director and have not attained the age of 18
  - parents

- a body corporate with which the director is connected, which is a body corporate in which he and the persons connected with him together:
  - are interested in at least 20% of the share capital, or
  - are entitled to exercise or control more than 20% of the voting power

- a person acting in his capacity as a trustee of a trust:
  - the beneficiaries of which include the director or a person connected with him, or
  - the terms of which confer a power on the trustees that may be exercised for the benefit of the director or any such person

- a person acting in his capacity as partner:
  - of the director, or
  - of a person who is connected with the director

- of a firm that is a legal person and in which:
  - the director is a partner
  - a partner is a person connected with the director, or
  - a partner is a firm of which the director is a partner or in which there is a partner who is connected with the director.

SUBSTANTIAL PROPERTY TRANSACTIONS WITH DIRECTORS – REQUIREMENT FOR MEMBERS' APPROVAL

5.87 The following arrangements are prohibited unless first approved by a resolution of the members of the company or unless made conditional on such approval being obtained:

- an arrangement under which a director of the company (or of its holding company), or a person connected with such a director, acquires or is to acquire from the company (directly or indirectly) a substantial non-cash asset

- an arrangement under which the company acquires or is to acquire a substantial non-cash asset (directly or indirectly) from such a director or a person so connected.

5.88 For these purposes an asset is a 'substantial' asset in relation to a company if its value:

- exceeds 10% of the company's asset value and is more than £5,000, or

- exceeds £100,000.

5.89 For this purpose a company's 'asset value' is determined as at the time the arrangement is entered into and is:

- the value of the company's net assets determined by reference to its most recent statutory accounts, or

- if no statutory accounts have been prepared, the amount of the company's called up share capital.

5.90 If the director or connected person is a director of the company's holding company or a person connected with such a director, the arrangement must also have been approved by a resolution of the members of the holding company, or be conditional upon such approval being obtained. No approval is required under this provision by members of:

- a wholly-owned subsidiary of another body corporate (which includes a body incorporated outside the UK), or

- a body corporate that is not a UK registered company.

SUBSTANTIAL PROPERTY TRANSACTIONS WITH DIRECTORS – EXCEPTIONS TO THOSE REQUIRING APPROVAL

5.91 Members' approval under this provision is not required:

- in relation to anything to which a director is entitled under his service contract

- in relation to payment for loss of office as defined in s 215 (to which separate requirements apply, see below)

- for a transaction between a company and a person in his character as a member of the company (eg a contract between the member and the company for the purchase of shares)

- for a transaction between a holding company and its wholly-owned subsidiary

- for a transaction between two wholly-owned subsidiaries of the same holding company

- for a transaction on a recognised investment exchange effected by a director, or a person connected with him, through the agency of an independent broker (that is, a person who independently selects the person with whom the transaction is effected)

- where a company is being wound up (unless the winding up is a members' voluntary winding up) or is in administration (within the meaning of Sch B1 to the Insolvency Act 1986 or the Insolvency (Northern Ireland) Order 1989):
  - on the part of members of that company, or
  - for an arrangement entered into by the company.

SUBSTANTIAL PROPERTY TRANSACTIONS WITH DIRECTORS – CONSEQUENCES OF CONTRAVENTION

5.92 Under provisions in s 195, if a company contravenes the requirements explained above, in basic terms, the effect is that:

- the arrangement is normally voidable at the instance of the company

- whether or not the arrangement is avoided each of the following persons is liable to account to the company for any gain that he has made and (jointly and severally) to indemnify the company for any loss; the persons are:

(a) any director of the company or its holding company with whom the company entered into the arrangement

(b) any person with whom the company entered into the arrangement who is connected with a director of the company or its holding company

(c) the director of the company or holding company with whom the director is connected, and

(d) any other director of the company who authorised the transaction

- the above liabilities are subject to the provisos that:
  – in the case of an arrangement between the company and a connected person of a director of the company or its holding company, that director is not liable if he shows that he took all reasonable steps to secure the company's compliance with the requirements
  – a connected person otherwise liable under (b), and a director otherwise liable under (d) is not so liable if he shows that, at the time the arrangement was entered into, he did not know the relevant circumstances constituting the contravention.

The effect of rules of law is explicitly preserved.

5.93 If the transaction or arrangement is subsequently affirmed by the members of the company, it may no longer be avoided under s 195.

DIRECTORS' SERVICE CONTRACTS LONGER THAN TWO YEARS – REQUIREMENT FOR MEMBERS' APPROVAL

5.94 Under provisions in s 198, if the guaranteed term of a director's employment under a director's service contract with the company of which he is a director is, or may be, longer than two years (or where he is director of a holding company, if the guaranteed term within the group of companies is, or may be, longer than 2 years) prior approval by resolution of the members of the company (and, in the case of a director of a holding company, by the directors of that company) is required. A memorandum setting out the proposed contract must be supplied to the members within required time limits.

5.95 If a company agrees to provision in a director's service contract in contravention of this requirement:

- the provision is void, to the extent of the contravention, and

- the contract is deemed to contain a term entitling the company to terminate it at any time by the giving of reasonable notice.

5.96 No approval is required under this provision by members of:

- a wholly-owned subsidiary of another body corporate (which includes a body incorporated outside the UK), or

- a body corporate that is not a UK registered company.

PAYMENTS FOR LOSS OF OFFICE – REQUIREMENT FOR MEMBERS' APPROVAL

5.97 There are also provisions (see s 215 onwards) requiring members' approval for payments to a director or past director by way of compensation for loss of office or as consideration in connection with his retirement, or as compensation for loss of (or as consideration in connection with retirement from) any other office or employment in connection with the management of the affairs of the company or of any subsidiary undertaking. These provisions also 'bite' on payment to a person connected with a director. Also, a company may not make a payment for loss of office to a director of its holding company unless approved by a resolution of the members of both those companies. There are further detailed provisions about:

- what is to be taken to be such a payment

- payments for loss of office made by any person in connection with the transfer of the undertaking or property of the company or the transfer of shares in it.

5.98 As usual, there is no requirement for approval by members of a wholly-owned subsidiary of another body corporate or a body corporate that is not a UK-registered company.

5.99 There are exceptions (which contain some detail) to the requirement for approval in respect of:

- payments in discharge of legal obligations (including by way of settlement or compromise of any claim arising in connection with the termination of a person's office or employment)

- payments not exceeding £200.

5.100 If a payment is made without the required approval, usually (but see exceptions in s 222):

- it is held by the recipient on trust for the company, and

- any director who authorised it is jointly and severally liable to indemnify the company for loss resulting from it.

LOANS TO DIRECTORS – REQUIREMENT FOR MEMBERS' APPROVAL

5.101   The Act introduced a major change in this area (see s 197 onwards), by allowing a company to make a loan to a director of the company or its holding company. It also allows a company to give a guarantee or provide security in connection with a loan made by any person to such a director. However any of these is subject to requirements for member approval. A resolution giving the required approval must not be passed unless a memorandum setting out required matters about the loan is made available to members:

* in the case of a written resolution, by being sent or submitted to every eligible member at or before the time at which the proposed resolution is sent to him

* in the case of a resolution at a meeting, by being made available for inspection by members of the company both:
  – at the company's registered office for not less than 15 days ending with the date of the meeting, and
  – at the meeting itself.

5.102   The matters to be disclosed in the memorandum are:

* the nature of the transaction

* the amount of the loan and the purpose for which it is required, and

* the extent of the company's liability under any transaction connected with the loan.

5.103   If the director is a director of the company's holding company, the transaction must also receive prior approval by a resolution of the members of the company's holding company. There are also provisions set out in s 203 requiring approval for related arrangements as defined therein.

5.104   As usual no such approval is required under this provision on the part of members of a body corporate that:

* is not a UK- registered company, or

* is a wholly-owned subsidiary of another body corporate.

QUASI-LOANS AND CREDIT TRANSACTIONS

5.105   There are detailed provisions on the Act regarding requirements for members' approval for quasi-loans to directors and credit transactions in favour of directors. However, these only apply to:

- a public company, or

- a private company associated with a public company.

Bodies corporate or companies are associated if:

- one is a subsidiary of another or both are subsidiaries of the same body corporate.

5.106 Because these provisions are only likely to apply to private companies in a minority of cases, the full provisions are not set out here. Please refer to ss 198–203.

LOANS TO DIRECTORS – EXCEPTIONS TO REQUIREMENT FOR MEMBERS' APPROVAL

5.107 The Act lists various exceptions to this requirement:

- **Exception for minor and business transactions** – if the aggregate value of the transaction and other related transactions and arrangements does not exceed £10,000 (or in relation to a credit transaction, if applicable, does not exceed £15,000 or is entered into in the ordinary course of the company's business to the normal value and terms).

- **Exceptions for money-lending companies** – if in the ordinary course of business to the normal value and terms.

- **Exception for expenditure on company business** – anything done to provide a director with funds to meet expenditure incurred by him (or to be incurred by him) for the purpose of the company or for the purpose of enabling him to properly perform his duties as an officer of the company; this exception does not apply if the aggregate value of the transaction and other relevant transactions or arrangements exceeds £50,000.

- **Exception for intra-group transactions** – loans, guarantees etc to an associated body corporate.

- **Exception for expenditure in defending proceedings** – anything done to provide the director with funds to defend any civil or criminal proceedings in connection with any alleged negligence, default, breach of duty or breach of trust by him in relation to the company or an associated company or in connection with an application for relief under s 661(3) or (4) (power of court to grant relief in case of acquisition of shares by innocent nominee) or s 1157 (general power of the court to grant relief in case of honest and reasonable conduct); there are provisions requiring repayment if the director is convicted, judgment is given against him or the court refuses to grant relief on the application.

- **Exception for expenditure in connection with regulatory action or investigation** – anything done to provide the director with funds to meet expenditure in defending himself against an investigation by a regulatory authority or against an action proposed to be taken by a regulatory authority in connection with any alleged negligence, default, breach of duty or breach of trust by him in relation to the company or an associated company.

LOANS TO DIRECTORS – CONSEQUENCES OF CONTRAVENTION

5.108 Under provisions in s 213, if a company contravenes the requirements explained above, in basic terms, the effect is that:

- the arrangement is normally voidable at the instance of the company

- whether or not the arrangement is avoided each of the following persons is liable to account to the company for any gain that he has made and (jointly and severally) to indemnify the company for any loss; the persons are:
  - (a) any director of the company or its holding company with whom the company entered into the arrangement
  - (b) any person with whom the company entered into the arrangement who is connected with a director of the company or its holding company
  - (c) the director of the company or holding company with whom the director is connected, and
  - (d) any other director of the company who authorised the transaction

- the above liabilities are subject to the provisos that:
  - – in the case of an arrangement between the company and a connected person of a director of the company or its holding company, that director is not liable if he shows that he took all reasonable steps to secure the company's compliance with the requirements
  - – a connected person otherwise liable under (b), and a director otherwise liable under (d) is not so liable if he shows that, at the time the arrangement was entered into, he did not know the relevant circumstances constituting the contravention.

The effect of rules of law is explicitly preserved.

5.109 If the transaction or arrangement is subsequently affirmed by the members of the company, it may no longer be avoided under s 213.

DIRECTORS' LIABILITIES – PROVISIONS TO PROTECT DIRECTORS FROM LIABILITY

5.110 The Act (see s 232) starts from the position that any provision (whether in the articles, any contract with the company, or otherwise):

- that purports to exempt a director from, or

- by which a company provides an indemnity for a director against,

liability in connection with negligence, default, breach of duty or breach of trust in relation to the company, is void.

5.111 It then provides for three exceptions to this rule:

- provision of insurance for a director

- qualifying third party indemnity provision

- qualifying pension scheme indemnity provision.

5.112 The intention of these exceptions is to deal with concerns about directors facing legal action from third parties in relation to their activities as directors of the company or as directors of a company that is a trustee of an occupational pension scheme. (They should be read in conjunction with the exceptions allowing companies to lend money to directors without the normal shareholder approval in order to defend proceedings (see above).)

5.113 The exemption for insurance is refreshingly simple. The Act states that the relevant provision does not prevent a company from purchasing and maintaining for a director of the company, or of an associated company, insurance against any such liability as is mentioned (ie any liability attaching to him in connection with any negligence, default, breach of duty or breach of trust in relation to the company). I would suggest that the company should have provision in its articles dealing with any conflict of interest issues that may arise in relation to insurance, QTPIPs or QPSIPs (see below).

QUALIFYING THIRD PARTY INDEMNITY PROVISION ('QTPIP')

5.114 The Act (see s 234) permits a company to indemnify a director against liability incurred by the director to a person other than the company or an associated company. This is subject to conditions. The QTPIP must not provide any indemnity against:

- any liability of the director to pay:

- a fine in any criminal proceedings, or
- a sum payable to a regulatory authority by way of a penalty in respect of non-compliance with any requirement of a regulatory nature, or

- any liability incurred by the director:
  - in defending criminal proceedings in which he is convicted, or
  - in defending civil proceedings brought by the company, or an associated company, in which judgment is given against him, or
  - in connection with an application for relief under s 661(3) or (4) (power of court to grant relief in case of acquisition of shares by innocent nominee) or s 1157 (general power of the court to grant relief in case of honest and reasonable conduct) in which the court refuses to grant him relief.

5.115 See below regarding disclosure in the directors' report.

QUALIFYING PENSION SCHEME INDEMNITY PROVISION ('QPSIP')

5.116 This provides for an almost identical exception for indemnifying a director of a company that is a trustee of an occupational pension scheme in connection with the company's activities as trustee of the scheme. It is subject to similar conditions. See below regarding disclosure in the director's report.

QUALIFYING INDEMNITY PROVISION – DISCLOSURE IN DIRECTORS' REPORT

5.117 The Act refers to QTPIPs and QPSIPs collectively as 'qualifying indemnity provisions'. Disclosure is required in the directors' report regarding these both by the company whose directors receive the benefit and by any company making such a provision for a director of an associated company. The disclosure requirements are as follows (see s 236):

- If when the directors' report is approved any qualifying indemnity provision (whether made by the company or otherwise) is in force for the benefit of one or more directors of the company, the report must state that such provision is in force.

- If at any time during the financial year a qualifying indemnity provision was in force for the benefit of one or more persons who were then directors of the company, the report must state that such provision was in force.

- If when the directors' report is approved a qualifying indemnity provision made by the company is in force for the benefit of one or more directors of an associated company, the report must state that such provision is in force.

- If at any time during the financial year a qualifying indemnity provision was in force for the benefit of one or more persons who were then directors of an associated company, the report must state that such provision was in force.

5.118 Qualifying indemnity provisions must also be open for inspection (by shareholders of both the company whose director(s) benefit from it and any associated company providing it) and kept for at least a year after ending, in the same way as directors' service contracts, so that shareholders can look at an indemnity provision in detail if they have concerns about it. A loan to a director by his company to enable him to pay his defence costs upfront may be a qualifying indemnity provision, and therefore have to be disclosed. Companies which choose not to indemnify directors will not have to make any disclosure and companies are not required to make any disclosure in relation to directors' liability insurance.

DIRECTORS' SERVICE CONTRACTS – RIGHT OF MEMBERS TO INSPECT ETC

5.119 For these purposes (see s 227) a director's 'service contract' in relation to a company means a contract under which:

- a director of the company undertakes personally to perform services (as director or otherwise) for the company, or for a subsidiary of the company, or

- services (as director or otherwise) that a director of the company undertakes personally to perform are made available by a third party to the company or to a subsidiary of the company,

and these provisions apply to the terms of a person's appointment as a director of the company.

5.120 A company must keep a copy of every director's service contract (as defined in s 227) (or if it is not in writing a written memorandum of its terms) with the company (or with a subsidiary of the company) available for inspection. Please see s 228 for precise requirements regarding where these must be kept and notice required to be given to the Registrar (the requirements are basically the same as for the register of directors, see **8.27**). The copy (or memorandum) must be open to inspection by any member without charge and on request and on payment of the prescribed fee, a copy of it must be provided to a member within seven days after a request is received by the company.

Copies must be kept for one year after termination or expiry of the contract and must be kept available for inspection during that time. Default in respect of the various requirements is an offence.

PROVISION FOR EMPLOYEES ON CESSATION OR TRANSFER OF BUSINESS

5.121 Section 247 (which is due to come into force on 1 October 2009 and replaces a similar provision previously contained in s 719 of the Companies Act 1985) provides that the powers of directors of a company include (if they would not otherwise do so) power to make provision for the benefit of persons employed or formerly employed by the company, or any of its subsidiaries, in connection with the cessation or transfer to any person of the whole or part of the undertaking of the company or that subsidiary. The power may only be exercised if sanctioned by a resolution of the company or by a resolution of the directors. Such a resolution of the directors must be authorised by the company's articles and is not sufficient sanction for payments to or for the benefit of directors, former directors or shadow directors. Any payment under s 247 must be made out of profits of the company that are available for dividend and before the commencement of any winding up of the company.

CONTRACT WITH A SOLE MEMBER WHO IS ALSO A DIRECTOR

5.122 Section 231 provides that special provisions apply where:

- a limited company having only one member enters into a contract with the sole member

- the sole member is also a director of the company, and

- the contract is not entered into in the ordinary course of the company's business.

In such a case, the company is required to ensure that the terms of the contract are either:

- set out in writing or in a written memorandum, or

- recorded in the minutes of the first meeting of the directors following the making of the contract.

Failure to comply is an offence, but it does not affect the validity of the contract.

THE COMPANY SECRETARY

5.123 Under previous legislation, every company was required to have a company secretary. The Act has changed this so that the requirement to appoint a company secretary no longer applies to a private company. So whilst a public company must have a company secretary, a private company may make a choice whether or not to have a company secretary. The appointment is optional. There are no qualification requirements to be a secretary of a private company (in contrast to the requirements under s 273 applicable to the secretary of a public company). The secretary can be an individual, a body corporate or a firm. A company can have joint secretaries.

5.124 If a private company appoints a company secretary:

- the secretary's particulars must be put on (and kept up to date on) the public record (whether appointment is on the formation of the company or at a later stage) and the company must maintain a register of its secretaries (see **8.35** for precise requirements)

- the secretary has the same status in relation to the company as the secretary of a plc, and in particular the secretary can be a co-signatory (with a director) for the execution of documents by the company (see **4.52, 4.57** regarding the execution of documents).

5.125 It will depend on the nature, size and activities of each private company whether it chooses to appoint a company secretary. Whatever the choice, it is important to note that the directors must decide how they are going to ensure that the company complies with statutory and other requirements applicable under company law. This is likely to involve delegation by the Board of day-to-day responsibility for such matters to an individual, firm or company. It then becomes a question of practicality whether it is useful to have that person named on the public record as holding that position, so that (for instance) third parties accept that person as a co-signatory with a director for the execution of documents by the company. Remember that, in any case, any director can cause the company to execute a document, by signing it himself in the presence of a witness who must sign to attest the signature. So signature by a company secretary (or a second director) is not necessary. If no secretary is appointed, it is good practice to make one of the directors responsible for overseeing the functions that would normally be carried out by the company secretary.

SUMMARY OF MAJOR CHANGES INTRODUCED BY THE ACT

1   Directors' duties to the company are listed in statute. Note that they are not identical to the former common law duties, although they are mostly derived from them. The new statutory duties have effect in place of the relevant common law rules and equitable principles on which they are based, but are to be interpreted and applied 'in the same way' and 'regard shall be had to the corresponding common law rules and equitable principles in interpreting and applying the general duties' (see ss 170–181). *Sections 170–174 and 178–181 came into force on 1 October 2007 and ss 175–177 came into force on 1 October 2008.*

2   Provisions for a derivative claim have been put in statutory form (see ss 260–269). *These came into force on 1 October 2007.*

3   There is a new directors' duty (which came into force on 1 October 2007) in s 172 stating:

> 'A director of a company must act in the way he considers, in good faith, would be most likely to promote the success of the company for the benefit of its members as a whole, and in doing so have regard (amongst other matters) to:
> (a)   the likely consequences of any decision in the long term
> (b)   the interests of the company's employees
> (c)   the need to foster the company's business relationships with suppliers, customers and others
> (d)   the impact of the company's operations on the community and the environment
> (e)   the desirability of the company maintaining a reputation for high standards of business conduct, and
> (f)   the need to act fairly as between members of the company.'

4   The provisions that deal with possible conflicts of interest between directors and their company and the requirement for shareholders' approval in some cases of such possible conflict have been re-written (see generally ss 170–239). *Mostly came into force on 1 October 2007, apart from ss 175–177 and ss 182–187 which came into force on 1 October 2008.*

5   It is now possible for a private company to make a loan to a director if the requisite members' approval is obtained (see ss 197–214). *These provisions came into force on 1 October 2007.*

6   All directors who are individuals will have a service address which will be on the register of directors and on the public record. However, where a director's residential address previously appeared on the public record, this will not be removed (see ss 163, 1141 and 242(2)). However, for those at risk of violence or intimidation application may be made to remove addresses filed on or after 1 January 2003 (see ss 243 and 1088 and the

Companies (Disclosure of Address) Regulations (which at the time of writing are available in draft on the BERR website). *These provisions are due to come into force on 1 October 2009.*

7   There will be a new register of directors' residential addresses (which will also be notified to the Registrar). Access to this information will be restricted. It will be kept as 'restricted information' which will only be available to certain parties (see ss 165–167 and 240–246). *These provisions are due to come into force on 1 October 2009.*

8   The previous statutory maximum age limit for directors has been abolished (see s 1295, Sch 16). *This came into force on 6 April 2007.*

9   There is a new minimum age limit for directors of 16 (see ss 157–159). *This came into force on 1 October 2008.*

10   Corporate directors are permitted, BUT every company must have at least one director who is a natural person (see ss 155 and 156). *This came into force on 1 October 2008 (subject to a transitional saving until 1 October 2010 for some companies that had only corporate directors on 8 November 2006).*

11   There is no longer any statutory requirement for a private company to appoint a company secretary. If a private company does have a company secretary, this must be notified to Companies House and details entered in a register of secretaries (see ss 270–280). *Sections 270–274 and 280 regarding the optional company secretary for private companies came into force on 6 April 2008. New provisions regarding the register of secretaries in ss 275–279 are due to come into force on 1 October 2009.*

Chapter 6

DECISIONS OF THE DIRECTORS

INTRODUCTION

6.1   The Board of directors has collective responsibility for the affairs of the company. The Board are the 'directing mind' of the company and it is their responsibility to further the interests of the company. In a commercial company this is likely to take the form of entrepreneurial leadership that adds value to the company without taking unreasonable risks that may seriously damage it. For a non-commercial company, this may take the form of furthering the company's purposes and interests, while again protecting against serious risk to the company. So the role of the board combines both 'positive/leadership' and 'risk control' aspects. At all times the directors need to be mindful of the 'collective' nature of the Board's responsibilities as well as their own direct responsibilities.

6.2   **Chapter 5** covers directors and their duties. This chapter is concerned with how the Board of directors makes and records its decisions. The Act has detailed provisions about how members make decisions. In contrast it has little to say about how directors make decisions (although it does have some requirements regarding the recording of such decisions). As under previous legislation, how directors make decisions is left to be covered by the company's articles. The decision-making processes of the directors have always been subject to less stringent formalities than the requirements applied to members.

6.3   Given modern business practice and the use of e-mail, the possibilities regarding how directors may reach a decision and agree matters are now much broader. The wording used in the draft regulations prescribing model articles of association for private companies limited by shares (which are available via BERR's website, see **Appendix 5**) recognises this to a certain extent. It is discussed in more detail further below.

6.4   If the articles allow, the Board may reach a decision:

• at a meeting of the directors at which a quorum of directors is physically present

• at a quorate meeting of the directors which one or more of the directors attend by telephone or video conference facility, so that each can hear and participate in all parts of the meeting

- by means of a resolution in writing that has been provided to all the directors for approval

- by a method provided for in rules made by the directors pursuant to clause 16 of the draft model articles.

6.5   The articles (or any rules made by the directors pursuant to clause 16 of the draft model articles or a similar provision in their own articles) may in each case provide that the decision (or particular types of decision) must be taken by a majority of the Board, or by a particular majority, or unanimously. In the past it has been usual for articles to provide that decisions taken at meetings may be taken by a majority of the Board and that written resolutions must be signed by every director.

6.6   This chapter summarises the statutory position regarding records and then explores the range of methods that might be used for directors' decision taking. Hopefully these will allow company decision taking to follow the reality of modern business practice, so that urgent decisions may be taken by the Board without delay.

RECORDS OF DIRECTORS' MEETINGS – BOARD MINUTES (SS 248 AND 249)

6.7   The Act contains provisions regarding records of directors' meetings. It does not contain provisions regarding records of directors' decisions made by other means – as to which see further below.

6.8   The Act requires every company to cause minutes of all proceedings at meetings of its directors to be recorded and kept for at least 10 years from the date of the meeting. Failure to comply with this requirement is an offence.

6.9   If such minutes purport to be authenticated by the chairman of that meeting (or by the chairman of the next directors' meeting), they are evidence (in Scotland, sufficient evidence) of the proceedings of the meeting.

6.10   Where such minutes have been made, then until the contrary is proved:

- the meeting is deemed duly held and convened

- all proceedings at the meeting are deemed to have duly taken place, and

- all appointments at the meeting are deemed valid.

6.11   Usual procedure is for someone at the meeting to be asked to take the minutes at the meeting. This person may be the company secretary (if any), but could be any person that the directors deem suitable. It is good and sensible practice to have someone other than one of the directors taking the minutes, but a director may do this.

6.12 It is usual practice for the minutes to be prepared after the meeting, checked with the chairman and then circulated to the directors in advance of the next meeting. Often an early item of business at the next directors' meeting will be formal approval of the minutes and the chairman will sign a hard copy of the minutes of the previous meeting at the close of that meeting. If the chairman is happy to sign the minutes without them being submitted to a subsequent meeting, he may do so. In some cases this may be necessary if a copy of the minute is required for another purpose. Note that the Act now only requires that the minutes be 'authenticated' by the Chairman to be evidence (see **6.14**).

6.13 Minutes are in draft form prior to signature or authentication. After they have been signed (or authenticated) they should not be altered. If a mistake is discovered in signed (or authenticated) minutes, then this should be reported to the Board and the decision of the Board that the former minutes were incorrect (and details of the inaccuracy) should be recorded in a later set of minutes (or other record of Board decision if appropriate, see below).

AUTHENTICATED

6.14 The Act uses the word 'authenticated' widely. It is defined in s 1146 in relation to a document (or information) sent or supplied by a person to a company in hard copy form or in electronic form.

6.15 A document or information sent or supplied in hard copy form is sufficiently authenticated if it is signed by the person sending or supplying it. So, for instance, a written resolution supplied to a director in hard copy should be signed by the director to show his agreement to it.

6.16 A document or information sent or supplied in electronic form is sufficiently authenticated:

- if the identity of the sender is confirmed in a manner specified by the company, or

- where no such manner has been specified by the company, if the communication contains or is accompanied by a statement of the identity of the sender and the company has no reason to doubt the truth of such statement.

6.17 This seems to give a great deal of flexibility to private companies to decide what they regard as sufficient authentication where documents or information are supplied in electronic form. This is discussed in **Chapter 7** in relation to decisions of the shareholders of a private company, but has equal application to the directors' decisions.

DIRECTORS' MEETINGS

6.18 Traditionally, company law assumed that Boards of directors made decisions at meetings after face to face discussion and debate. It is still the case that most active companies will have scheduled board meetings through the year where the directors meet to discuss matters.

6.19 The number of Board meetings in a year and the extent of formality connected with them will depend on the size, nature and activities of the company. It is necessary to give all the directors reasonable notice of the meeting, but this notice does not have to be in writing. It is usual (but not a requirement) for an agenda and supporting papers regarding matters to be discussed to be circulated to all the directors before the Board meeting. These can be dispatched by e-mail with attachments if the directors agree and provide a suitable e-mail address.

6.20 The company secretary (if any) or other person with responsibility for such matters should ensure that the necessary number of directors are present at the meeting to form a quorum, that any procedures provided for by the articles are followed, and that proper minutes are taken to record the proceedings of the meeting.

DIRECTORS' MEETINGS – ATTENDANCE BY TELEPHONE OR VIDEO CONFERENCE

6.21 Often a Board decision may be required when some directors are travelling and may be unable to come to a meeting. Because of this, it has become common practice for some directors to attend meetings by teleconference if they are unable to attend in person. In such cases it is important that all parties to the meeting can hear all the proceedings and take part in them by speaking and interjecting as if they were actually present.

6.22 In the past, companies have often chosen to include specific provision in their articles regarding attendance at Board meetings by telephone or video conference in order to ensure that this is permitted.

6.23 All the normal provisions regarding notice, minutes etc apply to such a meeting. It is a normal meeting of the Board; it is just that one or more directors is attending it by electronic means.

ALTERNATE DIRECTORS

6.24 The model articles (Table A) prescribed under the Companies Act 1985 made provision for a director to appoint an 'alternate director' to act in his appointer's place when the appointer was absent from meetings etc. The model articles provided that a director could either appoint (i) another director or (ii) somebody else approved by the directors to act as alternate director for him.

6.25 The increasing use of telephone conference facilities for meetings has made the appointment of alternates less common. However, many company articles contain provision for the appointment of alternate directors.

WRITTEN RESOLUTIONS OF THE DIRECTORS

6.26 Often a formal decision of the Board is required, but there is no real need for discussion about it. This may be either because the directors are already in agreement, but just need to make and record a formal decision of the Board, or because the decision is essentially a procedural one (eg opening a bank account).

6.27 The model articles (Table A) prescribed under the Companies Act 1985 allowed the use of written resolutions of the directors, but required them to be signed by all the directors (either in one document or by each signing different copies, or by a combination of those methods). This ensured that all the directors had received the written resolution, but could sometimes be inconvenient if one director was unavailable to sign.

6.28 Given that written resolutions of the members can now be passed by a majority, there seems to be no reason why articles should not also allow written resolutions of the directors to be passed by a majority, provided that there are safeguards to ensure that all directors have been made aware of the proposal.

MODEL ARTICLES OF ASSOCIATION FOR PRIVATE COMPANIES

6.29 The Department for Business, Enterprise and Regulatory Reform ('BERR') has issued draft regulations that contain draft model articles for:

- private companies limited by shares

- private companies limited by guarantee

- public companies.

The relevant model will apply to a company on its incorporation unless a company chooses to deliver its own articles.

6.30 The draft model articles for a private company limited by shares are designed for a small, stand alone business. They are unlikely to be suitable (unless added to or modified) for companies with more complicated needs. They do not contain provision for alternate directors (or partly paid shares). The model articles for private companies limited by guarantee are also likely to require modification to meet the needs of specific companies limited by guarantee. The model articles for public companies are unlikely to be adopted as such by many public companies, but they do contain useful clauses which could be used within the articles of private companies with more complicated needs or as part of specially drafted articles of public companies.

6.31 Note that the provisions below are still in draft. At the time of writing we still await the production of a final version of the regulations.

6.32 The draft new model articles for a private company limited by shares provide that (unless a company has only one director), any decision of the directors must be either:

- a unanimous decision, or

- a majority decision taken at a meeting.

If the private company has only one director (and the articles do not require it to have more than one director) then the rules do not apply (but a record of decisions must still be kept).

6.33 The draft model articles go on to provide that:

- directors take a unanimous decision when they all indicate to each other by any means that they share a common view on a matter, and

- a unanimous decision may take the form of a resolution in writing, copies of which have been signed by each director, or to which each director has otherwise indicated agreement in writing.

6.34 The model articles also contain provisions regarding directors' meetings, covering:

- calling a directors' meeting

- participation in directors' meetings

- quorum for directors' meetings (which, unless otherwise fixed by the directors, is two)

- chairing of directors' meetings

- the chairman's casting vote if there is an equality of votes

- conflicts of interest

- records of decisions, and

- directors' discretion to make further rules about how they take decisions.

6.35 The ability for directors to make further rules about how they make decisions is likely to be very useful. The above provisions are admirable in their concise wording and the flexibility that they grant the directors.

6.36 The challenge of the proposals is how private companies are going to keep adequate records of:

- decisions of the directors

- declarations of interests of directors

- how possible conflicts of interest have been dealt with.

6.37 Possibly some companies may formulate a procedure regarding a form of e-mail that:

- specifies the e-mail (or an enclosure) as a formal board resolution

- is sent to all the directors

- requires a response within a set time regarding agreement, disagreement or whether discussion is requested

- agrees to accept response by e-mail with a scanned copy of the signed resolution

- has some way of dealing with possible conflicts and declarations of interest.

Responses received would be kept and a responsible officer might then certify that the directors' resolution had been duly passed and ensure that this certified resolution and scanned copies of the signed resolution are kept with the directors' minutes.

6.38 The procedure adopted will depend on the circumstances of the company. The important thing is that companies may now have the flexibility to choose a system that accords with their business practice, provided that they institute a proper system of recording such decisions (and where necessary providing certified copies of them).

SUMMARY OF MAJOR CHANGES INTRODUCED BY THE ACT

1   Minutes of directors' meetings may be 'authenticated' (see s 1146 for definition) rather than just signed. However in most cases companies will wish to retain minutes in hard copy form. So they will still need to be signed in practice. *Sections 248 and 249 regarding minutes of directors' meetings came into force on 1 October 2007 and s 1146 regarding authentication came into effect on 20 January 2007.*

2   Minutes of directors' meetings must be kept for at least 10 years (see s 248). *Section 248 came into force on 1 October 2007 and applies to minutes of meetings held from then on.*

3   As with previous legislation, the Act contains very little regulation regarding directors' meetings and decisions. However, note the new provisions for model company articles proposed in the draft regulations available via the BERR website. Readers should keep under review whether these provisions appear in the final model articles when they are prescribed.

Chapter 7

DECISIONS OF THE MEMBERS (SHAREHOLDERS)

INTRODUCTION

7.1   Note that the term 'members' includes both shareholders in a company with share capital and members of a company limited by guarantee. As the provisions applicable to each type of company are generally the same, I shall follow the wording in the Act and use the term 'members' to refer to both shareholders and to members of a company without share capital.

7.2   The Act has introduced both changes of emphasis and changes of detail in how the members of a company take decisions. Mainly these changes were introduced with effect from 1 October 2007, although inevitably transitional provisions apply. Companies with articles designed to fit with older legislation in particular should take care in relation to meetings of members and decisions of members. The previous model form articles of association (Table A) was amended by statutory instrument (SI 2007/2541) with effect from 1 October 2007 to the extent necessary to take account of changes introduced by the Act on that date. So companies incorporated on or after that date should have articles that are suitable for these provisions regarding member decisions (although they may not be suitable in relation to other areas of the Act). However companies incorporated before 1 October 2007 will have (unless they have subsequently passed a members' resolution to alter their articles) articles of association that do not 'fit' with the new provisions. Such companies should exercise care and consider adopting new articles with effect on or after 1 October 2009 (when the remaining provisions of the Act are due to come into force) to 'fit' with all the provisions of the Act.

Companies whose articles adopt the 1985 Table A as it was before the 1 October 2007 amendments should in particular consider the following provisions in that Table A that will override the provisions in the Act regarding meetings (as these are areas where the Act is specifically stated to be subject to the articles in these respects):

- Regulation 38 requires (unless consent to short notice is given, see below) 21 clear days' notice for an annual general meeting or an extraordinary general meeting called for the passing of a special resolution or a resolution appointing a person as a director – (rather than the 14 days' notice of a general meeting of a private company provided for by s 307)

- Regulation 38 requires all the members entitled to vote to consent to short notice of an annual general meeting (if one is held) – (rather than the 90 per cent for any general meeting of a private company provided for by s 307)

- Regulation 38 requires members holding at least 95 per cent in nominal value of the shares giving the right to attend and vote to consent to short notice of any other general meeting – (rather than the 90 per cent for any general meeting of a private company provided for by s 307).

7.3   The Act recognises that all companies are likely to use electronic communications and that larger companies may use websites to provide information to their members. It therefore adopts wording that recognises and facilitates this. The provisions in Sch 5 regarding communications by the company and Sch 4 regarding communications to the company need to be taken into account.

7.4   The Act also recognises that members of private companies are less likely to want to take decisions of the members by a meeting; so it contains (for private companies) more extensive provision for the taking of decisions by written resolutions to which the members indicate their agreement. In some ways this has made such decisions easier – for instance:

- by moving closer to standardising the majorities required for written resolutions and for resolutions passed at meetings, and

- allowing consent to such resolutions to be authenticated more easily if the resolution is sent in electronic form.

However, the Act has also introduced additional detail in the requirements for passing written resolutions and makes non-compliance with them an offence, which many may see as a retrograde step.

7.5   Of course, it may still be appropriate for a private company to hold a meeting to take some decisions (or it may be a requirement under the company's articles to hold an AGM). Where meetings of the members are held, more provisions covering meetings are now contained in the Act. The intention may have been to remove the need for these to be contained in the company's articles. Some of the provisions override the company's articles, but others are specifically made subject to what is contained in the articles.

7.6   In general, provisions applicable to general meetings of the members also apply (with necessary modifications) to a meeting of holders of a class of shares in a company or meetings of a class of members of a company. However, this is subject to some exceptions.

7.7   As will be seen, decisions of the members of a company are subject to far more detailed regulation by the Act than decisions by directors.

7.8   Section 281(4) provides that nothing in the part of the Act dealing with resolutions and meetings affects any rule of law as to:

- things done otherwise than by passing a resolution

- circumstances in which a resolution is or is not treated as having been passed, or

- cases in which a person is precluded from alleging that a resolution has not been properly passed.

So it seems that, for instance, the existing common law rules regarding unanimous decisions of members have been preserved. Legal advice is required in this area.

RESOLUTIONS AND WHAT IS 'A RESOLUTION OF THE COMPANY' UNDER THE ACT

7.9   A resolution of the members (or a class of members) of a private company must be passed:

- as a written resolution in accordance with Chapter 2 of Part 13 of the Act, or

- at a meeting (to which the provisions of Chapter 3 of Part 13 of the Act apply).

So in either case it is necessary to be familiar with the detailed provisions contained in the Act.

7.10   Section 281(3) provides that where a provision of the Companies Acts:

- requires a resolution of a company, or of the members (or of a class of members) of a company, and

- does not specify what kind of resolution is required,

what is required is an ordinary resolution unless the company's articles require a higher majority (or unanimity).

7.11   If a resolution is passed at an adjourned meeting of a company, the resolution is treated as having been passed on the date on which it was in fact passed, and not on any earlier date (s 332).

ORDINARY RESOLUTIONS (S 282)

7.12 An ordinary resolution of the members (or of a class of members) is a resolution passed by a simple majority.

7.13 For a written resolution this means passed by members representing a simple majority of the total voting rights of the eligible members (ie those entitled to vote on the resolution on its circulation date, see **7.23**).

7.14 For a resolution passed at a meeting 'a simple majority' means:

- if the resolution is passed on a show of hands, passed by a simple majority of the members and duly appointed proxies who vote on the resolution, or

- if the resolution is passed on a poll, passed by a simple majority of the total voting rights of the members who vote (either in person or by proxy) on the resolution.

Note that proxies can (subject to any provision of the company's articles) vote on a show of hands and that in either case an ordinary resolution is passed by a simple majority of the votes validly cast. It does not require a majority of the votes capable of being cast. Contrast this with the requirement for written resolutions. See also below regarding notice required for meetings. Anything that may be done by ordinary resolution may also be done by special resolution.

SPECIAL RESOLUTIONS (S 283)

7.15 A special resolution of the members (or of a class of members) is a resolution passed by a majority of not less than 75 per cent. Special resolutions are listed in s 29 and therefore must be forwarded to the Registrar within 15 days of being passed (s 30). In addition, every copy of the company's articles issued by the company must (if the resolution is still in force) either be accompanied by a copy of the resolution or the effect of the resolution must be incorporated in the articles (s 36) (see **4.20** and **4.21**).

7.16 For a written resolution this means passed by members representing not less than 75 per cent of the total voting rights of the eligible members (ie those entitled to vote on the resolution on its circulation date, see **7.23**). Note that where a resolution of a private company is passed as a written resolution:

- the resolution is not a special resolution unless it stated that it was proposed as a special resolution, and

- if the resolution so stated, it may only be passed as a special resolution.

7.17 For a resolution passed at a meeting, 'passed by a majority of not less than 75 per cent' means:

- if the resolution is passed on a show of hands, passed by not less than 75 per cent of the members and duly appointed proxies who vote on the resolution, or

- if the resolution is passed on a poll, passed by not less than 75 per cent of the total voting rights of the members who vote (either in person or by proxy) on the resolution.

Note that proxies can (subject to any provision of the company's articles) vote on a show of hands and that in either case a special resolution is passed by a majority of not less than 75 per cent of the votes validly cast. It does not require a majority of the votes capable of being cast. Contrast this with the requirement for written resolutions.

7.18 Note that for a resolution passed at a meeting:

- the resolution is not a special resolution unless the notice of meeting included the text of the resolution and specified the intention to propose it as a special resolution, and

- if the notice of the meeting so stated, the resolution may only be passed as a special resolution.

7.19 The notice period required for a meeting to consider a special resolution is the same as that required for a meeting to consider an ordinary resolution (see below).

WRITTEN RESOLUTIONS OF PRIVATE COMPANIES IN ACCORDANCE WITH THE ACT

7.20 The requirements that must be satisfied in order to pass a valid written resolution of the members of a private company are that:

- copies of the proposed resolution are circulated to every eligible member in accordance with statutory requirements

- the required majority of all the eligible members indicate (in a manner consistent with the Act) that they agree to the resolution, and

- the resolution is passed within the period specified for this purpose in the company's articles or, if no period is specified in the articles, the period of 28 days beginning with the circulation date.

7.21 A resolution may be proposed as a written resolution –

- by the directors of a private company, or

- by the members of a private company.

7.22 A written resolution may not be used to:

- remove a director under s 168 before the expiration of his period of office

- remove an auditor under s 510 before the expiration of his period of office.

WRITTEN RESOLUTION PROPOSED BY THE DIRECTORS – CIRCULATION PROCEDURE (SS 288–291 AND 296–300)

7.23 These provisions apply to written resolutions proposed by the directors. They will apply in the vast majority of cases, but note the separate provisions that apply where members have required the company to circulate a written resolution (see **7.31**). The applicable statutory provisions for written resolutions proposed by the directors are:

- the company must send or submit a copy of the resolution to every eligible member (see below for definition) by:
    - sending copies at the same time (so far as reasonably practicable) to all eligible members in hard copy form, in electronic form or by means of a website, or
    - if it is possible to do so without undue delay, by submitting the same copy to each eligible member in turn (or different copies to each of a number of eligible members in turn), or
    - by a combination of the two methods above

- the copy of the resolution must be accompanied by a statement informing the member:
    - how to signify agreement to the resolution, and as to the date by which the resolution must be passed if it is not to lapse (see above).

Failure to comply with these requirements is an offence, but the validity of the resolution, if passed, is not affected by failure to comply with the above requirements.

WHO CAN VOTE ON A WRITTEN RESOLUTION? (SS 289 AND 290)

7.24 The **eligible members** to vote on a written resolution are the members who would have been entitled to vote on it on the circulation date. The circulation date is the date on which copies of it are sent or submitted to members in accordance with the statutory requirements (or if copies are sent or submitted to members on different days, the first of those days). If the persons so entitled to vote change during that day, the eligible members are the persons entitled to vote on the resolution at the time that the first copy of the resolution is sent or submitted to a member for his agreement.

7.25 Subject to any provision of the company's articles, on a vote on a written resolution:

- in the case of a company having share capital, every member has one vote for each share that he holds, or

- if the company has no share capital, every member has one vote

- if the company has issued 'stock' (which has a technical meaning and is very unusual) different provisions apply.

HOW DO THE MEMBERS INDICATE THAT THEY AGREE TO A WRITTEN RESOLUTION? (S 296)

7.26 The Act has broadened the way in which members may signify their agreement to a written resolution. A member signifies his agreement to a written resolution when the company receives from him (or from someone acting on his behalf) an authenticated document:

- identifying the resolution, and

- indicating his agreement to the resolution.

7.27 The document must be sent to the company either in hard copy or electronic form. Section 1146 of the Act provides clarification regarding what is meant by 'authenticated':

- a document supplied in hard copy is sufficiently authenticated if signed

- a document supplied in electronic form is sufficiently authenticated if:
  - the identity of the sender is confirmed in a manner specified by the company, or
  - where no such manner has been specified by the company, if the communication contains or is accompanied by a statement of the identity of the sender and the company has no reason to doubt that statement.

7.28 Section 1146 does not affect any provision in the company's articles under which, if the document is sent by one person on behalf of another, the company may require reasonable evidence of the authority of the former to act on behalf of the latter.

WRITTEN RESOLUTIONS – PRACTICAL POINTS

7.29 These provisions give private companies possibilities to speed up the decision-making process where a members' resolution is required. For instance, a private company with one member or a few members known to each other could as standard practice ask the member(s) to agree generally in advance to receive written resolutions by e-mail and specify an e-mail address for this. Then a proposed resolution could be sent out to all members simultaneously as an attachment to an e-mail. The e-mail (or the attachment) could request the member(s) to signify their consent by any of the following:

- signing and returning (or faxing to a specified number) a hard copy of the resolution

- signing, scanning and e-mailing a pdf of the resolution

- sending an e-mail to the return e-mail address of the company confirming that it is from (or sent on behalf of) the member and that the member agrees to the resolution.

7.30 If the member is a corporate body (for instance in the case of a wholly owned subsidiary), or where an e-mail consent is from somebody sending it on behalf of the member, the company receiving the assent to the resolution should have established (or then establish) that the sender has authority to act on behalf of the member.

7.31 It seems that in most cases, unless a meeting of the members is regarded as desirable, decisions of members of a private company will be made by written resolution.

WRITTEN RESOLUTIONS PROPOSED BY THE MEMBERS OF A PRIVATE COMPANY (SS 292–295)

7.32 The members of a private company holding at least 5 per cent (or such lower percentage as is specified in the company's articles) of the total voting rights of all members entitled to vote on the resolution may require the directors to circulate a proposed written resolution (together with a statement of up to 1,000 words) provided that:

- the resolution is not defamatory of any person

- the resolution is not frivolous or vexatious

- the resolution would, if passed, be legally effective.

7.33 The request:

- may be in hard copy or electronic form

- must identify the resolution and any accompanying statement

- must be authenticated by the person(s) making it.

7.34 The company is required **(subject to payment of costs, see below)** to circulate the resolution and statement within 21 days of receiving (a) request(s) from the required percentage of members. However, note that:

- the expenses of the company in complying with this requirement must be paid by the members who requisitioned the resolution unless the company resolves otherwise, and

- unless the company has previously so resolved, it is not bound to comply with the requisition unless there is deposited with or tendered to it a sum reasonably sufficient to meet its expenses in complying.

7.35 Other provisions regarding circulation of a resolution proposed by the members are similar to those for resolutions proposed by the directors (see above).

MEETINGS OF THE MEMBERS (SS 301–335)

7.36 It is still perfectly possible for private companies to take decisions by meetings of the members, which are known as 'general meetings'. Some companies may choose to hold meetings as a more suitable way of placing information and matters for decision before their members and some companies may be required by their articles to hold meetings of their members (for instance a requirement in the articles to hold an Annual General Meeting ('AGM')). Note that there is no statutory requirement under the Act for a private company to hold an AGM; so if a private company's articles require it, the AGM will be subject to the same statutory provisions as any other meeting of the members. It is usually the directors of a company who call a meeting of the members of the company (although there is provision for the required percentage of the members to require a meeting (see below)).

7.37 The Act contains provisions regarding meetings of the members, some of which may be overridden or supplemented by provisions in the articles. So it is necessary to check both the statutory provisions in the Act and the company's articles to gain a full picture of the provisions applicable to meetings of the members.

7.38   Section 301 provides that a resolution of the members of a company is validly passed at a general meeting if:

- notice of the meeting and of the resolution is given, and

- the meeting is held and conducted

in accordance with the relevant provisions in the Act and the company's articles.

NOTICE REQUIRED OF A MEETING OF MEMBERS (GENERAL MEETING)

7.39   The starting point in the Act is that there is a requirement to give the members of a private company at least 14 clear days' notice of a general meeting (s 307). In calculating any notice period, exclude the day that the notice is given (or deemed given) and exclude the day of the meeting – this is what is meant by 'clear days' (s 360). Note that it is possible for the company's articles to require a longer period of notice. For instance, reg 38 of the 1985 Table A as it was prior to amendment on 1 October 2007 (the model set of articles that is likely to apply to many private companies incorporated before that date) provides for at least 21 clear days' notice of an annual general meeting or a meeting at which a special resolution or a resolution to appoint a director is to be proposed. Whatever the period of notice required, it is possible to give a shorter period of notice if agreed to by a majority in number of the members who have the right to attend and vote at the meeting who together hold not less than 90 per cent (or such higher percentage, not exceeding 95 per cent, as may be specified in the company's articles) in nominal value of the shares giving the right to attend and vote at the meeting. For companies that adopted Table A prior to 1 October 2007, reg 38 requires 95 per cent. See also **7.2**.

7.40   The notice of a general meeting must be given:

- in hard copy form

- in electronic form, or

- by means of a website

or by a combination of the above methods. See also **7.91** regarding electronic communication with members and also use of a website for this purpose. Under those general provisions, if notice is given by means of a website, the company must notify the intended recipient. In addition, for a notice of meeting, the notification of the presence of the notice on the website must also:

- state that it concerns a notice of a company meeting, and

- specify the place, date and time of the meeting.

The notice of meeting must be available on the website throughout the period beginning with the date of that notification and ending with the conclusion of the meeting.

7.41   There must appear on the notice of meeting, with reasonable prominence, a statement informing the member of:

- his statutory right under s 324 to appoint another person as his proxy to exercise all his rights to attend and to speak and vote at a meeting of the company (which in the case of a company with share capital includes the right to appoint more than one proxy to exercise rights attached to a different share or shares held by him), and

- any more extensive rights conferred by the company's articles to appoint more than one proxy.

Failure to comply with this requirement is an offence, but it does not affect the validity of the meeting or of anything done at it (s 325).

7.42   The Act contains the following requirements.

1   The notice must be sent to every member and every director. This includes any person entitled to a share in consequence of the death or bankruptcy of a member, if the company has been notified of their entitlement.

2   The notice must state the time, date and place of the meeting and state the general nature of the business to be dealt with at the meeting.

3   Any accidental failure to give notice of the meeting or of a resolution to one or more persons is disregarded for the purposes of determining whether notice of the meeting (or resolution) is duly given. This is intended to deal with (for instance) an accidental omission in relation to one member.

These three provisions are all subject to any provision in the company's articles (save for the last in relation to meetings required or called by, and resolutions proposed by, the members).

7.43   Note that if a special resolution is to be proposed at the meeting, the notice must include the text of the resolution and specify the intention to propose it as a special resolution (see s 283 and **7.17**). Note also that in a very few cases, for certain specific resolutions, 'special notice' (meaning 28 clear days' notice to the company of intention to move a resolution) may be required. See **5.26** for an explanation of 'special notice' in the context of a resolution to remove a director from office.

MEMBERS' POWER TO REQUIRE DIRECTORS TO CALL A GENERAL MEETING (SS 303–305)

7.44   The members of a private company representing at least 10 per cent (subject to the exception below, when it may be 5 per cent) of the paid up share capital carrying the right to vote at general meetings (or for a company not having share capital, the required percentage of the total voting rights at general meetings) may require the directors to call a general meeting of the company. The request must state the general nature of the business to be dealt with at the meeting and may include the text of a proposed resolution provided that:

- the resolution is not defamatory of any person

- the resolution is not frivolous or vexatious

- the resolution would, if passed, be legally effective.

7.45   The request:

- may be in hard copy or electronic form

- must be authenticated (in accordance with s 1146 – see **7.27**) by the person(s) making it.

Note that if a special resolution is to be proposed, the text will need to be stated.

7.46   For a private company, the required percentage is 5 per cent if more than 12 months has elapsed since the last general meeting:

- called in pursuance of this requirement, or

- in relation to which the members had rights with respect to the circulation of a resolution no less extensive than they would have had if the meeting had been so called at their request.

7.47   The directors are required to within 21 days of the company receiving (a) request(s) from the required percentage of members to call a general meeting to be held not more than 28 days after the date of the notice convening the meeting. If the requests received identified a resolution to be moved at the meeting, the notice must include notice of the resolution (which if it is a special resolution, means the text of the resolution).

7.48 If the directors do not call the meeting as required, the members who requested the meeting (or any of them representing half of the total voting rights of all of them) may call a general meeting for a date not more than three months after the date on which the directors became subject to the requirement to call the meeting. Any reasonable expenses incurred by such members by reason of the failure of the directors to comply with the requirement to call the meeting **must** be reimbursed by the company. Any sum so reimbursed **shall** be retained by the company out of any sums due from the company by way of fees or remuneration in respect of the services of the directors in default.

MEMBERS' STATEMENTS – MEMBERS' POWER TO REQUIRE CIRCULATION OF A STATEMENT (SS 314–317)

7.49 The Act also gives the right to members to require the company to circulate to the members entitled to receive notice of a general meeting a statement of not more than 1,000 words with respect to:

- a matter referred to in a proposed resolution to be dealt with at that meeting, or

- other business to be dealt with at that meeting.

Note that normally the members requesting this will have to pay for it and deposit money in advance (see below).

7.50 The requirement applies once the company has received the request(s) from:

- members representing at least 5 per cent of the total voting rights of all the members who have a relevant right to vote, or

- at least 100 members who have a relevant right to vote and hold shares in the company on which there has been paid up an average sum, per member, of at least £100.

The request(s):

- may be in hard copy or electronic form

- must identify the statement to be circulated

- must be authenticated by the person or persons making it

- must be received by the company at least one week before the meeting to which it relates.

7.51 For a private company, in all cases (for a public company in some cases) the expenses of the company in circulating the statement must be paid by the members who requested it unless the company resolves otherwise. Also, unless the company has previously so resolved, the company **is not bound to circulate the statement unless there is deposited with or tendered to it, not later than one week before the meeting, a sum reasonably sufficient to meet its expenses** in doing so.

7.52 Note also that application may be made to the court (by the company or another person who claims to be aggrieved) claiming that these rights are being abused. If the court is satisfied that these rights are being abused, the company does not have to circulate the statement and the court may order the members who requested the circulation of the statement to pay the company's costs.

7.53 When the requirement to circulate a statement does apply, the company must circulate the statement in the same manner as the notice of meeting and at the same time as, or as soon as reasonably practicable after, it gives notice of the meeting. Failure to comply is an offence.

POWER OF COURT TO ORDER A MEETING (S 306)

7.54 The court has wide powers to order the holding and conducting of a meeting of the members. If for any reason it is impracticable:

- to call a meeting of a company in any manner in which meetings of that company may be called, or

- to conduct the meeting in the manner prescribed by the company's articles or the Act

then the court may, either if its own motion or on the application:

- of a director of the company, or

- of a member of the company who would be entitled to vote at the meeting

order a meeting to be called, held and conducted in any manner the court thinks fit (such directions may include a direction for there to be a quorum of one).

QUORUM AT GENERAL MEETINGS (S 318)

7.55 The 'quorum' is the number of persons required to be present in order to form a valid meeting. The Act provides that if a company has only one member (whether it is limited by shares or by guarantee) then one qualifying person present at a meeting is a quorum. This will override any provision in the articles.

7.56 Otherwise, **subject to the provisions of the company's articles**, two qualifying persons present at the meeting are a quorum. This is subject to two exceptions as follows. It does not apply if:

- the two are qualifying persons only because they are authorised representatives of the same corporation

- the two are qualifying persons only because they are proxies of the same member.

7.57 For these purposes 'qualifying person' means:

- an individual who is a member of the company

- an authorised representative of a corporation (see below), or

- a person appointed as proxy of a member in relation to the meeting.

AUTHORISED REPRESENTATIVE OF A CORPORATION (S 323)

7.58 The Act provides a statutory procedure for a corporation that is a member of a company to authorise a representative to act as its representative at a meeting of that company. A 'corporation' includes a body incorporated outside the United Kingdom. Note that as an alternative, a corporation may in any case appoint a proxy.

7.59 A corporation that is a member of a company may, by resolution of its board of directors or other governing body, authorise a person or persons to act as its representative or representatives at any meeting of the company. If the corporation authorises only one person, he is entitled to exercise the same powers on behalf of the corporation as it could exercise if it were an individual member of the company. If it authorises more than one person, any one of them can exercise those powers. If more than one authorised person purports to exercise a power of the corporation, and they purport to exercise that power in different ways, then it has no effect. This last provision has caused problems in relation to nominee holdings in public companies and is likely to be subject to amendment.

7.60   Often it may be difficult to appoint an authorised representative of a corporation by 'resolution of its directors or other governing body', so corporations have often chosen to appoint proxies instead. Given the wider powers that proxies now have, this may continue.

PROXIES (SS 324–331)

7.61   A proxy is a person appointed by a member of a company to exercise all or any of his rights to attend and to speak and to vote at a meeting of the company. The Act provides a statutory right for a member of any company (including a member of a company without share capital) to appoint a proxy (s 324).

7.62   Note the requirement for a notice of meeting to contain a statement of rights to appoint proxies (see **7.40**).

7.63   For a company having share capital, a member may appoint more than one proxy in relation to a meeting, provided that each proxy is appointed to exercise the rights attached to a different share or shares held by that member. This is designed for the case where the shareholder is holding different shares on behalf of different people, but there is no restriction in the Act on its use.

7.64   It is often practice to send out a form for appointment of (a) prox(y)(ies) with the notice of meeting, with instructions on how to complete and return it for an effective proxy appointment. The Act regulates how this is done. The provisions are:

- if there are issued at the company's expense invitations to appoint as proxy a specified person or a number of specified persons, the invitations must be issued to all the members entitled to vote at the meeting

- the above requirement is not contravened if:
  - there is issued to a member at his request a form of appointment naming the proxy or a list of persons willing to act as proxy, and
  - the form or list is available on request to all members entitled to vote at the meeting.

Failure to comply with this requirement is an offence.

7.65   Often a proxy form will give the opportunity on each resolution to either mandate the proxy to vote in a particular way on particular resolutions, or to give the proxy full discretion how (and whether) to cast the member's vote(s).

7.66   Section 327 regulates requirements in company articles relating to how early any appointment of a proxy must be received. These provisions also apply to any document necessary to show the validity of, or otherwise relating to, the appointment of a proxy. Any provision in a company's articles is void in so far as it would have the effect of requiring the proxy (or document) to be received by the company (or any other person) earlier than:

- in the case of a meeting or adjourned meeting, 48 hours before the time for holding the meeting (or adjourned meeting)

- in the case of a poll taken more than 48 hours after it was demanded, 24 hours before the time appointed for taking the poll

- in the case of a poll taken not more than 48 hours after it was demanded, the time at which it was demanded.

In calculating these periods, no account is taken of any part of a day that is not a working day.

7.67 If the member wishes to terminate the appointment of his proxy, such termination is only effective if notice of termination is received by the company (or other person specified in the company's articles) before the commencement of the meeting. The company's articles can specify an earlier time for receipt of the notice of termination, but such provisions are subject to the same restrictions as those stated above for provisions about when proxy appointments must be received (s 330).

7.68 Subject to any provisions in the company's articles, a proxy may be elected chairman of the meeting (s 328).

7.69 The appointment of a proxy to vote on a matter at a general meeting authorises the proxy to demand (or join in demanding) a poll on that matter (s 329).

7.70 Finally the Act provides that nothing in the relevant provisions regarding proxies prevents a company's articles from conferring more extensive rights on members or proxies than are conferred by those provisions (s 331).

7.71 See also the separate provisions regarding the specific requirements for proxies voting on resolutions, referred to below in the section on voting at a general meeting (see **7.73** onwards).

CHAIRMAN OF THE GENERAL MEETING

7.72 It is appropriate to have a person act as chairman of a general meeting in order to regulate the proceedings of that meeting. Subject to any provisions in the company's articles a member (which would include an authorised representative of a corporation) or a proxy may be elected to be the chairman of a general meeting by a resolution of the company passed at the meeting (s 328).

VOTING AT A GENERAL MEETING

7.73 Section 284 provides that subject to any provisions of the company's articles:

- on a vote on a resolution on a show of hands at a meeting:
  - every member present in person has one vote, and
  - every proxy present who has been duly appointed by a member entitled to vote on the resolution has one vote

- on a vote on a resolution on a poll taken at a meeting:
  - in the case of a company having share capital, every member has one vote for each share that he holds, and
  - if the company has no share capital, every member has one vote
  - if the company has issued 'stock' (which has a technical meaning and is very unusual) different provisions apply

- in the case of joint holders of shares, only the vote of the senior holder who votes (and any proxies duly authorised by him) may be counted by the company; the senior holder is determined by the order in which the joint holders appear in the register of members (s 286).

7.74 There are specific requirements that apply in respect of the votes of proxies. Regardless of what is in the articles:

- a proxy has the same number of votes on a show of hands as the member who appointed him would have had if present at the meeting

- if the member has appointed more than one proxy, the above provision applies as if the reference to the proxy were a reference to the proxies taken together (s 285).

7.75 There is also specific provision that regardless of what is in the articles a member has the same number of votes in relation to a resolution passed as a written resolution and on a poll on the resolution taken at a meeting (s 285).

7.76 Note also that none of these statutory provisions on voting affects:

- any provision in a company's articles
  - requiring an objection to a person's entitled to vote on a resolution to be made in accordance with the articles, and
  - for the determination of any such objection to be final and conclusive, or

- the grounds on which such a determination may be questioned in legal proceedings (s 287).

VOTING ON A SHOW OF HANDS – DECLARATION OF RESULT

7.77 If a resolution is voted on at a meeting on a show of hands, a declaration by the chairman that the resolution:

- has or has not been passed, or

- has been passed by a particular majority

is conclusive evidence of that fact. An entry of such a declaration in the minutes of the meeting is also conclusive evidence of that fact. However, these provisions do not have effect if a poll is demanded and this demand is not withdrawn (s 320).

VOTING ON A POLL

7.78 A poll may be demanded (regardless of provision in the articles) at a general meeting on any question other than:

- the election of the chairman of the meeting, or

- the adjournment of the meeting (s 321).

7.79 A demand for a poll is effective (regardless of provision in the articles):

- by a member or members representing not less than 10 per cent of the total voting rights of all the members having the right to vote on the resolution

- by not less than 5 members having the right to vote on the resolution

- by a member or members holding shares entitled to vote on the resolution, being shares on which the aggregate sum paid up is not less than 10 per cent of the total sum paid up on all the shares conferring that right (s 321).

7.80 A proxy is entitled to demand, or join in demanding, a poll as if he were the member who appointed him in respect of the voting rights that the proxy is entitled to exercise (s 329).

7.81 Note that it is possible for a company's articles to make different provision in each of the above cases, but the articles can only give the members wider rights, they cannot detract from the statutory rights given above. Often it is convenient for articles to provide that the chairman may demand a poll.

7.82 On a poll, unless the articles provide otherwise, every member in a company with share capital has in respect of each share held by him (different provisions apply to stock) one vote and every member in a company limited by guarantee has one vote. So in a company with shares, a poll is likely to be demanded to enable the different shareholdings to be counted so that they may affect the outcome of the vote. In a company limited by guarantee a poll is likely to be demanded if the vote on a show of hands at a well attended meeting appears close. The methods used for taking the poll at a general meeting are likely to vary depending on the numbers present.

7.83 On a poll at a general meeting, a member entitled to more than one vote need not, if he votes, use all his votes or cast all the votes that he uses in the same way (s 322). Remember also that a member can appoint a proxy (or, in the case of a company with share capital, more than one proxy in respect of different shares) to exercise these rights (see **7.60**).

RECORDS OF MEMBERS' RESOLUTIONS AND MEETINGS

7.84 Every company must keep records comprising:

- copies of all resolutions of members passed otherwise than at a general meeting

- minutes of all proceedings of general meetings, and

- details provided to the company in respect of decisions of a sole member (see below).

These records must be kept for at least 10 years. Failure to comply is an offence (s 355). There are also strong reasons for a company to keep appropriately signed records of resolutions and proceedings of general meetings (see immediately below).

7.85 If a record of a resolution passed otherwise than at a general meeting purports to be signed by a director or the company secretary, it is evidence of the passing of the resolution and, where there is a record of a written resolution of a private company, the requirements of the Act with respect to the passing of the resolution are deemed to be complied with unless the contrary is proved (s 356).

7.86 The minutes of proceedings of a general meeting, if purporting to be signed by the chairman of the meeting (or the chairman of the next general meeting), are evidence of the proceedings of the meeting. Where there is a record of proceedings of a general meeting then, until the contrary is proved:

- the meeting is deemed duly held and convened

- all proceedings at the meeting are deemed to have duly taken place, and

- all appointments at the meeting are deemed valid (s 356).

7.87 Similar provisions apply to records of decisions and meetings of holders of a class of shares or classes of members (s 359).

RECORDS OF DECISIONS BY A SOLE MEMBER

7.88 Where a company limited by shares or by guarantee has only one member and that member takes any decision that:

- may be taken by the company in general meeting, and

- has effect as if agreed by the company in general meeting

he must (unless that decision is taken by way of a written resolution) provide the company with details of that decision. Failure to comply is an offence, but does not affect the validity of any such decision. In practice, a sole member should ensure that such decisions are recorded as written resolutions. Although not a statutory requirement, the same practice should be adopted by a sole member of an unlimited company.

PROVISIONS IN ARTICLES TO NOMINATE ANOTHER PERSON TO EXERCISE A MEMBER'S RIGHTS

7.89 Section 145 applies if a company's articles contain provision enabling a member to nominate another person (or persons) as entitled to enjoy or exercise all or any specified rights of the member in relation to the company. This section gives effect to such a provision in relation to anything required or authorised by the Companies Acts. It is likely to be of more interest to public companies, where shares may be held by nominees. However, it applies to private companies as well.

7.90 The section applies in particular to the rights conferred by the following in the Act:

- right to be sent proposed written resolution (ss 291 and 293)

- right to require circulation of written resolution (s 292)

- right to require directors to call general meetings (s 303)

- right to notice of general meetings (s 310)

- right to require circulation of a statement (s 314)

- right to appoint a proxy to act at a meeting (s 324)

- right to be sent a copy of annual accounts and reports (s 423).

7.91 Note that s 145 and any provision in the company's articles:

- do not confer rights enforceable against the company by anyone other than the member, and

- do not affect the requirements for an effective transfer or other disposition of the whole or part of a member's interest in a company.

COMMUNICATIONS BY A COMPANY

7.92 The provisions of ss 1143–1148 and Schs 4 and 5 (known as 'the company communications provisions') have effect regarding how documents or information may be sent or supplied by or to a company. Schedule 5 of the Act sets out detailed provisions regarding how a company may validly send or supply documents or information. These cover:

- communications in hard copy form

- communications in electronic form, and

- communications by means of a website.

7.93 Paragraph 16 of Sch 5 applies in relation to documents or information to be sent or supplied to joint holders of shares or debentures of a company. It provides that subject to anything in a company's articles, anything authorised or required to be supplied to joint holders of shares or debentures may be sent or supplied either:

- to the holder whose name appears first in the register of members (or debentures), or

- to each of the joint holders.

Anything to be agreed to or specified by the holder must be agreed or specified by all the joint holders. This presumably includes consent to receive information electronically or by means of a website (see below).

7.94 Paragraph 17 of Sch 5 provides that subject to anything in a company's articles, following the death or bankruptcy of a shareholder, documents or information required or authorised to be sent or supplied to the member may be sent or supplied to the persons claiming to be entitled to the shares in consequence of the death or bankruptcy:

- by name, or

- by their title (eg representatives of the deceased, or trustee of the bankrupt etc)

at the address in the UK supplied for the purpose by those so claiming. Until such an address is supplied, a document or information may be sent or supplied as if the death or bankruptcy had not occurred.

COMMUNICATIONS IN HARD COPY FORM

7.95 A document or information sent by the company in hard copy form must be:

- handed to the recipient, or

- supplied by hand or sent by posting a prepaid envelope to an address as follows:
  - to an address specified for the purpose by the intended recipient
  - to a company at its registered office
  - to a person in his capacity as a member of the company at his address as shown in the company's register of members
  - to a person in his capacity as a director at his address as shown in the company's register of directors
  - to an address which any provision of the Companies Acts authorises the document or information to be sent or supplied.

Where the company is unable to obtain an address as above, the document or information may be sent or supplied to the intended recipient's last address known to the company (Sch 5, paras 3 and 4).

COMMUNICATIONS IN ELECTRONIC FORM

7.96 A document or information may only be sent or supplied by a company in electronic form:

- to a person who has agreed (generally or specifically) that the document or information may be sent or supplied in that form (and has not revoked that agreement), or

- to a company that is deemed to have so agreed by a provision in the Companies Acts (see 'Communications to a company' below).

The document or information must be sent or supplied to an address specified for that purpose by the intended recipient (generally or specifically) or, in the case of a company, deemed to be so specified by a provision in the Companies Acts. Where the document or information is in electronic form that is sent or supplied by hand or post, it may be handed to the recipient or the provisions applicable to hard copy apply. This might be the case if, for instance, the information was supplied on disc (Sch 5, paras 5–7).

7.97 The easiest way of dealing with electronic communications in a small private company would be to:

- ask each member and director to supply an e-mail address for the purpose of receiving all notices and information of any type from the company

- record the e-mail address, and

- to use the e-mail addresses supplied to send notices and information to the members and directors electronically.

COMMUNICATIONS BY MEANS OF A WEBSITE

7.98 There are detailed provisions enabling a company to communicate with its members by means of a website (Sch 5, paras 8–14). These may in time provide substantial cost savings for public companies and the few private companies with a large membership.

7.99 In brief summary:

- a company can ask its members to resolve (or alter its articles to contain provision) that the company may send or supply documents or information to members by making it available on a website

- a company can then ask each relevant person individually to agree that the company may send or supply documents or information to him by means of a website, and

- provided that the company's request states clearly the effect of failure to respond, if the recipient does not respond within 28 days then that person is taken to have agreed that the company may send or supply documents or information to him in that manner

- there must be a period of at least 12 months between requests to the member for the later request to be effective.

7.100 There are further provisions about:

- how a document or information may be sent or supplied by a website

- requiring the company to notify the intended recipient of information about each notification on a website, and

- the period of availability on the website.

It is also helpful to make use of the guidance supplied by the Institute of Chartered Secretaries and Administrators regarding electronic communications by a company.

DOCUMENTS AND INFORMATION SENT OR SUPPLIED TO A COMPANY

7.101   The provisions of Sch 5 (see above, 'Communications of a company') apply in relation to documents or information that are to be sent or supplied by one company to another.

7.102   Otherwise, Sch 4 of the Act regulates the supply of information **to** a company by someone other than another company.

7.103   Under Sch 4 a document or information in hard copy form may be sent or supplied by hand or by post in a prepaid envelope:

- to an address specified by the company for the purpose

- to the company's registered office

- to an address to which any provision of the Companies Acts authorises the document or information to be sent or supplied.

7.104   Under Sch 4 a document or information may be sent or supplied to a company in electronic form if:

- the company has agreed (generally or specifically) that the document or information may be sent or supplied in that form (and has not revoked that agreement), or

- the company is deemed to have so agreed by a provision in the Companies Acts.

The document or information must be sent or supplied to an address specified for that purpose by the company (generally or specifically) or deemed to be so specified by a provision in the Companies Acts. Where the document or information is in electronic form that is sent or supplied by hand or post, the provisions applicable to hard copy apply. This might be the case if, for instance, the information was supplied on disc.

SUMMARY OF MAJOR CHANGES INTRODUCED BY THE ACT

1   Private companies may pass written resolutions by a majority but the Act imposes further additional procedures for the passing of written resolutions. There is the possibility for more flexibility about how members indicate their assent to a written resolution. It seems likely that written resolutions will become the norm for small private companies (ss 288–300 and 1146*). Brought into force on 1 October 2007 by Commencement Order 3 (except s 1146 brought into force on 20 January 2007 by Commencement Order 1).*

2   Members may requisition the circulation of a written resolution (ss 292–295). *Brought into force on 1 October 2007 by Commencement Order 3.*

3   The Act includes detailed provisions regarding meetings of members. These are presumably intended to avoid the necessity for such provisions to be contained in a company's articles. Some of these provisions may be overridden or modified by a company's articles, and some apply regardless of what is contained in a company's articles (ss 301–335). *Brought into force on 1 October 2007 by Commencement Order 3 (except ss 308, 309 and 333 brought into force on 20 January 2007 by Commencement Order 1).*

4   The notice period for all general meetings of private companies is now 14 clear days (regardless of the type of resolution to be proposed, so special resolutions no longer require 21 days' notice), unless the articles require a longer period or unless special notice is required (ss 307, 360 and 312). *Brought into force on 1 October 2007 by Commencement Order 3.*

5   Extraordinary resolutions have been abolished. This is subject to a transitional provision that any reference to an extraordinary resolution in a provision of a company's memorandum or articles, or of a contract, continues to have effect and be construed in accordance with old legislation (Companies Act 1985, s 378). *Brought into force on 1 October 2007 by Commencement Order 3.*

6   Proxies may vote on a show of hands at a meeting (subject to any provision in the articles) and there are other detailed provisions regarding proxies (ss 284 and 324–331). *Brought into force on 1 October 2007 by Commencement Order 3 (except s 333 brought into force on 20 January 2007 by Commencement Order 1).*

7   In calculating periods for delivery of proxy forms, no account is taken of days that are not working days (s 327). *Note that ss 327(1), (2)(a) and (b) and (3) and s 330(1)–(5), (6)(a) and (b) and (7) were brought into force on 1 October 2007 by Commencement Order 3. It is understood that the remaining parts of these sections will not be commenced (as they are*

regarded as unworkable). The definition of 'working day' in s 1173 was brought into force for these purposes on 1 October 2007 by Commencement Order 3.

8   Records of members' resolutions and meetings must be kept for at least 10 years (s 355). *Brought into force on 1 October 2007 by Commencement Order 3.*

9   Schedule 5 contains detailed provision about how a company may communicate with its members, by hard copy or electronic form or by means of a website. In particular:
   (i)   a company can ask its members to resolve (or alter its articles to contain provision) that the company may send or supply documents or information to members by making it available on a website;
   (ii) a company can then ask each relevant person individually to agree that the company may send or supply documents or information to him by means of a website; and
   (iii) provided that the company's request states clearly the effect of failure to respond, if the recipient does not respond within 28 days then that person is taken to have agreed that the company may send or supply documents or information to him in that manner. *Brought into force on 20 January 2007 (with ss 1143–1148) by Commencement Order 1.*

10 There are also provisions regarding the supply of documents or information to a company, set out in Sch 4. Note that Sch 5 (and not Sch 4) applies to the provision of documents or information that are to be sent or supplied by one company to another. *Brought into force on 20 January 2007 (with ss 1143–1148) by Commencement Order 1.*

11 A company can have provision in its articles allowing a member to nominate another person to enjoy or exercise that member's rights, but this does not confer rights enforceable against the company by that other person, nor affect the requirement for a valid transfer of an interest (s 145). *Brought into force on 1 October 2007 by Commencement Order 3.*

Chapter 8

ANNUAL COMPLIANCE – REGISTERS, RECORDS, ANNUAL RETURN AND ACCOUNTS

INTRODUCTION

8.1   The incorporation of a company brings with it the requirement to comply with company law and the Companies Acts. At the lowest level, a company must comply with the annual compliance requirements and disclosure requirements imposed by the Act. These apply to a company even if it is not carrying on any activity and is dormant. This chapter deals with those requirements.

8.2   In relation to annual compliance, the Act requires a private limited company to:

- maintain and keep available for inspection certain registers containing required information

- keep other records, and in some cases keep them available for inspection

- deliver to the Registrar an annual return which gives information about the company on a specific date

- keep accounting records and prepare annual accounts and a directors' report that must be circulated to the members and (in most cases) sent to the Registrar within required time limits

- have a registered office (in England and Wales, Scotland or Northern Ireland, depending in which the company is registered) (see **2.38**).

8.3   Failure to deliver the annual return and annual accounts to the Registrar within required time limits is likely to result in action by the Registrar. Initially this is likely to take the form of reminders to the company (and then to the directors) regarding statutory obligations. Continued default may ultimately result in the company being struck off and dissolved or prosecution of the directors. If annual accounts are filed late, the company is liable to an automatic civil penalty.

8.4　Under previous legislation, there was a requirement to hold an Annual General Meeting ('AGM') of the shareholders, present the annual accounts to the shareholders and propose a resolution to re-appoint the auditors. Under the previous legislation, these requirements could be relaxed for a private company by means of 'elective resolutions', passed unanimously by the members. Under the Act, the requirements to hold an AGM and present the accounts to the shareholders in a meeting no longer apply to a private company and elective resolutions no longer exist. So the AGM and presentation of the accounts to a meeting is optional (in respect of annual accounts for financial years ending on or after 1 October 2007). However, companies should check their articles (and any shareholders' agreement) to see if they require an AGM etc. Companies with a large membership and many companies limited by guarantee may still choose to have an Annual General Meeting, present the annual accounts and re-appoint the auditors at that meeting, but this will no longer be on a statutory basis.

8.5　Of course, there are also many event related requirements, the more common of which are explained in **Chapter 10**.

REGISTERS – REQUIREMENTS AND FORM

8.6　The registers required for a private company are:

- register of members (s 113)

- register of directors (s 162)

- register of directors' residential addresses (s 165)

- register of company secretaries (if the company has a company secretary) (s 275)

- register of charges (ss 876 and 891)

- register of debenture holders (if the company issues debentures) (s 743; it is not a statutory requirement to keep this register, but if kept, statutory requirements apply).

A company may also choose to keep an overseas branch register in certain circumstances (s 129). See also **5.120** regarding the requirement to keep a copy of directors' service contracts available for inspection by the members. The requirement for a register of directors' interests in shares has been abolished by the Act, so it is no longer required for private companies. (The Financial Services Authority requires companies whose shares are traded on a regulated market to comply with parallel disclosure rules regarding directors' interests in shares introduced as part of the UK's implementation of the EU Market Abuse Directive, but these of course do not apply to private companies).

8.7   Most of the provisions in the Act regarding the keeping of registers are due to come into force on 1 October 2009. Provisions regarding the inspection of the register of members (ss 116–119) and all the provisions regarding the register of debentures (ss 738–754) are already in force.

8.8   The Act prescribes:

* what information must be kept in each register

* where it must be kept

* who has a right to inspect the register and/or require copies, and on what terms this may be done

* circumstances when information about the location of the register must be delivered to the Registrar.

8.9   The registers and records may be kept in hard copy or electronic form provided that electronic records are capable of being reproduced in hard copy form (s 1135).

8.10   The Act provides for Regulations to be made about where company registers are to be kept available for inspection and about such inspection and copying (ss 1136 and 1137). Two sets of regulations have at the time of writing been made under s 1137. The first is the *Companies (Fees for Inspection and Copying of Company records) Regulations 2007* (SI 2007/2612), which prescribes the fees that may be charged for inspection and copies of the register of members, and the provision of copies of various documents such as a copy of a director's service contract or qualifying indemnity provision, or copy resolutions. The second set of regulations is the *Companies (Fees for Inspection and Copying of Company Records) (No 2) Regulations 2007* (SI 2007/3535) which provides for fees for the inspection and copies of the register of debenture holders. The fees are not large and for a private company that does not have a large number of members, it is unlikely to be economic to even raise an invoice for them (eg the fee for provision of a copy of the register of members is £1 for the first 5 entries, with additional fees as the number of entries increases).

REGISTER OF MEMBERS – EVIDENCE OF MEMBERSHIP AND SHAREHOLDING

8.11   This is possibly the most important register maintained by a company. The reason is that it is this register which records who the members of the company are. Section 112 provides that the subscribers to the memorandum are automatically members of a company and must be entered in the register of members, but otherwise every person who has agreed to become a member and whose name is entered in the register of members, is a member of the company.

The register of members is prima facie evidence of the matters the Act directs or authorises to be in it. Note also that the issue of shares on allotment is completed by making the appropriate entry in the register of members (although the shares are allotted when a person acquires the unconditional right to be included in the company's register of members in respect of the shares) (s 558).

REGISTER OF MEMBERS – WHAT MUST BE IN IT? (SS 113 AND 115)

8.12   The following must be in the register:

- the names and addresses of the members

- the date on which each person was registered as a member, and

- the date at which any person ceased to be a member.

8.13   If the company has share capital, there must be entered, with the names and addresses of the members, a statement of:

- the shares held by each member and

- the amount paid on the shares of each member,

- distinguishing each share:
    - by its number (if it has a number – which is not required if all the issued shares of the company (or of that class) are fully paid up and have equal rights for all purposes), and
    - by its class (where the company has more than one class of shares).

8.14   If the company does not have share capital (in most cases this will be a company limited by guarantee) and it has more than one class of members, a statement of the class to which a member belongs must be entered with his name and address.

8.15   If the company has more than 50 members, unless the register is in such a form as to constitute an index of members, the company must keep an index of members. In practice, most registers of members are kept on software which itself constitutes an index, or where kept in hard copy are in that form.

8.16   If a limited company has only one member, a statement of this fact, together with the date on which the company became a single member company, must be entered in the register with the name and address of the sole member (s 123). Similarly, if the number of members increases from one, a statement of this fact and the date on which it happened must be entered with the name and address of the person who was formerly the sole member.

8.17   Section 126 provides that no notice of any trust shall be entered on the register of members of a company registered in England and Wales or Northern Ireland.

REGISTER OF MEMBERS – WHERE MUST IT BE KEPT? (S 114)

8.18   The company's register of members must be kept available for inspection:

- at its registered office, or

- at a place specified in regulations to be made (which will be known as an 'inspection place').

8.19   A company must give notice to the Registrar of the place where its register of members is kept available for inspection and of any change in that place. There is an exception to this requirement if the register has at all times since:

- in the case of a company registered in Great Britain, the creation of the register or 1 July 1948, and

- in the case of a company registered in Northern Ireland, the creation of the register or 1 April 1961

been kept available for inspection at the registered office.

8.20   It is an offence to fail to comply with either of these requirements.

REGISTER OF MEMBERS – RIGHTS TO INSPECT AND REQUIRE COPIES (SS 116–120)

8.21   In the past, concerns have arisen about the use made of information taken from registers of members. This has ranged from the use of lists of members for unwelcome mailshots to concerns about animal rights protestors. As a result, the Act has introduced additional requirements regarding requests to inspect or have a copy of the register (or any part of it). There are also restrictions on providing information obtained by such requests to other parties. These provisions are now in force.

8.22   The Act starts from the position that the register must be open to the inspection of any member without charge and any other person on payment of the prescribed fee (see **8.10**). Any person may require a copy of the register (or any part of it) on payment of the prescribed fee. However, any person seeking to exercise those rights must make a request to the company. The request must contain the following information:

- in the case of an individual, his name and address

- in the case of an organisation, the name and address of an individual responsible for making the request on behalf of the organisation

- the purpose for which the information is to be used, and

- whether the information is to be disclosed to any other person, and if so:
    - where that person is an individual, his name and address
    - where that person is an organisation, the name and address of an individual responsible for receiving the information on its behalf, and
    - the purpose for which the information is to be used by that person.

8.23   It is an offence for a person to knowingly or recklessly make in such a request a statement that is misleading, false or deceptive in a material particular. It is also an offence for a person in possession of information obtained by exercise of these rights of inspection and the provision of copies to do anything (or fail to do anything) that results in the information being disclosed to another person.

8.24   Where a company receives such a request for inspection or copies, it has the options of either complying with the request or applying to court on the basis that the inspection or copy is not sought for a proper purpose. The company must either comply or apply to the court within 5 working days, so quick action is required, particularly if a court application is the desired route. There is no definition in the Act of what is a 'proper purpose', but the Institute of Chartered Secretaries and Administrators has issued a guidance note on this area, which contains some helpful suggestions about what they believe might, or might not, be regarded as a 'proper purpose' in this context.

8.25   Where a person inspects the register or the index of members' names, or the company provides a copy, the company must inform him of the most recent date when alterations were made to the register and no further alterations were made, and (in the case of the index, whether there is any alteration to the register not reflected in the index). Failure to comply is an offence.

REGISTER OF MEMBERS – REMOVAL OF ENTRIES (S 121)

8.26   An entry relating to a former member can be removed after 10 years from when he ceased to be a member. Section 128 imposes a maximum 10-year time limit for claims in respect of entries (or failure to make entries) in the register. These provisions came into force on 6 April 2008. Transitional provisions require that old records of members that had left prior to that date must be kept for another 10 years after 6 April 2008 or until 20 years after that member ceased to be a member, whichever is earlier.

REGISTER OF DIRECTORS (SS 162–164)

8.27 Every company must keep a register of directors. Provisions to be brought into force on 1 October 2009 will alter some of the requirements regarding the content of this register. The major change will be the introduction of a service address for all directors (see **5.14**), but there are also some other alterations to detailed requirements. Under the new provisions in the Act this register must contain the required particulars of each person who is a director of the company. For an individual, the required particulars are:

- name and any former name(s)

- a service address (see also **5.14**)

- the country or state (or part of the UK) in which he is usually resident

- nationality

- business occupation (if any)

- date of birth.

In this context '**name**' means a person's Christian name (or other forename) and surname, except that in the case of a peer, or an individual usually known by a title, the title may be stated instead of his/her Christian name (or other forename) and surname or in addition to either or both of them. Note that '**former name**' means a name by which an individual was formerly known for business purposes and that where a person was formerly known by more than one such name, each of them must be stated. It is not necessary to include a former name: (i) in the case of a peer or an individual normally known by a British title, where the former name is one by which the person was known previous to the adoption of or succession to the title; or (ii) in the case of any person, where the former name was changed or disused before that person attained the age of 16 years or has been changed or disused for 20 years or more. This is a change from the previous law, which did not refer to 'a name by which the individual was formerly known for business purposes' and which provided that in the case of a married woman, the name by which she was known previous to marriage did not have to be stated. So the Act requires a married woman who has changed her name on marriage to state her former name if it was a name by which she was formerly known for business purposes.

8.28 For corporate directors and firms, the required particulars are:

- corporate or firm name

- registered or principal office

- in the case of an EEA company to which the first company law directive applies:
  - the public register in which the public file of the company is kept (including details of the relevant state)
  - the registration number

- in any other case:
  - the legal form of the company or firm and the law by which it is governed
  - if applicable, the register in which it is entered (including details of the state) and its registration number.

Remember that the company must have at least one director who is a natural person (see **5.12**).

8.29 The register must be kept available for inspection:

- at its registered office, or

- at a place specified in regulations to be made (which will be known as an 'inspection place').

A company must give notice to the Registrar of the place where its register of directors is kept available for inspection and of any change in that place unless it has at all times been kept at the registered office (s 162).

8.30 The register must be open to the inspection of any member of the company without charge and of any other person on payment of the prescribed fee (s 162).

8.31 It is an offence to fail to comply with the above requirements.

REGISTER OF DIRECTORS' RESIDENTIAL ADDRESSES (S 165) (SEE ALSO SS 240–246)

8.32 This is a new requirement imposed by the Act as a result of the introduction of the concept of directors' service addresses. It ensures that there is a record of the usual residential address of each director who is an individual. If a director's usual residential address is the same as his service address, this register need only contain an entry to that effect, but this does not apply if the service address is stated to be: 'The company's registered office'. This provision is due to be brought into force on 1 October 2009.

8.33 This register is not open to public inspection. The usual residential address of the director that is an individual (or, if applicable, the information that his service address is his usual residential address) is defined by the Act as 'protected information' (and it continues to be such after a person ceases to be a director). A company must not use or disclose such protected information except:

- for communicating with the director concerned

- in order to comply with any requirement of the Companies Acts as to particulars to be sent to Companies House, or

- in accordance with an order of the court for disclosure under s 244.

8.34 See **5.14** for a fuller explanation.

REGISTER OF COMPANY SECRETARIES (SS 275–279)

8.35 A private company is not required to have a company secretary. This provision came into force on 6 April 2008. However, many private companies may still choose to have a company secretary. A company must keep a register of secretaries. It must contain the required particulars of the person who is (or the persons who are) the secretary (or joint secretaries) of the company. The provisions in the Act regarding the content of the register of secretaries are due to come into force on 1 October 2009. Until then, the provisions regarding the content of this register are set out in the Companies Act 1985. The provisions set out below are those that are due to be in force from 1 October 2009 onwards.

8.36 In the case of an individual who is secretary the required particulars are:

- name and any former name

- address.

The address required to be stated in the register is a service address and may be stated to be: 'The company's registered office'.

8.37 The provisions regarding the meaning of 'name' and 'former name' are the same as for the register of directors.

8.38 It is quite common to appoint a company as secretary. In the case of a body corporate or a firm that is a legal person under the law by which it is governed, the required particulars of the secretary are the same details as those required of a corporate director.

8.39 If all the partners of a firm are joint secretaries, it is sufficient to state the particulars that would be required if the firm were a legal person and the firm had been appointed secretary. This would presumably apply to an English partnership, which is not a legal person. However, it is inadvisable to do this, as it is unlikely that all the partners in the firm will want to be joint secretaries.

8.40 The requirements about where to keep this register and to give notice to the Registrar of its whereabouts are the same as for the register of directors.

REGISTER OF CHARGES AND COPIES OF INSTRUMENTS CREATING A CHARGE (SS 876 AND 891)

8.41 There are detailed provisions in the Act relating to the registration of details of charges with the Registrar within the required time limit, so that they appear in a public register of charges maintained by the Registrar. These are outlined in **10.64**. The Act also requires every limited company to keep available for inspection a register of charges. These provisions are due to come into force on 1 October 2009 and will replace similar provisions currently contained in the Companies Act 1985. The provisions set out below are those that are due to be in force from 1 October 2009 onwards.

8.42 The register of charges must have entered in it:

- all charges specifically affecting property of the company, and

- all floating charges on the whole or part of the company's property or undertaking.

The entry must in each case give a short description of the property charged, the amount of the charge and, except in the cases of securities to bearer, the names of the persons entitled to it.

8.43 The company must also keep available for inspection a copy of every instrument creating a charge requiring registration with the Registrar. In the case of a series of uniform debentures, a copy of one of the series is sufficient (ss 875 and 890).

8.44 The requirements about where to keep this register (and copies of instruments) and to give notice to the Registrar of their whereabouts are the same as for the register of directors.

8.45 The register and copies of instruments must be open to the inspection of any creditor or member without charge, and any other person on payment of the prescribed fee (ss 877 and 892).

8.46 Failure to comply with these requirements is an offence.

REGISTER OF DEBENTURE HOLDERS (SS 743–748)

8.47 There is no requirement to have a register of debenture holders, but if a company does have one, the Act contains requirements applicable to it. In practice, a company will not have this register unless it has issued debentures. The term 'debenture' includes debenture stock, bonds and any other securities of a company, whether or not constituting a charge on the assets of a company.

8.48 Any register of debenture holders that is kept by a company is subject to generally the same (but not identical) requirements regarding where it is kept, notice to the Registrar about where it is kept, and inspection as applies to the register of members. Please refer to ss 743–748 for details.

OVERSEAS BRANCH REGISTER (SS 129–135)

8.49 Sections 129 to 135 allow a company (having share capital) that transacts business in a country or territory to which the provisions apply to keep and maintain there an overseas branch register that contains the required details of members resident there. The countries or territories listed include: Cyprus, Hong Kong, India, Ireland, Malta, Seychelles, Singapore, South Africa and Trinidad and Tobago, plus others (s 129). The overseas branch register is regarded as part of the company's main register of members but all entries and transactions relating to the shares in the overseas branch register must be entered in that register, not in the main register of members. These provisions are due to come into force on 1 October 2009 and will replace similar provisions currently contained in the Companies Act 1985. The provisions set out below are those that are due to be in force from 1 October 2009 onwards.

8.50 A transfer of shares registered in the overseas branch register is regarded as a transfer of property situated outside the UK. So if the transfer form is executed outside the UK and there is no other connection with the UK, the transfer may be able to escape liability to stamp duty. Advice on specific situations is required.

8.51 The Registrar must be notified within 14 days of the company beginning to keep, or discontinuing an overseas branch register. The company must keep with the main register in the UK a duplicate of the overseas branch register. The duplicate is treated for all purposes as part of the main register and so is open to inspection etc.

RECORDS OF RESOLUTIONS AND MEETINGS ETC (SS 355–359)

8.52 Every company must keep records comprising:

- copies of all resolutions of members passed otherwise than at general meetings

- minutes of all proceedings of general meetings

- records of decisions taken by a sole member that may be taken by the company in general meeting and have effect as if agreed by the company in general meeting.

These must be kept for at least 10 years from the date of the resolution, meeting or decision.

8.53 The records must be kept available for inspection:

- at its registered office, or

- at a place specified in regulations to be made.

A company must give notice to the Registrar of the place where these records are kept available for inspection and of any change in that place unless they have at all times been kept at the registered office.

8.54 The records must be open to the inspection of any member of the company without charge and a member may require a copy on payment of the prescribed fee.

8.55 Similar provisions apply in respect of class resolutions and meetings.

8.56 Failure to comply is an offence.

8.57 All companies are also required to record minutes of all proceedings at meetings of directors and keep them for at least 10 years from the date of the meeting (s 248). The company should also keep and retain in a similar manner records of decisions made by the directors otherwise than at a meeting.

ANNUAL RETURN (SS 854–859)

8.58 Every company is required to deliver an 'annual return' to the Registrar on not less than an annual basis. The annual return is a 'snapshot picture' of information about the company on a particular date – which must not be later than the 'return date'. The company's return date is initially the anniversary of its incorporation. So normally the return date is the company's 'birthday'. The annual return must be delivered to the Registrar within 28 days of the return date. Failure to comply is an offence and failure to comply with this requirement under previous legislation has in the past been an area where prosecution is more likely. Companies registered in England & Wales and Scotland can check online for the date by which the annual return must be delivered.

8.59 If you wish to change the return date (for instance to align all the companies in a group so that they have the same return date), then just deliver the annual return made up to that earlier date. So for instance, if a company is incorporated on 8 November, the default return date is 8 November and the first annual return must be delivered within 28 days after that date one year later. If you wish to change this date to, for instance, 31 March, just make up a return to the earlier date of 31 March and deliver it to the Registrar within 28 days after that. In subsequent years the company's return date will be 31 March.

8.60 The required contents of the annual return are:

- the date to which it is made up (ie the date of the 'snapshot picture' of the information)

- the address of the registered office

- the type of company and its principal business activities – regulations will prescribe classifying systems for this (eg SIC codes have been used previously)

- particulars of the directors and (if it has a secretary or secretaries) the company secretary or joint secretaries

- if the register of members (and/or register of debenture holders) is not kept available for inspection at the registered office, the address where it is kept available for inspection.

8.61 The annual return of a company having share capital must also contain:

- a statement of capital containing required details

- prescribed particulars of members of the company on the date to which the return is made up and the shares of each class held by each member

- prescribed particulars of persons who have ceased to be members since the last date to which the return was made up and the number of shares of each class transferred by each since that date (or, for the first annual return, since incorporation) and the dates of registration of the transfers.

Normally private companies choose to give all these particulars on every annual return. However, note that there is only a requirement to give complete details of all members and shareholdings every three years. If these details have been included in either of the two immediately preceding annual returns, only details of changes (ie persons ceasing to be or becoming members and shares transferred since the date of that return) are required.

8.62   The form of the annual return has been changed by statutory instrument to modify the requirements regarding members' addresses. For annual returns made up to a date from 1 October 2008 onwards it is no longer necessary for a private company to include the addresses of its shareholders.

8.63   The address of shareholders is only required in respect of companies whose shares are traded on a regulated market and even then only in respect of members holding at least 5 per cent of the issued shares of any class. This provision cannot apply to a private company.

ACCOUNTING RECORDS

8.64   Every company must keep adequate accounting records that are sufficient:

- to show and explain the company's transactions

- to disclose with reasonable accuracy, at any time, the financial position of the company at that time, and

- to enable the directors to ensure that any accounts required to be prepared (eg the annual accounts) comply with applicable requirements.

It is an offence to fail to comply (s 386).

8.65   The accounting records must be kept at the registered office or such other place as the directors think fit and must at all times be open to inspection by the company's officers. If the accounting records are kept outside the UK, accounts and returns must be sent to, and kept at, a place in the UK. The Act requires a private company to keep accounting records for three years (and a public company for six). However, in practice, for legal and tax reasons, the author recommends that accounting records should always be retained (in some form) for a minimum of six years.

ANNUAL ACCOUNTS AND REPORTS – INTRODUCTION

8.66   Companies are also required to prepare annual accounts and a directors' report, circulate them (or a summary of them) to the members, have them audited (in some cases) and (usually) deliver them (or part of them) to the Registrar, so that they are on the public record. All this must be done within required time limits. If accounts are not filed with the Registrar on time, the company will be subject to an automatic civil penalty.

8.67 The accounting provisions in the Act and the relevant statutory instruments made under the Act apply (mainly) only in respect of financial years beginning on or after 6 April 2008. The provisions set out below are those as contained in the Act unless otherwise stated.

8.68 The extent of the requirements that apply depend on whether the company is defined as:

- a small company

- a medium-sized company

- an unquoted company

- a quoted company (which, of necessity, will be a public company)

- an unlimited company.

Detailed provisions regarding the requirements for the annual accounts and reports are set out in the following statutory instruments and reference should be made to these as appropriate:

- SI 2008/409 *Small Companies and Groups (Accounts and Directors' Report) Regulations 2008*

- SI 2008/410 *Large and Medium-sized Companies and Groups (Accounts and Reports) Regulations 2008*

- SI 2008/393 *Companies Act 2006 (Amendment) (Accounts and Reports) Regulations 2008*

- SI 2008/374 *Companies (Summary Financial Statement) Regulations 2008*

- SI 2008/565 *Insurance Accounts Directive (Miscellaneous Insurance Undertakings) Regulations 2008*

- SI 2008/567 *Bank Accounts Directive (Miscellaneous Banks) Regulations 2008*

- SI 2008/373 *Companies (Revision of Defective Accounts and Reports) Regulations 2008*

The following was published by BERR in June 2008 and is also available: *Guidance on the Accounts and Reports Regulations under the Companies Act 2006*. At the time of writing all these may be accessed via BERR's website (see **Appendix 5**).

8.69 It is the duty of the directors to arrange for the preparation of the accounts etc in accordance with the Act. The Act and supporting statutory instruments contain detailed provisions regarding annual accounts and reports. The following sections contain an overview with some of the details. No mention is made of the requirements applicable to a quoted company (such as the requirement for a quoted company to produce a remuneration report).

ANNUAL ACCOUNTS AND REPORT

8.70 An individual private company must prepare:

- a balance sheet as at the last day of the financial year giving a true and fair view of the state of affairs of the company as at the end of the financial year

- a profit and loss account giving a true and fair view of the profit or loss of the company for the financial year, and

- a directors' report for each financial year.

8.71 There is also a duty in some cases (see below) for a parent company to prepare group accounts. Directors must not approve the annual accounts unless they are satisfied that they give a true and fair view. Accordingly they should be satisfied that they comply with applicable accounting standards and the Act's requirements.

GROUP ACCOUNTS

8.72 If at the end of a financial year a company is a parent company, it is required to prepare group accounts unless it is exempt from that requirement (although even if exempt it may choose to prepare group accounts). Group accounts are consolidated accounts of the parent company and its subsidiary undertakings.

8.73 The following are cases where the parent company is exempt from the requirement to prepare group accounts:

- if the parent company qualifies as a small company (to do so, the group must also qualify as a small group, see below)

- if the company is included in the EEA accounts of a larger group, drawn up and audited in accordance with EEC requirements or international accounting standards (see s 400 for precise requirements)

- if the company is included in the non-EEA accounts of a larger group, drawn up in accordance with EEC requirements or in a manner equivalent to consolidated accounts and annual reports so drawn up – the accounts must be audited but note that equivalent accounts do not need to conform with the detailed requirements of EEC directives so long as they meet the basic requirements and in particular give a true and fair view (see s 401 and UITF Abstract 43 issued by the Accounting Standards Board in October 2006)

- if all of its subsidiary undertakings could be excluded from consolidation in Companies Act group accounts.

8.74   In cases where the company is exempt because it is included in larger group accounts, the company must state in its individual accounts:

- that it is exempt from the obligation to prepare and deliver group accounts

- the name of the parent undertaking that draws up the group accounts, and:
    - if it is incorporated outside the UK, the country in which it is incorporated, or
    - if it is unincorporated, the address of its principal place of business.

8.75   The company must also deliver to the Registrar, within the period for filing its accounts and reports for the financial year in question, copies of:

- those group accounts, and

- where appropriate, the parent undertaking's annual report

together with the auditor's report on them.

8.76   Sections 398 to 408 contain detailed provisions regarding the above matters.

FINANCIAL YEAR, ACCOUNTING REFERENCE DATE AND ACCOUNTING REFERENCE PERIODS (SS 390–392)

8.77   The annual accounts are made up to the end of the company's financial year and cover the period of that financial year. The first financial year begins with the date of incorporation of the company and ends on its accounting reference date ('ARD') (or up to seven days either side of that date, as the directors may determine). Subsequent financial years begin with the day after the end of the previous financial year and end on its accounting reference date ('ARD') (or up to seven days either side of that date, as the directors may determine). The capability to flex the year end by seven days is useful for businesses that account in complete weeks.

8.78 On incorporation, a company's accounting reference date is automatically set as the last day of the month in which the anniversary of its incorporation falls. So if it is incorporated on 8 November 2007, its first accounting period will (if the ARD is not changed) cover the period from 8 November 2007 to 30 November 2008 (or end up to seven days either side of that date). Of course many companies choose to change this ARD which is set by default and may not suit their needs. This is possible, provided that it is done within the correct time limit and the correct information is delivered to the Registrar.

CHANGE OF ACCOUNTING REFERENCE DATE (S 392)

8.79 Section 392 provides that a company can change its accounting reference date ('ARD') by giving notice to the Registrar (which will be in the prescribed form). This is subject to restrictions. The notice may specify a new ARD for:

- the company's current accounting reference period (ie the one it is in) and subsequent periods, or

- the company's immediately previous accounting reference period (ie the one that has most recently come to an end) and subsequent periods.

The notice must state whether the relevant accounting reference period is to be shortened or extended. In the example in **8.76**, if the ARD was changed to 31 March, the accounting period could be shortened, so that it came to an end on 31 March 2008, or extended, so that it came to an end on 31 March 2009. A notice extending an accounting period is not effective if given earlier than five years after the end of a previous accounting reference period of the company that was extended in accordance with these provisions, unless:

- the notice is to align the ARD with the ARD of a subsidiary or parent undertaking that is established under the law of the UK or the law of any other EEA state, or

- the company is in administration under Part 2 of the Insolvency Act 1986 or Part 3 of the Insolvency (Northern Ireland) Order 1989 (SI 1989/2405 (NI 19)), or

- the Secretary of State directs that it should not apply.

Note also the following restrictions regarding change of ARD:

- it is not possible to give notice to alter the ARD for a previous accounting reference period if the time allowed for delivering the annual accounts in respect of that period to the Registrar has already expired, and

- an accounting reference period may not be extended so as to exceed 18 months unless the company is in administration under Part 2 of the Insolvency Act 1986 or Part 3 of the Insolvency (Northern Ireland) Order 1989 (SI 1989/2405 (NI 19)).

SMALL COMPANIES ACCOUNTS REGIME

8.80 The small companies regime for accounts and reports applies to a company for a financial year in relation to which the company:

- qualifies as small, **and**

- is not excluded from the regime.

Qualification as a small company (ss 381–384)

8.81 A company qualifies as small in relation to its first financial year if the qualifying conditions are met in that year. It qualifies as small in relation to a subsequent financial year:

- if the qualifying conditions are met in that year and the preceding financial year

- if the qualifying conditions are met in that year and the company qualified as small in relation to the preceding financial year

- if the qualifying conditions were met in the preceding financial year and the company qualified as small in that year.

8.82 The qualifying conditions are met by a company in a year in which it satisfies two or more of the following requirements:

- For financial years beginning before 6 April 2008:
  - turnover not more than £5.6 million
  - balance sheet total not more than £2.8 million
  - number of employees not more than 50.

- For financial years beginning on or after 6 April 2008:
  - turnover not more than £6.5 million
  - balance sheet total not more than £3.26 million
  - number of employees not more than 50.

For a period that is a company's financial year, but not in fact a year, the maximum figures for turnover must be proportionately adjusted.

8.83 If the company is a parent company, it can only qualify as a small company in relation to a financial year if the group headed by it qualifies as a small group. In very basic summary, to qualify as a small group, the aggregate figures for that group as a whole must fall within the qualifying conditions for a small company. See s 383 for precise requirements.

Companies excluded from the small companies regime

8.84   The small companies regime does not apply to a company that is, or was at any time within the financial year to which the companies relate:

- a public company

- a company that is an authorised insurance company, a banking company, an e-money insurer, an ISD investment firm or a UCITS management company

- a company that carries on insurance market activity, or

- a member of an ineligible group (save that such companies are entitled to small companies exemption in relation to the directors' report – see the *Companies Act 2006 (Amendment) (Accounts and Reports) Regulations 2008* (SI 2008/393).

8.85   A group is ineligible if any of its members is:

- a public company

- a body corporate whose shares are admitted to trading on a regulated market in an EEA state

- a person (other than a small company) who has permission under Part 4 of the Financial Services and Markets Act 2000 to carry on a regulated activity

- a small company that is an authorised insurance company, an e-money insurer, aMiFID investment firm or a UCITS management company, or

- a person who carries on insurance market activity.

EFFECTS OF SMALL COMPANIES REGIME

8.86   If a company is subject to the small companies regime:

- it may be audit exempt (ss 477–479) (see **8.102** onwards)

- it does not have to include a business review in its directors' report (see below) or the amount (if any) that the directors recommend should be paid as dividend (s 416(3))

- it does not have to deliver to the Registrar a copy of the company's profit and loss account (s 444)

- it does not have to deliver to the Registrar a copy of the directors' report (s 444), and

- it is subject to the requirements on the detailed format and content of the annual accounts and directors' report set out in the *Small Companies and Groups (Accounts and Directors' Report) Regulations 2008* (SI 2008/409).

8.87   Note that the small company may nevertheless choose to prepare fuller accounts than those required, or deliver a full set of accounts and directors' report to Companies House, but it is not a statutory requirement. There is also provision to file a balance sheet drawn up in accordance with regulations and a shorter form of profit and loss account. These are 'abbreviated accounts' (s 444).

MEDIUM-SIZED COMPANIES

8.88   The process for identifying whether a company is a medium-sized company is much the same as for identifying a small company (see above), save that the qualifying conditions are met by a medium-sized company in a year in which it satisfies two or more of the following requirements:

- For financial years beginning before 6 April 2008:
  - turnover not more than £22.8 million
  - balance sheet total not more than £11.4 million
  - number of employees not more than 250.

- For financial years beginning on or after 6 April 2008:
  - turnover not more than £25.9 million
  - balance sheet total not more than £12.9 million
  - number of employees not more than 250.

Again, for a parent company to qualify it must head a medium-sized group where the aggregate figures fall within the limits. See ss 465–467 for precise requirements to qualify as a medium-sized company.

8.89   A medium-sized company does not have to include in its business review in the directors' report analysis using key performance indicators in relation to non-financial information (such as environmental and employee matters) (s 417). It is also permitted to deliver a shorter form of profit and loss account as specified in regulations (see the *Large and Medium-sized Companies and Groups (Accounts and Reports) Regulations 2008* (SI 2008/410). These are 'abbreviated accounts' (s 445).

DIRECTORS' REPORT

8.90 The directors must prepare a directors' report for each financial year of the company and if the company is a parent company and prepares group accounts, then the directors' report must be a consolidated report (s 415). See the *Small Companies and Groups (Accounts and Directors' Report) Regulations 2008* (SI 2008/409) or the *Large and Medium-sized Companies and Groups (Accounts and Reports) Regulations 2008* (SI 2008/410) for precise requirements.

8.91 The directors' report must state:

- the names of the persons who, at any time during the financial year, were directors of the company, and

- the principal activities of the company (and, for a consolidated report, of the group undertakings)in the course of the year

- (unless it is subject to the small companies regime) the amount (if any) that the directors recommend should be paid by way of dividend

- (unless it is subject to the small companies regime) a business review, as detailed below.

8.92 Section 418 provides that unless the company is audit exempt (see below) and the directors take advantage of that exemption, the directors' report must also contain a statement to the effect that, in the case of each of the persons who are directors at the time the report is approved:

- so far as the director is aware, there is no relevant audit information of which the company's auditor is unaware, and

- he has taken all the steps that he ought to have taken as a director in order to make himself aware of any relevant audit information and to establish that the company's auditor is aware of that information.

8.93 'Relevant audit information' means information needed by the company's auditor in connection with preparing his report. In this context a director is regarded as having taken all the steps that he ought to have taken as a director if he has:

- made such enquiries of his fellow directors and of the company's auditors for that purpose, and

- taken such other steps (if any for that purpose),

as are required by his duty as a director of the company to exercise reasonable care, skill and diligence. If a directors' report containing the required statement is approved but the statement is false, every director who:

- knew that the statement was false, or was reckless as to whether it was false, and

- failed to take reasonable steps to prevent the report from being approved,

commits an offence.

8.94   There is provision for regulations to be made about the other contents of the directors' report. See the relevant statutory instruments from those listed in **8.66** above.

DIRECTORS' REPORT – THE BUSINESS REVIEW (S 417)

8.95   Section 417 applies to financial years commencing on or after 1 October 2007. It requires that unless the company is subject to the small business regime, the directors' report must contain a business review. The purpose of the business review is to inform members of the company and help them assess how the directors have performed their duty to promote the success of the company. The business review must contain:

- a fair review of the company's business, and

- a description of the principal risks and uncertainties facing the company.

8.96   The review required is a balanced and comprehensive analysis of:

- the development and performance of the company's business during the financial year, and

- the position of the company's business at the end of that year,

consistent with the size of the company's business.

8.97   The review must, to the extent necessary for an understanding of the development, performance or position of the company's business, include:

- analysis using key financial performance indicators, and

- where appropriate, analysis using other key performance indicators, including information relating to environmental matters and employee matters.

'Key performance indicators' means factors by reference to which the development, performance or position of the company's business can be measured effectively. Note that a medium-sized company need not comply with these requirements regarding key performance indicators so far as they relate to non-financial information.

8.98 The review must, where appropriate, include references to, and additional explanations of, amounts included in the company's annual accounts.

8.99 Nothing in the provisions detailing the required contents of the business review requires the disclosure of information about impending developments or matters in the course of negotiation if the disclosure would, in the opinion of the directors, be seriously prejudicial to the interests of the company (s 417(10)).

8.100 Quoted companies are subject to additional requirements regarding the content of the business review which are not set out here.

DIRECTORS' REPORT – LIABILITY

8.101 Section 463 came into force on 20 January 2007. It deals with liability for statements in the directors' report (and the directors' remuneration report, which is not required for private companies) and a summary financial statement derived from those reports. It provides that no person shall be subject to any liability to a person **other than the company** resulting from reliance, by that person or another, on information in such a report. It also provides that a director is liable to compensate the company for any loss suffered by it as a result of:

- any untrue or misleading statement in a such a report, or

- the omission from such a report of anything required to be included in it

but it also provides that a director is so liable only if:

- he knew the statement to be untrue or misleading or was reckless as to whether it was untrue or misleading, or

- he knew the omission to be dishonest concealment of a material fact.

AUDIT OF ACCOUNTS – REQUIREMENT, EXEMPTION AND BALANCE SHEET STATEMENT

8.102 Sections 475–481 of the Act apply to accounts for financial years beginning on or after 6 April 2008. Equivalent (but not identical) provisions under the Companies Act 1985 etc apply in respect of financial years beginning before that date.

8.103 Section 475 provides that a company's annual accounts must be audited unless the company is exempt from audit in accordance with the provisions applicable to:

- small companies

- dormant companies, or

- non-profit-making companies subject to public sector audit provided for by s 482.

8.104 A company is not entitled to audit exemption unless its balance sheet contains a statement by the directors to that effect and also to the effect that:

- the members have not required the company to obtain an audit of its accounts for the year in question in accordance with s 476, and

- the directors acknowledge their responsibilities for complying with the requirements of the Act with respect to accounting records and the preparation of accounts.

These statements must appear on the balance sheet above the director's signature (s 475).

8.105 There are separate provisions applicable to non-profit making bodies subject to public sector audit which are not covered in this book (ss 482 and 483). These provisions apply to accounts for financial years beginning on or after 1 April 2008.

RIGHT OF MEMBERS TO REQUIRE AN AUDIT (S 476)

8.106 In the case of a small or dormant company which would otherwise be entitled to audit exemption, the members may require an audit for a financial year. Members representing not less than 10 per cent in nominal value of the issued share capital (or any class of it) (or if the company does not have share capital, 10 per cent of the members) may require the audit by giving notice to the company. The notice may not be given before the financial year to which it relates and must be given not later than one month before the end of that year.

SMALL COMPANIES – CONDITIONS FOR EXEMPTION FROM AUDIT (SS 477–479)

8.107   To qualify for audit exemption as a small company for a financial year beginning on or after 6 April 2008:

*   the company must qualify as a small company in relation to that year

*   its turnover in that year must be not more than £6.5 million, and

*   its balance sheet total for that year must be not more than £3.26 million.

For a period that is a company's financial year, but not in fact a year, the maximum figures for turnover must be proportionately adjusted. If the company is in a group, note that it is unlikely to be entitled to audit exemption as a small company (see **8.109** and s 479).

8.108   A company is not entitled to audit exemption as a small company if it was at any time in the financial year in question:

*   a public company

*   a company that is an authorised insurance company, a banking company, an e-money insurer, a MiFID investment firm or a UCITS management company

*   a company that carries on insurance market activity, or

*   a special register body under Trade Union legislation or an employers' association.

8.109   If a company was a group company at any time in the financial year it will not be entitled to the audit exemption as a small company unless:

*   the group qualifies as a small group and it was not at any time in that year an ineligible group, and

*   the aggregate turnover and balance sheet totals meet the limits required for a small group, or

*   throughout the whole of the time during the financial year when it was a group company, it was both a subsidiary undertaking and dormant.

DORMANT COMPANIES – CONDITIONS FOR EXEMPTION FROM AUDIT

8.110 A company is defined by s 1169 as 'dormant' during any period when it has no transaction that is required to be entered in the company's accounting records. For these purposes the following are disregarded:

- any transaction arising from the taking of the subscriber shares by a subscriber to the memorandum as a result of an undertaking of his in connection with the formation of the company

- fees payable to the Registrar for the registration of the annual return, a change of name or re-registration, and

any penalty under s 453 payable to the Registrar for failure to file accounts.

8.111 A company is audit exempt under these provisions if:

- it has been dormant since its formation, or

- it has been dormant since the end of the previous financial year and the following conditions are met:
  - it is not required to prepare group accounts for that year, and
  - it is entitled to prepare accounts in accordance with the small companies regime (or would have been so entitled but for having been a public company or a member of an ineligible group).

8.112 So a plc or a company in a group can claim audit exemption by reason of being dormant. However, a company is not entitled to this exemption if it was at any time within the financial year a company that:

- is an authorised insurance company, a banking company, an e-money insurer, a MiFID investment firm or a UCITS management company, or

- carries on insurance market activity.

APPOINTMENT AND TERM OF OFFICE OF AUDITOR (SS 485–494)

8.113 The provisions in the Act regarding the appointment of auditors of a private company (ss 485–488) apply in relation to appointments for financial years beginning on or after 1 October 2007.

8.114 An auditor of a private company must be appointed for each financial year, unless the directors reasonably resolve otherwise on the ground that audited accounts are unlikely to be required (s 485).

8.115   The Act contains some detailed provisions about who should appoint the auditor, when the appointment should be made and in what circumstances the auditor is deemed re-appointed. In practice, unless the directors resolve that audited accounts are unlikely to be required, it is likely to be easiest if the members appoint the auditor by ordinary resolution. After that, the auditors will usually be deemed re-appointed.

Some may prefer the auditors to be initially appointed by the directors and afterwards re-appointed (perhaps each year) by the members. Some of the relevant detail contained in the Act regarding such appointments is set out below.

8.116   For each financial year for which an auditor is to be appointed (other than the company's first financial year), the appointment must be made before the end of the period of 28 days beginning with:

- the end of the time allowed for sending out the annual accounts and reports for the previous financial year (which is tied to the period for filing accounts, see **8.137** and **8.143** onwards), or

- if earlier, the day on which the annual accounts and reports for the previous year are sent out.

This is the 'period for appointing auditors' (s 485(2)).

8.117   The directors may appoint an auditor:

- at any time before the company's first period for appointing auditors

- following a period when the company was audit exempt and did not have an auditor, at any time before the company's next period for appointing auditors, or

- to fill a casual vacancy.

8.118   The members may appoint an auditor by ordinary resolution:

- during any period for appointing auditors

- if the company should have appointed auditors in the period for appointing auditors but has failed to do so, or

- where the directors had a power to appoint but failed to do so.

8.119   If no one is appointed before the end of the period for appointing auditors, the company must within one week give notice to the Secretary of State and the Secretary of State has a default power to make an appointment (s 486).

8.120 Where no auditor is appointed by the end of the next period for appointing auditors, any auditor in office is deemed re-appointed unless:

- he was appointed by the directors (save that where a private company had elected (under previous legislation) to dispense with the annual appointment of auditors, and that election was in force immediately before 1 October 2007, this does not apply in respect of auditors first appointed before 1 October 2007)

- the company's articles require actual re-appointment

- the deemed re-appointment is prevented by the members representing 5 per cent (or such lower percentage as is specified in the company's articles) of the total voting rights giving notice in accordance with s 488 that the auditor should not be re-appointed

- the members have resolved that he should not be re-appointed, or

- the directors have resolved that no auditor should be appointed for the financial year in question.

This is subject to provisions applicable to resignation or removal of an auditor (covered in **10.28** onwards).

8.121 The remuneration of an auditor appointed by the directors must be fixed by the directors. The remuneration of an auditor appointed by the members must be fixed by the members by ordinary resolution or in such manner as the members may by ordinary resolution determine (s 492). In practice, the members may choose to delegate to the directors the power to fix the auditor's remuneration.

8.122 There is provision to make regulations requiring disclosure of the terms on which the auditor is appointed and regulations about the disclosure regarding any services provided to the company by the auditor or by his associates (ss 493 and 494). Please see the *Companies (Disclosure of Auditor Remuneration and Liability Limitation Agreements) Regulations 2008* (SI 2008/489).

AUDITOR – INDEMNITIES AND LIABILITY LIMITATION AGREEMENTS (SS 532–538)

8.123 A company may indemnify an auditor against any liability incurred by him:

- in defending proceedings (whether civil or criminal) in which judgment is given in his favour or he is acquitted

- in connection with an application under s 1157 (power of court to grant relief in case of honest and reasonable conduct) in which relief is granted to him by the court, or

- in accordance with the provisions in ss 534–536 regarding 'liability limitation agreements'.

Otherwise, s 532 prohibits provisions protecting auditors to any extent from liability.

8.124   Sections 534–538 allow a company to enter into a 'liability limitation agreement' with its auditor. Such agreements can limit the liability of the auditor for negligence, default, breach of duty or breach of trust occurring in the course of the audit. Such an agreement can only apply in respect of one financial year (so a new one would be needed for each audit). There is provision for regulations regarding such agreements. The provisions regarding auditor liability limitation agreements came into force on 6 April 2008.

8.125   There are provisions in s 536 requiring authorisation of a liability limitation agreement by members of the company by passing a resolution:

- before the company enters into the agreement, waiving the need for approval

- before the company enters into the agreement, approving the agreement's principal terms, or

- after the company enters into the agreement, approving the agreement.

A resolution authorising a liability limitation agreement is still effective even if passed before 6 April 2008 (when this provision came into force), provided that it complied with the requirements of that section.

8.126   Section 537 restricts the effect of such agreements by reference to a 'fair and reasonable' test.

8.127   Regulations to be made may require disclosure of such agreements, in particular in a note to the accounts (s 538). Please see the *Companies (Disclosure of Auditor Remuneration and Liability Limitation Agreements) Regulations 2008* (SI 2008/489), which set out the disclosure requirements.

THE AUDIT REPORT

8.128   The audit report is made by the auditor to the company's members. It must include several items including a statement whether, in the auditor's opinion, the annual accounts give a true and fair view and have been properly prepared in accordance with the relevant financial reporting framework and in accordance with the requirements of the Act (and, where applicable, the relevant International Accounting Standards provision).

8.129   The auditor's report must be either qualified or unqualified and must include a reference to any matters to which the auditor wishes to draw attention by way of emphasis without qualifying the report (s 495). The auditor must also state in his report whether in his opinion the information given in the directors' report is consistent with the accounts for the financial year (s 496). The auditor is subject to a number of duties set out in s 498.

8.130   The auditor is entitled to full access to the company's books, accounts and vouchers (in whatever form they are held) and may require information from a range of persons regarding the company and its subsidiaries as set out in ss 499 and 500. It is an offence to knowingly or recklessly make a statement or convey information to an auditor that is misleading, false or deceptive in a material particular (s 501). The auditor is entitled to receive written resolutions proposed to be agreed by a private company and receive notice of, attend and speak at general meetings (s 502).

AUDIT REPORT – SIGNATURE AND THE SENIOR STATUTORY AUDITOR

8.131   The auditor's report must (subject to the exception in s 506 explained in **8.133**) state the name of the auditor and be signed and dated. If the auditor is an individual, the report must be signed by him. If the auditor is a firm, it must be signed by the senior statutory auditor in his own name, and for and on behalf of the auditor (s 503). Every copy of the audit report published by or on behalf of the company must (subject to s 506) state the name of the auditor and (where the auditor is a firm) the name of the person who signed it as senior statutory auditor (s 505).

8.132   The senior statutory auditor means the person identified by the firm as such in relation to that audit (s 504).

8.133   Pursuant to s 506 the auditor's name and (where applicable) the name of the senior statutory auditor may be omitted from published copies of the audit report and the copy delivered to the Registrar if the company:

- considering on reasonable grounds that statement of the name would create or be likely to create a serious risk that the auditor or senior statutory auditor, or any other person, would be subject to violence or intimidation has resolved that the name should not be stated, and

- has given notice to the Registrar stating:
  - the name and registered number of the company
  - the financial year to which the report relates, and

  - the name of the auditor and (if applicable) the name of the senior statutory auditor who signed the report.

APPROVAL AND SIGNING OF ACCOUNTS AND DIRECTORS' REPORT

8.134 The company's annual accounts must be approved by the Board and signed on behalf of the Board by a director (s 414). The signature must be on the balance sheet. The directors' report must be approved by the Board and signed on behalf of the Board by a director or the company secretary (s 419). Any copy of either of these documents that is published by or on behalf of the company must state the name of the signatory (s 433).

8.135 In each case an offence is committed if the accounts or report do not comply with requirements by every director who:

- knew that they (or it) did not comply, or was reckless as to whether they (or it) complied, and

- failed to take reasonable steps to secure compliance with those requirements or, as the case may be, prevent the accounts (or report) from being approved.

CIRCULATION OF ANNUAL ACCOUNTS AND DIRECTORS' REPORT

8.136 Section 423 provides that every company must send a copy of its annual accounts and reports to:

- every member of the company

- every holder of the company's debentures, and

- every person who is entitled to receive notice of general meetings.

This is subject to the option to send out a summary financial statement as an alternative (see below).

8.137 Section 424 requires a private company to comply with this requirement not later than:

- the end of the period for filing accounts and reports with the Registrar (see **8.143**), or

- if earlier, the date on which it actually delivers the accounts and reports to the Registrar.

8.138 Failure to comply is an offence.

SUMMARY FINANCIAL STATEMENT

8.139 The Act provides that in cases specified in regulations to be made, a company may provide a summary financial statement instead of copies of the annual accounts and reports. Please refer to ss 426 and 427 for more detail of applicable requirements. Please also see the *Companies (Summary Financial Statement) Regulations 2008* (SI 2008/374) for further detail.

8.140 Note that full annual accounts and reports must be sent to an entitled person who wishes to receive them (s 426(2)).

FILING ACCOUNTS AND REPORTS WITH THE REGISTRAR (SS 441–453)

8.141 All companies (other than some unlimited companies) must file annual accounts and reports with the Registrar within the required time limit. The extent of what must be filed by a private company varies according to whether the company is:

- a company subject to the small companies regime – only balance sheet and auditor's report (if any) required and possibility of filing abbreviated accounts drawn up in accordance with regulations (s 444; see also ss 449 and 450)

- a medium-sized company – annual accounts and directors' report with auditor's report (if any), with the possibility of filing abbreviated accounts drawn up in accordance with regulations (s 445; see also ss 449 and 450)

- neither of the above (an unquoted company) – the company's annual accounts and directors' report with auditor's report (if any) (s 446).

Companies may choose to file full accounts, directors' report and auditor's report even when not required to do so.

8.142 In each case, the copies of the balance sheet and directors' report delivered must state the name of the person who signed it on behalf of the Board. The copy of the auditor's report must either:

- state the name of the auditor and (where the auditor is a firm) the name of the person who signed it as senior statutory auditor, or

- if the conditions in s 506 are met (see **8.133**), state that a resolution has been passed and notified to the Secretary of State in accordance with that section.

PERIOD ALLOWED FOR FILING ACCOUNTS AND REPORTS WITH THE REGISTRAR (SS 442 AND 443)

8.143 Companies registered in England & Wales and Scotland can check online at the Companies House website for the date by which the accounts and reports must be delivered.

8.144

Normally, for financial years beginning on or after 6 April 2008, a private company must deliver required accounts and reports to the Registrar within 9 months after the end of the relevant accounting reference period. For financial years beginning before 6 April 2008, for '9 months' substitute '10 months'.

8.145 If the relevant accounting reference period is the company's first and is a period of more than 12 months, the accounts and reports must be delivered within:

- 9 months from the first anniversary of the date of incorporation of the company, or

- 3 months of the end of the accounting reference period, whichever expires last.

As an accounting period cannot exceed 18 months, for a private company this effectively means within 21 months of incorporation. For financial years beginning before 6 April 2008, for '9 months' substitute '10 months'.

8.146 If the relevant accounting reference period has been shortened because the accounting reference date has been changed, the accounts and reports must be delivered within:

- the period calculated under the applicable provisions above, or

- three months from the date of the notice of change,

whichever last expires.

8.147 If application is made to the Secretary of State before the end of the period allowed for delivery, he may, if for any special reason he thinks fit, extend the filing period (s 442(5)). In practice, this is only likely to happen in exceptional circumstances that are beyond the control of the company (eg if accounting records have been destroyed in a fire).

8.148   Prior to the Act, a common law rule (referred to as 'the same day rule') regarding calculation of the months' period for filing accounts sometimes caused confusion amongst companies. The Act modifies this rule to remedy this. Consequently, under the Act, when calculating the period of months allowed for filing, if counting from the last day of a month, the period of months also expires on the last day of the relevant month. So, for instance, if calculating 9 months from 30 June, the Act provides that the period will expire on 31 March. Additional provisions apply in respect of February to achieve a similar result. However, in other cases, when not dealing with month ends, the period ends on the corresponding date (s 443).

8.149   It is an offence to fail to file the required accounts and reports within the required period.

UNLIMITED COMPANIES – ACCOUNTS FILING (S 448)

8.150   Unlimited companies are only required to file accounts with the Registrar in certain circumstances. The circumstances in which an unlimited company will have to file its accounts are:

- if within the accounting period it was (to its knowledge) at any time a subsidiary of an undertaking (defined in s 1161) the liability of whose members was then limited (which I shall refer to as a 'limited undertaking')

- if within the accounting period at any time (to its knowledge) two or more limited undertakings could exercise rights which, if exercisable by one of them, would have made the company a subsidiary undertaking of it

- if within the accounting period the company has at any time been a parent company of a limited undertaking

- the company is a banking or insurance company (or is the parent company of a banking or insurance group)

- the company is a qualifying company within the meaning of the Partnerships and Unlimited Companies (Accounts) Regulations 1993 (SI 1993/1820).

The references above to an undertaking being limited at a particular time are to an undertaking (under whatever law established) the liability of whose members is at that time limited.

CIVIL PENALTY FOR FAILURE TO FILE ACCOUNTS AND REPORTS WITHIN THE REQUIRED TIME LIMIT (S 453)

8.151   Section 453 provides that if the accounts and reports are not filed with the Registrar within the period required, the company is liable to a civil penalty. This is in additional to such failure being a criminal offence. The civil penalty will be payable by the company automatically, without any further action being required. The civil penalty is levied upon the late receipt of accounts by the Registrar.

8.152   The amount of the civil penalty is prescribed by the *Companies (Late Filing Penalties) and Limited Liability Partnerships (Filing Periods and Late Filing Penalties) Regulations 2008* (SI 2008/497). The penalties will change and increase in respect of accounts that are filed late on or after 1 February 2009. Below are Tables setting out the prescribed automatic civil penalties for accounts filed late but before 1 February 2009 and for accounts filed late after that date.

Accounts filed late but before 1 February 2009

How late accounts are received	Public company	Private company
Not more than 3 months	£500	£100
Between 3 and 6 months	£1,000	£250
Between 6 and 12 months	£2,000	£500
More than 12 months	£5,000	£1,000

Accounts filed late on or after 1 February 2009

How late accounts are received	Public company	Private company
Not more than 1 months	£750	£150
Between 1 and 3 months	£1,500	£375
Between 3 and 6 months	£3,000	£750
More than 6 months	£7,500	£1,500

So in summary, for accounts filed late on or after 1 February 2009 the penalties will increase at a much earlier stage of lateness and all penalties have been increased by 50 per cent. Please also note that for accounts drawn up under the Act (ie for accounting periods beginning on or after 6 April 2008), if these accounts are filed late and the previous accounts drawn up under the Act (ie also for an accounting period beginning on or after 6 April 2008) were also filed late, then the penalty imposed will be double that shown in the Table.

8.153 The changes to the penalties are designed to encourage greater compliance in filing accounts and deal with those who have in the past habitually filed accounts late.

VOLUNTARY REVISION OF ACCOUNTS

8.154 The Act contains provision for the voluntary revision of accounts if it appears to the directors that they did not comply with the Act. See s 454 and the *Companies (Revision of Defective Accounts and Reports) Regulations 2008* (SI 2008/373) for details.

SUMMARY OF MAJOR CHANGES INTRODUCED BY THE ACT

1   The Annual General Meeting and presentation of accounts to a meeting is no longer a statutory requirement for private companies, so it is now optional. Elective resolutions are abolished; the AGM is still required for public companies (ss 1295 and Sch 16 and ss 336–354). *Provisions relating to private companies came into force for private companies on 1 October 2007, subject to transitional provisions (see **Chapter 12**).*

2   An auditor must be appointed for each financial year, unless the directors reasonably resolve otherwise on the ground that audited accounts are unlikely to be required. New provisions apply about who may appoint the auditor and when. If appointed by the members the auditor is deemed re-appointed unless certain circumstances apply. If appointed by the directors, the auditor needs to be re-appointed by the members (ss 485–494). *Provisions relating to private companies came into force for private companies on 1 October 2007, subject to transitional provisions (see **Chapter 12**).*

3   A person seeking to inspect or have copies of the register of members must give required information and is subject to criminal penalty for false information. The company can apply to the court to prevent inspection etc (ss 116–120). *Subject to staged implementation from 1 October 2007 – now fully in force.*

4   Entries in the register of members can be removed after 10 years (s 121). *This came into force on 6 April 2008 subject to transitional provisions – see **8.26**.*

5   The content of information in the register of directors is changed. This includes a requirement for a service address and usual country of residence as well as a different definition of 'former name' (ss 163 and 164). *Due to come into force on 1 October 2009.*

6   Provision for a register of directors' residential addresses and provision about the limited circumstances in which this information may be disclosed (but old information about residential addresses will remain accessible on the public record) (ss 165–167 and 240–246). *Due to come into force on 1 October 2009.*

7   There is more detail easily accessible regarding overseas branch registers (ss 129–135). *Due to come into force on 1 October 2009.*

8   The appointment of a company secretary is now optional for a private company (ss 270–274 & 280). *This came into force on 6 April 2008.*

9   Records of resolutions etc must be kept for at least 10 years (s 355). *This came into force on 1 October 2007.*

10   New wording regarding requirements about annual accounts and reports – but no simplification. Detailed requirements for a business review in the directors' report, but these do not apply to small companies (ss 380–484). *These provisions mainly came into force on 6 April 2008, but many provisions regarding accounts only apply to financial years beginning on or after that date.*

11   Private company accounts are required to be delivered to the Registrar in 9 months rather than 10. The 'same day rule' previously applicable in calculating 'months' has been modified (ss 441–443). *This applies in respect of financial years beginning on or after 6 April 2008.*

12   Section 463 limits directors' liability in relation to statements made in the directors' report etc. *This came into force on 20 January 2007.*

13   If the auditor is a firm, the audit report must be signed by the 'senior statutory auditor' in his own name and for and on behalf of the auditor. There is an exception to this if the company considers on reasonable grounds that statement of the name would create or be likely to create a serious risk that the auditor or senior statutory auditor, or any other person, would be subject to violence or intimidation and the company has resolved that the name should not be stated (and notified the Registrar) (ss 503–506). *These provisions apply in respect of financial years beginning on or after 6 April 2008.*

14   The Act allows a 'liability limitation agreement' with the auditor (subject to controls and disclosure) (ss 532–538). *These provisions came into force on 6 April 2008.*

15   The register of directors' interests in shares is no longer required (s 1177). *This came into force on 6 April 2007.*

Chapter 9

SHARE CAPITAL – ISSUE, TRANSFER AND OTHER MATTERS

INTRODUCTION

9.1 The Act will introduce several far reaching changes to the previous law regarding share capital and private companies. The changes are designed to make the administration and re-organisation of private companies easier and in many respects they achieve this goal. Many of these provisions are due to come into force on 1 October 2009, but some provisions (particularly those that were seen as helpful) have been commenced earlier. Please see the summary of changes at the end of this chapter or **Appendix 3** for further detail about this. Some of the more important implementation dates are also referred to in the text.

9.2 Under previous legislation, companies had an 'authorised share capital' which was the total number of shares available to be allotted by a company. This concept is no longer contained in the Act. A company formed under the Act may simply allot and issue shares in accordance with the provisions of the Act, with no statutory 'ceiling' on the number of shares that may be issued. There is also a new requirement to file a 'statement of capital' with the Registrar on the formation of a company with share capital and (in general terms) if there are changes, so that the public record of the share capital of the company is clear and kept up to date. All these provisions are due to come into force on 1 October 2009.

9.3 However, note that it is proposed that under transitional provisions the authorised share capital of existing companies will continue to operate as a restriction on the number and nominal value of shares that the directors may allot. On implementation of this part of the Act, existing companies will need to either pass an ordinary resolution (in accordance with a transitional provision to be prescribed) or modify their articles to remove the old restriction of authorised share capital, if they no longer wish for the restriction to apply. This seems to be another reason to consider adopting new articles framed by reference to the Act.

9.4 Private companies are still prohibited from issuing shares to the public, but the effects of contravention of this prohibition are changed by the Act. These provisions came into effect on 6 April 2008.

9.5   There are no longer any provisions in the Act prohibiting a private company from giving financial assistance for the purchase of its shares or shares in another private company. There are new provisions enabling a private company to reduce its share capital by a simpler method making use of a special resolution and a 'solvency statement'. Both these changes came into effect on 1 October 2008. There are also new provisions enabling the redenomination of shares (due to come into force on 1 October 2009) and many other changes of detail.

SHARES – GENERAL BACKGROUND

9.6   References in the Companies Acts to 'a company having share capital' are to a company that has power under its constitution to issue shares (s 545).

9.7   Shares in a limited company having share capital must each have a fixed nominal value and an allotment of a share that does not have a fixed nominal value is void and an offence (s 542). Typically the nominal value of each share will be £1. However this does not have to be the case. Shares can be denominated in any currency (eg US dollars or Euros). Different classes of shares may be denominated in different currencies or amounts (but note that special requirements apply to public companies). Sometimes one sees shares denominated in fractions of a penny or fractions of another currency.

9.8   Typically a private company will issue one class of shares called 'Ordinary shares' which have equal rights to participate in profits, vote and participate in the distribution of any surplus assets if the company is wound up. However, it is possible for a company to issue shares of different classes with different rights. For instance shares issued to an external investor may give preferential rights to receive dividends paid out to the profits of the company and/or preferential rights if the company is wound up. Different classes of shares may be entitled to different voting rights. There can be a great deal of flexibility regarding the rights that different classes of shares have and drafting of such rights requires professional advice.

9.9   Shares are personal property (in Scotland, moveable property) (s 541) and are transferable in accordance with the company's articles and applicable legal requirements (s 544) (see **9.99**).

9.10   If all the issued shares in a company (or all the issued shares in a particular class) are fully paid up and have equal rights, then the shares do not need to have individual numbers for so long as they remain fully paid up and subject to equal rights. However, if the shares are not all fully paid with exactly the same rights, each share must be distinguished by its appropriate number (s 543).

PROHIBITION OF PUBLIC OFFERS OF SHARES BY PRIVATE COMPANIES (SS 755–760)

9.11 Private companies limited by shares (and the few remaining private companies limited by guarantee with share capital) are prohibited from offering their shares or debentures to the public. This specifically includes an offer to any section of the public. Note that a large range of circumstances may be deemed to be 'an offer to the public'. The Act sets out certain circumstance where an offer is not to be regarded as an offer to the public (see below). If in any doubt, take professional advice on this matter. These provisions came into effect (replacing previous legislation) on 6 April 2008.

9.12 Section 756 states that an offer is not regarded as an offer to the public if it can properly be regarded in all the circumstances as:

- not being calculated to result, directly or indirectly, in securities of the company becoming available to persons other than those receiving the offer, or

- otherwise being a private concern of the person receiving it and the person making it.

An offer is to be regarded (unless the contrary is proved) as being a private concern of the person making it and the person receiving it if it is made to:

- an existing member or employee of the company

- a member of the family of a person who is or was a member or employee

- the widow, widower or surviving civil partner of a person who was a member or employee

- an existing debenture holder, or

- a trustee of a trust where the principal beneficiary is one of the above

and the rights to receive the shares may only be renounced in favour of another such connected person (if they are allowed to be renounced at all). An offer to subscribe for securities to be held under an employee share scheme (with restricted rights to renounce) is similarly regarded as a private concern.

9.13 The Act enables members, creditors or the Secretary of State to apply to the court to restrain a private company from contravening this prohibition. If a private company has already breached the prohibition, certain members, certain creditors or the Secretary of State can apply to the court and the court may (depending on the circumstances) order that the company re-register as a public company or that it be wound up. A court can also order any person knowingly concerned in the contravention to offer to purchase the relevant shares on terms specified by the court. None of this affects the validity of the allotment (ss 757–760).

CHANGES TO SHARE CAPITAL – SUBSCRIBER SHARES, ALLOTMENT, ISSUE, REDUCTION, CONSOLIDATION, SUB-DIVISION, REDENOMINATION

9.14 A limited company having share capital can increase its share capital by allotting and issuing shares in accordance with the provisions of the Act (s 617). A share is 'allotted' when a person acquires the unconditional right to be entered in the company's register of members in respect of the share (s 558). A share is 'issued' when the entry has been made in that register. References in the Act to allotted or issued share capital include shares taken on the formation of the company by subscribers to the company's memorandum (s 546). However, note that the provisions regarding the allotment of shares in the Act have no application to the taking of the subscriber shares (s 559). The subscribers to the memorandum are deemed to have agreed to become members of the company, and on its registration become members and must be entered as such in its register of members (s 112). These provisions are due to come into force (replacing previous legislation with some changes) on 1 October 2009. Under previous legislation companies had an 'authorised share capital' of shares that could be issued and once these were all issued, the authorised share capital could only be increased by resolution of the members. Note that previous law is still in force until 1 October 2009 and that even after that it is proposed that companies incorporated prior to 1 October 2009 will still be subject to this restriction unless they pass an ordinary resolution of the members to amend or revoke this restriction, or adopt new articles without an authorised share capital. It is proposed that an ordinary resolution to remove this restriction will be subject to Chapter 3 of Part 3 of the Act and therefore will be required to be filed at Companies House.

9.15 A limited company can only reduce its share capital by one of the methods provided for by the Act. Companies may also consolidate and sub-divide the nominal value of shares and redenominate shares in accordance with provisions in the Act. These matters are covered in more detail below.

ALLOTMENT AND ISSUE OF SHARES – SUMMARY OF REQUIRED STEPS

9.16 The provisions of the Act regarding the allotment and issue of shares are due to come into force on 1 October 2009. Prior to that, provisions under previous legislation apply. The steps set out below relate to procedure and law after the Act's provisions come into force.

1   Check that the directors have authority to allot shares (which usually they will have automatically under the Act if this is a private company with one class of shares).

2   Check provisions in the company's articles.

3   For companies incorporated prior to 1 October 2009, check:
     –   whether the company still has the restriction of an authorised share capital in force (see above), and
     –   whether the powers for directors to allot shares given by s 550 of the Act apply to the company (see below).

4   Consider whether the statutory pre-emption rights on allotment apply.

5   The directors make the decision to allot shares, which must be properly made and recorded either as a written resolution of the directors or by means of minutes of the decision taken at a Board meeting.

6   The shares are offered to the allottees and usually under the terms of allotment paid for then.

7   The company completes the issue by making entries in the register of members.

8   A return of allotment and statement of capital must be sent to the Registrar within one month.

9   A share certificate must be issued within two months.

ALLOTMENT OF SHARES – AUTHORITY FOR ALLOTMENT (SS 549–551)

9.17   Under previous legislation, for all companies, if the directors wished to allot shares (other than for an employees' share scheme), they were required to obtain authority from the shareholders (either by means of the company's articles or by resolution of the shareholders) for the directors to allot shares. This was often referred to as a 'section 80 authority' after the relevant section number in the Companies Act 1985. The 2006 Act abolishes this statutory requirement for private companies with one class of shares, but retains it in other cases. The directors may in any case allot shares in pursuance of an employees' share scheme (or grant rights to subscribe for, or convert any security into, shares so allotted) without any further authority (s 549).

9.18   If a private company has only one class of shares, the directors may exercise any power of the company to allot shares of that class (or grant rights to subscribe for or convert any security into such shares) except to the extent that they are prohibited from doing so by the company's articles (s 550). Note that this provision will not apply to a company incorporated prior to 5 October 2009 unless the members of the company have resolved that the directors should have this power. Such a resolution will be subject to Chapter 3 of Part 3 of the Act and therefore will be required to be filed at Companies House.

9.19 If a private company will have more than one class of shares after a proposed allotment, then the directors must be authorised to allot shares in the company (or grant rights to subscribe for or to convert any security into shares in the company) by the company's articles or by resolution of the company (s 551). The authorisation to allot shares etc:

- may be a general authority (subject to the limitations below) or may be given for a particular allotment of shares

- may be unconditional (subject to the limitations below) or subject to conditions

- **must** state the maximum amount of shares that may be allotted under it **and** specify the date on which it will expire, which **must** not be more than 5 years later, and

- may be renewed, revoked or varied by resolution of the company and any renewal must again state the maximum number of shares to which it relates and expire not more than 5 years later.

9.20 A resolution to give, vary, revoke or renew authority to allot shares etc under this provision may be an ordinary resolution, even though it amends the company's articles. Chapter 3 of Part 3 of the Act (resolutions affecting a company's constitution) applies to such a resolution (see s 29 and **4.20**). Typically, in the past, a private company would have a general allotment authority for a period of 5 years in its articles on incorporation and this would be renewed by ordinary resolution when required. It may be that in the future, as such allotment authorities normally will only be required where there is to be more than one class of shares, the allotment authorities given will become more specific.

9.21 BERR has proposed that at the date when these provisions of the Act come into force (which is expected to be 1 October 2009) transitional provisions will provide that any existing allotment authority given by a company under previous legislation will continue to have legal effect as if given under s 551. However, if previously existing private companies with one class of share wish to take advantage of the authority to allot shares granted by s 550, an enabling resolution of the members will be required (see **9.18** above).

PRE-EMPTION RIGHTS ON THE ALLOTMENT OF SHARES (SS 560–577)

9.22　In order to protect the position of existing shareholders, the Act contains detailed provisions which (when they apply) require the company to first offer shares that are to be allotted to existing holders of ordinary shares in proportion to their existing shareholdings. This is designed to ensure that existing shareholders do not have their proportion of shareholding in the company diminished without first having the opportunity to take up new shares themselves and thereby maintain the proportion of shares that they hold. These provisions are detailed and also may in any case be excluded by provisions in a private company's articles or in some cases by shareholder resolution. Many private companies have in the past chosen to exclude the statutory provisions but substitute their own provisions in their articles. It is useful, as a matter of practice, to first check the allotment provisions in the company's articles.

9.23　The statutory pre-emption rights do not apply to:

- the allotment of bonus shares (s 564)

- a particular allotment of shares for a non-cash consideration (s 565)

- the allotment of shares for an employee share scheme (s 566)

- the allotment of shares that are not 'equity securities' (s 561).

'Equity securities' are ordinary shares (or rights to subscribe for, or convert securities into, ordinary shares of the company). 'Ordinary shares' means shares other than shares that as respects dividend and capital carry a right to participate only up to a specified amount in a distribution (s 560). 'Equity share capital' is defined by s 548 as issued share capital excluding any part of that capital that, neither as respects dividend nor as respects capital, carries any right to participate beyond a specified amount in a distribution.

9.24　If the statutory pre-emption provisions apply, then:

- a company must not allot equity securities to a person unless it has made an offer to each person who holds ordinary shares to allot to him (on the same or more favourable terms) a proportion of those securities that is (as nearly as practicable) equal to the proportion in nominal value held by him of the ordinary share capital of the company (s 561)

- the offer may be on terms that allows the offeree to renounce the right to allotment (s 561)

- there are detailed provisions about the communication of the offer and the period for acceptance (at least 21 days, but can be altered by regulations) (s 562)

- the company must have either received replies to every offer or the period for acceptance must have expired before the company may allot the shares to another person (s 561).

9.25 Where a private company has only one class of shares, the statutory pre-emption rights may be excluded by a special resolution (as an alternative to exclusion by the articles) (s 569).

9.26 Otherwise, if the private company has more than one class of shares, if the directors are generally authorised to allot shares, they may be given power by a special resolution (or by the articles) to allot equity securities pursuant to that authorisation as if the statutory pre-emption rights did not apply to that allotment. This exclusion of the statutory pre-emption rights is tied to that particular authority to allot shares, so the exclusion will expire when the authority expires (s 570).

9.27 There are further alternative detailed provisions under which the statutory pre-emption provisions may be excluded by special resolution where the directors are authorised to allot shares either generally or specifically. This exclusion may be more specific in its terms, but it may only be proposed if recommended by the directors and supported by a directors' written statement that complies with requirements set out in the Act (see ss 571 and 572 for precise requirements).

ALLOTMENT OF SHARES – DIRECTORS' DECISION

9.28 If the directors have authority to allot shares (see above) then it is up to them to make the decision to allot shares. This will be done in accordance with normal procedures (see **Chapter 6** 'Decisions of directors'). In allotting shares the directors must comply with any applicable pre-emption rights and must also act in accordance with the articles and their duties as directors. Shares may be allotted on terms that the directors decide (see below regarding payment).

ALLOTMENT OF SHARES – PAYMENT AND SHARE PREMIUM

9.29 A company, if so authorised by its articles, may (normally by decision of the directors):

- make arrangements on the issue of shares for a difference between the shareholders in the amounts and times of payment of calls (for payment) on their shares

- accept from any member the whole or part of the amount remaining unpaid on any shares held by him, although no part of that amount has been called up

- pay a dividend in proportion to the amount paid up on each share where a larger amount is paid on some shares than on others (s 548).

9.30 The most normal situation is that shares are paid for in full at par at the time of allotment. However, shares may be issued on terms that only part of the money due to the company in respect of them is immediately payable (and so long as only partly paid for are referred to as 'partly paid shares') or on terms that all monies due may be paid later (and for so long as no payment has been made to the company are referred to as 'nil paid shares'). It is for the directors to decide at the time of allotment how much is to be paid for the shares, how it is to be paid and on what terms. They may decide that the amounts should be paid on specific dates or at any time when a call for the money is made by the company. Any unpaid amounts on shares are owed to the company if it goes into liquidation.

9.31 In the majority of cases, shares are allotted for payment in cash. Section 583 provides that 'cash consideration' means:

- cash received by the company

- a cheque received by the company in good faith that the directors have no reason for suspecting will not be paid

- a release of a liability to the company for a liquidated sum

- an undertaking to pay cash to the company at a future date, or

- payment by other means giving rise to a present or future entitlement (of the company or a person acting on the company's behalf) to a payment, or credit equivalent to a payment, in cash.

9.32 Shares can be issued for non-cash consideration (including goodwill and know-how) and in such cases the directors should be properly satisfied that the non-cash consideration is a proper payment of the sums required. There are extensive requirements regarding the allotment of shares for a non-cash consideration by a public company, but these do not apply to a private company. However, if directors allot shares for inadequate non-cash consideration they may be in breach of their duties.

9.33 There is a general prohibition of commissions, discounts and allowances in respect of the allotment of shares (s 552). This is subject to an exception regarding permitted commission (as set out in s 553).

9.34 The directors may decide to issue shares at a premium (for a sum greater than their nominal value). The amount in excess of the nominal value of the shares constitutes the share premium. If a company issues shares at a premium (whether for cash or otherwise) a sum equal to the aggregate amount or value of the premiums on those shares must be transferred to a special account known as 'the share premium account' (s 610). In general the same restrictions apply to any reduction in the share premium account as apply to any reduction in share capital (s 610(4)). The exceptions to this rule are:

- it may be used to pay up shares for a bonus issue of shares to the members

- it may be used to write off expenses and commission paid on the issue of the shares that generated the premium

- group reconstruction relief (see s 611), and

- merger relief (see ss 612 and 613).

RETURN OF THE ALLOTMENT AND STATEMENT OF CAPITAL

9.35 If a limited company allots shares, it must within one month of making the allotment of shares deliver to the Registrar a return of the allotment (s 555). The return must contain the prescribed information and be accompanied by a statement of capital. The statement of capital must state with respect to the company's share capital at the date to which the return is made up:

- the total number of shares of the company

- the aggregate nominal value of those shares

- for each class of shares:
    - the prescribed particulars of the rights attached to the shares
    - the total number of shares of that class, and
    - the aggregate nominal value of the shares of that class, and

- the amount paid up and the amount (if any) unpaid on each share (whether on account of the nominal value of the share or by way of premium) (s 555).

9.36   An unlimited company is only required to make a return of allotments where it allots shares of a different class. The return of allotments by an unlimited company is only required to contain prescribed particulars of the rights attaching to the shares (s 556).

9.37   It is an offence to fail to make a return in accordance with requirements. Note that a return of allotment is not required in respect of the shares taken by subscribers on the formation of the company (s 556) (this information is detailed in the statement of capital and initial shareholdings delivered on formation of the company, see **2.47** and s 10).

SUB-DIVISION OR CONSOLIDATION OF SHARES

9.38   These provisions (replacing provisions under earlier legislation) are expected to come into force on 1 October 2009. A limited company having share capital may:

- sub-divide its shares (or any of them) into shares of a smaller nominal amount than its existing shares, or

- consolidate and divide all or any of its share capital into shares of a larger nominal amount than its existing shares

provided that the same proportion between the amount paid and the amount (if any) unpaid on each resulting share is the same as it was in the case of the share from which that share was derived (s 618).

9.39   A company can only exercise any of the above powers if its members have passed a resolution authorising it to do so. Such a resolution can either be in very general terms or be specific. It can authorise a company:

- to exercise more than one of these powers

- to exercise a power on more than one occasion

- to exercise a power at a specified time or in specified circumstances (s 618).

9.40   The company's articles may exclude or restrict the ability to exercise of any of these powers (s 618).

9.41   If a company does sub-divide or consolidate its shares, it must within one month give notice to the Registrar accompanied by a statement of capital (see **9.35** for contents) (s 619). Failure to comply is an offence.

REDENOMINATION OF SHARE CAPITAL (SS 622–627)

9.42 The Act will introduce statutory provisions to enable the redenomination of a company's share capital (or any class of its share capital). This means the conversion of shares from having a fixed nominal value in one currency to having a fixed nominal value in another currency (for instance the conversion of £ shares to US $ shares, or £ shares to € shares). A company's articles may prohibit or restrict the exercise of this power. These provisions are expected to come into force on 1 October 2009.

9.43 The redenomination is by resolution of the company. The conversion is made at the appropriate spot rate of exchange specified in the resolution. This rate must be either:

- a rate prevailing on a day specified in the resolution, or

- a rate determined by taking the average of rates prevailing on each consecutive day of a period specified in the resolution.

The day or period specified for determining the above rate must be within the period of 28 days ending on the day before the resolution is passed (s 622).

9.44 The redenomination takes effect:

- on the day on which the resolution is passed, or

- on such later day as may be determined in accordance with the resolution (subject to a statutory 28 day time limit, see below).

The resolution may specify conditions which must be met before the redenomination takes effect, but the resolution will in any case lapse if the redenomination has not taken effect within 28 days of the date of the resolution.

9.45 Section 623 provides that for each class of share the new nominal value of each share is calculated as follows:

Step 1   Take the aggregate of the old nominal value of all the shares of that class

Step 2   Translate that amount into the new currency at the rate of exchange specified in the resolution

Step 3   Divide that amount by the number of shares in the class.

9.46 Section 626 provides that a limited company may, for the purpose of adjusting the nominal values of the redenominated shares to obtain values that are, in the opinion of the company, more suitable, reduce its share capital. Any such reduction requires a special resolution, which must be passed within three months of the resolution effecting the redenomination. The amount by which the company's share capital is reduced under this provision must not exceed 10 per cent of the nominal value of the company's allotted share capital immediately after the reduction. The amount by which the share capital is reduced must be transferred to a reserve, called 'the redenomination reserve' (s 628). The same restrictions apply to any reduction in the redenomination reserve as apply to any reduction in share capital, save that it may be used to pay up shares for a bonus issue of fully paid shares to the members.

9.47 A resolution redenominating the share capital must be forwarded to the Registrar within 15 days after it is passed and forms part of the company's constitution (so it is subject to the provisions of s 29 in Part 3 Chapter 3 of the Act, see **4.20**) (s 622(8)). Also, within one month after the redenomination, the company must give notice to the Registrar accompanied by a statement of capital. Failure to comply is an offence (s 625).

9.48 If there is a reduction of capital in connection with the redenomination the company must give to the Registrar within 15 days after the resolution is passed (in addition to the required copy of the special resolution):

- notice containing required information

- a statement of capital

- a statement by the directors confirming that the reduction is in accordance with s 626.

The reduction in capital is not effective until the notice and statement of capital are registered by the Registrar (s 627(5)). Failure to comply with the filing requirements is also an offence.

VARIATION OF CLASS RIGHTS (SS 629–640)

9.49 It is possible to have different classes of shares that have different rights regarding such matters as dividends, voting and rights on a winding up etc. The Act also recognises that companies without share capital can have different classes of members. The Act contains provisions designed to protect both types of class rights so that, subject to any provisions contained in a company's articles, such rights can only be altered in accordance with procedures laid down in the Act. These sections (replacing provisions under previous legislation) are expected to come into force on 1 October 2009.

9.50 Class rights can only be varied:

- in accordance with provision in the company's articles for the variation of those rights, or

- where the company's articles contain no such provision:

- with the consent in writing from the holders of at least three-quarters of the nominal value of the issued shares of that class (or in the case of a company without share capital, three-quarters of the members of that class), or
- by a special resolution passed at a separate meeting of that class of shareholders (or members).

9.51 There are also further provisions giving holders of 15 per cent of the issued shares of that class (or 15 per cent of the members of that class for a company without share capital) the right to apply to the court to have the variation cancelled.

9.52 Where a new name or other designation is assigned to a class of shares (or in the case of a company without share capital a new class of members is created or a new name or designation is assigned to a class of members), the company must within one month deliver the required notice to the Registrar. If class rights are varied (either for a class of shares or a class of members), the company must give notice to the Registrar within one month. Failure to comply with these requirements is an offence (ss 636–640).

REDUCTION IN SHARE CAPITAL – GENERAL

9.53 A private company limited by shares is subject to restrictions on how it may reduce its share capital. It is possible for the company's articles also to impose further restrictions on such a reduction (or prohibit it) (s 641) but this is likely to be unusual. The commentary below refers to the statutory provisions only.

9.54 The Act substantially eases the procedures for reduction in share capital by a solvent private limited company by providing a new alternative procedure. It enables a private company limited by shares to reduce its share capital by special resolution supported by a solvency statement made by the directors. This acts as an alternative to the possibility of reducing share capital by special resolution confirmed by the court, which is also in the Act. In appropriate cases the reduction supported by solvency statement is likely to be substantially simpler than the alternative procedure requiring an application to the court. The Act also contains provisions regarding the purchase by a company of its own shares (see **9.74**). This book does not deal with Treasury shares (which are applicable in the case of some public companies).

9.55 By following one of the two procedures above a private company limited by shares may reduce its share capital in any way, provided that after the reduction it has some issued shares other than redeemable shares. In particular, a company may:

- repay any paid-up share capital in excess of the company's wants

- cancel any paid-up share capital that is lost or unrepresented by available assets

- extinguish or reduce the liability on any of its shares in respect of share capital not paid up (s 641).

9.56 An unlimited company may reduce its share capital without following the additional procedures required by the Act. All companies are subject to the restriction that a company may not reduce its share capital if as a result of the reduction there would no longer be any member of the company holding shares other than redeemable shares (s 641(2)).

REDUCTION OF CAPITAL SUPPORTED BY SOLVENCY STATEMENT

9.57 The procedure for a private limited company to reduce its share capital by special resolution supported by a solvency statement came into force on 1 October 2008 and is as follows.

Solvency statement (ss 642 and 643)

9.58 The directors must make a solvency statement not more than 15 days before the date on which the special resolution is passed. The solvency statement must:

- be in writing

- indicate that it is a solvency statement for the purposes of s 642 of the Act, and

- be signed by each of the directors.

The solvency statement is a statement that each of the directors:

- has formed the opinion, as regards the company's situation at the date of the statement, that there is no ground on which the company could then be found to be unable to pay (or otherwise discharge) its debts; and

- has also formed the opinion:
  - if it is intended to commence the winding up of the company within 12 months, that the company will be able to pay or discharge its debts in full within 12 months of the commencement of the winding-up, or
  - in any other case, that the company will be able to pay or discharge its debts as they fall due during the year following the date of the statement.

In forming those opinions, the directors must take into account all the company's liabilities, including contingent or prospective liabilities. If the directors make a solvency statement without having reasonable grounds for the opinions expressed in it, and the statement is delivered to the Registrar, an offence is committed by every director who is in default. Conviction may make a director liable to imprisonment. So it is important for the directors to conduct a full enquiry about the company's affairs, and where appropriate take professional advice, before making a solvency statement.

Circulation/availability of the solvency statement (ss 642 and 644)

9.59   The solvency statement must be made available to the members as follows. If the special resolution is proposed as a written resolution, a copy of the solvency statement must be sent or submitted to every eligible member (ie those entitled to vote) at or before the time at which the proposed resolution is sent or submitted to him. If the special resolution is proposed at a general meeting, a copy of the solvency statement must be made available for inspection by the members throughout the meeting. Note that the validity of a resolution is not affected by a failure to comply with these requirements but that if they are not complied with it is an offence to deliver the solvency statement to the Registrar.

Special resolution (s 641)

9.60   The company must pass a special resolution to reduce its share capital by the chosen method. The resolution cannot provide for the reduction to take effect later than the date on which the resolution has effect under the Act (see **9.61**). See also **7.14** and **4.20**. Note also that under transitional provisions, for the period from 1 October 2008 until 1 October 2009, due to the staged implementation of the Act, the special resolution must make any necessary alterations of the company's memorandum of association by reducing the amount of its share capital and of its shares.

Registration of resolution and supporting documents (s 644)

9.61   The following must be delivered to the Registrar within 15 days of passing the resolution:

- the special resolution

- a copy of the solvency statement

- a statement of capital

- a statement by the directors confirming that the solvency statement was:
    - made not more than 15 days before the date on which the resolution was passed, and
    - provided to members as required by the Act.

The reduction takes effect on registration of the first three documents above by the Registrar. The validity of a resolution is not affected by failure to deliver the first three items within 15 days, or by a failure to provide the fourth document. However, it is an offence to fail to comply with all the registration requirements. See also **4.20** and **4.21** regarding requirements applicable to special resolutions. Note also that under transitional provisions, for the period from 1 October 2008 until 1 October 2009, due to the staged implementation of the Act, the requirement for a statement of capital is replaced by a requirement for a memorandum of capital that must show with respect to the company's share capital as reduced by the resolution:

- the amount of share capital

- the number of shares into which it is to be divided, and the amount of each share, and

- the amount (if any) at the date of the registration deemed to be paid up on each share.

REDUCTION OF CAPITAL APPROVED BY THE COURT (SS 645–649)

9.62 The alternative procedure applicable to all limited companies having share capital is to pass a special resolution to reduce share capital and then apply to the court for an order confirming the reduction. The court will be concerned to protect the interests of creditors. The procedure will normally involve preparation of a list of creditors and debts. The provisions in the Act for this are due to come into force on 1 October 2009 and will replace similar provisions in previous legislation.

9.63 If the court makes an order confirming the resolution, the order and a statement of capital must be delivered to the Registrar. The reduction will take effect on registration of the order and statement of capital (or if it forms part of a compromise or arrangement sanctioned by the court, on delivery of those documents unless the court orders otherwise).

GENERAL RULE AGAINST A COMPANY ACQUIRING ITS OWN SHARES (SS 658–676)

9.64 Section 658 provides that a limited company must not acquire its own shares except in accordance with provisions of that part of the Act. Any contravention is an offence and a purported contravention is void. Where shares are purported to be held by a nominee for the company, the nominee is regarded as holding them on his own account and the company is treated as having no interest in them. There are various exceptions to the rule that a company must not acquire its own shares, which include:

- the acquisition of shares in a reduction of capital duly made (see above)

- the redemption of shares issued as redeemable shares (see below)

- the purchase of own shares in accordance with the Act (see below)

- the forfeiture etc of shares in pursuance of the company's articles for failure to pay any sum payable in respect of the shares

- the purchase of shares in pursuance of certain types of court order

- the acquisition of the company's own fully paid shares otherwise than for valuable consideration.

Section 658 (which will replace similar provisions in earlier legislation) is due to come into force on 1 October 2009.

FINANCIAL ASSISTANCE FOR ACQUISITION OF A COMPANY'S SHARES

9.65 The statutory provisions prohibiting private companies giving financial assistance for the purchase of their own shares (or the shares of their holding company) are abolished by the Act. This abolition came into force on 1 October 2008.

9.66 Under previous legislation there were detailed provisions that prohibited companies from giving financial assistance for the purchase of their own shares (or the shares of their holding company) except in restricted circumstances. This often caused issues and problems during normal transactions. The Act contains provisions regarding the prohibition of financial assistance, but these are only applicable to public companies (so they will still apply in respect of a private company subsidiary giving financial assistance for the acquisition of shares in its public holding company, or a public company giving financial assistance for the acquisition of shares in itself or in its holding company) (ss 677–683). However, note that, although the statutory provisions regarding financial assistance have been abolished for private companies, it is still necessary when carrying out transactions to consider other legal questions such as the directors' duty to promote the interests of the company and restrictions on distributions.

REDEEMABLE SHARES (SS 684–689)

9.67 The Act's provisions regarding redeemable shares will replace provisions contained in earlier legislation and are due to come into force on 1 October 2009. The Act permits a limited company having share capital to issue shares that are to be redeemed (or are liable to be redeemed) at the option of the company or the shareholder. These are known as 'redeemable shares' and are commonly used when a company receives investment from a third party who desires a defined exit route. Note that shares that have already been issued cannot be converted into redeemable shares. The articles of a private company may exclude or restrict the issue of redeemable shares. Redeemable shares cannot be issued at a time when there are no issued shares of the company that are not redeemable.

9.68 There are two alternative methods of determining the terms, conditions and manner of redemption of the redeemable shares.

1   The directors may determine them if they are authorised to do so:
    - by the company's articles, or
    - by a resolution of the company (which may be an ordinary resolution even though it amends the company's articles).
    Where the directors are so authorised, they must determine the terms, conditions and manner of redemption of the redeemable shares before the shares are allotted. These must also be set out in any statement of capital that the company is required to send to the Registrar (as for instance when it allots the redeemable shares).

2   Where the directors are not so authorised, the terms, conditions and manner of redemption of any redeemable shares must be stated in the company's articles.

REDEEMABLE SHARES – REDEMPTION, PAYMENT, CAPITAL REDEMPTION RESERVE AND NOTICE TO THE REGISTRAR

9.69 Redeemable shares in a limited company may not be redeemed unless they are fully paid. The terms of redemption may provide that the amount payable on redemption may, by agreement between the company and the holder of the shares, be paid on a date after the redemption date. However, unless the terms of redemption contain such a provision, the shares must be paid for on redemption (s 686).

9.70 In practice the mechanics of redemption will have been set out in the terms under which the redeemable shares were originally issued. If the shares are being redeemed by payment out of distributable profits, the company only needs to follow these in order to effect the redemption.

9.71 Subject to the exception applicable for the redemption or purchase of shares out of capital (as to which see **9.86**), redeemable shares of a limited company may only be redeemed out of distributable profits or the proceeds of a fresh issue of shares made for the purposes of the redemption. Where they are redeemed wholly (or partly) out of profits, that amount by which the capital is diminished (or the amount by which the proceeds of the fresh issue is less than the nominal value of the shares redeemed) must be transferred to the capital redemption reserve. This requirement is modified if there is a permitted payment out of capital.

9.72 Any premium payable on redemption normally must be paid from distributable profits. This is subject to an exception where the redeemable shares were issued at a premium, as set out in ss 687(4) and (5).

9.73 When shares are redeemed, they are treated as cancelled and the company's issued share capital is diminished accordingly. Within one month after redemption the company must give notice to the Registrar with a statement of capital. Failure to comply is an offence.

PURCHASE OF OWN SHARES (SS 690–708)

9.74 The Act's provisions regarding purchase of own shares by a private company will replace provisions contained in earlier legislation and are due to come into force on 1 October 2009. Subject to any restriction or prohibition in its articles, a limited company may purchase its own shares if it follows the detailed provisions set out in the Act. It may not purchase its own shares if, after the purchase, the only issued shares of the company would be redeemable shares (or, in the case of a public company, redeemable shares and treasury shares). The shares to be purchased must be fully paid and must be paid for at the time of purchase.

9.75 Where a private limited company purchases its own shares, the shares so purchased are treated as cancelled and the amount of the company's issued share capital is diminished accordingly.

9.76 A private company will be making what is known as an 'off-market' purchase. In order to do this, the terms of the contract for the purchase must be authorised by special resolution. This special resolution is subject to several special requirements:

- a copy of the contract (or if it is not in writing a memorandum of its terms containing specified details) must be made available to members:
  - in the case of a written resolution, by being sent or submitted to every eligible member (ie those entitled to vote) at or before the time at which the proposed resolution is sent or submitted to him

> – if the special resolution is proposed at a general meeting, by being made available for inspection by the members both at the company's registered office for not less than 15 days ending with the date of the meeting and at the meeting itself.

The resolution is not effective if this is not complied with.

- where the resolution is proposed as a written resolution, a member who holds shares to which the resolution relates is not an eligible member

- where the resolution is proposed at a meeting, it is not effective if:
  - any member of the company holding shares to which the resolution relates exercises the voting rights carried by any of those shares in voting on the resolution, and
  - the resolution would not have been passed if he had not done so.

9.77 Similar requirements apply to any variation or release of a contract for an off-market purchase.

PURCHASE OF OWN SHARES – RETURN TO REGISTRAR

9.78 Where a company purchases shares in accordance with these provisions it must deliver a return to the Registrar within 28 days beginning with the date on which the shares are delivered to it. The private company must also give notice of the cancellation of the shares to the Registrar, together with a statement of capital. Failure to comply is an offence. The special resolution authorising the terms of the contract must be forwarded to the Registrar within 15 days of it being passed (see **10.17** and also **4.20** and **4.21**).

9.79 The return notifying the purchase of own shares is subject to stamp duty as if it was a share transfer. So the return must be stamped by the Stamp Office. The stamp duty will be payable on the consideration paid for the shares (the current rate is £5 per £1,000 (or part thereof) of consideration paid).

PURCHASE OF OWN SHARES – RETENTION AND INSPECTION OF CONTRACT (S 702)

9.80 A copy of the contract (or if it was not in writing, the memorandum of its terms) must be kept available for inspection from the conclusion of the contract until the end of the period of 10 years beginning with:

- the date on which the purchase of all the shares in pursuance of the contract is completed, or

- the date on which the contract otherwise determines.

9.81   The copy or memorandum must be kept available for inspection:

- at the company's registered office, or

- at a place specified in regulations to be made.

It must be open to inspection without charge by any member of the company (and in the case of a public company, by any other person).

9.82   Failure to comply with these requirements is an offence. The same provisions apply to any variation of the contract.

PURCHASE AND REDEMPTION OF OWN SHARES – FINANCING AND THE CAPITAL REDEMPTION RESERVE (SS 692 AND 733–737)

9.83   Subject to the exception applicable for the redemption or purchase of shares out of capital (as to which see below), a limited company may only purchase its own shares out of distributable profits or the proceeds of a fresh issue of shares made for the purposes of the purchase.

9.84   Where shares of a limited company are redeemed or purchased wholly (or partly) out of profits, that amount by which the capital is diminished (or the amount by which the proceeds of the fresh issue is less than the nominal value of the shares redeemed) must be transferred to the capital redemption reserve. This requirement is modified if there is a permitted payment out of capital (see **9.99**).

9.85   Any premium payable on the purchase (or redemption) normally must be paid from distributable profits. This is subject to an exception where the shares to be purchased (or redeemed) were issued at a premium, as set out in ss 692(3) and (4) (and 687(4) and (5)). See also **9.71** and **9.72**.

POWER OF A PRIVATE LIMITED COMPANY TO REDEEM OR PURCHASE ITS OWN SHARES OUT OF CAPITAL AND THE 'PERMISSIBLE CAPITAL PAYMENT' (SS 709–723)

9.86   Subject to any restriction or prohibition in its articles, a private limited company may make a payment in respect of the redemption or purchase of its own shares otherwise than out of distributable profits or the proceeds of a fresh issue of shares. However, this is subject to detailed requirements in the Act. This is referred to as 'a payment out of capital'.

9.87 If making a payment out of capital in respect of a purchase of own shares, the company will have to comply with both the purchase of own shares requirements (see **9.74**) and the payment out of capital requirements (see **9.89**). The timetable for achieving this needs to be planned carefully and in practice a first step is likely to be a conversation with the company's auditor.

9.88 Before making any such payment, the company must first calculate the 'permissible capital payment'. The company must first apply any available profits and the proceeds of any fresh issue of shares made for the purpose of the redemption or purchase. The permissible capital payment is the amount required to meet the price of the redemption or purchase after the company has applied such available profits and proceeds of the fresh issue made for the purpose. In this context 'available profits' means profits available for distribution calculated by reference to accounts not more than three months old at the time when the directors make the required directors' statement (as to which see **9.91**). These accounts must be such as to enable a reasonable judgement to be made as to the amounts of the matters mentioned in s 712(2) (in summary: profits, losses, assets and liabilities, provisions and share capital and reserves). Note the requirement to involve the company's auditor (see **9.93**).

REQUIREMENTS FOR PAYMENT OUT OF CAPITAL

9.89 The requirements for a payment out of capital are complex and in some respects harsher than the requirements for a reduction in share capital by special resolution supported by a solvency statement (see **9.57**). Because of this, depending on the circumstances, private companies may in many cases prefer to undertake a reduction of share capital rather than a purchase of own shares with a payment out of capital.

9.90 A payment out of capital by a private company for the redemption or purchase of its own shares is not lawful unless several requirements are met as follows.

Directors' statement and auditor's report (ss 714 and 715)

9.91 The directors must make a statement in the prescribed form specifying the permissible capital payment and stating that, having made full enquiry into the affairs and prospects of the company, the directors have formed the opinion:

- as regards its initial situation immediately following the date on which the payment out of capital is proposed to be made, that there will be no grounds on which the company could then be found unable to pay its debts, and

- as regards its prospects for the year immediately following that date, that having regard to:
  - their intentions with respect to the management of the company business during that year, and
  - the amount and character of the financial resources that will in their view be available to the company during that year,

  the company will be able to continue to carry on business as a going concern (and will accordingly be able to pay its debts as they fall due) throughout that year.

9.92 The directors are required to take into account all the company's liabilities (including contingent and prospective liabilities). If the directors make the statement without having reasonable grounds for the opinion expressed in it, an offence is committed by every director who is in default. Conviction may make a director liable to imprisonment. So it is important for the directors to conduct a full enquiry about the company's affairs, and where appropriate take professional advice, before making this statement.

9.93 The directors' statement must have annexed to it a report addressed to the directors from the company's auditor stating that:

- he has enquired into the company's state of affairs

- the amount specified in the statement as the permissible capital payment is in his view properly determined, and

- he is not aware of anything to indicate that the opinion expressed by the directors in their statement is unreasonable in all the circumstances.

Special resolution (ss 716–718)

9.94 The payment out of capital must be approved by a special resolution of the company. The resolution is subject to special requirements as follows:

- it must be passed on, or within the week immediately following, the date on which the directors make the statement referred to above

- a copy of the directors' statement and auditor's report must be made available to members
  - in the case of a written resolution, by being sent or submitted to every eligible member (ie those entitled to vote) at or before the time at which the proposed resolution is sent or submitted to him
  - if the special resolution is proposed at a general meeting, by being made available for inspection by the members at the meeting.

  The resolution is not effective if this is not complied with.

- where the resolution is proposed as a written resolution, a member who holds shares to which the resolution relates is not an eligible member

- where the resolution is proposed at a meeting, it is not effective if:
  - any member of the company holding shares to which the resolution relates exercises the voting rights carried by any of those shares in voting on the resolution, and
  - the resolution would not have been passed if he had not done so.

Public notice in Gazette and a national newspaper (s 719)

9.95 Within the week immediately following the date of the resolution, the company must publish in the Gazette a notice:

- stating that the company has approved a payment out of capital for the purpose of acquiring its own shares by redemption or purchase (as the case may be)

- specifying the amount of the permissible capital payment and the date of the resolution

- stating where the directors' statement and auditor's report are available for inspection, and

- stating that any creditor may at any time within 5 weeks immediately following the date of the resolution apply to the court for an order preventing the payment.

Unless the company gives notice in writing to that effect to all its creditors, the company must publish the same notice in an appropriate national newspaper.

A copy of the directors' statement and auditor's report to be delivered to the Registrar (s 719)

9.96 A copy of the directors' statement and auditor's report must be delivered to the Registrar not later than the day on which the company first publishes the notice. Note that there is also a requirement to forward a copy of the special resolution to the Registrar within 15 days of it being passed.

Directors' statement and auditor's report to be available for inspection (s 720)

9.97 The directors' statement and auditor's report must be kept available for inspection by any member or creditor throughout the period beginning with the day on which the company first publishes the notice under s 719 and ending 5 weeks after the date of the resolution approving the payment out of capital. They must be kept available at the registered office or at a place specified in regulations.

Timing of payment out of capital (s 723)

9.98   The payment out of capital must be made no earlier than 5 weeks after the date on which the resolution approving the payment out of capital was passed and no later than 7 weeks after that date. This is presumably because any member or creditor can within 5 weeks after the passing of the resolution apply to the court for cancellation of the resolution.

CAPITAL REDEMPTION RESERVE AND PAYMENT OUT OF CAPITAL (S 734)

9.99   Where shares of a limited company are redeemed or purchased wholly (or partly) out of profits, that amount by which the capital is diminished (or the amount by which the proceeds of the fresh issue is less than the nominal value of the shares redeemed) must be transferred to the capital redemption reserve (see **9.83**). This requirement is modified if there is a permitted payment out of capital. If the permissible capital payment is less than the nominal amount of the shares redeemed or purchased, the amount of the difference must be transferred to the capital redemption reserve. If the permissible capital payment is greater than the nominal amount of the shares redeemed or purchased:

- the amount of any capital redemption reserve, share premium account or fully paid share capital of the company, and

- any amount representing unrealised profits in any revaluation reserve

may be reduced accordingly. For the purposes of making these calculations, the proceeds of a fresh issue that are used for a redemption or purchase of shares are aggregated with the permissible capital payment. Refer to s 734 for precise requirements.

TRANSFER OF SHARES

9.100   The person transferring shares to another person is the 'transferor'. The person to whom the shares are being transferred is the 'transferee'. To transfer shares in a private company from an existing living shareholder to another person the usual steps are:

1   Check the articles of the company (and any shareholders' agreement) to see if any special requirements apply. For instance, in some cases the articles may require shares that are to be transferred to be offered to the other existing shareholders as a prior first step. Comply with any such requirements or ensure that all the other shareholders waive them in writing.

2   The existing shareholder signs a share transfer form (if the shares are fully paid, this is normally a form that follows the format prescribed under the Stock Transfer Act 1963; if the shares are not fully paid, the transfer will be in a slightly different format that requires the transferee to sign as well). If the share is held jointly, all the joint holders must sign.

3   Stamp duty is paid to HMRC unless the transfer is exempt from stamp duty and certified as such in accordance with applicable requirements or a stamp duty exemption has been applied for and the transfer has been adjudicated and stamped as not chargeable. Stamp Duty is paid via the relevant Stamp Office (see **Appendix 5**) and an orange stamp is impressed on the share transfer form to show that payment has been made. Normally the stamp duty is paid by the transferee (subject to any agreement to the contrary). Stamp duty payable is based on the consideration paid for the shares. Currently where the consideration for a transfer on sale is £1,000 or less and the transfer is certified appropriately no stamp duty is payable. Where the consideration paid is above £1,000, duty is charged at 0.5 per cent of the consideration rounded up to the nearest £5.

4   The stamped (or certified) share transfer form and the share certificate in respect of the relevant shares are submitted to the company. This is normally done by the transferee, but can be done by the transferor (s 772).

5   The company should check that the documents are correctly completed, that the share certificate has been surrendered with the transfer form, that stamp duty appears to have been correctly dealt with and that the shares are registered in the name of the transferor. If the relevant share certificate has been lost, the company may choose to accept an appropriate indemnity instead.

6   The company should check that the articles have been (or will be) complied with. Often the articles of association of private companies give the directors absolute discretion to refuse to register the transfer of a share. In any case, normally the transfer will be submitted to the directors for approval. If the company refuses to register the transfer, special requirements apply (see **9.101**). The transfer must either be registered or refused as soon as practicable and in any event within two months after it is lodged with the company (s 771).

7   If the transfer is approved, the transfer will be registered in the register of members, the company will cancel and retain the old share certificate and the company will issue a new share certificate to the transferee. This must be issued within two months of the date of lodgement of the transfer with the company (s 776) (unless the transfer is refused, see **9.101**). If the transfer is registered but not all the shares comprised in the old share

certificate have been transferred, the company will also issue a share certificate to the transferor in respect of the remaining shares not transferred.

TRANSFER OF SHARES – REFUSAL TO REGISTER

9.101 Often, private company articles may give the directors absolute discretion to refuse a transfer without giving reasons. The Act has introduced new provisions governing refusals to register a transfer that came into effect on 6 April 2008.

9.102 If a company refuses to register a transfer, it **must** provide the transferee with such further information about the reasons for the refusal as the transferee may reasonably request. This does not include copies of minutes of meetings of the directors. If the company does not comply with this requirement, an offence is committed (s 771).

9.103 This is a new provision and it is possible that the full extent of its meaning may be tested in the courts. When reasons are given, this may open up the possibility of further legal challenge. Companies are recommended to take legal advice prior to refusing to register a transfer (unless the reason for refusal is a clear failure to comply with procedural requirements).

TRANSFER OF THE SHARES OF A DECEASED PERSON (TRANSFER BY PERSONAL REPRESENTATIVES)

9.104 If a share was held jointly, on the death of one of the joint holders, the company will (after the production of the death certificate) recognise the survivor(s) as entitled to the share.

9.105 Where a shareholder (other than a joint shareholder) has died, his property will be dealt with by his personal representative(s). The Act provides that a personal representative of the deceased shareholder may sign the share transfer as if that personal representative were the member. It also provides that the production to the company of any document that is by law sufficient evidence of the grant of:

- probate of the will of a deceased person

- letters of administration of the estate of a deceased person, or

- confirmation as executor of a deceased person

shall be accepted by the company as sufficient evidence of the grant.

9.106 The normal procedure on the death of a shareholder would be:

- to advise the company of the death by producing the death certificate

- once the relevant grant has been obtained, produce an office copy of that to the company; the company should note its production in the register of members and this will normally entitle the personal representative(s) to receive notice of general meetings (see s 310)

- the personal representative(s) will (in due course) sign a share transfer form and submit it to the company – the company should then follow the same procedure as on any transfer of a share (but note that the transfer is likely to be exempt from stamp duty).

SHARE WARRANTS (SS 779–781 AND 122)

9.107 Sections 779–781 came into force on 6 April 2008. If a company limited by shares is so authorised by its articles, it may issue with respect to any fully paid shares a warrant (a 'share warrant') stating that the bearer of the warrant is entitled to the shares specified in it. A share warrant issued under the company's common seal (or executed by the company in accordance with the statutory procedure) (or in the case of a company registered in Scotland, executed in accordance with the Requirements of Writing Act (Scotland) Act 1995) entitles the bearer to the shares specified in it and may be transferred by delivery of the warrant.

9.108 This means that once a share warrant is validly issued, whoever has the warrant is entitled to the shares specified in it. Those shares can be transferred to another person by handing over the share warrant (in a similar way to the transfer of money by handing over a bank note). It is not necessary to go through the transfer procedure to transfer the shares specified in the warrant.

9.109 Note that special provisions apply requiring (in some cases) the payment of stamp duty by the company prior to the issue of a share warrant. Specialist advice is required. This requirement is presumably to make up for the fact that no stamp duty is payable on the subsequent transfers of the shares whilst they are comprised in the warrant.

9.110 On the issue of a share warrant the company must:

- enter in the register of members:
  - the fact of the issue of the warrant
  - a statement of the shares included in the warrant, distinguishing each share by its number so long as it has a number, and
  - the date of the issue of the warrant

and

- amend the register, if necessary, so that no person is named on the register as the holder of the shares specified in the warrant.

9.111 The company is responsible for any loss incurred by a person by reason of the company entering in the register the name of a bearer of a share warrant in respect of the shares specified in it without the warrant being surrendered and cancelled (s 122).

9.112 The bearer of a share warrant:

- may, if the articles so provide, be deemed a member of the company within the meaning of the Act, either to the full extent or for any purposes defined in the articles

- is entitled, on surrendering it for cancellation, to have his name entered as a member in the register of members.

9.113 On the surrender of a share warrant, the date of the surrender must be entered in the register.

9.114 A company that issues a share warrant may, if so authorised by its articles, provide (by coupons or otherwise) for the payment of future dividends on the shares included in the warrant.

SUMMARY OF MAJOR CHANGES INTRODUCED BY THE ACT

1   The statutory concept of 'authorised share capital' is to be abolished for companies formed under the Act. When these provisions are brought into force, it is proposed that the authorised share capital of existing companies will continue to operate as a restriction in the company's articles under transitional provisions unless an appropriate resolution is passed. *These provisions are due to come into force on 1 October 2009.*

2   There is a requirement to deliver a 'statement of capital' to the Registrar on the happening of certain events (which, in basic terms, are any change to the share capital). *These provisions are due to come into force on 1 October 2009.*

3   The Act enables a private company limited by shares to reduce its share capital by special resolution supported by a solvency statement made by the directors (ss 641–644). *This provision came into force on 1 October 2008.*

4   There is abolition of the statutory prohibition of a private company giving financial assistance for the purchase of its shares, but provisions still apply to public companies and private company subsidiaries giving financial assistance for the acquisition of shares in public companies (ss 677–683). *This provision came into force on 1 October 2008.*

5   If a private company will only have one class of shares, there is no requirement for the directors to be authorised to allot shares (subject to provisions in the articles). However, such authority is required if the company has (or will have after the allotment) more than one class of shares (ss 549–551). When these provisions are brought into force, it is proposed that existing companies will need to pass a resolution of the members to take advantage of the provisions of s 550 relating to the power of the directors of a private company with one class of shares to allot shares. *These provisions are due to come into force on 1 October 2009.*

6   The sanctions if a private company offers its shares to the public (which is prohibited) have changed (ss 755–760). *These provisions came into force on 6 April 2008.*

7   There are different provisions regarding the mechanics of how a company may subdivide or consolidate its share capital (ss 617–619). *These provisions are due to come into force on 1 October 2009.*

8   There are detailed new provisions that enable a company to redenominate its share capital (ss 622–628). *These provisions are due to come into force on 1 October 2009.*

9   There are new provisions for determining the terms, conditions and manner of redemption of redeemable shares (ss 684 and 685). *These provisions are due to come into force on 1 October 2009.*

10   The Act provides that if a company refuses to register a transfer, it **must** provide the transferee with such further information about the reasons for the refusal as the transferee may reasonably request (s 771). *This provision came into force on 6 April 2008.*

11   The Act provides that a personal representative of a deceased shareholder may sign a share transfer as if that personal representative were the member (s 773). So this has moved from a provision in the articles onto a statutory footing. *This provision came into force on 6 April 2008.*

Chapter 10

EVENT RELATED COMPLIANCE

INTRODUCTION

10.1 The Act contains numerous event related compliance requirements. It is not possible to summarise them all here but the intention is to cover the main ones that are likely to be encountered by a private company. Generally they require the company to make entries in its registers and deliver information to the Registrar. **Chapter 8** contains more detailed information about the various registers to be maintained by a company.

10.2 Some compliance requirements have been covered in more detail in other chapters. In such cases, only the primary compliance requirements are mentioned here and reference is made to the other chapter. For some items not covered elsewhere, such as declaration of a dividend, the detail is contained in this chapter.

10.3 Please also refer to **Appendix 4** – 'Table of main changes to annual and event driven compliance for private companies'.

THE REGISTRAR OF COMPANIES AND DELIVERY OF DOCUMENTS

10.4 There is a Registrar of Companies for each of:

- England & Wales

- Scotland, and

- Northern Ireland

Information, notices or documents required to be delivered to the Registrar must be delivered to the Registrar for the part of the UK where the company is registered and has its registered office. Contact details for the main office of each of the Registrars (and website addresses, that provide useful information) are included in **Appendix 5**.

10.5 The Government is currently consulting on a proposal to create a UK-wide Register of Companies through the integration of the Northern Ireland Registry with Companies House. It is proposed that:

- the system would operate in much the same way as Companies House currently works with Scotland

- the Registrar in Northern Ireland and the office in Belfast will remain in the same way as there is currently a Registrar in Scotland and an office in Edinburgh

- the systems, hardware, processes, corporate standards and fees will be common with those of Companies House

- there will be common filing and search services covering the whole of the UK.

10.6 The Registrar has power to impose requirements as to the form and manner of delivery of documents and how they are to be authenticated. In recent years there has been an increasing shift from the use of paper forms to electronic delivery of information to the Registrar. This shift to greater use of electronic delivery will continue. The Act also empowers the Secretary of State to make regulations to actually require documents to be delivered by electronic means. Users should access the relevant website for up-to-date information about the methods of delivery, as this is likely to develop and change from time to time.

10.7 The Act gives the Registrar wider powers about how to deal with defective documents. These give more flexibility to the Registrar and no doubt will enable defective documents to be dealt with more efficiently. There are also new provisions enabling the Registrar to deal with inconsistencies on the register and rectification of the register. Section 1112 provides a new offence of knowingly or recklessly delivering to the Registrar information which is misleading, false or deceptive in a material particular.

CHANGE OF REGISTERED OFFICE

10.8 See **2.38** regarding the importance of the registered office and more detail regarding changing the registered office.

10.9 The registered office may be changed by giving notice in the prescribed form to the Registrar. The change takes effect upon the change being registered by the Registrar, but until the end of the period of 14 days beginning with the date on which it is registered a person may validly serve any document on the company at the address previously registered.

10.10 It is good practice, but not a requirement, for the change in registered office to be a directors' decision.

APPOINTMENT OF A DIRECTOR

10.11 How a director is appointed is governed by a company's articles. These normally state that a director may be appointed by ordinary resolution of the shareholders or by a decision of the directors. However some articles may contain other provisions. See **5.16** for more detail and check the company's articles.

10.12 Note the restrictions on who can be a director (no one under 16 can be appointed; corporate directors are permitted but there must be at least one natural person as a director) as set out in more detail in **Chapter 5**.

10.13 When a new director is appointed, the company must enter the director's details and the date of his appointment in the Register of directors and (with effect from 1 October 2009) appropriate details in the Register of directors' residential addresses. See **Chapter 8** for details of the entries to be made in these registers.

10.14 The company must within 14 days of the appointment, give notice to the Registrar of the appointment, the date on which it occurred and the details regarding the director that are entered in the above registers. This must include consent by the person appointed director to act as such.

TERMINATION OF A DIRECTOR'S APPOINTMENT

10.15 The most usual method of termination of appointment is for a director to resign by notice in writing to the company. See **5.20** for more detail about the procedures regarding resignation or removal of a director.

10.16 It is appropriate to enter in the Register of directors the date on which that person ceased to be a director.

10.17 The company must within 14 days of a person ceasing to be a director, give notice to the Registrar of that fact and the date of cessation (s 167).

CHANGE OF DIRECTORS' PARTICULARS

10.18 The company must give notice to the Registrar within 14 days of the occurrence of any change in the particulars registered in the register of directors or (with effect from 1 October 2009) the register of directors' residential addresses (for instance a change of service or residential address). With effect from 1 October 2009, where a company gives notice of a change of a director's service address, if the notice is not accompanied by a notice of any resulting change in the register of directors' residential addresses, then the notice must state that no such change is required.

SPECIAL RESOLUTIONS AND RESOLUTIONS OR AGREEMENTS AFFECTING A COMPANY'S CONSTITUTION

10.19   A copy of any of the following must be forwarded to the Registrar within 15 days after it is passed or made:

• any special resolution

• any resolution or agreement agreed to by all the members that, if not so agreed to, would not have been effective for its purpose unless passed as a special resolution

• any resolution or agreement agreed to by all the members of a class of shareholders that, if not so agreed to, would not have been effective for its purpose unless passed by some particular majority or otherwise in some particular manner

• any resolution or agreement that effectively binds all members of a class of shareholders though not agreed to by all those members

• any other resolution or agreement to which Chapter 3 of Part 3 of the Act applies by virtue of any enactment.

Items required to be forwarded under the last category include a resolution to redenominate share capital in accordance with s 622 and a resolution that a company may send or supply documents etc by making them available on the company's website pursuant to para 10 of Sch 5. See also **4.20** and **4.21**. Note that the third Commencement Order allows for the passing of an extraordinary resolution pursuant to a provision in a company's memorandum or articles or a contract (as such provisions for elective resolutions continue to have effect) and the fifth Commencement Order requires these to be forwarded to the Registrar under the last category.

CHANGE OF NAME OF A COMPANY

10.20   A company may change its name by special resolution of the members or (with effect from 1 October 2009) by other means provided for in the company's articles (s 77).

10.21   With effect from 1 October 2009, where a change of name has been agreed to by special resolution, the company must give notice to the Registrar (s 78). This is in addition to the requirement to forward a copy of the resolution to the Registrar. Where a change of name has been made by other means provided by a company's articles, the company must again give notice to the Registrar and this notice must be accompanied by a statement that the change of name has been made by means provided for in the company's articles (s 79). The Registrar may rely on this statement.

10.22 A change of a company's name has effect on the date on which a new certificate is issued by the Registrar.

10.23 See **Chapter 3** for more details about company names generally and in particular **3.33–3.36** regarding changes of name and conditional change of name resolutions.

APPOINTMENT OF AN AUDITOR

10.24 See **8.113** which contains more detail on this. If the company is not going to appoint an auditor for any financial year, because it believes that it will be audit exempt, then the directors must reasonably resolve not to appoint auditors on the ground that audited accounts are unlikely to be required (s 485).

10.25 Section 487 provides that where no auditor has been appointed by the end of the next period for appointing auditors, any auditor in office is deemed re-appointed, unless:

- he was appointed by the directors

- the company's articles require actual re-appointment

- the deemed re-appointment is prevented by the members representing 5 per cent (or such lower percentage as is specified in the company's articles) of the total voting rights giving notice in accordance with s 488 that the auditor should not be re-appointed

- the members have resolved that he shall not be re-appointed, or

- the directors have resolved that no auditor should be appointed for the financial year in question.

Note that under transitional provisions, where a private company had elected to dispense with the annual appointment of auditors, and this election was in force immediately before 1 October 2007, the first bullet point above (he was appointed by the directors) does not prevent the deemed re-appointment of auditors first appointed before 1 October 2007.

10.26 The 'period for appointing auditors' is defined by s 485 as the end of the period of 28 days beginning with:

- the end of the time allowed for sending out copies of the company's annual accounts for the previous financial year to the members, or

- if earlier, the day on which the copies of the company's annual accounts for the previous financial year are sent out.

10.27 See also the special provisions at **10.41** that apply if the company is changing its auditor by appointing a new auditor in the place of an outgoing auditor whose term of office has expired (or is to expire).

RESIGNATION OR REMOVAL ETC OF AUDITOR

Resignation

10.28 An auditor can resign by depositing notice of resignation in writing at the company's registered office (s 516). This must be accompanied by a statement in accordance with s 519 (see **10.30**). The company must within 14 days of the deposit of the resignation send a copy to the Registrar (s 517). Failure to comply is an offence.

10.29 If the auditor has stated that there are circumstances connected with his resignation that should be brought to the attention of members or creditors (in accordance with s 519), then he may require the directors to convene a general meeting of the members and circulate a statement to its members (see s 518).

Section 519 statement by auditor of circumstances connected with cessation of office

10.30 This statement is required on any occasion when an auditor ceases to hold office as auditor. The statement from the outgoing auditor of an unquoted company must be deposited at the company's registered office and must state either:

- that he considers that there are no circumstances in connection with his ceasing to hold office that need to be brought to the attention of members or creditors of the company, or

- a statement of circumstances connected with his ceasing to hold office.

In contrast, the outgoing auditor of a quoted company must deposit a statement of the circumstances connected with his ceasing to hold office (but the requirements relating to quoted companies are not covered by this book).

10.31 This statement must be deposited:

- in the case of resignation, along with the notice of resignation

- in the case of failure to seek re-appointment, not less than 14 days before the end of the time allowed for next appointing an auditor

- in any other case, not later than the end of the period of 14 days beginning with the date on which he ceases to hold office.

10.32 If the auditor makes a statement of circumstances connected with his ceasing to hold office (instead of stating that there are none that need to be brought to the attention of members or creditors) then further requirements apply to both the auditor and the company to ensure that these circumstances are brought to the attention of those with an interest.

10.33 First, unless the auditor receives notice of an application to the court within 21 days of its deposit with the company (see **10.34**), he must within a further 7 days send a copy of the statement to the Registrar (s 521).

10.34 Secondly, if the statement states the circumstances connected with the auditor ceasing to hold office, then the company must within 14 days of its deposit either send a copy of it to every person entitled to receive a copy of the annual accounts, or apply to the court for relief on the basis that the auditor is using these provisions to secure needless publicity for defamatory matter (s 520).

10.35 It is an offence for both the auditor (in relation to requirements applying to the auditor under ss 519 and 521) and the officers of the company (in relation to requirements applying to the company under s 520) to fail to comply with these requirements.

Duty of auditor and company to notify appropriate audit authority (ss 522 and 523)

10.36 In the case of a 'major audit', where an auditor **ceases for any reason to hold office**, the auditor ceasing to hold office must notify the appropriate audit authority. Section 522 defines 'major audit' as a statutory audit conducted in respect of:

- a company whose securities have been admitted to the official list, or

- any other person in whose financial condition there is a major public interest.

If the audit is not a major audit (as will almost always be the case for a private company), the auditor ceasing to hold office must still notify the appropriate audit authority if he **ceases to hold office before the end of his term of office**, meaning that he must so notify only if he has resigned or has been dismissed.

10.37 The notification by the auditor to the audit authority must be accompanied by a copy of the s 519 statement. If that s 519 statement to the company said that there were no circumstances that needed to be brought to the attention of members or creditors, the notice to the audit authority must also be accompanied by a statement of the reasons for the auditor ceasing to hold office.

10.38   It is an offence for a person ceasing to hold office as auditor to fail to comply with these requirements.

10.39   Section 523 imposes a similar duty on the company to notify the appropriate audit authority where an auditor ceases to hold office before the end of his term of office (ie he resigns or is dismissed). The notice must either be accompanied:

- by a statement by the company of the reasons for the auditor ceasing to hold office, or

- by a copy of the s 519 statement deposited by the auditor (provided that the s 519 statement is a statement of circumstances that need to be brought to the attention of members or creditors).

This notification must be made not later than 14 days after the s 519 statement is deposited at the company's registered office by the auditor.

10.40   Section 524 provides that the audit authority on receiving notice under s 522 or 523 must inform the accounting authorities.

Failure to re-appoint auditor – special procedures for resolution to appoint an auditor other than the outgoing auditor

10.41   Special procedures apply if a company is proposing a resolution to appoint an auditor in place of an auditor whose term of office has expired or is to expire. These will apply if changing the auditor from one financial year to the next. The procedures are set out in ss 514 and 515 and are aimed at ensuring that the outgoing auditor has the chance to make representations which are seen by the members. The special procedures apply to a private company appointing a new auditor if:

- no period for appointing auditors has ended since the outgoing auditor ceased to hold office, or

- such a period has ended and an auditor should have been appointed but was not.

The 'period for appointing auditors' is defined by s 485 as the end of the period of 28 days beginning with:

- the end of the time allowed for sending out copies of the company's annual accounts for the previous financial year to the members, or

- if earlier, the day on which the copies of the company's annual accounts for the previous financial year are sent out.

10.42 If the resolution is to be proposed as a written resolution, the company must send a copy of the proposed resolution to the person proposed to be appointed and to the outgoing auditor. The outgoing auditor is entitled, within 14 days of receipt, to require the company to circulate written representations and the company must circulate these to the members with the written resolution.

10.43 If the resolution is to be proposed at a general meeting, special notice of it is required. See **5.26** and s 312 regarding the requirements of special notice. In basic terms, this requires notice of the resolution to be given to the company at least 28 days before the meeting at which it is to be proposed. In this case, on receipt of the notice of the intended resolution the company must forthwith send a copy of it to the person proposed to be appointed and the outgoing auditor. Again, the auditor may require the company to circulate representations in writing to the members. The auditor is entitled to attend the meeting and be heard in any case under general auditor's rights (s 502).

10.44 In each case, the company may apply to the court not to circulate the representations on the basis that the auditor is using the statutory provisions to secure needless publicity for defamatory matter.

Removal of an auditor (ss 510–513)

10.45 The company may remove an auditor from office, but this can only be done by ordinary resolution passed at a meeting. Again, special notice of the meeting is required (see **10.43, 5.26** and s 312). The statutory provision does not deprive the auditor from any entitlement to damages in respect of the termination of the auditor's appointment as auditor or the termination of any appointment terminating with that as auditor.

10.46 Again, on receipt of the special notice the company must send a copy of it to the person proposed to be removed. Again, the auditor has the right to require written representations to be circulated to the members, and again the company may apply to the court for relief. In any case the auditor can attend and be heard at the meeting (s 502).

10.47 Where a resolution is passed to remove an auditor from office, the company must give notice of that fact to the Registrar within 14 days. It is an offence to fail to comply (s 512).

10.48 An auditor who has been removed from office has the right to attend and be heard at any general meeting of the company at which it is proposed to fill the vacancy caused by his removal (s 513).

ISSUE AND TRANSFER OF SHARES

10.49 See **Chapter 9** for detail on these subjects. Note that when a company issues shares it must complete the issue by making appropriate entries in its register of members. The company must register the allotment as soon as practicable and in any event within 2 months (s 554) (different provisions apply if the company issues a share warrant). The company must also complete and have ready for delivery the appropriate share certificates within the 2 month period (s 769).

10.50 Within one month of the allotment a limited company must deliver to the Registrar a return of allotment and also (with effect from 1 October 2009) a statement of capital. The statement of capital will give the required details of the company's current share capital, which are:

- the total number of shares of the company

- the aggregate nominal value of those shares

- for each class of shares:
    - prescribed particulars of the rights attached to those shares
    - the total number of shares of that class, and
    - the aggregate nominal value of the shares of that class

- the amount paid up and the amount (if any) unpaid on each share (whether on account of the nominal value of the share or by way of premium).

10.51 Under provisions due to come into force on 1 October 2009, an unlimited company only needs to deliver a return of allotments if it issues shares with different rights. The return will contain only the prescribed particulars regarding the share rights.

10.52 Where a transfer of shares is lodged with a company, it must as soon as practicable and in any event within 2 months either register the transfer or give notice of refusal to register **together with reasons for the refusal** (s 771). If the company refuses to register the transfer, it must provide the transferee with such further information about the reasons for the refusal as the transferee may reasonably request (s 771(2)).

10.53 The company must complete and have ready for delivery the share certificate within 2 months of the transfer being lodged with the company (s 776). There is no requirement to make any return to the Registrar when shares are transferred. Details of the transfer will only appear on the public record when the next annual return is submitted (see **8.56**). However, interested parties may inspect the register of members maintained by the company (see **8.19**).

DIVIDENDS – DISTRIBUTABLE PROFITS AND DECLARATION

10.54 As under previous legislation, the Act contains detailed provisions regulating when a company can make a distribution. The provisions are generally the same, but note that the Act clarifies the position regarding intra-group transfers at book value (see **10.66**).

10.55 A dividend is a distribution. It is necessary to determine whether the company has sufficient distributable profits to lawfully declare and pay the dividend prior to actually declaring it. See below for further detail on this. If at the time of an unlawful distribution a member knows or has reasonable grounds for believing that a distribution is unlawful, he is liable to repay it to the company (s 847).

10.56 The directors should also be satisfied that, given the company's current and projected financial situation, it is appropriate and in accordance with their duties to declare the dividend.

10.57 The mechanics of how a dividend may be declared will be set out in the company's articles. Under the 1985 Table A, the directors could decide to declare a dividend or they could recommend that a dividend be declared by resolution of the shareholders. Under these provisions a dividend declared by the shareholders could not exceed an amount recommended by the directors.

10.58 If a dividend is to be paid immediately upon declaration, it is simpler for it to be declared by the directors. The draft model articles for a private company limited by shares produced for consultation (and intended to apply to private companies limited by shares incorporated on or after 5 October 2009) provide that if the directors act in good faith, they do not incur any liability to the holders of shares carrying preferred rights for any loss they may suffer by the lawful payment of an interim dividend on shares with deferred or non-preferred rights. Note that at the time of writing, these model articles are in draft form.

DISTRIBUTIONS

10.59 The Act defines a 'distribution' as 'every description of distribution of a company's assets to its members, whether in cash or otherwise, subject to the following exceptions' (s 829):

- an issue of shares as fully or partly paid bonus shares

- the reduction of share capital:
  - by repaying paid up share capital, or
  - by extinguishing or reducing the liability of any of the members on any of the company's shares in respect of share capital not paid up

- the redemption or purchase of any of the company's own shares out of capital (including the proceeds of any fresh issue of shares) or out of unrealised profits in accordance with Chapter 3, 4 or 5 of Part 18 of the Act

- a distribution of assets to the members of the company on its winding up.

10.60 So a dividend (whether satisfied in cash or by distribution of assets) is definitely a distribution within the terms of the Act. Note that a transfer at undervalue to a shareholder or holding company (or a transfer to another subsidiary of the same holding company at undervalue) is likely to be in contravention of these distribution rules. Professional advice is required prior to making such transfers. See also **10.66** and **10.67** below.

DISTRIBUTABLE PROFITS

10.61 A company may only make a distribution out of profits available for the purpose. A company's profits available for distribution are its accumulated, realised profits (so far as not previously utilised by distribution or capitalisation) less its accumulated, realised losses (so far as not previously written off in a reduction or reorganisation of capital duly made) (s 830). Note that distributions by investment companies (and public companies) are subject to slightly modified rules (ss 831–835).

DISTRIBUTABLE PROFITS – JUSTIFICATION BY REFERENCE TO RELEVANT ACCOUNTS (SS 836–853)

10.62 Whether a company may make a distribution is determined by reference to the required items as stated in the 'relevant accounts' (s 836).

10.63 The required items are:

- profits, losses, assets and liabilities

- provisions of the following kinds:
  - where the relevant items are Companies Act accounts, provisions of a kind specified for this purpose in regulations about accounts
  - where the relevant accounts are IAS accounts, provisions of any kind

- share capital and reserves (including undistributable reserves).

10.64 The 'relevant accounts' are the company's last **annual accounts**, except that:

- where the distribution would be found to contravene the Act by reference to the last annual accounts, it may be justified by reference to '**interim accounts**', and

- where the distribution is proposed to be declared during the company's first accounting reference period, or before any accounts have been circulated to members in respect of that period, it may be justified by reference to '**initial accounts**'.

10.65 Particular requirements apply to each of these accounts where they are used to justify a distribution as follows.

For annual accounts used for this purpose (s 836):

- they must be the last annual accounts circulated to members (or if a summary financial statement was circulated, the accounts on which that statement was based)

- the accounts must have been properly prepared in accordance with the Act (or have been so prepared subject only to matters that are not material for determining by reference to the required items whether the distribution would contravene these requirements)

- unless the company is exempt from audit and the directors take advantage of that exemption, the auditor must have made his report on the accounts

- if the auditor's report was qualified:
  - the auditor must have stated in writing (either at the time of the report or subsequently) whether in his opinion the matters in respect of which his report is qualified are material for determining whether a distribution would contravene these requirements, and
  - a copy of the statement must have been circulated to the members.

For interim accounts and initial accounts:

- these must be accounts that enable a reasonable judgement to be made as to the amounts of the required items (if using management accounts, make sure that all provisions and other such items that have to be included in annual accounts are taken into account) (also note that additional requirements apply in respect of public companies).

DISTRIBUTIONS IN KIND – DETERMINATION OF AMOUNT

10.66 In the past, following the decision in *Aveling Barford Ltd v Perion Ltd* [1989] BCLC 626 there were sometimes concerns about whether a company could transfer assets at book value to another company in the same group without making an unlawful distribution. Sections 845 and 846 attempt to clarify the law in this area. In summary, they provide that if a company has profits available for distribution (of whatever amount), then it may transfer assets in such a way at book value without contravening the distribution rules.

10.67 Section 851 preserves the existing common law rules on unlawful distributions, apart from the changes made by ss 845 and 846.

REDUCTIONS IN SHARE CAPITAL, ISSUE OF REDEEMABLE SHARES, PURCHASE OF A COMPANY'S OWN SHARES, REDENOMINATION OF SHARES

10.68 See **Chapter 9** for requirements in these areas.

REGISTRATION OF A CHARGE ETC

10.69 The provisions regarding the registration of charges are generally the same as under previous legislation (with some changes about who may deliver documents and verify them). However, note that there has been consultation on wholesale changes to this area and the Act contains provision for the Secretary of State to make such changes by regulations. So it may be that we will see further changes in this area in the future.

10.70 A detailed examination of these provisions is beyond the scope of this book, so what follows is an overview of what is in the Act in relation to companies registered in England and Wales or Northern Ireland. Similar provisions apply to companies registered in Scotland which are worded differently to take account of differences in Scottish law. These provisions (contained in ss 860–894) are due to come into effect on 1 October 2009.

10.71 In various places in this section, the Act requires a document to be 'verified'. Section 1111 of the Act empowers the Registrar to impose requirements as to the person (or description of person) by whom the verification is to be given.

10.72 The provisions regarding registration of charges are contained in Part 25, ss 860–894 of the Act. Companies should take legal advice regarding the requirements applicable to charges and their registration.

10.73 A company that creates a charge to which these provisions relate must deliver the prescribed particulars of the charge (together with the instrument by which it is created or evidenced) to the Registrar within 21 days beginning with the day after the day on which the charge is created (ss 860 and 870). Failure to comply means that the charge is void against a liquidator, administrator or creditor of the company, and the money secured by it immediately becomes payable. Such failure is also an offence. In practice registration is normally effected by the person taking the benefit of the charge. The Act (s 860(2)) allows registration to be effected on the application of a person interested in it.

10.74 The Registrar will enter particulars of the charge on the public register and issue a certificate of registration to the company. This certificate acts as conclusive evidence that the registration requirements have been satisfied (s 869).

10.75 These requirements apply to the following charges (s 860):

- a charge on land or any interest in land, other than a charge for any rent or other periodical sum issuing out of land

- a charge created or evidenced by an instrument which, if executed by an individual, would require registration as a bill of sale

- a charge for the purpose of securing any issue of debentures

- a charge on uncalled share capital of the company

- a charge on calls made but not paid

- a charge on book debts of the company

- a floating charge on the company's property or undertaking

- a charge on a ship or aircraft, or any share in a ship

- a charge on goodwill or on any intellectual property.

10.76 Where a company acquires property which is subject to such a charge, it must register it with the Registrar within 21 days beginning with the day after the day on which the acquisition is completed (s 870).

10.77 There are various provisions dealing with cases where the charge is created outside the United Kingdom or may need to be registered in different places or it may be difficult to register the original charge within the time required. In some cases the 21-day period instead will begin with the day after the day on which the instrument by which the charge is created could, in due course of post (and if despatched with due diligence), have been received in the United Kingdom. In other cases a verified copy of the instrument by which the charge is created may be delivered instead of the original (see s 870 for precise requirements).

10.78 Where a charge is created outside the United Kingdom comprising property situated outside the United Kingdom, a verified copy of the instrument by which the charge is created may be delivered instead of the original (s 866).

10.79 Where a charge is created in the United Kingdom but comprises property outside the United Kingdom, the instrument may be sent for registration even if further proceedings may be necessary to make the charge valid or effectual according to the law of the country in which the property is situated (s 866).

10.80 If a charge comprises property in a part of the United Kingdom other than the part in which the company is registered, and registration is necessary in that other part to make the charge valid or effectual, delivery of a verified copy of the instrument, together with a certificate that the charge was presented for registration in that other part of the United Kingdom on the date that it was so presented, has the same effect as delivery of the instrument itself (s 867).

10.81 If a charge is not registered within the period required, it is possible to apply to the court for relief to allow late registration in accordance with s 873.

10.82 There are also requirements for the company itself to keep a register of charges and copies of the instruments creating the charges available for inspection. See **8.41** for further details.

MEMORANDUM OF SATISFACTION OF A CHARGE

10.83 If a statement is delivered to the Registrar verifying with respect to a registered charge:

- that the debt has been paid or satisfied (in whole or in part), or

- that part of the property or undertaking has been released from the charge or ceased to form part of the company's property or undertaking

the Registrar may enter a memorandum of satisfaction on the public record and if required and it is a memorandum of satisfaction of whole, send the company a copy (s 872).

REGISTRATION OF ENFORCEMENT OF SECURITY (S 871)

10.84 If a person obtains an order for the appointment of a receiver or manager of a company's property, or appoints a receiver or manager under powers contained in an instrument, he is required within seven days to give notice of this fact to the Registrar. Where a person appointed receiver or manager of a company's property under powers contained in an instrument ceases to act as such receiver or manager, he is required to give notice to the Registrar.

PROTECTION OF MEMBERS AGAINST UNFAIR PREJUDICE

10.85 Section 994 provides that a member of a company may apply to the court on the ground that the company's affairs are being or have been conducted in a manner that is unfairly prejudicial to the interests of the members generally or of some part of its members (including at least himself), or that an actual or proposed act or omission of the company is or would be so prejudicial.

10.86 This is not a compliance requirement but should at all times be borne in mind by the directors in carrying out their duties as officers of the company.

RE-REGISTRATION OF A COMPANY

10.87 Sections 89–111 (which are due to come into force on 1 October 2009) deal with re-registration as a means of altering a company's status. They allow for:

- a private company to become a public company

- a public company to become a private company

- a private limited company to become unlimited

- an unlimited private company to become limited, and

- a public company to become private and unlimited.

The possibility for a public company to re-register as a private unlimited company without having to first re-register as a private limited company is a new addition made by the Act. Generally the provisions are similar to that under the previous legislation. Statements of compliance replace the previous statutory declarations and there is a new requirement for a statement of proposed secretary where a private company without a company secretary wishes to re-register as a public company.

POLITICAL DONATIONS AND EXPENDITURE

10.88 Sections 362–379 deal with the control of political donations and expenditure. In the main, they restate the previously existing provisions. However, the Act simplifies the position for groups of companies (see **10.89** and **10.90**). The Act provides greater clarity about the provision of facilities to trade union officials by introducing a specific exemption for donations to and expenditure for trade unions (other than a contribution to the union's political fund) (s 374). Paid leave for local councillors does not constitute a political donation or expenditure.

10.89 In summary, companies continue to be prohibited from making a donation to a political party or other political organisation or from incurring political expenditure unless the donation or expenditure has been authorised by a resolution of the company's members. There is an exception for donations that do not exceed £5,000 in a 12-month period (group donations are aggregated) (s 378). The resolution may authorise the making of donations and incurring expenditure for a period of not more than four years up to a value specified in the resolution. If the company is a subsidiary, the expenditure must also be authorised by a resolution of the members of the company's 'relevant holding company'. A 'relevant holding company' is a UK-registered company that is not a subsidiary of another UK-registered company. So the requirement only applies to the holding company highest up the chain that is a UK-registered company.

10.90 Section 367(1) provides that a holding company may seek authorisation for both itself and one or more subsidiaries in one resolution. Indeed the resolution can relate to all the subsidiaries of the holding company at any time during the period for which the resolution has effect, without identifying them individually (s 367(2)).

10.91 If a company makes a political donation or incurs political expenditure without the required authorisation, the directors in default (which may in some cases include directors of the relevant holding company) are jointly and severally liable to make good to the company and to compensate it for loss (ss 369–373).

TAKEOVERS – 'SQUEEZE-OUT' AND 'SELL-OUT'

10.92 Sections 974–991 are designed to address the problems of, and for, residual minority shareholders following a successful takeover bid. 'Squeeze out' provisions enable a successful bidder to compulsorily purchase the shares of the remaining minority shareholders in certain circumstances and 'sell-out' provisions enable minority shareholders, following such a bid, to require the majority shareholder to purchase their shares in certain circumstances. The sections restate previous law, but also contain changes to reflect alterations required to meet requirements of the EU Takeovers directive. Please refer to the sections for full requirements.

SUMMARY OF MAJOR CHANGES INTRODUCED BY THE ACT

1   The Act now also extends to Northern Ireland (s 1299). *When provisions are brought into force in almost all cases they also apply to Northern Ireland.*

2   The Registrar has wider powers to impose requirements as to the form and manner of delivery of documents and how they are to be authenticated and verified. The Act empowers the Secretary of State to make regulations to actually require documents to be delivered by electronic means (ss 1060–1120, in particular 1068–1076, 1093–1094, 1111 and 1117). *Again, these provisions have in most cases been brought into force as necessary to fit with other parts of the Act. They are due to come into force fully for all purposes on 1 October 2009.*

3   The Act gives the Registrar wider powers about how to deal with defective documents (ss 1072–1076). *Due to come fully into force on 1 October 2009.*

4   Requirement to notify changes to details in the register of directors' service addresses (s 167). *Due to come into force on 1 October 2009.*

5   A company may change its name by means provided in the company's articles (or by special resolution) (s 77). *Due to come into force on 1 October 2009.*

6   New list of documents required to be forwarded to the Registrar (special resolutions etc) – similar but not identical to the old list (ss 29 and 30). *This came into force on 1 October 2007 and has been subject to minor changes in effect by later commencement orders.*

7   New provisions regarding the detail of the appointment of an auditor (ss 485–494). *Sections 485–488 regarding the appointment of auditors of private companies came into effect on 1 October 2007 and apply in relation to the appointment of auditors of private companies for financial years beginning on or after that date. Sections 489 and 490 regarding the appointment of auditors of public companies came into force on 6 April 2008 and apply to the appointment of auditors of public companies for financial years beginning on or after that date.*

8   New requirements on the departing auditor and the company to notify the appropriate audit authority if an auditor resigns or is dismissed (or ceases to hold office in the case of a major audit) (ss 522–525). *These provisions came into effect on 6 April 2008.*

9   Requirement to give reasons for refusal to register the transfer of shares (s 771). *This came into effect on 6 April 2008.*

10 Statutory confirmation that if a company has profits available for distribution, it may transfer assets at book value without making an unlawful distribution (ss 845 and 846). *This came into effect on 6 April 2008.*

11 Provision for the Registrar to specify who may verify in relation to documents delivered for the registration of a charge or notice of satisfaction of the charge (s 1111). *This came into effect on 1 January 2007.*

12 A public company may re-register as a private unlimited company (ss 109–111). *This is due to come into force on 1 October 2009.*

13 There are some changes regarding political donations and expenditure authorisation requirements (ss 362–379). *These came into effect in England, Wales and Scotland (with exceptions for independent candidates) on 1 October 2007. The same provisions came into effect in Northern Ireland on 1 November 2007. Provisions regarding independent candidates came into effect on 1 October 2008.*

14 There are some changes regarding the precise requirements of 'squeeze-out' and 'sell-out' provisions following takeovers (ss 974–991). *These provisions came into effect on 6 April 2007.*

Chapter 11

STRIKING OFF COMPANIES

INTRODUCTION

11.1 Forming a new company is very easy, but closing them down can be much more time consuming, expensive and difficult. This chapter looks at the provisions in the Act dealing with the striking off and restoration of a company. Note that this is only a small part of the total picture. Striking off is essentially an administrative procedure that may either:

- be instituted by the Registrar where a company appears to be no longer in business or operation, or

- applied for by the company in appropriate cases (voluntary application for strike off).

11.2 Before a company makes a voluntary application to be struck off it is necessary to ensure that this is a suitable route for that company. If the company is insolvent, this method should not be used and immediate professional advice is required. If the directors continue trading when the company is insolvent, it is possible for them to become personally liable. Such matters are not covered by this book. Even if the company is solvent, in some cases it may be more suitable to dissolve the company by means of a members' voluntary winding up, involving a liquidator.

11.3 The Act essentially carries over the process for striking off from previous legislation but will introduce some changes, particularly in relation to restoration of a struck off company to the Register (see **11.28**). The statutory provisions are contained in ss 1000–1034 and are due to come into force on 1 October 2009. See the end of this chapter for the main changes to the existing statutory provisions that are to be introduced.

STRIKE OFF INSTITUTED BY THE REGISTRAR

11.4 If the Registrar has reasonable cause to believe that a company is not carrying on business or in operation, the Registrar may send to the company a series of letters and notices (in accordance with the timetable provided for by s 1000) which culminate in the strike off of that company from the Register.

11.5   The Registrar must first enquire whether the company is in business or operation, then state that notice will be published in the Gazette with a view to striking the company's name off the Register and then finally give notice (which must be published in the Gazette) that at the expiration of 3 months, the company will, unless cause is shown to the contrary, be struck off the Register and the company will be dissolved. When the company is struck off the Registrar must publish a further notice in the Gazette.

11.6   This process is likely to be instituted if a company fails to file its annual accounts and/or annual return within a reasonable period after the time permitted.

11.7   Section 1001 also gives the Registrar power to institute a strike off procedure where a company is being wound up and the Registrar has reasonable cause to believe that no liquidator is acting or that the affairs of the company are fully wound up.

STRIKE OFF, VOLUNTARY APPLICATION – WHEN IS THIS SUITABLE?

11.8   Even if the company is solvent, it is necessary to undertake a series of checks to ensure that striking off is suitable. The alternative methods to dissolve a solvent company so that it ceases to exist are:

* members voluntary winding up (involving a liquidator), or

* striking off.

Which is more suitable will depend upon the particular circumstances of the particular company. Companies should seek advice on this. This book does not deal with the winding up of companies.

11.9   In basic summary, striking off is lower in cost and can be much simpler. A members' voluntary liquidation ('MVL') is a more expensive and formal process, but deals with possible creditors and is likely to be more suitable for companies with a trading history or where the company's history is unknown and there might be claims against the company.

11.10   In some cases a voluntary application for strike off may be suitable, particularly if the company has always been dormant (or dormant for many years), it has no assets or creditors, and there is no likelihood of future claims against it.

11.11   If it is intended to make a voluntary application to strike off a company, it is appropriate to conduct a series of internal checks prior to making the application. These might include the following questions:

- are the company's tax affairs complete?

- will the dissolution have any effect regarding VAT (or group VAT)?

- are there any regulatory issues?

- does the company have any assets or liabilities (remember to check land ownership and rights, intellectual property rights and contractual rights; also consider intra group debtors and creditors)?

- does the company own any shares (whether in its own right or as nominee or beneficial owner)?

- has the company assigned any leases that may give rise to future liability if the assignee defaults?

- does the company have a bank account?

- does the company have any creditors, debtors, claims or realistic likelihood of claims against it?

- does the company have employees or a pension fund?

- has the company changed its name or made a disposal or done anything or engaged in any activity in the last 3 months other than one 'necessary or expedient' for the purpose of:
    - complying with any statutory requirement
    - concluding the affairs of the company, or
    - making the application to strike off (or deciding whether to do so)?

STRIKE OFF, VOLUNTARY APPLICATION – WHEN PERMITTED

11.12 The application must not be made if, at any time in the previous 3 months the company has:

- changed its name

- traded or otherwise carried on business

- made a disposal for value of property or rights that, immediately before ceasing to trade or otherwise carry on business, it held for the purpose of disposal or gain in the normal course of trading or otherwise carrying on business, or

- engaged in any other activity, except one which is:

- necessary or expedient for making the application (or deciding whether to do so)
- necessary or expedient for concluding the affairs of the company, or
- necessary or expedient for the purpose of complying with any statutory requirement.

11.13 A company is not treated as trading or carrying on business by virtue only of the fact that it makes a payment in respect of a liability incurred in the course of trading or carrying on business.

11.14 Section 1005 prohibits an application if certain proceedings are before a court or if the company is involved in certain insolvency matters. Please refer to the section of the specific matters listed.

11.15 It is an offence to make an application in contravention of the above requirements (s 1005(4)).

STRIKE OFF, VOLUNTARY APPLICATION – PROCEDURE

11.16 The application must be made on the company's behalf by the company's directors (or at least a majority of them) and must contain the prescribed information (s 1003). In practice it will be made on the prescribed form.

11.17 A person who makes the application on behalf of a company must secure that within 7 days from the day on which the application is made, a copy of the application is given to every person who at any time on that day is:

- a member

- an employee

- a creditor (including a contingent or prospective creditor)

- a director

- a manager or trustee of any pension fund established for the benefit of any employees of the company.

Failure to comply is an offence (s 1006).

11.18 If, at any time before the application is dealt with or withdrawn, a person becomes any of the above (ie member, employee, creditor, director, manager/trustee of a pension fund, etc), then each director is under a duty to secure that a copy of the application is given to that person within 7 days. Again, failure to comply is an offence (s 1007).

11.19   Section 1008 sets out provisions regarding the service of documents to comply with the above requirements. It permits them to be sent by post to the proper address.

11.20   There are provisions set out in s 1009 requiring the application to be withdrawn in certain circumstances. In summary these apply if, before the application is dealt with or withdrawn, the company does, or becomes involved in, any of the things that would have made it prohibited from making the application in the first place.

11.21   After receipt of the application, the Registrar will publish a notice in the Gazette stating that after the expiration of 3 months the company may be struck off and inviting any person to show cause why this should not be done. When the company is struck off the Registrar must publish a further notice in the Gazette.

STRIKE OFF – EFFECT ON PROPERTY OF COMPANY

11.22   When a company is dissolved any property vested in it immediately before dissolution is deemed to be bona vacantia and accordingly belongs to the Crown (or the Duchy of Lancaster or the Duchy of Cornwall if the registered office of the company fell within one of their areas of jurisdiction for this purpose) (s 1012). This includes all property and rights vested in or held on trust for the company (including leasehold property), but does not include property held by the company on trust for another person.

11.23   It is important to ensure that the company does not have any assets before applying for, or allowing it to be, struck off and dissolved (see **11.11**). It is a common occurrence that companies allow themselves to be stuck off (or even make a voluntary application to be struck off) only to find afterwards that there is some property owned by the company. If the company has by then been dissolved, the only course is to apply for it to be restored to the Register (see **11.32**).

11.24   Property passing bona vacantia to the Crown will be administered by the Treasury Solicitor whose website gives information about bona vacantia (see **Appendix 5** for website addresses).

11.25   The Act introduces (in s 1013) new provisions giving the Crown a longer period to disclaim property. A notice of disclaimer must be executed within 3 years after:

- the date on which the fact that the property may have vested in the Crown first comes to the notice of the Crown representative, or

- if ownership of the property is not established on that date, the end of the period reasonably necessary for the Crown representative to establish the ownership of the property.

If an application in writing is made to the Crown representative, requiring him to decide whether he will disclaim, any notice of disclaimer must be executed within 12 months or such further period allowed by the court.

11.26 The Crown's disclaimer operates so as to terminate the rights, interests and liabilities in or in respect of the properties disclaimed. It is possible for a court to make an order in respect of disclaimed property (see s 1021).

11.27 In some cases a company may be subsequently restored to the Register. Restoration does not include any disposition of property made by the person in whom it was vested whilst the property was bona vacantia. However there are provisions under s 1034 whereby the consideration received for the property (less costs) may be paid to the company.

RESTORATION TO THE REGISTER – ADMINISTRATIVE PROCEDURE (SS 1024–1028)

11.28 The Act introduces a new administrative procedure for the restoration of a company to the Register after it has been struck off. Note that this new procedure only applies where the company has been struck off by the procedure instituted by the Registrar. It does not apply where a company is struck off after voluntary application by the company. In those cases it is still necessary to apply to the court for restoration.

11.29 The administrative application may be made by a former member or former director of the company within 6 years from the date of dissolution of the company. The application is made to the Registrar (s 1024).

11.30 The Registrar shall restore the company if, and only if, the following conditions are met (s 1025):

- the company was carrying on business or in operation at the time of its striking off

- if any property or right vested in or held on trust for the company has vested as bona vacantia, the Crown representative has signified to the Registrar in writing consent to the company's restoration to the Register (the applicant must obtain such consent and pay any costs)

- the applicant has delivered to the Registrar the necessary documents to bring the company's records kept by the Registrar up to date and paid any late filing penalties in relation to the late filing of accounts that were outstanding at the date of dissolution or strike off (the company is not liable for late penalties in respect of accounts due to be filed after strike off and before restoration)

- the application must be accompanied by a statement of compliance stating that the person making the application has standing to apply (ie is a former member or director) and that the requirements for administrative restoration are met.

11.31 The Registrar must give notice to the applicant of the decision on an application. If the decision is that the company should be restored, the restoration takes effect from the date that the notice is sent, entry will be made on the public record and an advertisement placed in the Gazette. The effect of the restoration is that the company is deemed to have continued in existence as if it had not been dissolved or struck off the Register. The company is not liable for accounts late filing penalties in respect of the period between dissolution and restoration.

RESTORATION TO THE REGISTER – APPLICATION TO THE COURT (SS 1029–1032)

11.32 If a company has been:

- dissolved after winding up

- deemed to have been dissolved following administration

- struck off at the instigation of the Registrar, or

- struck off following an application by the company

it is possible to make an application to the court to restore the company to the Register. Such an application generally may only be made within 6 years from dissolution of the company, save that an application may be made at any time for the purpose of bringing proceedings against the company for damages for personal injury (ss 1029 and 1030).

11.33 The application to the court for restoration may be made by:

- the Secretary of State

- any former director of the company

- any person having an interest in land in which the company had a superior or derivative interest

- any person having an interest in land or other property:

-     that was subject to rights vested in the company, or
-     that was benefited by obligations owed by the company

- any person who but for the company's dissolution would have been in a contractual relationship with it

- any person with a potential legal claim against the company

- any manager or trustee of a pension fund established for the benefit of employees of the company

- any former member of the company (or the personal representatives of such a person)

- any person who was a creditor of the company at the time of its striking off or dissolution

- any former liquidator of the company

- where the company was struck off on application of the company, any person designated by regulations as entitled to receive a copy of the notice of application for strike off, or

- any other person appearing to the court to have an interest in the matter.

11.34 The Treasury Solicitor's website (see **Appendix 5**) has useful guidance on how to make an application to the court.

11.35 The court may order the restoration of a company to the Register if:

- the company was struck off at the instigation of the Registrar and the company was (at the time of the striking off) carrying on business or in operation

- the company was struck off following an application by the company and any of the requirements set out in ss 1004 to 1009 were not complied with

- in any other case the court considers it just to do so.

Normally the applicant will be required to pay the costs of the Registrar and the Crown representative.

11.36 If the court does order restoration, this will take effect on an office copy of the order being delivered to the Registrar (s 1031). The general effect of the restoration is that the company is deemed to have continued in existence as if it had not been dissolved or struck off the Register (s 1032). The company is not liable for accounts late filing penalties in respect of the period between dissolution and restoration (s 1032). The court is also empowered to give further directions etc as seems just for placing the company and all other persons in the same position (as nearly as may be) as if the company had not been dissolved or struck off (s 1032).

RESTORATION TO THE REGISTER – COMPANY NAME

11.37 Normally a company is restored to the Register with the same name. However, there may be difficulty if the name is no longer available for registration as another company has been registered with that name. Section 1033 makes provision for such cases. In summary, the company must be restored under another name.

SUMMARY OF MAJOR CHANGES INTRODUCED BY THE ACT

All the changes below are due to be introduced with effect from 1 October 2009.

1   There is a new procedure for administrative restoration of a company that has been struck off that may be used if the strike off was instigated by the Registrar. This does not apply if the company voluntarily applied to be struck off as in such cases a court application is still required (ss 1024–1028).

2   The period to apply to the court for restoration of a company is standardised at 6 years (or at any time for the purpose of bringing proceedings against the company for damages for personal injury) regardless of whether the company was (i) wound up or dissolved following administration under the Insolvency Act or (ii) struck off under the Companies Act (s 1030). *The new 6-year time limit applies to companies dissolved on or after 1 October 2007. It does not enable an application to be made in respect of a company dissolved before that date. If a company was struck off and dissolved by administrative procedure under previous legislation, s 1030(4) does not prevent an application to restore being made at any time before (1) 1 October 2015 (ie six years after commencement), or (2) 20 years after publication of the dissolution in the Gazette, whichever occurs first. There is no time bar in respect of cases of personal injury.*

3   There is a wider list of persons in the Act entitled to make application to the court for restoration of a company to the Register (s 1029).

4   Public companies may apply to the Registrar to be struck off the Register and dissolved (s 1003).

5   The Crown representative has a longer period to disclaim property passing bona vacantia to the Crown and there are further provisions regarding disclaimed property (s 1013).

Chapter 12

COMING INTO FORCE AND
APPLICATION TO EXISTING COMPANIES

INTRODUCTION

12.1 The implementation of the Companies Act 2006 has been a protracted process. The Act received Royal Assent on 8 November 2006. A small number of provisions were brought into force on that date. Since then there have been eight commencement orders bringing sections of the Act into force. Details of these and the commencement dates are given in **Appendix 3**. At the time of writing it is anticipated that the final provisions of the Act will be brought into force on 1 October 2009 and a draft eighth commencement order is available via the BERR website (see **Appendix 5**). Details of the items proposed to be implemented by this order are also included in **Appendix 3**.

12.2 In many areas the Act provides for regulations to be made regarding detail and other matters. Lists of regulations made or before Parliament and draft proposed regulations are also available via the BERR website (see **Appendix 5**). The main areas covered by regulations are:

- **Model articles of association** – Table A was modified with effect from 1 October 2007 to take account of the changes to the law introduced on that date regarding resolutions and meetings etc. This 'transitional' Table A only applies to companies formed on or after that date or companies that choose to alter their articles to adopt it. Further minor amendments were made to Tables C and E with effect from 6 April 2008. It is intended that new model articles of association will be introduced by statutory instrument with effect from 1 October 2009. Again, these will only apply to companies formed under the Act, unless previously existing companies adopt them.

- **Accounts and Reports** – The requirements for accounts and reports are mainly set out in regulations, which generally came into effect on 6 April 2008 for financial years commencing on or after that date (see **8.68**).

- **Auditors** – There are regulations setting out the requirements for disclosure of auditor remuneration and liability limitation agreements and also dealing with 'third country auditors'.

- **Trading disclosures** – the company law requirements for information about the company to be set out on websites, notepaper, invoices etc and requirements with respect to display of the company name are now set out in regulations.

- **Late filing penalties** – the civil penalties for delivering accounts late to the Registrar are prescribed by regulations.

- **Company Names Adjudicator Rules** – these regulations cover objections to 'opportunistic' registrations of company names.

- **Various other matters** – these include regulations in relation to reduction of capital, the annual return, fees for inspection and copying of company records, company and business names, political expenditure and the minimum share capital for public companies.

Relevant statutory instruments are referred to in more detail in the parts of this book that deal with the items they cover. Many more statutory instruments can be expected in relation to the implementation of the final parts of the Act on 1 October 2009.

12.3 One of the areas of difficulty in the implementation of the new Act has been its application to existing companies. Transitional provisions mean that not only is it necessary to understand the changes that have been introduced to company law but also to understand:

- when such changes came into force

- whether the changes automatically apply to existing companies

- whether existing companies need to take some action to take advantage of the changes (for instance by passing a resolution or altering articles)

- whether the changes only apply in respect of financial years beginning on or after a certain date (or in some cases ending on or after a certain date)

- whether any other transitional provisions apply, and if so, whether they will cease to apply when the remaining parts of the Act come into force.

12.4 Readers are recommended to check the current situation on implementation issues and statutory instruments by accessing the BERR website (see **Appendix 5** for website address).

PROVISIONS THAT WILL BE LEFT BEHIND IN PREVIOUS ACTS

12.5 As stated previously, the Act is a consolidating Act. However some non-core provisions have been left behind in previous Acts. These are summarised by BERR as follows.

Parts of previous Companies Acts to do with non-company law items

12.6

- Some Scots law provisions, which are now devolved to the Scottish Parliament, and which are being replaced by the Scottish Parliament.

- Provisions about the Financial Reporting Council which are about the operation of that body and its subsidiaries, not about how companies generally conduct themselves.

- Provisions about assisting overseas regulatory authorities, about financial markets, about the Financial Reporting Review Panel, and about insolvency all of which relate more to financial services law than company law.

In the 1985 Act

12.7

- Company investigations.

- Orders imposing restrictions on shares following an investigation.

- Provisions about Scottish floating charges and receivers.

In the 1989 Act

12.8

- Powers to require information and documents to assist overseas regulatory authorities.

- Provisions about Scottish incorporated charities.

- Amendments and savings consequential upon the changes in the law made by the 1989 Act.

- Provisions about financial markets and insolvency.

In the 2004 Act

12.9

- The provisions extending the functions of the Financial Reporting Review Panel ('FRRP') to interim accounts and reports.

- Provisions about the financing and liability of the Financial Reporting Council ('FRC') and its subsidiary bodies.

- Community interest companies.

APPLICATION TO EXISTING COMPANIES – BACKGROUND

12.10 In 2006 the Government issued a paper seeking views on the application of the new law to existing companies. The Government's approach to implementing the provisions was stated to be guided by three main objectives:

- the new provisions should apply to existing companies as well as new ones (so generally law comes into force for existing companies and companies formed under the Act at the same time and should apply to existing companies in the same way)

- to ensure so far as possible that existing bargains are not overridden (so that existing provisions in articles and decisions made by members' resolution are preserved), and

- make it as easy as possible for existing companies to comply with the new requirements and take advantage of the new freedoms.

This follows the model of previous changes to company legislation.

12.11 In some areas the Government recognised a conflict between its objectives. This is apparent from the transitional provisions that have been applied as the Act has been implemented. In many cases previously existing companies cannot automatically take advantage of the Act's provisions. This can raise many difficulties when attempting to determine the detail of the law that applies to a particular company.

12.12 In the author's view, many of these questions are best dealt with by a company adopting new articles that are designed to fit with, and take advantage of, the provisions of the Act when (or with effect from, or after) the final provisions of the Act come into force on 1 October 2009.

ELECTRONIC COMMUNICATIONS

12.13 An address notified by a person to a company for the purposes of receiving certain types of information by means of electronic communications which was effective immediately before 20 January 2007 continues to have effect in relation to the matters to which it relates. However, note that previous legislation only related to the supply of far more limited types of information by electronic means. To take advantage of the far wider terms contained in Schs 4 and 5 to the Act, it appears that it is necessary to obtain a new wider general consent to the sending or supply of any document or information in electronic form. See SI 2006/3428, Sch 5, paras 4 and 5.

COMPANY CONSTITUTIONS

12.14 See **Chapter 4** for a fuller discussion regarding this issue. To avoid existing companies having to update their constitutional documentation, existing companies will be treated as having a new-style constitution, without having to do anything to achieve this. Relevant provisions in the old style memorandum of an existing company will automatically be deemed to form part of its articles.

12.15 Objects clauses of an existing company's memorandum will be treated as provisions of its articles. An objects clause drafted as a list of things that the company is empowered to do will, in future, be read as a restriction on what the company can do. The Government's view is that there is no need for an existing company to change its constitution. As discussed in **Chapter 4**, active companies may, following consultation with their advisers, take the view that it is desirable to update their articles in any case.

12.16 Transitional provisions will preserve existing absolute entrenchment provisions for existing companies that already have them. Such absolute entrenchment provisions are rare.

ABOLITION OF AUTHORISED SHARE CAPITAL

12.17 See **Chapter 9** for fuller discussion on this issue. Existing companies will have a statement of authorised share capital of shares available for issue, which will in future be deemed to be part of their articles. New companies formed under the Act will not be required to have an authorised share capital (but may do so if they wish – which is likely to be very unusual).

12.18 After consultation, the Government has concluded that the authorised share capital of an existing company should continue to act as a restriction on the shares that could be allotted, as a restriction contained in the company's articles. Transitional arrangements will allow shareholders to remove this restriction by ordinary resolution, rather than by special resolution as is normally the case for changes to the articles. Such a resolution must be filed at Companies House.

RESTRICTIONS IN THE ARTICLES AS TO ALTERATIONS TO A COMPANY'S SHARE CAPITAL

12.19 Previous legislation generally required that a company could only make an alteration to its share capital (eg reduction, purchase of own shares etc) if authorised by its articles. The Act generally reverses this position, so that such alterations may be made by a private company unless there is a restriction in the company's articles.

12.20 The possible concern is in relation to existing companies that did not have an authorisation for such alterations to share capital in their articles. Is this to be taken as deliberate and if so should such companies be restricted regarding such alterations to share capital? After consultation the Government has eventually concluded that where articles of existing companies did not contain a relevant authorisation, such companies should still be able to take advantage of the provisions in the Act regarding:

- reduction of share capital with court approval

- the issue of redeemable shares

- purchase of the company's own shares

- purchase of the company's own shares out of capital.

The Government concluded that such previously existing companies without provision in their articles were few and that members were adequately protected as all these measures require a members' resolution in any case. So no alteration of the articles is required to take advantage of these provisions.

SUBSISTING AUTHORITY UNDER COMPANIES ACT 1985, S 80

12.21 See **Chapter 9** for a fuller discussion regarding this. Currently directors must be authorised by the members in accordance with statutory requirements before they may allot shares. Under the Act, companies with one class of shares will no longer require this authority but companies with more than one class of shares will still require it under replacement provisions in the Act (see ss 549 to 551).

12.22   Under transitional provisions, any existing authority under s 80 of the Companies Act 1985 will continue to have effect. However, if previously existing private companies with one class of share wish to take advantage of the authority to allot shares granted by s 550, an enabling resolution of the members will be required.

12.23   If an existing private company has (or after the allotment would have) more than one class of shares, then a new authority will be required in accordance with the Act's provisions.

ANNUAL GENERAL MEETING ('AGM') AND PRESENTATION OF ANNUAL ACCOUNTS TO THE MEMBERS

12.24   See **Chapter 8** for a fuller discussion on this. The Act abolishes the requirement for a private company to have an AGM. However some companies may have a provision in their articles requiring an AGM.

12.25   Any express provision in articles requiring an AGM will continue to have effect. However, mere reference to an AGM in the articles (eg a requirement for directors to retire at the AGM) will not operate to require the company to hold an AGM. In such cases such directors' appointments continue until terminated. See SI 2007/2194, Sch 3, para 32. The 1985 Table A does not specifically require an AGM. The 1948 Table A does explicitly require an AGM. However, if a company that had a specific requirement in its articles to hold an AGM (such as a company whose articles adopted the 1948 Table A) had previously passed an elective resolution to dispense with this requirement, and this elective resolution was in force immediately prior to 1 October 2007, then the company is not treated as one whose articles require it to hold an AGM and no AGM is required (see SI 2007/3495, Sch 5, para 2(6)).

12.26   The repeal of the requirement for private companies to lay accounts and reports before a general meeting has effect in relation to annual accounts and reports for financial years ending on or after 1 October 2007. Provisions under previous legislation apply in respect of annual accounts and reports for financial years ending before that date (see SI 2007/2194, Sch 3, para 49).

COMPANY SECRETARIES

12.27   Some companies may have specific provisions in their articles requiring a company secretary or assuming that it has one. Such provisions will continue to have effect without any need for transitional provisions.

12.28   Existing company secretaries will simply continue in office until the appointment is terminated.

CHAIRMAN'S CASTING VOTE AT GENERAL MEETINGS

12.29   Due to changes introduced by the Act to the definition of resolutions etc (see ss 281–287) the chairman does not have a second or casting vote on resolutions of the members unless the company's articles included such a power before 1 October 2007. If they did, it continues to apply or, if it has been removed after 1 October 2007, may be reinstated. For companies that are not entitled to this transitional provision, it may be possible to achieve a similar result by the insertion of other provisions into the company's articles. In such cases specialist advice is required. See SI 2007/3495, Sch 5, para 2.

EXTRAORDINARY RESOLUTIONS

12.30   Any reference to an extraordinary resolution in a provision:

- of a company's memorandum or articles, or

- of a contract

continues to have effect and an extraordinary resolution (as defined by s 378 of the Companies Act 1985) may still be passed in accordance with that provision in the memorandum, articles or contract. Such extraordinary resolutions must be filed with the Registrar and are subject to the provisions of Chapter 3 of Part 3 of the Act. See SI 2007/2194, Sch 3, para 23 as amended by SI 2007/3495, Sch 5, para 2.

CORPORATE DIRECTORS

12.31   Any private company that had only corporate directors on 8 November 2006 (when the Act received Royal Assent) may continue to have only corporate directors until 1 October 2010 (instead of having to meet the requirement to have at least one natural person on the Board from 1 October 2008). See SI 2007/3495, Sch 4, para 46.

DIRECTORS' CONFLICTS OF INTEREST

12.32   See **Chapter 5** for a fuller discussion on this. The Act introduced important changes in this area with effect from 1 October 2008. Private companies in existence prior to 1 October 2008 (when the relevant provision came into force) are required to pass an ordinary resolution before they may take advantage of the provision in s 175 that allows directors to authorise s 175 type conflicts. Such a resolution is required to be filed at Companies House.

12.33 Note that s 180(4) carries over common law rules regarding authorisation of conflicts, so that authorisation by the members in accordance with the common law is still permitted and in many cases may be the preferable route. Section 180(4) also provides that where the company's articles contain provisions for dealing with conflicts of interest, the general duties that directors owe to their company are not infringed by anything done (or omitted) by the directors, or any of them, in accordance with those articles.

DIRECTORS' TRANSACTIONS WITH THE COMPANY

12.34 The consultation referred to the interaction between existing provisions in a company's articles regarding this (eg Reg 85 of the 1985 Table A) and the provisions in the Act. Companies that have adopted Reg 85 of the 1985 Table A already allow a director to be a party to a transaction with the company subject to disclosure safeguards.

12.35 Provisions in companies' articles dealing with conflicts of interest continue to have effect as does the existing rule of law that members may authorise such transactions and conflicts (s 180(4)).

ACCOUNTS, REPORTS AND AUDIT

12.36 A business review in accordance with s 417 of the Act is required in the directors' report for financial years beginning on or after 1 October 2007 (unless the company can claim the small company accounts exemption then applicable) – see SI 2007/2194, Sch 3, para 43).

12.37 Generally the requirements on the form and content of accounts and reports in Part 15 of the Companies Act 2006 and new regulations made under it are commenced with effect for accounts and reports for periods beginning on or after 6 April 2008. Accounts and reports for periods beginning before then continue to be prepared in accordance with the Companies Act 1985 and the Companies (Northern Ireland) Order 1986. The new provisions regarding the turnover and balance sheet totals for determining whether a company is small or medium-sized, the new requirements regarding signature of the audit report and the reduced time period for delivering accounts to Companies House also apply to accounts for financial years beginning on or after 6 April 2008. See SI 2007/3495, Sch 4, paras 6–19 and SI 2008/393 para 2 regarding details.

12.38 Sections 475–481 (general provisions about audit), apply to accounts for financial years beginning on or after 6 April 2008. Note that ss 482 and 483 (companies subject to public sector audit) apply to accounts for financial years beginning on or after 1 April 2008. See SI 2007/3495, Sch 4, para 9.

12.39 With regard to the appointment of auditors, the new provisions regarding the appointment of auditors of private companies apply to the appointment of auditors for financial years beginning on or after 1 October 2007 (see SI 2007/2194, Sch 3, para 44) and the new provisions regarding the appointment of auditors of public companies apply to appointments for financial years beginning on or after 6 April 2008.

12.40 If a private company had elected to dispense with the annual re-appointment of auditors, and this election was in force immediately before 1 October 2007, s 487(2)(a) (no deemed re-appointment of auditors appointed by the directors) does not prevent the deemed re-appointment under that subsection of auditors first appointed before 1 October 2007. See SI 2007/2194, Sch 3, para 44.

LATE FILING PENALTIES

12.41 Increased late filing penalties automatically applicable when annual accounts are received by the Registrar late, apply in respect of any accounts received late on or after 1 February 2009, regardless of the financial year that they cover. See SI 2008/497.

ANNUAL RETURNS

12.42 For annual returns by private companies made up to a date on or after 1 October 2008 it is no longer necessary to include the addresses of members and a new form of annual return has been prescribed. See SI 2008/1659.

RESTORATION TO THE REGISTER

12.43 Section 1030(4) provides that the period to apply to the court for restoration of a company to the Register is to be standardised at 6 years (or at any time for the purpose of bringing proceedings against the company for damages for personal injury) regardless of whether the company was (i) wound up or dissolved following administration under the Insolvency Act or (ii) struck off under the Companies Act (s 1030). The new 6-year time limit applies with effect from 1 October 2009 to companies dissolved on or after 1 October 2007. It does not enable an application to be made in respect of a company dissolved before that date. If a company was struck off and dissolved by administrative procedure under previous legislation, s 1030(4) does not prevent an application to restore being made at any time before (1) 1 October 2015 (ie 6 years after commencement), or (2) 20 years after publication of the dissolution in the Gazette, whichever occurs first. There is no time bar in respect of cases of personal injury.

OTHER PROVISIONS IN THE DRAFT EIGHTH COMMENCEMENT ORDER

12.44   At the time of writing, the Government is consulting on the draft eighth commencement order that will bring the final parts of the Act into effect on 1 October 2009. The proposed transitional provisions in this draft commencement order that have not been mentioned above include:

- There may be a few companies which will be incorporated under the 1985 Act but where the incorporation will not occur until after 30 September 2009. These will be companies where the applications for incorporation were made just before 1 October 2009. These companies are referred to as 'transitional companies' in the final Commencement Order and slightly different transitional provisions apply to them.

- Existing companies will not be affected with regard to their existing names by any changes to the rules regarding permitted names etc that come into force then.

- The existing address held by the Registrar as a director's address (either a service address under a confidentiality order or the director's existing notified residential address) will automatically become that director's service address – so if a director wishes to use a different service address it will be necessary to notify the Registrar on or after 1 October 2009, otherwise no notification is required.

- The entry by a company in the new register of residential addresses of information that immediately before that date was contained in the register of directors does not give rise to a duty to notify the Registrar – so again no notification is required.

- For existing directors and secretaries, the requirements under the Act for the registers of them to contain additional specified particulars will not be mandatory until the next annual return date, but the requirement to have a register of directors' residential addresses is immediate.

- Directors who already receive the protection of a confidentiality order will automatically receive the higher protections that apply after a successful application not to disclose an address to a credit reference agency under s 243(4) of the Act.

Appendix 1

TABLE OF ORIGINS

Companies Act 2006

Origins

Notes

1. This table shows the origin of the company law provisions of the Companies Act 2006 by reference to the enactments in force on the date that Act received Royal Assent (subject to the note to the origins for Part 28). The Act received Royal Assent on 8 November 2006. Where an enactment had been amended before that date, the reference is to the text at that date; the table does not show the source of such amendments.

2. The origin of a provision of the Companies Act 2006 in the Companies (Northern Ireland) Order 1986 is acknowledged where it makes significantly different provision in relation to Northern Ireland than in relation to England and Wales or, as the case may be, Great Britain.

3. In the table —
    "1985" means the Companies Act 1985 (c. 6);
    "IA 1986" means the Insolvency Act 1986 (c. 45);
    "1986" means the Companies (Northern Ireland) Order 1986 (S.I. 1096/1032 (N.I. 6));
    "ICTA" means the Income and Corporation Taxes Act 1988 (c. 1);
    "1989" means the Companies Act 1989 (c.40).

4. The entry "drafting" indicates a new provision of a mechanical or editorial nature - for example, a provision defining an expression to avoid repetition or indicating where other relevant provisions are to be found.

5. A reference followed by "(changed)" means that the provision referred to has been re-enacted with one or more changes. In general, a change is noted only in the primary context affected and not in every provision where a consequential change results. The table does not show changes in the maximum penalties for offences.

6. The entry "new" indicates a provision which has no predecessor in the repealed legislation or which is fundamentally different from its predecessor.

7. The entries in the table are intended only as a general indication of what has changed and what is new. They should not be read as expressing any view as to the application or otherwise of any provision relating to enactments repealed and re-enacted.

Section of 2006 Act	*Origin*
PART 1 GENERAL INTRODUCTORY PROVISIONS	
1(1)	1985 s. 735(1)(a) and (b)
(2) and (3)	drafting

Section of 2006 Act	Origin
2(1) and (2)	1985 s. 744 (changed)
3(1) to (4)	1985 s. 1(2)
4(1) and (2)	1985 s. 1(3)
(3)	1985 s.1(3), 1986 art.12(3)
(4)	drafting
5(1)	1985 s. 1(4)
(2)	1984 s.1(4), 1986 art.12(4)
(3)	1985 s. 15(2)
6(1) and (2)	drafting
PART 2 COMPANY FORMATION	
7(1) and (2)	1985 s. 1(1) (changed)
8(1)	new
(2)	1985 s. 3(1)
9(1)	1985 s. 10(1) (changed)
(2)	1985 s. 2(1)(a) and (b), (2) and (3) (changed)
(3)	1985 s. 10(4)
(4)	new
(5)	1985 s. 10(1) and (6)
(6)	1985 s. 10(1)
10(1) to (5)	new
11(1)	drafting
(2)	new
(3)	1985 s. 2(4) (changed)
12(1)	1985 s. 10(2) (changed)
(2)	new
(3), first sentence	1985 s. 10(3)
(3), second sentence	new
13(1) and (2)	1985 s.12(3) and (3A) (changed)
14	1985 s. 12(1) and (2)
15(1)	1985 s. 13(1)

Section of 2006 Act	Origin
(2)	new
(3)	1985 s. 13(2)
(4)	1985 s. 13(7)(a)
16(1)	drafting
(2)	1985 s13(3) (changed)
(3)	1984 s13(4)
(4)	new
(5)	new
(6)	1985 s. 13(5)

PART 3 A COMPANY'S CONSTITUTION

Chapter 1 Introductory

17	new

Chapter 2 Articles of association

18(1)	new
(2)	1985 s. 7(1) (changed)
(3)	1985 s. 7(3) (changed)
(4)	1985 s. 744
19(1) to (3)	1985 s. 8(1) and (4) (changed)
(4)	1985, s. 8(3)
(5)	1985 s. 8(5)
20(1) and (2)	1985 s. 8(2) (changed)
21(1)	1985 s. 9(1)
(2) and (3)	drafting
22(1) to (3)	new
23(1) and (2)	new
24(1) to (4)	new
25(1)	1985 s. 16(1)
(2)	1985 s. 16(2)
26(1)	1985 s. 18(2) (changed)
(2)	new

Section of 2006 Act	Origin
(3) and (4)	1985 s. 18(3) and Sch. 24
27(1) to (5)	new
28(1) to (3)	new

Chapter 3 Resolutions and agreements affecting a company's constitution

29(1)	1985 s. 380(4) (changed)
(2)	1985 s. 380(4A)
30(1)	1985 s. 380(1)
(2) and (3)	1985 s. 380(5) and Sch. 24
(4)	1985 s. 380(7)

Chapter 4 Miscellaneous and supplementary provisions

31(1) to (5)	new
32(1)	1985 s.19(1) (changed)
(2)	new
(3) and (4)	1985 s.19(2) (changed) and Sch. 24
33(1)	1985 s. 14(1) (changed)
(2)	1985 s. 14(2) (changed)
34(1)	drafting
(2)	1985 s. 18(1) (changed)
(3)	1985 s. 18(2) (changed)
(4)	new
(5) and (6)	1985 s. 18(3) and Sch. 24
35(1) to (5)	new
36(1) and (2)	1985 s. 380(2) (changed)
(3) and (4)	1985 s. 380(6) (changed) and Sch. 24
(5)	1985 s. 380(7)
37	1985 s. 15(1)
38	Companies (Single Member Private Limited Companies) Regulations 1992 (S.I. 1992/1699) (changed)

PART 4 A COMPANY'S CAPACITY AND RELATED MATTERS

39(1)	1985 s.35(1) (changed)

Section of 2006 Act	Origin
(2)	1985 s.35(4)
40(1)	1985 s.35A(1)
(2)	1985 s.35A(2) and 35B
(3)	1985 s.35A(3)
(4)	1985 s.35A(4)
(5)	1985 s.35A(5)
(6)	1985 s.35A(6)
41(1)	1985 s.322A(1) and (4)
(2)	1985 s.322A(1) and (2)
(3)	1985 s.322A(3)
(4)	1985 s.322A(5)
(5)	1985 s.322A(6)
(6)	1985 s.322A(7)
(7)	1985 s.322A(8)
42(1)	Charities Act 1993 s.65(1)
(2)	Charities Act 1993 s.65(2)
(3)	Charities Act 1993 s.65(3)
(4)	Charities Act 1993 s.65(4)
(5)	drafting
43(1) and (2)	1985 s.36
44(1)	1985 s.36A(1) to (3)
(2)(a), (3) and (4)	1985 s.36A(4)
(2)(b)	new
(5)	1985 s.36A(6) (changed)
(6)	1985 s.36A(4A)
(7)	1985 s.36A(8)
(8)	1985 s.36A(7)
45(1)	1985 s.36A(3)
(2)	1985 s.350(1)
(3)	1985 s.350(1) (changed)

Section of 2006 Act	Origin
(4) and (5)	1985 s.350(2) and Sch.24
(6)	drafting
46(1)	1985 s.36AA(1)
(2)	1985 s.36AA(2)
47(1)	1985 s.38(1) (changed) and (3)
(2)	1985 s.38(2) (changed)
48(1)	Requirements of Writing (Scotland) Act 1995 (c. 7) s.15(3)
(2)	1985 s.36B(1)
(3)	1985 s.36B(2)
49(1)	1985 s.39(1) (changed)
(2)	1985 s.39(1)
(3)	1985 s.39(2) and (2A)
(4)	1985 s.39(3)
(5)	1985 s.39(4)
(6)	1985 s.39(5)
50(1) and (2)	1985 s.40(1)
51(1)	1985 s.36C(1)
(2)	1985 s.36C(2)
52	1985 s.37

PART 5 A COMPANY'S NAME

Chapter 1 General requirements

53	1985 s.26(1)(d) and (e)
54(1) to (3)	1985 s.26(2)(a) and second sentence (changed)
55(1)	1985 s.26(2)(b) and 29(1)(a)
(2)	1985 s.29(6)
56(1)	1985 s.29(1)(b) (changed)
(2)	1985 s.29(2)
(3) and (4)	1985 s.29(3) (changed)
(5)	drafting

Section of 2006 Act	Origin
57(1) to (5)	new
Chapter 2 Indications of company type or legal form	
58(1)	1985 s.25(1) and 27(4)(b)
(2)	1985 s.25(1) and 27(4)(d)
(3)	drafting
59(1)	1985 s.25(2) (opening words) and 27(4)(a)
(2)	1985 s.25(2)(b) and 27(4)(c)
(3)	1985 s.25(2)(a)
(4)	drafting
60(1)(a) and (b)	new
(1)(c)	drafting
(2)	1985 s.30(5B)
(3)	1985 s.30(4)
(4)	new
61(1)	1985 s.30(2), 1986 art.40(2)
(2) to (4)	1985 s.30(2) and (3) (changed)
62(1) to (3)	1985 s.30(2) and (3) (changed)
63(1)	1985 s.31(1)
(2) and (3)	1985 s.31(5) and Sch.24
(4) and (5)	new
64(1) to (3)	1985 s.31(2) first sentence
(4)	1985 s.31(2) second sentence (changed)
(5) and (6)	1985 s.31(6) and Sch.24
(7)	1985 s. 31(3)
65(1) to (5)	1985 s.26(1)(a), (b), (bb) and (bbb) (changed)
Chapter 3 Similarity to other names	
66(1)	1985 s.26(1)(c)
(2) and (3)	1985 s.26(3) (changed)
(4) to (6)	new
67(1)	1985 s.28(2)

Section of 2006 Act	Origin
(2) to (6)	new
68(1)	drafting
(2)	1985 s.28(2) full out
(3)	1985 s.28(4)
(4)	1985 s.28(2) full out and (4)
(5) and (6)	1985 s.28(5) and Sch.24
69(1) to (7)	new
70(1) to (6)	new
71(1) to (4)	new
72(1) and (2)	new
73(1) to (6)	new
74(1) to (5)	new
Chapter 4 Other powers of the Secretary of State	
75(1) and (2)	1985 s.28(3)
(3)	1985 s.28(4)
(4)	1985 s28(3)
(5) and (6)	1985 s.28(5) and Sch.24
76(1)	1985 s.32(1)
(2)	new
(3)	1985 s.32(2)
(4) and (5)	1985 s.32(3)
(6) and (7)	1985 s.32(4) (changed) and Sch.24
Chapter 5 Change of name	
77(1)(a)	1985 s.28(1)
(1)(b)	new
(2)	drafting
78(1) to (3)	new
79(1) and (2)	new
80(1) and (2)	1985 s.28(6) and 32(5) (changed)
(3)	1985 s.28(6) and 32(5)

Section of 2006 Act	Origin
81(1)	1985 s.28(6) and 32(5)
(2) and (3)	1985 s. 28(7) and 32(6)
Chapter 6 Trading disclosures	
82(1) and (2)	1985 ss.348(1), 349(1), 351(1) and (2), Business Names Act 1985 s.4(1) (changed)
(3) to (5)	new
83(1) and (2)	Business Names Act 1985 s.5(1)
(3)	Business Names Act 1985 s.5(2)
84(1) and (2)	1985 ss.348(2), 349(2) and (3), 351(5), Business Names Act 1985 s.7 (changed)
(3)	new
85(1) and (2)	new
PART 6 A COMPANY'S REGISTERED OFFICE	
86	1985 s.287(1)
87(1)	1985 s.287(3)
(2)	1985 s.287(4)
(3)	1985 s.287(5)
(4)	1985 s.287(6)
88(1)	drafting
(2)	1985 s. 2(2)
(3) and (4)	new
PART 7 RE-REGISTRATION AS A MEANS OF ALTERING A COMPANY'S STATUS	
89	drafting
90(1)	1985 s.43(1) (changed)
(2)	1985 s.43(1); drafting
(3)	1985 s.43(2)
(4)	1985 s.48(1) and (2)
91(1)	1985 s.45(1) to (4)
(2)	1985 s.45(5), 1986 art.55(5)
(3)	1985 s.45(6)
(4)	1985 s.45(7)

Section of 2006 Act	Origin
(5)	1985 s.47(3) (changed)
92(1)	1985 s.43(3)(b) and (c), (4)
(2)	1985 s.43(e)(ii)
(3) and (4)	1985 s.46(2) and (3)
(5) and (6)	1985 s.46(4)
93(1)	1985 s.44(1)
(2)	1985 s.44(2), drafting
(3) to (5)	1985 s.44(4) and (5)
(6)	1985 s.44(6) and (7)(b)
(7)	1985 s.44(2) and (7)(a)
94(1)	new
(2)	1985 s.43(3)(a) to (d)
(3)	1985 s.43(e)(i)
(4)	1984 s.47(2)
95(1) to (3)	new
96(1) and (2)	1985 s.47(1)
(3)	new
(4) and (5)	1985 s.47(4) and (5)
97(1)	1985 s.53(1) (changed)
(2)	new
(3)	1985 s.53(2)
98(1)	1985 s.54(1) and (2)
(2)	1985 s.54(3)
(3) and (4)	1985 s.54(5)
(5)	1985 s.54(6)
(6)	1985 s.54(8)
99(1) and (2)	1985 s.54(4) (changed)
(3)	1985 s.54(7)
(4) and (5)	1985 s.54(10), Sch.24
100(1)	new

Section of 2006 Act	*Origin*
(2)	1985 s.53(1)(b) (changed)
(3) and (4)	new
101(1) and (2)	1985 s.55(1)
(3)	new
(4) and (5)	1985 s.55(2) and (3)
102(1)	1985 s.49(1), (4), (8)(a) (changed)
(2)	1985 s.49(2)
(3)	1985 s.49(5) to (7) (changed)
(4)	1985 s.49(9)
(5)	new
103(1)	new
(2)	1985 s.49(8)(a), (c) and (d)
(3) and (4)	1985 s.49(8)(b), (8A) (changed)
(5)	new
104(1) and (2)	1985 s.50(1)(b)
(3)	new
(4) and (5)	1985 s.50(2) and (3)
105(1)	1985 s.51(1) (changed)
(2)	1985 s.51(2)
(3) and (4)	1985 s.51(3)
106(1)	new
(2)	1985 s.51(5) (changed)
(3) to (5)	new
107(1) and (2)	1985 s.52(1)
(3)	new
(4) and (5)	1985 s.52(2) and (3)
108(1) to (5)	new
109(1) to (5)	new
110(1) to (5)	new
111(1) to (5)	new

Section of 2006 Act	Origin
PART 8 A COMPANY'S MEMBERS	
Chapter 1 The members of a company	
112(1)	1985 s.22(1) (changed)
(2)	1985 s.22(2)
Chapter 2 Register of members	
113(1) and (2)	1985 s.352(1) and (2)
(3) and (4)	1985 s.352(3)
(5)	new
(6)	1985 s.352(4)
(7) and (8)	1985 s.352(5), Sch.24
114(1)	1985 s.353(1) (changed)
(2)	1985 s.353(2)
(3)	1985 s.353(3)
(4)	1985 s.353(3), 1986 art.361(3)
(5) and (6)	1985 s.353(4), Sch.24
115(1) and (2)	1985 s.354(1)
(3)	1985 s.354(2)
(4)	1985 s.354(3) (changed)
(5) and (6)	1985 s.354(4), Sch.24
116(1)	1985 s.356(1) (changed)
(2)	1985 s.356(3) first branch
(3) and (4)	new
117(1) to (5)	new
118(1) and (2)	1985 s.356(5), Sch. 24 (changed)
(3)	1985 s.356(6)
119(1) to (3)	new
120(1) to (4)	new
121	1985 s.352(6) (changed)
122(1)	1985 s.355(1) (changed)
(2)	1985 s.355(4)

Section of 2006 Act	Origin
(3)	1985 s.355(5)
(4) and (5)	1985 s.355(2) and (3)
(6)	1985 s.355(4)
123(1)	new
(2) and (3)	1985 s.352A(1) and (2) (changed)
(4) and (5)	1985 s.352A(3), Sch.24
124(1) and (2)	1985 s.352(3A)
125(1) to (4)	1985 s.359(1) to (4)
126	1985 s.360
127	1985 s.361
128(1) and (2)	1985 s.352(7)
Chapter 3 Overseas branch registers	
129(1)	1985 s.362(1), (2) opening words
(2)	1985 Sch.14 Pt.1
(3) and (4)	new
(5)	1985 s.362(2)(b) and (c)
130(1)	1985 s.362(3), Sch.14 Pt.2 para.1(1), (2)
(2) and (3)	1985 s.362(3), Sch.14 Pt.2 para.1(3), Sch.24
131(1)	1985 s.362(3), Sch.14 Pt.2 para.2(1)
(2) and (3)	new
(4)	1985 s.362(3), Sch.14 Pt.2 para.7
132(1) and (2)	1985 s.362(3), Sch.14 Pt.2 para.4(1) (changed)
(3) and (4)	1985 s.362(3), Sch.14 Pt.2 para.4(2), Sch.24
133(1) and (2)	1985 s.362(3), Sch.14 Pt.2 para.5
(3)	1985 s.362(3), Sch.14 Pt.2 para.8
134(1) and (2)	1985 s.362(3), Sch.14 Pt.2 para.3(1) (changed)
(3)	1985 s.362(3), Sch.14 Pt.2 para.3(2)
135(1) and (2)	1985 s.362(3), Sch.14 Pt.2 para.6
(3)	1985 s.362(3), Sch.14 Pt.2 para.1(1), (2)
(4) and (5)	1985 s.362(3), Sch.14 Pt.2 para.1(3), Sch.24

Section of 2006 Act	Origin
Chapter 4 Prohibition on subsidiary being member of its holding company	
136(1)	1985 s.23(1)
(2)	drafting
137(1)	1985 s.23(4) and (5)
(2)	1985 s.23(4), 1986 art.33(4)
(3) and (4)	1985 s.23(6)
138(1) and (2)	1985 s.23(2), Sch.2 para.4(1) and (2); drafting
139(1) to (4)	1985 Sch.2 para.1(1) to (4)
(5)	1985 Sch.2 para.5(2)
(6)	1985 Sch.2 para.5(2) and (3)
140(1) and (2)	1985 Sch.2 para.3(1) and (2)
(3) and (4)	1985 Sch.2 para.5(2) and (3)
141(1) and (2)	1985 s.23(3)
141(3) and (4)	1985 s.23(3A) and (3B)
(5)	1985 s.23(3BA)
142(1) and (2)	1985 s.23(3C)
143	1985 s.23(8)
144	1985 s.23(7)
PART 9 EXERCISE OF MEMBERS' RIGHTS	
145(1) to (4)	new
146(1) to (5)	new
147(1) to (6)	new
148(1) to (8)	new
149(1) to (3)	new
150(1) to (7)	new
151(1) to (3)	new
152(1) to (4)	new
153(1) and (2)	new
PART 10 A COMPANY'S DIRECTORS	
Chapter 1 Appointment and removal of directors	

Section of 2006 Act	Origin
154(1)	1985 s.282(3)
(2)	1985 s.282(1) (changed)
155(1) and (2)	new
156(1) to (7)	new
157(1) to (6)	new
158(1) to (5)	new
159(1) to (4)	new
160(1) to (4)	1985 s.292(1) to (4)
161(1) and (2)	1985 s.285 (changed)
162(1) to (3)	1985 s.288(1) (changed)
(4)	new
(5)	1985 s.288(3)
(6)	1985 s.288(4) and (6)
(7)	1985 s.288(4), Sch.24
(8)	1985 s.288(5)
163(1)	1985 s.289(1)(a) (changed)
(2)	1985 s.289(2)(a)
(3)	new
(4)	1985 s.289(2)(b) (changed)
(5)	new
164	1985 s.289(1)(b) (changed)
165(1) to (6)	new
166(1) and (2)	new
167(1) and (2)	1985 s.288(2) (changed)
(3)	new
(4)	1985 s.288(4) and (6)
(5)	1985 s.288(4), Sch.24
168(1)	1985 s.303(1) (changed)
(2) to (5)	1985 s.303(2) to (5)
169(1) and (2)	1985 s.304(1)

Section of 2006 Act	Origin
(3) and (4)	1985 s.304(2) and (3)
(5)	1985 s.304(4) (changed)
(6)	1985 s.304(5)

Chapter 2 General duties of directors

170(1) to (5)	new
171	new
172(1)	1985 s.309(1) (changed)
(2) and (3)	new
173(1) and (2)	new
174(1) and (2)	new
175(1) to (7)	new
176(1) to (5)	new
177(1) to (6)	new
178(1) and (2)	new
179	new
180(1) to (5)	new
181(1) to (5)	new

Chapter 3 Declaration of interest in existing transaction or arrangement

182(1)	1985 s.317(1) and (5) (changed)
(2)	1985 s.317(2) (changed)
(3) to (6)	new
183(1)	1985 s.317(7)
(2)	1985 s.317(7), Sch.24
184(1) to (5)	new
185(1) and (2)	1985 s.317(3) (changed)
(3)	new
(4)	1985 s.317(4)
186(1) and (2)	new
187(1) to (4)	1985 s.317(8) (changed)

Chapter 4 Transactions with directors requiring approval of members

Section of 2006 Act	Origin
188(1)	1985 s.319(1) (changed)
(2)	1985 s.319(3) (changed)
(3)	1985 s.319(1) (changed)
(4)	1985 s.319(2) (changed)
(5)	1985 s.319(5), para.7 of Sch.15A (changed)
(6)	1985 s.319(4)
(7)	1985 s.319(7)(a)
189	1985 s.319(6)
190(1) and (2)	1985 s.320(1) (changed)
(3)	new
(4)	1985 s.321(1)
(5) and (6)	new
191(1) to (5)	1985 s.320(2) (changed)
192	1985 s.321(2)(a) and (3) (changed)
193(1) and (2)	1985 s.321(2)(b) (changed)
194(1) and (2)	1985 s.321(4)
195(1)	1985 s.322(1) and (3)
(2)	1985 s.322(1) and (2)(a) and (b)
(3)	1985 s.322(3) and (4)
(4)	1985 s.322(3)
(5)	1985 s.322(4)
(6)	1985 s.322(5)
(7)	1985 s.322(6)
(8)	1985 s.322(4)
196	1985 s.322(2)(c)
197(1)	1985 s.330(2) (changed)
(2) to (5)	new
198(1)	1985 s.330(3), s.331(6)
(2)	1985 s.330(3)(a) and (c) (changed)
(3) to (6)	new

Section of 2006 Act	Origin
199(1)	1985 s.331(3)
(2) and (3)	1985 s.331(4)
200(1)	1985 s.330(3), s.331(6)
(2)	1985 s.330(3)(b) and (c) (changed)
(3) to (6)	new
201(1)	1985 s.330(4), s.331(6)
(2)	1985 s.330(4) (changed)
(3) to (6)	new
202(1)	1985 s.331(7)
(2)	1985 s.331(9)(b)
(3)	1985 s.331(8) and (10)
203(1)	1985 s.330(6) and (7) (changed)
(2) to (5)	new
(6)	1985 s.330(6)
204(1)	1985 s.337(1) and (2) (changed)
(2)	1985 s.337(3), s.339(1) and (2) (changed)
205(1)	1985 s.337A(1) and (3) (changed)
(2)	1985 s.337A(4)
(3)	1985 s.337A(5)
(4)	1985 s.337A(6)
(5)	1985 s.337A(2)
206	new
207(1)	1985 s.334, s.339(1) and (2) (changed)
(2)	1985 s.335(1), s.339(1) and (2) (changed)
(3)	1985 s.335(2)
208(1)	1985 s.333, s.336(a) (changed)
(2)	1985 s.336(b) (changed)
209(1)	1985 s.338(1) and (3)
(2)	1985 s.338(2)
(3) and (4)	1985 s.338(6) (changed)

Section of 2006 Act	Origin
210(1)	1985 s.339(1)
(2)	1985 s.339(2)
(3)	1985 s.339(2) and (3)
(4)	1985 s.339(2) and (3)
(5)	1985 s.339(5)
211(1)	1985 s.339(6) and s.340(1)
(2)	1985 s.340(2)
(3)	1985 s.340(3)
(4)	1985 s.340(6)
(5)	1985 s.340(4)
(6)	1985 s.340(5)
(7)	1985 s.340(7) (changed)
212	1985 s.331(9)(a) to (d)
213(1) and (2)	1985 s.341(1)
(3) and (4)	1985 s.341(2)
(5)	1985 s.341(3)
(6)	1985 s.341(4)
(7)	1985 s.341(5)
(8)	1985 s.341(3)
214	new
215(1)	1985 s.312, s.313(1), s.314(1) (changed)
(2) to (4)	new
216(1) and (2)	1985 s.316(2) (changed)
217(1)	1985 s.312
(2)	new
(3)	1985 s.312 (changed)
(4)	new
218(1)	1985 s.313(1)
(2)	new
(3)	1985 s.313(1) (changed)

Section of 2006 Act	Origin
(4)	new
(5)	1985 s.316(1)
219(1)	1985 s.314(1), s.315(1)(b) (changed)
(2)	1985 s.315(1)(b)
(3) and (4)	new
(5)	1985 s.315(3)
(6)	new
(7)	1985 s.316(1)
220(1)	1985 s.316(3) (changed)
(2) to (5)	new
221(1) to (4)	new
222(1)	new
(2)	1985 s.313(2)
(3)	1985 s.315(1)
(4) and (5)	new
223(1)	1985, s.319(6), 320(3), 330(5)
(2)	new
224(1) and(2)	new
225(1) to (3)	new
226	new
Chapter 5 Directors' service contracts	
227	new
228(1)	1985 s.318(1)
(2)	1985 s.318(2) and (3) (changed)
(3)	new
(4)	1985 s.318(4)
(5)	1985 s.318(8) (changed)
(6)	1985 s.318(8), Sch.24
(7)	1985 s.318(10)
229(1)	1985 s.318(7)

Section of 2006 Act	Origin
(2)	new
(3)	1985 s.318(8) (changed)
(4)	1985 s.318(8), Sch.24
(5)	1985 s.318(9) (changed)
230	1985 s.318(6)
Chapter 6 Contracts with sole members who are directors	
231(1)	1985 s.322B(1) and (2) (changed)
(2)	1985 s.322B(1)
(3)	1985 s.322B(4) (changed)
(4)	1985 s.322B(4), Sch.24
(5)	1985 s.322B(3)
(6)	1985 s.322B(6)
(7)	1985 s.322B(5)
Chapter 7 Directors' liabilities	
232(1)	1985 s.309A(1) and (2)
(2)	1985 s.309A(1) and (3) (changed)
(3)	1985 s.309A(6)
(4)	new
233	1985 s.309A(5)
234(1)	1985 s.309A(4)
(2)	1985 s.309B(1) and (2)
(3)	1985 s.309B(3) and (4)
(4)	1985 s.309B(5)
(5)	1985 s.309B(6) and (7)
(6)	1985 s.309B(4)(c)
235(1) to (6)	new
236(1)	1985 s.309C(1) (changed)
(2) and (3)	1985 s.309C(2)
(4) and (5)	1985 s.309C(3)
237(1)	1985 s.309C(4) and (5)

Section of 2006 Act	*Origin*
(2)	1985 s.309C(5), s.318(1)
(3)	1985 s.309C(5), s.318(2) and (3) (changed)
(4)	new
(5)	1985 s.309C(5), s.318(4)
(6)	1985 s.309C(5), s.318(8) (changed).
(7)	1985 s.309C(5), s.318(8), Sch.24
(8)	1985 s.309C(5), s.318(10)
(9)	new
238(1)	1985 s.309C(5), s.318(7)
(2)	new
(3)	1985 s.309C(5), s.318(8) (changed)
(4)	1985 s.309C(5), 1985 s.318(8), Sch.24
(5)	1985 s.309C(5), s.318(9) (changed)
239(1) to (7)	new

Chapter 8 Directors' residential addresses: protection from disclosure

240(1) to (3)	new
241(1) and (2)	new
242(1) to (3)	new
243(1) to (8)	new
244(1) to (4)	new
245(1) to (6)	new
246(1) to (7)	new

Chapter 9 Supplementary provisions

247(1)	1985 s.719(1)
(2)	1985 s.719(2) (changed)
(3)	new
(4)	1985 s.719(3)
(5)	1985 s.719(3) (changed)
(6)	1985 s.719(3)
(7)	1985 s.719(4) (changed)

Section of 2006 Act	Origin
248(1)	1985 s.382(1)
(2)	new
(3)	1985 s.382(5) (changed)
(4)	1985 s.382(5), Sch.24
249(1)	1985 s.382(2)
(2)	1985 s.382(4)
250	1985 s.741(1)
251(1) and (2)	1985 s.741(2)
(3)	1985 s.741(3)
252(1)	1985 s.346(1)
(2)	1985 s.346(2) and (3) (changed)
(3)	1985 s.346(2)
253(1)	drafting
(2)	1985 s.346(2) and (3) (changed)
(3)	new
254(1)	1985 s.346(1)
(2)	1985 s.346(4)
(3)	1985 s.346(7)
(4)	1985 s.346(8)
(5)	1985 s.346(4)
(6)	1985 s.346(6)
255(1)	1985 s.346(1)
(2)	1985 s.346(5)
(3)	1985 s.346(7)
(4)	1985 s.346(8)
(5)	1985 s.346(5)
(6)	1985 s.346(6)
256	new
257(1) and (2)	new
258(1)	1985 s.345(1)

Section of 2006 Act	Origin
(2)	1985 s.345(2)
(3)	1985 s.345(3)
259	1985 s.347

PART 11 DERIVATIVE CLAIMS AND PROCEEDINGS BY MEMBERS

Chapter 1 Derivative claims in England and Wales or Northern Ireland

260(1) to (5)	new
261(1) to (4)	new
262(1) to (5)	new
263(1) to (7)	new
264(1) to (5)	new

Chapter 2 Derivative proceedings in Scotland

265(1) to (7)	new
266(1) to (5)	new
267(1) to (5)	new
268(1) to (6)	new
269(1) to (5)	new

PART 12 COMPANY SECRETARIES

270(1) and (2)	new
(3)	1985 s.283(3) (changed)
271	1985 s.283(1) (changed)
272(1) to (7)	new
273(1) and (2)	1985 s.286(1) (changed)
(3)	1985 s.286(2)
274	1985 s.283(3) (changed)
275(1) to (3)	1985 s.288(1) (changed)
(4)	new
(5)	1985 s.288(3)
(6)	1985 s.288(4) and (6)
(7)	1985 s.288(4), Sch.24
(8)	1985 s.288(5)

Section of 2006 Act	Origin
276(1) and (2)	1985 s.288(2)
(3)	1985 s.288(4) and (6) (changed)
(4)	1985 s.288(4), Sch.24
277(1)	1985 s.290(1)(a) (changed)
(2)	1985 s.289(2)(a), s.290(3)
(3)	new
(4)	1985 s.289(2)(b), s.290(3) (changed)
(5)	new
278(1)	1985 s.290(1)(b) (changed)
(2)	1985 s.290(2)
279(1) and (2)	new
280	1985 s.284

PART 13 RESOLUTIONS AND MEETINGS

Chapter 1 General provisions about resolutions

281(1) to (4)	new
282(1) to (5)	new
283(1)	1985 s.378(1) and (2) (changed)
(2) and (3)	new
(4)	1985 s.378(1) and (2) (changed)
(5)	1985 s.378(1), (2) and (5) (changed)
(6)	1985 s.378(2) (changed)
284(1)	1985 s.370(6)
(2)	Table A, para.54 (changed)
(3)	1985 s.370(6), Table A, para.54 (changed)
(4)	1985 s.370(1), Table A, para.54
285(1) to (3)	new
286(1) to (3)	Table A, para.55
287	new

Chapter 2 Written resolutions

Section of 2006 Act	Origin
288(1)	new
(2)	1985 s.381A(7), Sch.15A, para.1
(3)	new
(4)	1985 s.381A(1) (changed)
(5)	1985 s.381A(4)
289(1)	1985 s.381A(1) (changed)
(2)	new
290	new
291(1) to (7)	new
292(1) to (6)	new
293(1) to (7)	new
294(1) and (2)	new
295(1) and (2)	new
296(1)	1985 s.381A(2) (changed)
(2) to (4)	new
297(1) and (2)	new
298(1) and (2)	new
299(1) and (2)	new
300	1985 s.381C(1)
Chapter 3 Resolutions at meetings	
301	1985 s.378(6) (changed)
302	Table A, para.37
303(1)	1985 s.368(1)
(2)	1985 s.368(1), (2) and (2A)
(3)	1985 s.368(2) (changed)
(4)	1985 s.368(3) (changed)
(5)	new
(6)	1985 s.368(3) (changed)
304(1)	1985 s.368(4) and (8)
(2) and (3)	new

Section of 2006 Act	Origin
(4)	1985 s.368(7)
305(1)	1985 s.368(4)
(2)	new
(3)	1985 s.368(4)
(4)	1985 s.368(5)
(5)	new
(6) and (7)	1985 s.368(6)
306(1) and (2)	1985 s.371(1)
(3) and (4)	1985 s.371(2)
(5)	1985 s.371(3)
307(1)	new
(2)	1985 s.369(1) and (2) (changed)
(3)	1985 s.369(1) and (2)
(4)	1985 s.369(3) (changed)
(5) and (6)	1985 s.369(4) (changed)
(7)	drafting
308	1985 s.369(4A), (4B) (changed)
309(1)	1985 s.369(4B)
(2)	1985 s.369(4C) (changed)
(3)	1985 s.369(4B)(d)
310(1)	1985 s.370(2), Table A, para.38 (changed)
(2)	Table A, para.38 (changed)
(3)	new
(4)	1985 s.370(1), Table A para.38
311(1) and (2)	Table A, para.38
312(1)	1985 s.379(1)
(2)	1985 s.379(2)
(3)	1985 s.379(2) (changed)
(4)	1985 s.379(3)
313(1) and (2)	1985 Table A, para.39 (changed)

Section of 2006 Act	Origin
314(1)	1985 s.376(1)(b)
(2) and (3)	1985 s.376(2) (changed)
(4)	1985 s.376(1), s.377(1)(a) (changed)
315(1)	1985 s.376(3) and (5)
(2)	1985 s.376(1)
(3)	1985 s.376(7)
(4)	1985 s.376(7), Sch.24
316(1)	new
(2)	1985 s.376(1), s.377(1)(b) (changed)
317(1)	1985 s.377(3) (changed)
(2)	1985 s.377(3)
318(1)	1985 s.370A
(2)	1985 s.370(1) and (4) (changed)
(3)	1985 s.370A (changed)
319(1)	1985 s.370(5)
(2)	1985 s.370(1)
320(1)	1985 s.378(4), Table A, para.47
(2)	Table A, para.47
(3)	1985 s.378(4), Table A, paras.47 and 48 (changed)
321(1)	1985 s.373(1)(a)
(2)	1985 s.373(1)(b) (changed)
322	1985 s.374
323(1)	1985 s.375(1)(a)
(2) and (3)	1985 s.375(2) (changed)
(4)	new
324(1)	1985 s.372(1) (changed)
(2)	1985 s.372(2)(b) (changed)
325(1)	1985 s.372(3) (changed)
(2)	new
(3)	1985 s.372(4)

Section of 2006 Act	Origin
(4)	1985 s.372(4), Sch.24
326(1) and (2)	1985 s.372(6)
(3)	1985 s.372(6) (changed)
(4)	1985 s.372(6), Sch.24
327(1)	1985 s.372(5)
(2)	1985 s.372(5) (changed)
(3)	new
328(1) and (2)	new
329(1)	1985 s.373(2)
(2)	1985 s.373(2) (changed)
330(1) to (7)	Table A, para.63 (changed)
331	new
332	1985 s.381
333(1) to (4)	new
334(1) to (3)	1985 s.125(6) (changed)
(4)	1985 s.125(6)(a)
(5)	new
(6)	1985 s.125(6)(b)
(7)	1985 s.125(7) and (8)
335(1) to (6)	new

Chapter 4 Public companies: additional requirements for AGMs

Section of 2006 Act	Origin
336(1)	1985 s.366(1) (changed)
(2)	new
(3)	1985 s.366(4) (changed)
(4)	1985 s.366(4), Sch.24
337(1)	1985 s.366(1)
(2)	1985 s.369(3)(a)
338(1)	1985 s.376(1)(b)
(2)	new
(3)	1985 s.376(2) (changed)

Section of 2006 Act	Origin
(4)	1985 s.376(1), s.377(1)(a) and (2) (changed)
339(1)	1985 s.376(3) and (5)
(2)	1985 s.376(1)
(3)	1985 s.376(6)
(4)	1985 s.376(7)
(5)	1985 s.376(7), Sch.24
340(1)	new
(2)	1985 s.376(1), s.377(1)(b) (changed)

Chapter 5 Additional requirements for quoted companies

Section of 2006 Act	Origin
341(1) to (6)	new
342(1) to (4)	new
343(1) to (6)	new
344(1) to (4)	new
345(1) to (6)	new
346(1) to (5)	new
347(1) to (4)	new
348(1) to (4)	new
349(1) to (5)	new
350(1) to (5)	new
351(1) to (5)	new
352(1) and (2)	new
353(1) to (5)	new
354(1) to (4)	new

Chapter 6 Records of resolutions and meetings

Section of 2006 Act	Origin
355(1)	1985 s.382(1), s.382A(1) (changed)
(2)	new
(3)	1985 s.382(5) (changed)
(4)	1985 s.382(5), Sch.24
356(1)	drafting
(2) and (3)	1985 s.382A(2)

Section of 2006 Act	Origin
(4)	1985 s.382(2)
(5)	1985 s.382(4)
357(1) and (2)	1985 s.382B(1)
(3)	1985 s.382B(2)
(4)	1985 s.382B(2), Sch.24
(5)	1985 s.382B(3)
358(1)	1985 s.383(1) (changed)
(2)	new
(3)	1985 s.383(1)
(4)	1985 s.383(3) (changed)
(5)	1985 s.383(4) (changed)
(6)	1985 s.383(4), Sch.24
(7)	1985 s.383(5)
359	new

Chapter 7 Supplementary provisions

360(1) and (2)	new
361	new

PART 14 CONTROL OF POLITICAL DONATIONS AND EXPENDITURE

362	1985 s.347A(1) (changed)
363(1)	1985 s.347A(6), (7)(a) and (9)
(2)	1985 s.347A(6)(b) and (7)(b) and (c) (changed)
(3)	new
(4)	drafting
364(1)	drafting
(2)	1985 s.347A(4)
(3)	new
(4)	new
365(1)	1985 s.347A(5) (changed)
(2)	new
366(1)	1985 s.347C(1) (changed)

Section of 2006 Act	Origin
(2)	1985 s.347C(1), 347D(1), (2) and (3) (changed)
(3)	1985 s.347D(3) (changed)
(4)	new
(5)	1985 s.347A(10), s.347C(1), s.347D(2) and (3)
(6)	1985 s.347C(6), s.347D(9)
367(1) and (2)	new
(3)	1985 s.347C(2), s.347D(4) (changed)
(4)	new
(5)	1985 s.347C(4), s.347D(6)
(6)	1985 s.347C(2), s.347D(4) (changed)
(7)	new
368(1)	1985 s.347C(3)(b), s.347D(5)
(2)	1985 s.347C(3), s.347D(5)
369(1)	1985 s.347F(1)
(2)	1985 s.347F(2), (3) and (4)
(3)	1985 s.347F(2) and (6) (changed)
(4)	new
(5)	1985 s.347F(3)
(6)	1985 s.347F(5)
370(1)	1985 s.347I(1) (changed)
(2)	1985 s.347I(1)
(3)	1985 s.54(2), s.347I(2) (changed)
(4)	1985 s.347I(3)
(5)	new
371(1)	1985 s.347I(3)
(2)	1985 s.347I(4) and (5)
(3)	1985 s.347I(6)
(4)	1985 s.347I(7)
(5)	1985 s.347I(8)
372(1)	1985 s.347J(1)

Section of 2006 Act	Origin
(2)	1985 s.347J(2)
(3)	1985 s.347J(3)
(4)	1985 s.347J(4) and (5)
(5)	1985 s.347J(6)
373(1)	1985 s.347K(1)
(2)	1985 s.347K(2)
374(1) to (3)	new
375(1)	1985 s.347B(1)
(2)	1985 s.347B(2) (changed)
376(1) and (2)	1985 s.347B(3)
377(1)	1985 s.347B(8)
(2)	1985 s.347B(10)
(3)	1985 s.347B(9)
(4)	1985 s.347B(11)
378(1)	1985 s.s.347B(4), (6) and (7) (changed)
(2)	new
(3)	1985 s.347B(5)
379(1)	1985 s.347A(3) and (8)
(2)	1985 s.347A(10)

PART 15 ACCOUNTS AND REPORTS

Chapter 1 Introduction

380(1) to (4)	drafting
381	drafting
382(1)	1985 s.247(1)(a)
(2)	1985 s.247(1)(b) and (2)
(3) and (4)	1985 s.247(3) and (4)
(5)	1985 s.247(5) (changed)
(6)	1985 s.247(6), Sch.4 para.56(2) and (3)
(7)	drafting
383(1)	1985 s.247A(3)

Section of 2006 Act	Origin
(2)	1985 s.249(1)(a)
(3)	1985 s.249(1)(b) and (2)
(4)	1985 s.249(3)
(5) and (6)	1985 s.249(4)
(7)	1985 s.249(5) and (6)
384(1)	1985 s.247A(1) to (1B)
(2)	1985 s.247A(2) (changed)
(3)	1985 s.247A(2A)
385(1)	new
(2)	1985 s.262(1) "quoted company"
(3)	drafting
(4) to (6)	new
Chapter 2 Accounting records	
386(1) and (2)	1985 s.221(1)
(3) to (5)	1985 s.221(2) to (4)
387(1) and (2)	1985 s.221(5)
(3)	1985 s.221(6), Sch.24
388(1) to (3)	1985 s.222(1) to (3)
(4) and (5)	1985 s.222(5)
389(1) and (2)	1985 s.222(4)
(3)	1985 s.222(6)
(4)	1985 s.222(4) and (6), Sch.24
Chapter 3 A company's financial year	
390(1) to (5)	1985 s.223(1) to (5)
391(1)	1985 s.224(1)
(2)	1985 s.224(2) and (3)
(3)	1986 art.232(2) and (3)
(4)	1985 s.224(3A), 1986 art.232(3A)
(5) to (7)	1985 s.224(4) to (6)
392(1)	1985 s.225(1)

Section of 2006 Act	Origin
(2) to (6)	1985 s.225(3) to (7)
Chapter 4 Annual accounts	
393(1) and (2)	new
394	1985 s.226(1)
395(1) to (5)	1985 s.226(2) to (6)
396(1) and (2)	1985 s.226A(1) and (2)
(3)	1985 s.226A(3) (changed)
(4)	1985 s.226A(4)
(5)	1985 s.226A(5) and (6)
397	1985 s.226B
398	1985 ss.227(8), 248(1) (changed)
399(1) and (2)	1985 ss.227(1) and (8), 248(1) and (2) (changed)
(3)	1985 s.227(8)
(4)	new
400(1) and (2)	1985 s.228(1) and (2)
(3)	1985 s.228(5)
(4)	1985 s.228(3)
(5)	1985 s.228(4)
(6)	1985 s.228(6)
401(1) and (2)	1985 s.228A(1) and (2)
(3)	1985 s.228A(5)
(4)	1985 s.228A(3)
(5)	1985 s.228A(4)
(6)	1985 s.228A(6)
402	1985 s.229(5)
403(1) to (6)	1985 s.227(2) to (7)
404(1) and (2)	1985 s.227A(1) and (2)
(3)	1985 s.227A(3) (changed)
(4)	1985 s.227A(4)
(5)	1985 s.227A(5) and (6)

Section of 2006 Act	Origin
405(1) and (2)	1985 s.229(1) and (2)
(3) and (4)	1985 s.229(3)
406	1985 s.227B
407(1) to (5)	1985 s.227C(1) to (5)
408(1)	1985 s.230(1) (changed)
(2)	1985 s.230(2) (changed)
(3) and (4)	1985 s.230(3) and (4)
409(1) and (2)	1985 s.231(1) and (2) (changed)
(3) and (4)	1985 s.231(3) (changed)
(5)	1985 s.231(4)
410(1) and (2)	1985 s.231(5)
(3)	1985 s.231(6)
(4) and (5)	1985 s.231(7), Sch.24
411(1)	1985 ss.231A(1), 246(3)(b)(ai)
(2)	1985 s.231A(5)
(3) to (5)	1985 s.231A(2) to (4)
(6)	1985 s.231A(7), Sch.4 para.94(1) and (2)
(7)	1985 s.231A(6)
412(1) to (4)	new
(5)	1985 s.232(3)
(6)	1985 s.232(4), Sch.24
413(1) to (8)	new
414(1) and (2)	1985 s.233(1) and (2)
(3)	1985 s.246(8)
(4) and (5)	1985 s.233(5) (changed), Sch.24
Chapter 5 Directors' report	
415(1)	1985 s.234(1)
(2) and (3)	1985 s.234(2) and (3)
(4) and (5)	1985 s.234(5), Sch.24
416(1)	1985 s.234ZZA(1)(a) and (b)

Section of 2006 Act	Origin
(2)	1985 s.234ZZA(2)
(3)	1985 ss.234ZZA(1)(c), 246(4)(a)
(4)	1985 s.234ZZA(3) and (4) (changed)
417(1)	1985 ss.234(1)(a), 246(4)(a)
(2)	new
(3) and (4)	1985 s.234ZZB(1) and (2)
(5)	new
(6)	1985 s.234ZZB(3) and (5)
(7)	1985 s.246A(2A)
(8)	1985 s.234ZZB(4)
(9)	1985 s.234ZZB(6)
(10) and (11)	new
418(1)	1985 s.234ZA(1)
(2)	1985 ss.234(1)(b), 234ZA(2)
(3) and (4)	1985 s.234ZA(3) and (4)
(5) and (6)	1985 s.234ZA(6), Sch.24
419(1)	1985 s.234A(1)
(2)	1985 s.246(8)(b)
(3) and (4)	1985 ss.234(5), 234A(4) (changed), Sch.24

Chapter 6 Quoted companies: directors' remuneration report

420(1)	1985 s.421(1)
(2)	1985 s.234B(3) and (4) (changed)
(3)	1985 s.234B(3), Sch.24
421(1) and (2)	1985 s.234B(1) and (2) (changed)
(3)	1985 s.234B(5) and (6)
(4)	1985 s.234B(6), Sch.24
422(1)	1985 s.234C(1)
(2) and (3)	1985 s.234C(4) (changed), Sch.24

Chapter 7 Publication of accounts and reports

423(1)	1985 s.238(1) and (1A)

Section of 2006 Act	Origin
(2) and (3)	new
(4)	1985 s.238(3)
(5)	1985 s.238(6)
(6)	drafting
424(1) to (3)	1985 s.238(1) (changed)
(4)	1985 s.238(4) (changed)
(5)	new
(6)	drafting
425(1) and (2)	1985 s.238(5), Sch.24
426(1)	1985 s.251(1)
(2) and (3)	1985 s.251(2)
(4)	drafting
(5)	new
(6)	1985 s.251(5)
427(1)	1985 s.251(1) "summary financial statement"
(2)	1985 s.251(3)
(3)	1985 s.251(3A)
(4)	1985 s.251(4)
(5)	new
(6)	1985 s.251(5)
428(1)	1985 s.251(1) "summary financial statement"
(2)	1985 s.251(3)
(3)	1985 s.251(3A)
(4)	1985 s.251(4)
(5)	new
(6)	1985 s.251(5)
429(1) and (2)	1985 s.251(6), Sch.24
430(1) to (7)	new
431(1) and (2)	1985 s.239(1) and (2)
(3) and (4)	1985 s.239(3), Sch.24

Section of 2006 Act	Origin
432(1) and (2)	1985 s.239(1) and (2)
(3) and (4)	1985 s.239(3), Sch.24
433(1) to (3)	1985 ss.233(3), 234A(2) and 234C(2)
(4) and (5)	1985 ss.233(6)(a), 234A(4)(a) and 234C(4)(a), Sch.24
434(1)	1985 s.240(1) (changed)
(2)	1985 s.240(2) (changed)
(3)	1985 s.240(5)
(4) and (5)	1985 s.240(6), Sch.24
(6)	1985 s.251(7)
435(1) and (2)	1985 s.240(3) (changed)
(3)	1985 s.240(5) (changed)
(4)	new
(5) and (6)	1985 s.240(6), Sch.24
(7)	1985 s.251(7)
436(1) and (2)	1985 ss.233(3), 234A(2), 234C(2), 240(4) (changed)

Chapter 8 Public companies: laying of accounts and reports before general meeting

437(1)	1985 s.241(1) (changed)
(2)	1985 s.241(2)
(3)	drafting
438(1) to (3)	1985 s.241(2) to (4)
(4)	1985 s.241(2), Sch.24

Chapter 9 Quoted companies: members' approval of directors' remuneration report

439(1)	1985 s.241A(1) and (3)
(2)	1985 s.241A(4)
(3)	1985 s.241A(5) and (7)
(4)	1985 s.241A(6)
(5)	1985 s.241A(8)
(6)	1985 s.241A(2) and (12)
440(1)	1985 s.241A(9)
(2) and (3)	1985 s.241A(10) and (11)

Section of 2006 Act	Origin
(4)	1985 s.241A(9) and (10), Sch.24
(5)	1985 s.241A(2) and (12)
Chapter 10 Filing of accounts and reports	
441(1)	1985 s.242(1)
(2)	drafting
442(1)	drafting
(2) and (3)	1985 s.244(1) and (2) (changed)
(4) and (5)	1985 s.244(4) and (5)
(6)	new
(7)	1985 s.244(6)
443(1) to (5)	new
444(1)	1985 ss.242(1)(a) and (b), 246(5)
(2)	1985 ss.242(1)(d), 249E(1)(b) (changed)
(3)	1985 s.246(5) and (6) (changed)
(4)	1985 s.247B(2)
(5)	1985 s.246(8)
(6)	1985 ss.233(4), 234A(3), 246(7)
(7)	1985 s.236(3)
445(1)	1985 ss.242(1)(a) and (b), 246A(1)
(2)	1985 ss.242(1)(d), 249E(1)(b) (changed)
(3)	1985 s.246A(2) and (3) (changed)
(4)	1985 s.247B(2)
(5)	1985 ss.233(4), 234A(3) (changed)
(6)	new
(7)	drafting
446(1)	1985 s.242(1)(a) and (b)
(2)	1985 ss.242(1)(d), 249E(1)(b)
(3)	1985 ss.233(4), 234A(3) (changed)
(4)	new

Section of 2006 Act	Origin
(5)	drafting
447(1)	1985 s.242(1)(a), (b) and (c)
(2)	1985 ss.242(1)(d)
(3)	1985 ss.233(4), 234A(3), 234C(3) (changed)
(4)	new
448(1) to (3)	1985 s.254(1) to (3)
(4)	1985 s.254(4)
(5)	1985 s.244(6)
449(1) to (5)	1985 s.247B(1) to (5)
450(1) and (2)	1985 ss.233(1) and (2), 246(7)
(3)	1985 s.246(8), 246A(4)
(4) and (5)	1985 s.233(5), Sch.24
451(1)	1985 s.242(2)
(2) and (3)	1985 s.242(4) and (5)
(4)	1985 s.242(2), Sch.24
452(1) and (2)	1985 s.242(3)
453(1)	1985 s.242A(1)
(2)	1985 s.242A(2) (changed)
(3) and (4)	1985 s.242A(3) and (4)
(5)	new

Chapter 11 Revision of defective accounts and reports

454(1) to (3)	1985 s.245(1) to (3)
(4)	1985 s.245(4) (changed)
(5)	1985 s.245(5)
455(1) and (2)	1985 s.245A(1)
(3) to (5)	1985 s.245A(2) to (4)
456(1) to (3)	1985 s.245B(1) to (3)
(4)	1985 s.245B(3A)
(5) to (8)	1985 s.245B(4) to (7)
457(1)	1985 s.245C(1)

Section of 2006 Act	Origin
(2) and (3)	1985 s.245C(2) and (3)
(4)	1985 s.245C(4B)
(5)	1985 s.245C(1A) and (4A)
(6)	1985 s.245C(5)
(7)	1985 s.245C(4)
458(1)	1985 s.245D(1) and (3)
(2)	1985 s.245D(2)
(3)	1985 s.245E(1) and (2)
(4)	1985 s.245E(3) and (4) (changed)
(5)	1985 s.245E(3), Sch.24
459(1) to (8)	1985 s.245F(1) to (8)
460(1) and (2)	1985 s.245G(1) and (2)
(3)	drafting; 1985 s.245G(3) and (10)
(4)	1985 s.245G(7)(a) and (8)
(5)	1985 s.245G(7)(b), Sch.24
461(1)	1985 s.245G(3)
(2)	1985 s.245G(3)(a)
(3)	1985 s.245G(3)(b), Sch.7B Pt.1
(4)	1985 s.245G(3)(c), Sch.7B Pt.2
(5) and (6)	1985 s.245G(3)(d), Sch.7B Pt.3
(7)	1985 s.245G(11)
462(1) to (3)	1985 s.245G(4) to (6)

Chapter 12 Supplementary provisions

463(1) to (6)	new
464(1) and (2)	1985 s.256(1) and (2)
(3)	1985 s.256(4)
465(1)	1985 s.247(1)(a)
(2)	1985 s.247(1)(b) and (2)
(3) and (4)	1985 s.247(3) and (4)
(5)	1985 s.247(5) (changed)

Section of 2006 Act	Origin
(6)	1985 s.247(6), Sch.4 para.56(2) and (3)
(7)	drafting
466(1)	1985 s.247A(3)
(2)	1985 s.249(1)(a)
(3)	1985 s.249(1)(b) and (2)
(4)	1985 s.249(3)
(5) and (6)	1985 s.249(4)
(7)	1985 s.249(5) and (6)
467(1)	1985 s.247A(1) to (1B)
(2)	1985 s.247A(2)
(3)	1985 s.247A(2A)
468(1) to (5)	new
469(1) to (4)	1985 s.242B(1) to (4) (changed)
470(1)	1985 s.255D(1)
(2)	1985 s.255D(2), (2A)
(3)	1985 s.255D(5)
(4)	1985 s.255D(4)
471(1)	1985 s.262(1) "annual accounts"
(2) and (3)	1985 s.238(1A); drafting
472(1) and (2)	1985 s.261(1) and (2)
473(1) to (4)	1985 s.257(2), (3) (changed)
474(1)	1985 ss.262(1), 744 "regulated activity"
(2)	1985 s.262(2)

PART 16 AUDIT

Chapter 1 Requirement for audited accounts

475(1)	1985 s.235(1) (changed)
(2) and (3)	1985 s.249B(4)
(4)	1985 s.249B(5)
476(1) to (3)	1985 s.249B(2)
477(1)	1985 s.249A(1)

Section of 2006 Act	Origin
(2)	1985 s.249A(3)
(3)	1985 s.249A(6)
(4)	1985 s.249A(3)(a) and (7)
(5)	drafting
478	1985 s.249B(1)(a) to (e)
479(1) to (3)	1985 s.249B(1)(f) and (1A) to (1C)
(4)	drafting
(5) and (6)	1985 s.249B(1)(C)
480(1) and (2)	1985 s.249AA(1) and (2)
(3)	drafting
481	1985 s.249AA(3)
482(1) to (4)	new
483(1) to (5)	new
484(1)	1985 s.257(1)
484(2)	1985 s.257(4)(c)
484(3)	1985 s.257 (2)(b) and (d)
484(4)	1985 s.257 (3)
Chapter 2 Appointment of auditors	
485(1)	1985 s.384(1)
(2) to (5)	new
486(1) and (2)	1985 s.387(1) and (2)
(3) and (4)	1985 s.387(2), Sch.24
487(1) to (4)	new
488(1) to (3)	new
489(1)	1985 s.384(1) (changed)
(2)	1985 ss.384(2), 385(2)
(3)	1985 ss.385(3), 388(1) (changed)
(4)	1985 s.385(2) and (4) (changed)
(5)	drafting
490(1) and (2)	1985 s.387(1) and (2)

Section of 2006 Act	Origin
(3) and (4)	1985 s.387(2), Sch.24
491(1)	1985 s.385(2) (changed)
(2)	drafting
492(1)	1985 s.390A(1)
(2) and (3)	1985 s.390A(2)
(4) and (5)	1985 s.390A(4) and (5)
493(1) to (4)	new
494(1)	1985 s.390B(1), (8)
(2) to (4)	1985 s.390B(2) to (4)
(5)	1985 s.390B(5)(a)
(6)	1985 s.390B(9)
Chapter 3 Functions of auditor	
495(1)	1985 s.235(1); drafting
(2)	1985 s.235(1A)
(3)	1985 s.235(1B), (2)
(4)	1985 s.235(2A)
496	1985 s.235(3)
497(1) and (2)	1985 s.235(4) and (5)
498(1) to (4)	1985 s.237(1) to (4)
(5)	1985 s.237(4A)
499(1) and (2)	1985 s.389A(1) and (2)
(3)	1985 s.389A(6)
(4)	1985 s.389A(7)
500(1) to (3)	1985 s.389A(3) to (5)
(4)	1985 s.389A(6)
(5)	1985 s.389A(7)
501(1)	1985 s.389B(1)
(2)	1985 s.389B(1), Sch.24
(3)	1985 s.389B(2), (3) (changed)
(4)	1985 s.389B(4)

Section of 2006 Act	Origin
(3) and (4)	1985 s.387(2), Sch.24
491(1)	1985 s.385(2) (changed)
(2)	drafting
492(1)	1985 s.390A(1)
(2) and (3)	1985 s.390A(2)
(4) and (5)	1985 s.390A(4) and (5)
493(1) to (4)	new
494(1)	1985 s.390B(1), (8)
(2) to (4)	1985 s.390B(2) to (4)
(5)	1985 s.390B(5)(a)
(6)	1985 s.390B(9)
Chapter 3 Functions of auditor	
495(1)	1985 s.235(1); drafting
(2)	1985 s.235(1A)
(3)	1985 s.235(1B), (2)
(4)	1985 s.235(2A)
496	1985 s.235(3)
497(1) and (2)	1985 s.235(4) and (5)
498(1) to (4)	1985 s.237(1) to (4)
(5)	1985 s.237(4A)
499(1) and (2)	1985 s.389A(1) and (2)
(3)	1985 s.389A(6)
(4)	1985 s.389A(7)
500(1) to (3)	1985 s.389A(3) to (5)
(4)	1985 s.389A(6)
(5)	1985 s.389A(7)
501(1)	1985 s.389B(1)
(2)	1985 s.389B(1), Sch.24
(3)	1985 s.389B(2), (3) (changed)
(4)	1985 s.389B(4)

Section of 2006 Act	Origin
(2) and (3)	1985 s.392(3), Sch.24
518(1) to (4)	1985 s.392A(1) to (4)
(5)	1985 s.392A(5)
(6) and (7)	1985 s.392(5), Sch.24
(8) to (10)	1985 s.392A(6) to (8)
519(1) to (3)	1985 s.394(1) (changed)
(4)	1985 s.394(2) (changed)
(5) and (6)	1985 s.394A(1) and (2)
(7)	1985 s.394(1), Sch.24
520(1)	drafting
(2) and (3)	1985 s.394(3) and (4)
(4)	1985 s.394(6)
(5)	1985 s.394(7) (changed)
(6)	1985 s.394A(4)
(7)	new
(8)	1985 s.394A(4), Sch.24 (changed)
521(1)	1985 s.394(5)
(2)	1985 s.394(7)
(3) and (4)	1985 s.394A(1) and (2)
(5)	1985 s.394A(1), Sch.24
522(1) to (8)	new
523(1) to (6)	new
524(1) to 4)	new
525(1) to (3)	new
526	1985 s.388(2)

Chapter 5 Quoted companies: right of members to raise audit concerns at accounts meeting

527(1) to (6)	new
528(1) to (5)	new
529(1) to (4)	new

Section of 2006 Act	Origin
530(1) and (2)	new
531(1) and (2)	new
Chapter 6 Auditors' liability	
532(1)	1985 s.310(1) (changed)
(2)	1985 s.310(2), drafting
(3)	1985 s.310(1)
(4)	new
533	1985 s.310(3)(b)
534(1) to (3)	new
535(1) to (5)	new
536(1) to (5)	new
537(1) to (3)	new
538(1) to (3)	new
Chapter 7 Supplementary provisions	
539	1985 ss.262(1)
PART 17 A COMPANY'S SHARE CAPITAL	
Chapter 1 Shares and share capital of a company	
540(1)	1985 s.744 ("share")
(2) and (3)	new
(4)	1985 s.744 ("share"), drafting
541	1985 s.182(1)(a)
542(1) to (5)	new
543(1) and (2)	1985 s.182(2)
544(1) and (2)	1985 s.182(1)(b)
(3)	drafting
545	new
546(1) and (2)	new
547	1985 s.737(1) and (2)
548	1985 s.744 ("equity share capital")
Chapter 2 Allotment of shares: general provisions	

Section of 2006 Act	Origin
549(1)	1985 s.80(1), (2) (changed)
(2) and (3)	1985 s.80(2)
(4)	1985 s.80(9)
(5)	1985 s.80(9), Sch.24
(6)	1985 s.80(10) (changed)
550	new
551(1)	1985 s.80(1), (2)
(2)	1985 s.80(3)
(3)	1985 s.80(4)
(4)	1985 s.80(4) and (5)
(5)	1985 s.80(5)
(6)	1985 s.80(6)
(7)	1985 s.80(7)
(8)	1985 s.80(8)
(9)	drafting
552(1)	1985 s.98(1)
(2)	1985 s.98(2)
(3)	1985 s.98(3)
553(1)	1985 s.97(1)
(2)	1985 s.97(2)(a)
(3)	1985 s.98(4)
554(1) to (5)	new
555(1)	1985 s.88(1)
(2)	1985 s.88(2) (changed)
(3) and (4)	new
556(1)	1985 s.128(1) and (2) (changed)
(2) and (3)	1985 s.128(1)
(4)	1985 s.128(2)
557(1)	1985 s.88(5), s.128(5) (changed)
(2)	1985 s.88(5), s.128(5), Sch.24

Section of 2006 Act	Origin
(3)	1985 s.88(6) (changed)
558	1985 s.738(1)
559	1985 s.80(2)(a)

Chapter 3 Allotment of equity securities: existing shareholders' right of pre-emption

560(1)	1985 s.94(2) and (5)
(2)	1985 s.94(3) and (3A)
561(1)	1985 s.89(1)
(2)	1985 s.89(4)
(3)	1985 s.94(3)
(4)	1985 s.89(6)
(5)	drafting
562(1)	1985 s.90(1)
(2)	new
(3)	1985 s.90(5) (changed)
(4)	1985 s.90(6)
(5)	1985 s.90(6) (changed)
(6) and (7)	new
563(1) and (2)	1985 s.92(1)
(3)	1985 s.92(2)
564	1985 s.94(2)
565	1985 s.89(4)
566	1985 s.89(5)
567(1) and (2)	1985 s.91(1)
(3) and (4)	1985 s.91(2)
568(1)	1985 s.89(2) and (3)
(2)	1985 s.89(3)
(3)	1985 s.90(1)
(4)	1985 s.92(1)
(5)	1985 s.92(2)
569(1) and (2)	new

Section of 2006 Act	Origin
570(1) and (2)	1985 s.95(1)
(3)	1985 s.95(3)
(4)	1985 s.95(4)
571(1) and (2)	1985 s.95(2)
(3)	1985 s.95(3)
(4)	1985 s.95(4)
(5) and (6)	1985 s.95(5)
(7)	1985 s.95(5), Sch.15A para.3(1) and (2)
572(1) and (2)	1985 s.95(6)
(3)	1985 s.95(6), Sch.24
573(1)	1985 s.95(2A)
(2)	1985 s.95(1) and (2A)
(3)	1985 s.95(1), (2A) and (4)
(4)	1985 s.95(2) and (2A)
(5)	1985 s.95(1), (2A), (4) and (5), Sch.15A para.3(1) and (2)
574(1) and (2)	1985 s.94(7)
575(1)	1985 s.93(1)
(2)	1985 s.93(2)
576(1)	1985 s.96(1) and (2)
(2)	1985 s.96(3)
(3)	1985 s.96(4)
577	1985 s.94(2)

Chapter 4 Public companies: allotment where issue not fully subscribed

Section of 2006 Act	Origin
578(1)	1985 s.84(1)
(2)	1985 s.84(2)
(3)	1985 s.84(3) (changed)
(4)	1985 s.84(4)
(5)	1985 s.84(4) and (5)
(6)	1985 s.84(6)

Section of 2006 Act	Origin
579(1) and (2)	1985 s.85(1)
(3)	1985 s.85(2)
(4)	1985 s.85(3)
Chapter 5 Payment for shares	
580(1)	1985 s.100(1)
(2)	1985 s.100(2)
581	1985 s.119
582(1)	1985 s.99(1)
(2)	1985 s.99(4)
(3)	1985 s.99(1)
583(1)	drafting
(2) to (3)(d)	1985 s.738(2)
(3)(e) and (4)	new
(4)	new
(5)	1985 s.738(3)
(6)	1985 s.738(4)
(7)	new
584	1985 s.106
585(1)	1985 s.99(2)
(2)	1985 s.99(3)
(3)	1985 s.99(5)
586(1)	1985 s.101(1)
(2)	1985 s.101(2)
(3)	1985 s.101(3) and (4)
(4)	1985 s.101(5)
587(1)	1985 s.102(1)
(2)	1985 s.102(2)
(3)	1985 s.102(3) and (4)
(4)	1985 s.102(5) and (6)
(5)	1985 s.102(7)

Section of 2006 Act	Origin
588(1)	1985 s.112(1) and (5)(a)
(2)	1985 s.112(3)
(3)	1985 s.112(4)
(4)	1985 s.112(5)(b)
589(1) and (2)	1985 s.113(1)
(3)	1985 s.113(2) and (3) (changed)
(4)	1985 s.113(4)
(5)	1985 s.113(5)
(6)	1985 s.113(6) and (7)
590(1)	1985 s.114
(2)	1985 s.114. Sch.24
591(1) and (2)	1985 s.115(1)
592(1) and (2)	1985 s.107

Chapter 6 Public companies: independent valuation of non-cash consideration

593(1)	1985 s.103(1)
(2)	1985 s.103(2)
(3)	1985 s.103(6)
(4)	drafting
594(1) to (3)	1985 s.103(3)
(4) and (5)	1985 s.103(4)
(6)	1985 s.103(7)
595(1) and (2)	1985 s.103(5)
(3)	1985 s.103(7)(b)
596(1)	drafting
(2)	1985 s.108(4)
(3)	1985 s.108(6)
(4) and (5)	1985 s.108(7)
597(1) and (2)	1985 s.111(1)
(3) and (4)	1985 s.111(3), Sch.24
(5) and (6)	1985 ss.88(6), 111(3)

Section of 2006 Act	Origin
598(1)	1985 s.104(1)
(2)	1985 s.104(2)
(3)	drafting
(4)	1985 s.104(6)(a)
(5)	1985 s.104(6)(b)
599(1)	1985 s.104(4)(a), (b) and (d)
(2)	1985 s.104(5)(a)
(3)	1985 s.104(4)(d)
(4)	1985 s.104(5)(b)
600(1)	drafting
(2)	1985 s.109(2)(a) and (b)
(3)	1985 s.108(6)(a), (b) and (c), 109(2)(c) and (d)
(4) and (5)	1985 s.109(3)
601(1) and (2)	1985 s.104(4)(c) and (d)
(3)	1985 s.104(4)(c) (changed)
602(1)	1985 s.111(2)
(2) and (3)	1984 s.111(4), Sch.24
603	1985 s.104(3)
604(1)	1985 s.105(1)
(2)	1985 s.105(2)
(3)	1985 s.105(3)
605(1)	1985 s.112(1)
(2)	1985 s.112(2)
(3)	1985 s.112(3)
(4)	1985 s.112(4)
606(1)	1985 s.113(1)
(2)	1985 s.113(2) and (3) (changed)
(3)	1985 s.113(4)
(4)	1985 s.113(5)
(5)	1986 s.113(6) and (7)

Section of 2006 Act	Origin
(6)	1986 s.113(8)
607(1)	drafting
(2)	1985 s.114
(3)	1985 s.114, Sch.24
608(1) and (2)	1985 s.115(1)
609(1) and (2)	1985 s.107
Chapter 7 Share premiums	
610(1)	1985 s.130(1)
(2) and (3)	1985 s.130(2) (changed)
(4)	1985 s.130(3)
(5) and (6)	1985 s.130(4)
611(1)	1985 s.132(1)
(2)	1985 s.132(2)
(3)	1985 s.132(3)
(4)	1985 s.132(4)
(5)	1985 s.132(5)
612(1)	1985 s.131(1)
(2)	1985 s.131(2)
(3)	1985 s.131(3)
(4)	1985 s.131(1), 132(8)
613(1)	drafting
(2) and (3)	1985 s.131(4)
(4)	1985 s.131(5)
(5)	1985 s.131(6)
614(1)	1985 s.134(1)
(2)	1985 s.134(3)
615	1985 s.133(1)
616(1)	1985 s.131(7), 133(4)
(2)	1985 s.133(2)
(3)	1985 s.133(3)

Section of 2006 Act	Origin
Chapter 8 Alteration of share capital	
617(1)	1985 s.121(1) (changed)
(2)	1985 s.121(2)(a) (changed)
(3)	1985 s.121(2)(b), (c) and (d) (changed)
(4) and (5)	new
618(1)	1985 s.121(2)(b) and (d)
(2)	1985 s.121(3) (changed)
(3)	1985 s.121(4) (changed)
(4) and (5)	new
619(1)	1985 s.122(1)(a) and (d)
(2) and (3)	1985 s.122(1) (changed)
(4)	1985 s.122(2)
(5)	1985 s.122(2), Sch.24
620(1)	1985 s.121(2)(c) (changed)
(2)	1985 s.121(4) (changed)
(3)	new
621(1)	1985 s.122(1)(c)
(2) and (3)	new
(4)	1985 s.122(2)
(5)	1985 s.122(2), Sch.24
622(1) to (8)	new
623	new
624(1) to (3)	new
625(1) to (5)	new
626(1) to (6)	new
627(1) to (8)	new
628(1) to (3)	new
Chapter 9 Classes of share and class rights	
629(1)	new
(2)	1985 s.128(2)

Section of 2006 Act	Origin
630(1)	1985 s.125(1)
(2) to (4)	1985 s.125(2) (changed)
(5)	1985 s.125(7)
(6)	1985 s.125(8)
631(1) to (6)	new
632	1985 s.126 (changed)
633(1)	1985 s.127(1)(b)
(2)	1985 s.127(2) and (2A)
(3)	1985 s.127(2)
(4)	1985 s.127(3)
(5)	1985 s.127(4)
(6)	1985 s.127(6)
634(1) to (6)	new
635(1) to (3)	1985 s.127(5)
636(1)	1985 s.128(4) (changed)
(2)	1985 s.128(5)
(3)	1985 s.128(5), Sch.24
637(1)	1985 s.128(3) (changed)
(2)	1985 s.128(5)
(3)	1985 s.128(5), Sch.24
638(1)	1985 s.129(1) (changed)
(2)	1985 s.129(4)
(3)	1985 s.129(4), Sch.24
639(1)	1985 s.129(3) (changed)
(2)	1985 s.129(4)
(3)	1985 s.129(4), Sch.24
640(1)	1985 s.129(2) (changed)
(2)	1985 s.129(4)
(3)	1985 s.129(4), Sch.24

Chapter 10 Reduction of share capital

Section of 2006 Act	Origin
641(1) to (3)	1985 s.135(1) (changed)
(4)	1985 s.135(2)
(5) and (6)	new
642(1) to (4)	new
643(1) to (5)	new
644(1) to (9)	new
645(1)	1985 s.136(1)
(2)	1985 s.136(2) and (6)
(3)	1985 s.136(6)
(4)	1985 s.136(2)
646(1)	1985 s.136(3)
(2) and (3)	1985 s.136(4)
(4) and (5)	1985 s.136(5)
647(1)	1985 s.141 (changed)
(2)	1985 s.141, Sch.24
648(1) and (2)	1985 s.137(1)
(3)	1985 s.137(2)(b)
(4)	1985 s.137(2)(a) and (3)
649(1)	1985 s.138(1) (changed)
(2)	new
(3)	1985 s.138(2) (changed)
(4)	1985 s.138(3) (changed)
(5)	1985 s.138(4) (changed)
(6)	1985 s.138(4)
650(1)	1985 s.139(1)
(2)	1985 s.139(2)
(3)	drafting
651(1) and (2)	1985 s.139(3)
(3)	1985 s.139(4) (changed)
(4)	1985 s.139(5)

Section of 2006 Act	Origin
(5)	new
(6)	1985 s.139(5)(a)
(7)	1985 s.139(5)(b)
652(1)	1985 s.140(1) (changed)
(2)	drafting
(3)	1985 s.140(5)
653(1)	1985 s.140(2)
(2)	1985 s.140(3)
(3)	1985 s.140(4)
(4)	drafting

Chapter 11 Miscellaneous and supplementary provisions

654(1) to (3)	new
655	1985 s.111A
656(1) to (3)	1985 s.142(1)
(4)	1985 s.142(2) (changed)
(5)	1985 s.142(2), Sch.24
(6)	1985 s.142(3)
657(1) to (4)	new

PART 18 ACQUISITION BY LIMITED COMPANY OF ITS OWN SHARES

Chapter 1 General provisions

658(1)	1985 s.143(1)
(2)	1985 s.143(2)
(3)	1985 s.143(2), Sch.24
659(1) and (2)	1985 s.143(3)
660(1) and (2)	1985 s.144(1) (changed)
(3)	1985 s.145(1) and (2)(a)
661(1) and (2)	1985 s.144(2) (changed)
(3)	1985 s.144(3)
(4)	1985 s.144(4)
(5)	1985 s.145(2)(a)

Section of 2006 Act	Origin
662(1)	1985 s.146(1)
(2)	1985 s.146(2)
(3)	1985 s.146(2) and (3)
(4)	1985 s.147(1)
(5) and (6)	1985 s.146(4)
663(1)	1985 s.122(1)(f)
(2) and (3)	new
(4)	1985 s.122(2)
(5)	1985 s.122(2), Sch.24
664(1) and (2)	1985 s.147(2) (changed)
(3)	new
(4)	1985 s.147(3) (changed)
(5) and (6)	new
665(1) and (2)	1985 s.147(4)
(3)	new
(4)	1985 s.147(4)(a) (changed)
(5)	1985 s.147(4)(b)
666(1) and (2)	1985 s.149(1)
667(1) and (2)	1985 s.149(2)
(3)	1985 s.149(2), Sch.24
668(1) and (2)	1985 s.148(1)
(3)	1985 s.148(2)
669(1) and (2)	1985 s.148(4)
670(1)	1985 s.150(1)
(2)	1985 s.150(2)
(3)	1985 s.150(3)
(4)	1985 s.150(4)
671	1985 s.145(3), s.146(1), s.148(3)
672(1)	1985 Sch.2 para.1(1)
(2)	1985 Sch.2 para.1(2)

Section of 2006 Act	Origin
(3)	1985 Sch.2 para.1(3)
(4)	1985 Sch.2 para.1(4)
(5)	1985 Sch.2 para.2(3)
(6)	1985 Sch.2 para.2(4)
673(1)	1985 Sch.2 para.3(1)(a) and (2)
(2)	1985 Sch.2 para.3(1)(b) and (2)(a)
674	1985 Sch.2 para.4(1) and (3)
675(1) and (2)	1985 Sch.2 para.5(1) and (2)
676	1985 Sch.2 para.5(1) and (3)

Chapter 2 Financial assistance for purchase of own shares

Section of 2006 Act	Origin
677(1)	1985 s.152(1)(a)
(2) and (3)	1985 s.152(2)
678(1)	1985 s.151(1) (changed)
(2)	1985 s.153(1)
(3)	1985 s.151(2) (changed)
(4)	1985 s.153(2)
(5)	drafting
679(1)	1985 s.151(1) (changed)
(2)	1985 s.153(1) (changed)
(3)	1985 s.151(2) (changed)
(4)	1985 s.153(2) (changed)
(5)	drafting
680(1)	1985 s.151(3)
(2)	1985 s.151(3), Sch.24
681(1) and (2)	1985 s.153(3)
682(1)	1985 s.153(4), s.154(1)
(2)	1985 s.153(4)
(3) and (4)	1985 s.154(2)
(5)	1985 s.153(5)
683(1)	1985 s.152(1)(b) and (c)

Section of 2006 Act	Origin
(2)	1985 s.152(3)
Chapter 3 Redeemable shares	
684(1)	1985 s.159(1) (changed)
(2)	new
(3)	1985 s.159(1) (changed)
(4)	1985 s.159(2)
685(1) to (4)	new
686(1) to (3)	1985 s.159(3) (changed)
687(1) to (3)	1985 s.160(1)
(4) and (5)	1985 s.160(2)
(6)	1985 s.160(1)
688	1985 s.160(4) (changed)
689(1)	1985 s.122(1)(e)
(2) and (3)	new
(4)	1985 s.122(2)
(5)	1985 s.122(2), Sch.24
Chapter 4 Purchase of own shares	
690(1)	1985 s.162(1) (changed)
(2)	1985 s.162(3)
691(1) and (2)	1985 s.159(3), s.162(2)
692(1) and (2)	1985 s.160(1), s.162(2)
(3) and (4)	1985 s.160(2), s.162(2)
(5)	1985 s.160(1), s.162(2)
693(1)	1985 s.164(1), s.166(1)
(2)	1985 s.163(1)
(3)	1985 s.163(2)
(4)	1985 s.163(3)
(5)	1985 s.163(4) and (5)
694(1)	1985 s.164(1)
(2)	1985 s.164(2), s.165(2) (changed)

Section of 2006 Act	Origin
(3)	1985 s.165(1)
(4)	1985 s.164(3), 165(2)
(5)	1985 s.164(4), 165(2)
(6)	drafting
695(1)	1985 s.164(5), 165(2)
(2)	1985 Sch.15A para.5(1) and (2)
(3) and (4)	1985 s.164(5), s.165(2)
696(1)	1985 s.164(6), s.165(2)
(2)	1985 s.164(6), s.165(2), Sch.15A, para.5(3) and (4)
(3) to (5)	1985 s.164(6), s.165(2)
697(1) and (2)	1985 s.164(7)
(3)	1985 s.164(3) and (7)
(4)	1985 s.164(4) and (7)
(5)	drafting
698(1)	1985 s.164(5) and (7)
(2)	1985 Sch.15A, para.5(1) and (2)
(3) and (4)	1985 s.164(5) and (7)
699(1)	1985 s.164(6) and (7)
(2)	1985 s.164(6) and (7), Sch.15A para.5(3)
(3) to (6)	1985 s.164(6) and (7)
700(1) and (2)	1985 s.167(2)
(3)	1985 s.164(3) and (7), s.167(2)
(4)	1985 s.164(4) and (7), s.167(2)
(5)	1985 s.164(5), (6) and (7), s.167(2)
701(1)	1985 s.166(1)
(2)	1985 s.166(2)
(3)	1985 s.166(3)(a) and (b)
(4)	1985 s.166(4)
(5)	1985 s.166(3)(c) and (4)
(6)	1985 s.166(5)

Section of 2006 Act	Origin
(7)	1985 s.166(6)
(8)	1985 s.166(7)
702(1) to (4)	1985 s.169(4) (changed)
(5)	new
(6)	1985 s.169(5)
(7)	1985 s.169(9)
703(1)	1985 s.169(7) (changed)
(2)	1985 s.169(7), Sch.24
(3)	1985 s.169(8)
704	1985 s.167(1)
705(1)	1985 s.168(1)
(2)	1985 s.168(2)
706	1985 s.160(4), s.162(2) and (2B)
707(1) to (3)	1985 s.169(1), (1A) and (1B) (changed)
(4)	1985 s.169(2)
(5)	1985 s.169(3)
(6)	1985 s.169(6)
(7)	1985 s.169(6), Sch.24
708(1)	1985 s.169(1), (1A) and (1B) (changed)
(2) and (3)	new
(4)	1985 s.169(6)
(5)	1985 s.169(6), Sch.24
Chapter 5 Redemption or purchase by private company out of capital	
709(1)	1985 s.171(1) (changed)
(2)	1985 s.171(2)
710(1) and (2)	1985 s.171(3)
711(1) and (2)	1985 s.172(1)
712(1)	drafting
(2)	1985 s.172(2)
(3)	1985 s.172(4)

Section of 2006 Act	Origin
(4)	1985 s.172(5)
(5)	drafting
(6)	1985 s.172(3)
(7)	1985 s.172(6)
713(1) and (2)	1985 s.173(1)
714(1) to (3)	1985 s.173(3) (changed)
(4)	1985 s.173(4) (changed)
(5) and (6)	1985 s.173(5) (changed)
715(1)	1985 s.173(6)
(2)	1985 s.173(6), Sch.24
716(1)	1985 s.173(2)
(2)	1985 s.174(1)
(3)	drafting
717(1)	drafting
(2)	1985 Sch.15A para.6(1) and (2)
(3)	1985 s.174(2)
(4)	1985 s.174(3) and (5)
718(1)	drafting
(2)	1985 s.174(4), Sch.15A para.6(1) and (3)
(3)	1985 s.174(4)
719(1)	1985 s.175(1)
(2)	1985 s.175(2)
(3)	1985 s.175(3)
(4)	1985 s.175(4) and (5)
720(1)	1985 s.175(4) and (6)(a)
(2)	1985 s.175(6)(a) (changed)
(3)	new
(4)	1985 s.175(6)(b)
(5)	1985 s.175(7) (changed)
(6)	1985 s.175(7), Sch.24

Section of 2006 Act	Origin
(7)	1985 s.175(8)
721(1)	1985 s.176(1)
(2)	1985 s.176(1) and (2)
(3)	1985 s.177(1)
(4) and (5)	1985 s.177(2)
(6)	1985 s.177(3)
(7)	1985 s.177(4)
722(1)	new
(2)	1985 s.176(3)(a)
(3)	1985 s.176(3)(b)
(4)	1985 s.176(4)
(5)	1985 s.176(4), Sch.24
723(1)	1985 s.174(1)
(2)	drafting
Chapter 6 Treasury shares	
724(1)	1985 s.162(2B)
(2)	1985 s.162(4)
(3)	1985 s.162A(1)
(4)	1985 s.162A(2)
(5)	1985 s.162A(3)
725(1)	1985 s.162B(1)
(2)	1985 s.162B(2)
(3)	1985 s.162B(3)
(4)	1985 s.143(2A)
726(1)	1985 s.162C(1)
(2)	1985 s.162C(2) and (3)
(3)	1985 s.162C(4)
(4)	1985 s.162C(5)
(5)	1985 s.162C(6)
727(1)	1985 s.162D(1)(a) and (b)

Section of 2006 Act	Origin
(2)	1985 s.162D(2) (changed)
(3)	1985 s.162D(3)
(4) and (5)	new
728(1)	1985 s.169A(1)(b)(ii) and (2)
(2)	1985 s.169A(2)
(3)	1985 s.169A(3)
(4)	1985 s.169A(4)
(5)	1985 s.169A(4), Sch.24
729(1)	1985 s.162D(1)(c)
(2)	1985 s.162E(1)
(3)	1985 s.162E(2)
(4)	1985 s.162D(4)
(5)	1985 s.162D(5)
730(1)	1985 s.169A(1)(b)(i) and (2)
(2)	1985 s.169A(2)
(3)	1985 s.169A(3)
(4) and (5)	new
(6)	1985 s.169A(4)
(7)	1985 s.169A(4), Sch.24
731(1)	1985 s.162F(1)
(2)	1985 s.162F(2)
(3)	1985 s.162F(3)
(4)	1985 s.162F(4) and (5)
732(1)	1985 s.162G (changed)
(2)	1985 s.162G

Chapter 7 Supplementary provisions

733(1) and (2)	1985 s.170(1)
(3)	1985 s.170(2) and (3)
(4)	1985 s.170(1)
(5) and (6)	1985 s.170(4)

Section of 2006 Act	Origin
734(1)	drafting
(2)	1985 s.171(4)
(3)	1985 s.171(5)
(4)	1985 s.171(6)
735(1)	1985 s.178(1)
(2)	1985 s.178(2) and (3)
(3)	1985 s.178(3)
(4)	1985 s.178(4)
(5)	1985 s.178(5)
(6)	1985 s.178(6)
736	1985 s.181(a)
737(1) to (4)	new
PART 19 DEBENTURES	
738	1985 s.744 ("debenture")
739(1) and (2)	1985 s.193
740	1985 s.195
741(1) to (4)	new
742	1985 s.197
743(1)	new
(2)	1985 s.190(5) (changed)
(3)	1985 s.190(6)
(4) and (5)	new
(6)	1985 s.190(1) and (5)
744(1)	1985 s.191(1)
(2)	1985 s.191(2)
(3) and (4)	new
(5)	1985 s.191(6)
(6)	new
745(1) to (5)	new
746(1)	1985 s.191(4) (changed)

Section of 2006 Act	Origin
(2)	1985 s.191(4), Sch.24
(3)	1985 s.191(5)
747(1) to (3)	new
748(1)	1985 s.191(7) (changed)
(2)	1985 s.191(7)
749(1)	1985 s.191(3)
(2)	1985 s.191(4)
(3)	1985 s.191(4), Sch.24
(4)	1985 s.191(5)
750(1)	1985 s.192(1)
(2)	1985 s.192(2)
(3)	1985 s.192(1)
751(1)	1985 s.192(3)
(2)	1985 s.192(3), 1986 art.201(3)
(3) and (4)	1985 s.192(4)
752(1)	1985 s.194(1)
(2)	1985 s.194(2)
(3)	1985 s.194(4)
(4)	1985 s.194(5)
753	1985 s.194(3)
754(1)	1985 s.196(1)
(2)	1985 s.196(2)
(3)	1985 s.196(3)
(4)	1985 s.196(4)

PART 20 PUBLIC AND PRIVATE COMPANIES

Chapter 1 Prohibition of public offers by private companies

755(1)	1985 s.81(1) (changed)
(2)	1985 s.58(3)
(3) and (4)	new
(5)	drafting

Section of 2006 Act	Origin
756(1) and (2)	1985 s.742A(1)
(3)	1985 s.742A(2)
(4)	1985 s.742A(3), (4), and (5)
(5)	1985 s.742A(3)(a) and (6)(b) (changed)
(6)	1985 s.742A(6)(a)
757(1) to (3)	new
758(1) to (4)	new
759(1) to (5)	new
760	1985 s.81(3)
Chapter 2 Minimum share capital requirement for public companies	
761(1)	1985 s.117(1)
(2)	1985 s.117(2) (changed)
(3)	1985 s.117(4)
(4)	1985 s.117(6) (changed)
762(1)	1985 s.117(3) (changed)
(2)	new
(3)	1985 s.117(5)
763(1)	1985 s.118(1) (changed)
(2) to (6)	new
764(1)	1985 s.118(1) (changed)
(2)	new
(3)	1985 s.118(2)
(4)	1985 s.118(3)
765(1) to (4)	new
766(1) to (6)	new
767(1)	1985 s.117(7)
(2)	1985 s.117(7), Sch.24
(3)	1985 s.117(8)
(4)	new
PART 21 CERTIFICATION AND TRANSFER OF SECURITIES	

Section of 2006 Act	Origin
Chapter 1 Certification and transfer of securities: general	
768(1)	1985 s.186(1)(a)
(2)	1985 s.186(1)(b) and (2)
769(1)	1985 s.185(1)(a)
(2)	1985 s.185(1), (4)(a) and (b)
(3)	1985 s.185(5)
(4)	1985 s.185(5), Sch.24
770(1)	1985 s.183(1)
(2)	1985 s.183(2)
771(1) to (6)	new
772	1985 s.183(4)
773	1985 s.183(3)
774	1985 s.187
775(1) and (2)	1985 s.184(1)
(3)	1985 s.184(2)
(4)	1985 s.184(3)
776(1)	1985 s.185(1)(b)
(2)	1985 s.185(2)
(3)	1985 s.185(1) and (4)(c)
(4)	drafting
(5)	1985 s.185(5)
(6)	1985 s.185(5), Sch.24
777(1) and (2)	1985 s.185(3)
778(1)	1985 s.185(4) and (4A)
(2)	1985 s.185(4B) and (4C)
(3)	1985 s.185(4D)
779(1)	1985 s.188(1)
(2)	1985 s.188(2)
(3)	1985 s.188(3)
780(1) to (4)	new

Section of 2006 Act	Origin
781(1)	1985 s.189(1)
(2)	1985 s.189(2)
(3)	1985 s.189(1), Sch.24
(4)	1985 s.189(2), Sch.24
782(1)	1985 s.185(6)
(2) and (3)	1985 s.185(7)
Chapter 2 Evidencing and transfer of title to securities without written instrument	
783	1989 s.207(1) and (10)
784(1) and (2)	new
(3)	1989 s.207(9)
785(1)	1989 s.207(1)
(2)	1989 s.207(2)
(3)	1989 s.207(3)
(4)	1989 s.207(4)
(5)	1989 s.207(5)
(6)	1989 s.207(6)
786(1) to (5)	new
787(1) to (3)	new
788	1989 s.207(7)
789	new
790	new
PART 22 INFORMATION ABOUT INTERESTS IN A COMPANY'S SHARES	
791	new
792(1)	1985 s.198(2) (changed)
(2)	1985 s.198(2)(b)
793(1) and (2)	1985 s.212(1) (changed)
(3)	1985 s.212(2)(a)
(4)	1985 s.212(2)(b)
(5)	1985 s.212(3)
(6)	1985 s.212(2)(c)

Section of 2006 Act	Origin
(7)	1985 s.212(4)
794(1)	1985 s.216(1)
(2)	1985 s.216(1B)
(3)	1985 s.216(1A)
(4)	drafting
795(1)	1985 s.216(3)
(2)	1985 s.216(4)
(3)	1985 s.216(3), Sch.24
796(1) and (2)	1985 s.216(5)
797(1)	1985 s.454(1)
(2)	1985 s.454(2)
(3)	1985 s.454(3)
(4)	1985 s.454(2) and (3)
798(1) and (2)	1985 s.455(1)
(3)	1985 s.455(2)
(4)	1985 s.455(2), Sch.24
(5)	1985 s.455(1) and (2)
799(1)	1985 s.456(1A)
(2)	1985 s.456(2)
(3)	1985 s.456(1A)
800(1)	1985 s.456(1)
(2)	1985 s.456(2)
(3)	1985 s.456(3)
(4)	1985 s.456(6)
(5)	1985 s.456(7)
801(1) and (2)	1985 s.456(4)
(3) and (4)	1985 s.456(5)
(5)	1985 s.457(3)
802(1) and (2)	1985 s.457(1)
(3)	1985 s.457(2)

Section of 2006 Act	Origin
(4)	1985 s.457(3)
803(1) and (2)	1985 s.214(1) (changed)
(3)	1985 s.214(2) (changed)
804(1)	1985 s.214(4)
(2)	1985 s.214(5) (changed)
(3)	1985 s.214(5), Sch.24
805(1)	1985 s.215(1) and (3)
(2)	1985 s.215(2)
(3)	1985 s.215(2) and (3)
(4)	1985 s.215(7) (changed)
(5)	new
(6)	1985 s.215(5)
(7)	1985 s.215(6)
806(1) and (2)	new
(3)	1985 s.215(8) (changed)
(4)	1985 s.215(8), Sch.24
807(1)	1985 s.215(7)(b), s.219(1)
(2)	1985 s.215(7)(b), s.219(2)
(3)	1985s.215(7)(b), s.219(3)
(4)	1985s.215(7)(b), s.219(3), Sch.24
(5)	1985 s.215(7)(b), s.219(4)
808(1)	1985 s.213(1)
(2)	1985 s.211(3), s.213(1) and (3)
(3)	1985 s.213(1) (changed)
(4)	1985 s.211(5), s.213(3)
(5)	1985 s.211(10), s.213(3)
(6)	1985 s.211(10), s.213(3), Sch.24
(7)	1985 s.211(4), s.213(3)
809(1)	1985 s.211(8), s.213(3) (changed)
(2) and (3)	s.211(8), s.213(3), s.325(5), Sch.13, para.27

Section of 2006 Act	Origin
(4) and (5)	new
810(1) to (3)	1985 s.211(6), s.213(3)
(4)	1985 s.211(8), s.213(3)
(5) and (6)	new
811(1)	1985 s.211(8)(b), s.213(3), s.219(1)
(2)	1985 s.211(8)(b), s.213(3), s.219(2) (changed)
(3)	new
(4)	new
812(1) to (7)	new
813(1)	1985 s.211(8)(b), s.213(3), s.219(3) (changed)
(2)	1985 s.211(8)(b), s.213(3), s.219(3), Sch.24
(3)	1985 s.211(8)(b), s.213(3), s.219(4)
814(1) to (3)	new
815(1)	1985 s.218(1)
(2)	1985 s.218(2)
(3)	1985 s.218(3)
(4)	1985 s.218(3), Sch.24
816	1985 s.217(1) (changed)
817(1)	1985 s.217(2) (changed)
(2) and (3)	1985 s.217(3)
(4)	1985 s.217(5)
818(1) and (2)	1985 s.217(4)
(3)	1985 s.217(5)
819(1)	1985 s.211(7), s.213(3)
(2)	1985 s.211(10), s.213(3)
(3)	1985 s.211(10), s.213(3), Sch.24
820(1)	1985 s.208(1), s.212(5)
(2)	1985 s.208(2), s.212(5)
(3)	1985 s.208(3), s.212(5)
(4)	1985 s.208(4), s.212(5)

Section of 2006 Act	Origin
(5)	1985 s.208(6), s.212(5)
(6)	1985 s.208(5), s.212(5)
(7)	1985 s.208(7), s.212(5)
(8)	1985 s.208(8), s.212(5)
821(1) and (2)	1985 s.212(6)
822(1) and (2)	1985 s.203(1), s.212(5)
823(1)	1985 s.203(2), s.212(5)
(2)	1985 s.203(3), s.212(5)
(3)	1985 s.203(4), s.212(5)
824(1)	1985 s.204(1) and (2), s.212(5)
(2)	1985 s.204(2), s.212(5)
(3)	1985 s.204(3), s.212(5)
(4)	1985 s.204(4), s.212(5)
(5)	1985 s.204(5), s.212(5)
(6)	1985 s.204(6), s.212(5)
825(1)	1985 s.205(1), s.212(5)
(2)	1985 s.205(2), s.212(5)
(3)	1985 s.205(3), s.212(5)
(4)	1985 s.205(4), s.212(5)
826(1)	1985 s.211(9), s.213(3), s.215(4)
(2)	1985 s.215(4)
827	1985 s.220(2) (changed)
828(1) and (2)	1985 s.210A(1)
(3)	1985 s.210A(5)

PART 23 DISTRIBUTIONS

Chapter 1 Restrictions on when distributions may be made

829(1) and (2)	1985 s.263(2)
830(1)	1985 s.263(1)
(2) and (3)	1985 s.263(3)
831(1)	1985 s.264(1)

Section of 2006 Act	Origin
(2) and (3)	1985 s.264(2)
(4)	1985 s.264(3)
(5)	1985 s.264(4)
(6)	1985 s.264(1)
832(1) to (3)	1985 s.265(1)
(4)	1985 s.265(2)
(5)	1985 s.265(4) and (6)
(6)	1985 s.265(4A) and (5)
(7)	1985 s.265(3)
833(1)	1985 s.266(1)
(2)	1985 s.266(2)
(3)	1985 s.266(2A)
(4) and (5)	1985 s.266(3)
834(1)	1985 s.266(2)(b)
(2)	1985 s.266(4), ICTA s.842(1A)
(3)	1985 s.266(4), ICTA s.842(2)
(4)	1985 s.266(4), ICTA s.842(3)
(5)	1985 s.266(4), ICTA s.838, s.842(1A) and (4)
835(1)	1985 s.267(1)
(2)	1985 s.267(2)(b)

Chapter 2 Justification of distribution by reference to accounts

836(1)	1985 s.270(1) and (2)
(2)	1985 s.270(3) and (4)
(3) and (4)	1985 s.270(5)
837(1)	1985 s.270(3)
(2)	1985 s.271(2)
(3)	1985 s.271(3)
(4)	1985 s.271(3) and (4)
(5)	1985 s.271(5)
838(1)	1985 s.270(4)

Section of 2006 Act	Origin
(2)	1985 s.272(1)
(3)	1985 s.272(2)
(4) and (5)	1985 s.272(3)
(6)	1985 s.272(4) and (5)
839(1)	1985 s.270(4)
(2)	1985 s.273(1)
(3)	1985 s.273(2)
(4)	1985 s.272(3), s.273(3)
(5)	1985 s.273(4)
(6)	1985 s.273(4) and (5)
(7)	1985 s.273(6) and (7)
840(1)	1985 s.274(1) and (2)
(2)	1985 s.274(2)
(3)	1985 s.274(3) ("financial assistance")
(4)	1985 s.154(2)(a), s.274(3) ("net assets" and "net liabilities")
(5)	1985 s.154(2)(b), s.274(3) ("net liabilities")
Chapter 3 Supplementary provisions	
841(1) and (2)	1985 s.275(1)
(3)	1985 s.275(1A)
(4)	1985 s.275(4), (5) and (6)
(5)	1985 s.275(2)
842	1985 s.275(3)
843(1)	1985 s.268(1)
(2)	1985 s.268(1)(a)
(3)	1985 s.268(2)(aa), (a)
(4)	1985 s.268(1)(b), (2)(b)
(5)	1985 s.268(1)
(6)	1985 s.268(3)(a)
(7)	1985 s.268(3)(b) and (4)

Section of 2006 Act	Origin
844(1)	1985 s.269(1)
(2) and (3)	1985 s.269(2)
845(1) to (5)	new
846(1) and (2)	1985 s.276 (changed)
847(1) and (2)	1985 s.277(1)
(3) and (4)	1985 s.277(2)
848(1)	1985 s.278
(2)	1985 s.278, 1986 art.286
849	1985 s.263(4)
850(1) and (2)	1985 s.263(5)
(3)	1985 s.263(5), 1986 art.271(5)
851(1)	1985 s.281 (changed)
(2) and (3)	new
852	1985 s.281
853(1)	1985 s.280(1)
(2)	1985 s.280(3)
(3)	1985 s.280(2)
(4) and (5)	1985 s.262(3), s.742(2)
(6)	1985 s.262(1), s.742(1)

PART 24 A COMPANY'S ANNUAL RETURN

854(1) and (2)	1985 s.363(1)
(3)	1985 s.363(2) (changed)
855(1)	1985 s.364(1) (changed)
(2)	1985 s.364(2)
(3)	1985 s.364(3)
856(1)	1985 s.364A(1)
(2)	1985 s.364A(2) and (3) (changed)
(3)	1985 s.364A(4) (changed)
(4)	1985 s.364A(5)
(5)	1985 s.364A(6)

Section of 2006 Act	Origin
(6)	1985 s.364A(8)
857(1) and (2)	1985 s.365(1)
(3)	1985 s.365(2)
858(1)	1985 s.363(3) and (4) (changed)
(2)	1985 s.363(3) and (4), Sch.24
(3)	1985 s.363(3)
(4)	1985 s.363(4)
(5)	new
859	1985 s.365(3)

PART 25 COMPANY CHARGES

Chapter 1 Companies registered in England and Wales or in Northern Ireland

860(1)	1985 ss.395(1), 399(1)
(2)	1985 s.399(1)
(3)	1985 s.399(2)
(4) to (6)	1985 s.399(3), Sch.24 (changed)
(7)	1985 s.396(1)
861(1)	1985 s.396(3)
(2)	1985 s.396(1)(d)
(3)	1985 s.396(2)
(4)	1985 s.396(3A)
(5)	1985 ss.395(1) ("company"), 396(4) ("charge"), 400(1) ("company")
862(1)	1985 s.400(1)
(2) and (3)	1985 s.400(2)
(4) and (5)	1985 s.400(4), Sch.24 (changed)
863(1) to (4)	1985 s.397(1)
(5)	1985 s.399(1) to (3)
864(1)	1985 s.397(2)
(2)	1985 s.397(3)
(3)	1985 s.397(2)

Section of 2006 Act	Origin
865(1)	1985 s.402(1)
(2)	1985 s.402(2)
(3) and (4)	1985 s.402(3), Sch.24
866(1)	1985 s.398(1)
(2)	1985 s.398(3)
867(1) and (2)	1985 s.398(4)
868(1) and (2)	1986 art.408(1)
(3)	1986 art.408(2)
(4)	1986 art.408(3)
(5)	Drafting
869(1)	1985 s.401(1) (opening words)
(2)	1985 s.401(1)(a)
(3)	1986 art.409(2)(b)
(4)	1985 s.401(1)(b)
(5) and (6)	1985 s.401(2)
(7)	1985 s.401(3)
870(1)	1985 ss.395(1), 398(2)
(2)	1985 s.400(2) and (3)
(3)	1985 s.397(1)
871(1)	1985 s.405(1)
(2)	1985 s.405(2)
(3)	1985 s.405(1) and (2)
(4) and (5)	1985 s.405(4), Sch.24
872(1) and (2)	1985 s.403(1) (changed)
(3)	1985 s.403(2)
873(1)	1985 s.404(1)
(2)	1985 s.404(2)
874(1) and (2)	1985 s.395(1)
(3)	1985 s.395(2)
875(1)	1985 s.406(1), 1986 art.414(1)

Section of 2006 Act	Origin
(2)	1985 s.406(2)
876(1)	1985 s.407(1)
(2)	1985 s.407(2)
(3) and (4)	1985 s.407(3), Sch.24
877(1)	1985 s.408(1)
(2)	1985 ss.406(1), 407(1), 408(1) (changed)
(3)	new
(4)	1985 s.408(1) and (2) (changed)
(5) and (6)	1985 s.408(3), Sch.24 (changed)
(7)	1985 s.408(4)
Chapter 2 Companies registered in Scotland	
878(1)	1985 ss.410(2), 415(1)
(2)	1985 s.415(1)
(3)	1985 s.415(2)
(4) to (6)	1985 s.415(3), Sch.24 (changed)
(7)	1985 s.410(4)
879(1)	1985 s.410(4)(a)
(2)	1985 s.413(1)
(3)	1985 s.410(4)(a)
(4)	1985 s.412
(5)	1985 s.410(5)
(6)	1985 s.410(5) ("company")
880(1) and (2)	1985 s.416(1)
(3) and (4)	1985 s.416(3), Sch.24 (changed)
881(1)	1985 s.414(1)
(2) and (3)	1985 s.414(2)
882(1) to (4)	1985 s.413(2)
(5)	1985 s.415(1) to (3)
883(1) to (3)	1985 s.413(3)
884	1985 s.411(2)

Section of 2006 Act	Origin
885(1)	1985 s.417(1)
(2)	1985 s.417(2)
(3)	1985 s.417(3)
(4)	1985 s.418(1) and (2)(b)
(5)	1985 s.418(2)(a) and (c)
(6)	1985 s.417(4)
886(1)	1985 ss.410(2), 411(1)
(2)	1985 s.416(1) and (2)
(3)	1985 s.413(2)
887(1)	1985 s.419(1) (changed)
(2)	1985 s.419(1B)(a) and (c), (3) (changed)
(3)	1985 s.419(1)
(4)	1985 s.419(2)
(5)	1985 s.419(4)
888(1) and (2)	1985 s.420
889(1)	1985 s.410(2)
(2)	1985 s.410(3)
890(1)	1985 s.421(1)
(2)	1985 s.421(2)
891(1)	1985 s.422(1)
(2)	1985 s.422(2)
(3) and (4)	1985 s.422(3), Sch.24
892(1)	1985 s.423(1)
(2)	1985 ss.421(1), 422(1), 423(1) (changed)
(3)	new
(4)	1985 s.423(1) and (2) (changed)
(5) and (6)	1985 s.423(3), Sch.24 (changed)
(7)	1985 s.423(4)

Chapter 3 Powers of the Secretary of State

893(1) to (9)	new

Section of 2006 Act	Origin
894(1) and (2)	new
PART 26 ARRANGEMENTS AND RECONSTRUCTIONS	
895(1)	1985 s.425(1)
(2)	1985 ss.425(6), 427(6)
(3)	drafting
896(1) and (2)	1985 s.425(1)
897(1)	1985 s.426(1), (2) and (3)
(2)	1985 s.426(2)
(3)	1985 s.426(4)
(4)	1985 s.426(5)
(5) to (8)	1985 s.426(6), Sch.24
898(1) to (3)	1985 s.426(7), Sch.24
899(1)	1985 s.425(2)
(2)	new
(3)	1985 s.425(2)
(4)	1985 s.425(3)
900(1)	1985 s.427(1) and (2)
(2)	1985 s.427(2) and (3)
(3) and (4)	1985 s.427(4)
(5)	1985 s.427(6)
(6) to (8)	1985 s.427(5), Sch.24
901(1) and (2)	new
(3) and (4)	1985 s.425(3) (changed)
(5) and (6)	1985 s.425(4), Sch.24
PART 27 MERGERS AND DIVISIONS OF PUBLIC COMPANIES	
Chapter 1 Introductory	
902(1)	1985 s.427A(1)
(2)	drafting
(3)	1985 s.427A(4)
903(1)	1985 s.427A(1)

Section of 2006 Act	Origin
(2) and (3)	drafting
Chapter 2 Merger	
904(1)	1985 s.427A(2) Cases 1 and 2
(2)	drafting
905(1)	1985 Sch.15B para.2(1)(a)
(2) and (3)	1985 Sch.15B para.2(2)
906(1) and (2)	1985 Sch.15B para.2(1)(b)
(3)	1985 Sch.15B para.2(1)(c)
907(1)	1985 s.425(2), Sch.15B para.1
(2)	1985 s.427A(1) closing words, Sch.15B para.1 opening words
908(1)	1985 Sch.15B para.3(a)
(2)	1985 Sch.15B para.4(1)
(3)	1985 Sch.15B para.3 opening words
909(1)	1985 Sch.15B para.3(d)
(2)	1985 Sch.15B para.5(1)
(3)	1985 Sch.15B para.5(1) and (2)
(4)	1985 Sch.15B para.5(3)
(5)	1985 Sch.15B para.5(7)
(6)	1985 Sch.15B para.5(8)
(7)	1985 Sch.15B para.3 opening words
910(1)	1985 Sch.15B para.6(1)(e)
(2)	1985 Sch.15B para.6(2)
(3)	1985 Sch.15B para.6(3) (changed)
(4)	1985 Sch.15B para.6(4)
911(1) and (2)	1985 Sch.15B para.3(e)
(3)	1985 Sch.15B para.6(1)
(4)	1985 Sch.15B para.3 opening words
912	1985 Sch.15B para.3(f)
913(1)	1985 Sch.15B para.8(1)

Section of 2006 Act	Origin
(2)	1985 Sch.15B para.8(2)
914	1985 Sch.15B para.7
915(1)	1985 Sch.15B para.12(1)
(2)	1985 Sch.15B para.12(2)
(3) to (5)	1985 Sch.15B para.12(3)
(6)	1985 Sch.15B para.12(1)(a) and (b)
916(1)	1985 Sch.15B para.14(1)
(2)	1985 Sch.15B para.14(2)
(3) to (5)	1985 Sch.15B paras.10(2), 14(3)
(6)	1985 Sch.15B para14(1)(a) and (b)
917(1)	1985 Sch.15B para.12(1)
(2)	1985 Sch.15B para.12(4)
(3) to (5)	1985 Sch.15B para.12(5)
(6)	1985 Sch.15B para.12(1)(a) and (b)
918(1)	1985 Sch.15B para.10(1)
(2) to (4)	1985 Sch.15B para.10(2)
Chapter 3 Division	
919(1)	1985 s.427A(2) Case 3
(2)	drafting
920(1)	1985 Sch.15B para.2(1)(a)
(2)	1985 Sch.15B para.2(2)
(3)	1985 Sch.15B para.2(3)
921(1) and (2)	1985 Sch.15B para.2(1)(b)
(3)	1985 Sch.15B para.2(1)(c)
(4)	1985 Sch.15B para.2(1)(b) and (c) opening words
922(1)	1985 s.425(2), Sch.15B para.1
(2)	1985 s.427A(1) closing words, Sch.15B para.1 opening words
923(1)	1985 Sch.15B para.3(a)
(2)	1985 Sch.15B para.4(1)

Section of 2006 Act	*Origin*
(3)	1985 Sch.15B para.4(2)
(4)	1985 Sch.15B para.3 opening words
924(1)	1985 Sch.15B para.3(d)
(2)	1985 Sch.15B para.5(1)
(3)	1985 Sch.15B para.5(1) and (2)
(4)	1985 Sch.15B para.5(3)
(5)	1985 Sch.15B para.5(7)
(6)	1985 Sch.15B para.5(8)
(7)	1985 Sch.15B para.3 opening words
925(1)	1985 Sch.15B para.6(1)(e)
(2)	1985 Sch.15B para.6(2)
(3)	1985 Sch.15B para.6(3) (changed)
(4)	1985 Sch.15B para.6(4)
(5)	1985 Sch.15B para.3 opening words
926(1) and (2)	1985 Sch.15B para.3(e)
(3)	1985 Sch.15B para.6(1)
(4)	1985 Sch.15B para.3 opening words
927(1)	1985 Sch.15B para.3(b)
(2)	1985 Sch.15B para.3(c)
(3)	1985 Sch.15B para.3 opening words
928	1985 Sch.15B para.3(f)
929(1)	1985 Sch.15B para.8(1)
(2)	1985 Sch.15B para.8(2)
930	1985 Sch.15B para.7
931(1)	1985 Sch.15B para.13(1)
(2)	1985 Sch.15B para.13(2)
(3)	1985 Sch.15B paras.12(5)(a), 13(3)(a)
(4)	1985 Sch.15B para.13(3)(b)
(5)	1985 Sch.15B paras.12(5)(c), 13(3)(a)
(6)	1985 Sch.15B para.13(3)(c)

Section of 2006 Act	Origin
932(1)	1985 Sch.15B para.10(1)
(2) to (4)	1985 Sch.15B para.10(2)
(5)	1985 Sch.15B para.10(2) opening words
933(1) to (3)	1985 Sch.15B para.11(1) and (2)
934(1)	1985 Sch.15B para.11(1) and (3)
(2)	1985 Sch.15B para.11(4)(a) and (b)
(3)	1985 Sch.15B para.11(4)(c)
(4)	1985 Sch.15B para.11(4)(d)

Chapter 4 Supplementary provisions

935(1)	1985 Sch.15B para.5(4) (changed)
(2)	1985 Sch.15B para.5(6)
936(1) to (4)	new
937(1) to (6)	new
938(1) and (2)	1985 s.427A(3)
939(1)	1985 Sch.15B para.9(1) and (2)
(2)	1985 Sch.15B para.9(2)
(3) and (4)	1985 Sch.15B para.9(3)
(5)	1985 Sch.15B para.9(4)
940(1)	1985 Sch.15B para.15(1)
(2)	1985 Sch.15B para.15(2)
(3)	1985 Sch.15B para.15(1)
941	1985 ss.427(6), 427A(8)

PART 28 TAKEOVERS ETC

[Note: The Takeovers Directive (Interim Implementation) Regulations 2006 (S.I. 2006/ 1183) are based on the provisions of this Part. So although the regulations came into force on 20 May 2006 and so before the date of Royal Assent to the Companies Act 2006, they are not cited as origins for those provisions.]

Chapter 1 The Takeover Panel

942(1) to (3)	new
943(1) to (9)	new
944(1) to (7)	new

Section of 2006 Act	Origin
945(1) and (2)	new
946	new
947(1) to (10)	new
948(1) to (9)	new
949(1) to (3)	new
950(1) and (2)	new
951(1) to (5)	new
952(1) to (8)	new
953(1) to (9)	new
954(1) and (2)	new
955(1) to (4)	new
956(1) to (3)	new
957(1) and (2)	new
958(1) to (8)	new
959	new
960	new
961(1) to (3)	new
962(1) and (2)	new
963(1) and (2)	new
964(1) to (6)	new
965	new
Chapter 2 Impediments to takeovers	
966(1) to (8)	new
967(1) to (7)	new
968(1) to (8)	new
969(1) to (3)	new
970(1) to (4)	new
971(1) and (2)	new
972(1) to (4)	new
973	new

Section of 2006 Act	Origin
Chapter 3 "Squeeze-out" and "sell-out"	
974(1) to (3)	1985 s.428(1), drafting
(4) and (5)	1985 s.428(2)
(6)	1985 s.428(2A)
(7)	1985 s.428(7)
975(1) and (2)	1985 s.428(5) (changed)
(3)	1985 s.428(6) (changed)
(4)	1985 s.430E(1)
976(1)	1985 s.428(3)
(2)	new
(3)	1985 s.428(4)
977(1)	1985 s.429(8) (changed)
(2)	1985 s.430E(1) (changed)
(3)	drafting
978(1) to (3)	new
979(1) and (2)	1985 s.429(1) (changed)
(3) and (4)	1985 s.429(2) (changed)
(5) to (7)	new
(8)	1985 s.429(8) (changed)
(9)	1985 ss.429(8), 430E(2) (changed)
(10)	1985 s.429(8) (changed)
980(1)	1985 s.429(4)
(2)	1985 s.429(3) (changed)
(3)	new
(4)	1985 s.429(4)
(5)	1985 s.429(5)
(6)	1985 s.429(6)
(7)	1985 s.429(7)
(8)	1985 s.429(6), Sch.24
981(1)	1985 s.430(1)

Section of 2006 Act	Origin
(2)	1985 s.430(2)
(3)	1985 s.430(3)
(4)	1985 s.430(4)
(5)	1985 s.430(4) (changed)
(6)	1985 s.430(5) and (8)
(7)	1985 s.430(6)
(8)	1985 s.430(7)
(9)	1985 s.430(9), drafting
982(1)	drafting
(2) and (3)	1985 s.430(10)
(4) and (5)	1985 s.430(11)
(6)	1985 s.430(12)
(7)	1985 s.430(13)
(8)	1985 s.430(14)
(9)	1985 s.430(15)
983(1)	1985 s.430A(1), (1A)
(2) and (3)	1985 s.430A(1) (changed)
(4)	1985 s.430A(2) (changed)
(5)	1985 s.430A(2A)
(6) and (7)	new
(8)	1985 s.430E(3)
984(1)	1985 s.430A(1)
(2)	1985 s.430A(4) (changed)
(3)	1985 s.430A(3)
(4)	1985 s.430A(5)
(5)	1985 s.430A(6)
(6)	1985 s.430A(7)
(7)	1985 s.430A(6), Sch.24
985(1)	1985 s.430B(1)
(2)	1985 s.430B(2)

Section of 2006 Act	Origin
(3)	1985 s.430B(3)
(4)	1985 s.430B(4)
(5)	1985 s.430B(4) (changed)
986(1)	1985 s.430C(1)
(2)	1985 s.430C(1), (2)
(3)	1985 s.430C(3)
(4)	new
(5)	1985 s.430C(4)
(6) to (8)	new
(9) and (10)	1985 s.430C(5)
987(1)	1985 s.430D(1)
(2) and (3)	1985 s.430D(2) (changed)
(4)	1985 s.430D(4) (changed)
(5) and (6)	1985 s.430D(3)
(7)	1985 s.430D(4)
(8)	1985 s.430D(5)
(9)	1985 s.430D(6)
(10)	1985 s.430D(7)
988(1)	1985 s.430E(4) and (8)
(2)	1985 s.430E(5)
(3)	1985 s.430E(6) and (7)
(4)	1985 ss.204(2)(a), 430E(4)(d)
(5)	1985 ss.204(6), 430E(7)
(6)	1985 s.204(3)
(7)	1985 ss.204(5), 430E(7)
989(1)	1985 s.430F(1)
(2)	1985 s.430F(2)
990(1) to (3)	new
991(1)	1985 s.428(8) ("the company" and "the offeror"), new ("date of the offer", "non-voting shares", "voting rights" and "voting shares")

Section of 2006 Act	Origin
(2)	new
Chapter 4 Amendments to Part 7 of the Companies Act 1985	
992(1) to (6)	new (amends 1985 Pt7)
PART 29 FRAUDULENT TRADING	
993(1) to (3)	1985 s.458, Sch.24
PART 30 PROTECTION OF MEMBERS AGAINST UNFAIR PREJUDICE	
994(1)	1985 s.459(1)
(2)	1985 s.459(2)
(3)	1985 s.459(3)
995(1)	1985 s.460(1A)
(2) and (3)	1985 s.460(1)
(4)	1985 s.460(2)
996(1)	1985 s.461(1)
(2)	1985 s.461(2) and (3)
997	1985 s.461(6)
998(1) to (4)	1985 s.461(5)
999(1) to (5)	new
PART 31 DISSOLUTION AND RESTORATION TO THE REGISTER	
Chapter 1 Striking off	
1000(1)	1985 s.652(1)
(2)	1985 s.652(2)
(3)	1985 s.652(3)
(4) to (6)	1985 s.652(5)
(7)	1985 s.652(6)
1001(1)	1985 s.652(4)
(2) to (4)	1985 s.652(5)
(5)	1985 s.652(6)
1002(1) to (3)	1985 s.652(7)
1003(1)	1985 s.652A(1) (changed)
(2)	1985 s.652A(2) (changed)

Section of 2006 Act	Origin
(3)	1985 s.652A(3)
(4)	1985 s.652A(4)
(5)	1985 s.652A(5)
(6)	1985 s.652A(6) and (7)
1004(1)	1985 s.652B(1)
(2)	1985 s.652B(2)
(3)	1985 s.652B(9)
(4)	1985 s.652D(5)(c)
(5)	1985 s.652E(1)
(6)	1985 s.652E(3)
(7)	1985 s.652E(1), Sch.24
1005(1)	1985 s.652B(3)
(2)	1985 s.652B(4)
(3)	1985 s.652B(5)
(4)	1985 s.652E(1)
(5)	1985 s.652E(3)
(6)	1985 s.652E(1), Sch.24
1006(1)	1985 ss.652B(6), 652D(5)(c)
(2)	1985 s.652B(7)
(3)	1985 s.652B(8)
(4)	1985 s.652E(1) and (2)
(5)	1985 s.652E(4)
(6)	1985 s.652E(1), Sch.24
(7)	1985 s.652E(2), Sch.24
1007(1)	1985 s.652C(1)
(2)	1985 ss.652C(2), 652D(5)(c)
(3)	1985 s.652C(3)
(4)	1985 s.652E(1) and (2)
(5)	1985 s.652E(5)
(6)	1985 s.652E(1), Sch.24

Section of 2006 Act	Origin
(7)	1985 s.652E(2), Sch.24
1008(1) and (2)	1985 s.652D(1)
(3)	1985 s.652D(2) and (3)
(4)	1985 s.652D(4)
1009(1)	1985 s.652C(4)
(2)	1985 s.652C(5)
(3)	1985 s.652C(7)
(4)	1985 ss.652C(6), 652D(5)(c)
(5)	1985 s.652E(1)
(6)	1985 s.652E(5)
(7)	1985 s.652E(1), Sch.24
1010	1985 s.652D(6)
1011	1985 s.652D(8)

Chapter 2 Property of dissolved company

1012(1)	1985 s.654(1)
(2)	1985 s.654(2)
1013(1)	1985 s.656(1)
(2)	1985 s.656(2) (changed)
(3) to (5)	1985 s.656(3) (changed)
(6) and (7)	1985 s.656(5)
(8)	1985 s.656(6)
1014(1)	1985 s.657(1)
(2)	drafting
1015(1) and (2)	1985 s.657(2), IA 1986 s.178(4)
1016(1)	1985 s.657(2), IA 1986 s.179(1)
(2)	1985 s.657(2), IA 1986 s.179(2)
(3)	drafting
1017(1)	1985 s.657(2), 1A 1986 s.181(2) and (3)
(2)	1985 s.657(2), 1A 1986 s.181(3)
(3)	1985 s.657(2), 1A 1986 s.181(4)

Section of 2006 Act	Origin
(4)	1985 s.657(2), 1A 1986 s.181(3)
(5)	1985 s.657(2), 1A 1986 s.181(6)
1018(1)	1985 s.657(2), 1A 1986 s.182(1)
(2)	1985 s.657(2), 1A 1986 s.182(2)
(3)	1985 s.657(2), 1A 1986 s.182(4)
(4) and (5)	1985 s.657(2), 1A 1986 s.182(3)
1019	1985 s.657(2), 1A 1986 s.180(1) and (2)
1020(1) and (2)	1985 s.657(4)
1021(1) and (2)	1985 s.657(5)
(3)	1985 s.657(6)
1022(1)	1985 Sch.20 para.5
(2)	1985 Sch.20 para.6
(3)	1985 Sch.20 para.7
(4) and (5)	1985 Sch.20 para.8
(6)	1985 Sch.20 para.9
1023(1)	1985 s.658(1), IA s.180(1)
(2)	1985 s.658(1), IA s.180(2)
(3)	1985 s.658(2)

Chapter 3 Restoration to the register

1024(1) to (4)	new
1025(1) to (6)	new
1026(1) to (3)	new
1027(1) to (4)	new
1028(1) to (4)	new
1029(1) and (2)	new
1030(1) to (6)	new
1031(1) to (4)	new
1032(1) to (5)	new
1033(1) to (7)	new
1034(1)	1985 s.655(1)

Section of 2006 Act	Origin
(2)	1985 s.655(2)
(3)	new
(4)	1985 s.655(3)
(5)	1985 s.655(4)
(6)	drafting

PART 32 COMPANY INVESTIGATIONS: AMENDMENTS

1035(1) to (5)	new (inserts 1985 ss.446A and 446B; amends1985 ss.431, 432, 437 and 442)
1036	new (inserts 1985 ss.446C and 446D)
1037(1) to (3)	new (inserts 1985 s.446E; amends 1985 ss.451A and 452)
1038(1) and (2)	new (amends 1985 ss.434 and 447)
1039	new (amends Company Directors Disqualification Act 1986 s.8)

PART 33 UK COMPANIES NOT FORMED UNDER THE COMPANIES LEGISLATION

Chapter 1 Companies not formed under companies legislation but authorised to register

1040(1)	1985 s.680(1)(a) and (b), (1A) and (2)
(2) and (3)	1985 s.680(1) (closing words)
(4)	1985 s.680(3) and (4)
(5)	1985 s.680(5)
(6)	1985 s.680(1) (closing words)
1041(1)	1985 s.683(1)
(2)	1985 s.683(2)
1042(1) to (3)	new

Chapter 2 Unregistered companies

1043(1)	1985 s.718(1) and (2)
(2)	1985 s.718(3) (changed)
(3)	1985 s.718(1) (changed)
(4)	1985 s.718(5)
(5)	1985 s.718(1) and (3)
(6)	1985 s.718(6)

Section of 2006 Act	Origin
PART 34 OVERSEAS COMPANIES	
1044	1985 s.744 ("overseas company") (changed)
1045(1) and (2)	1989 s.130(6)
1046(1) to (8)	new
1047(1) to (6)	new
1048(1) and (2)	1985 s.694(4) (changed)
(3) to (5)	1985 s.694(5)
1049(1) to (4)	new
1050(1) to (6)	new
1051(1) to (5)	new
1052(1) to (6)	new
1053(1) to (6)	new
1054(1) to (4)	new
1055	new
1056	new
1057(1) to (3)	new
1058(1) to (4)	new
1059	1985 s.695A(4)
PART 35 THE REGISTRAR OF COMPANIES	
1060(1) and (2)	1985 s.704(2)
(3)	1985 s.744 ("the registrar of companies" and "the registrar")
(4)	drafting
1061(1) to (3)	drafting
1062	1985 s.704(4) (changed)
1063(1) to (3)	1985 s.708(1) (changed)
(4)	1985 s.708(2) and (3) (changed)
(5)	1985 s.708(5) (changed)
(6)	1985 s.708(4)
(7)	new

Section of 2006 Act	Origin
1064(1) to (3)	1985 s.711(1)(a) (changed)
1065	1985 s.710
1066(1) to (3)	1985 s.705(1) to (3)
(4) and (5)	1985 s.705(4)
(6)	1985 s.705(5)(za)
1067(1)	1985 s.705A(1) and (2) (changed)
(2)	1985 s.705A(3)
(3)	1985 s.705A(4)
(4) and (5)	1985 s.705A(5)
1068(1) to (7)	new
1069(1) to (3)	new
1070(1) to (3)	new
1071(1) and (2)	new
1072(1) and (2)	new
1073(1) to (6)	new
1074(1) to (5)	new
1075(1) to (7)	new
1076(1) to (4)	new
1077(1)	1985 s.711(1) opening words
(2) and (3)	new
1078(1)	drafting
(2) and (3)	1985 s.711(1) (changed)
(4)	new
(5) and (6)	new
1079(1) to (3)	1985 s.42(1)
(4)	1985 s.711(2) (changed)
1080(1) and (2)	drafting
(3)	new
(4)	1985 s.707A(1)
(5)	new

Section of 2006 Act	Origin
1081(1) to (7)	new
1082(1) to (5)	new
1083(1)	1985 s.707A(2) (changed)
(2) and (3)	new
1084(1) to (3)	1985 s.707A(3) (changed)
(4)	1985 s.707A(4)
(5)	1985 s.707A(3)
1085(1)	1985 s.709(1) opening words
(2)	1985 s.709(2) (changed)
(3)	drafting
1086(1)	1985 s.709(1)(a) and (b)
(2)	new
(3)	drafting
1087(1) to (3)	new
1088(1) to (6)	new
1089(1) and (2)	new
1090(1) to (4)	new
1091(1) and (2)	new
(3)	1985 s.709(3)
(4)	new
(5)	1985 s.709(4)
1092(1) and (2)	1985 s.709(5)
1093(1) to (4)	new
1094(1) to (5)	new
1095(1) to (6)	new
1096(1)(1) to (6)	new
1097(1) to (5)	new
1098(1) and (2)	new
1099(1) to (3)	1985 s.714(1) (changed)
(4) and (5)	1985 s.714(2)

Section of 2006 Act	Origin
1100	1985 s.709(1) opening words
1101(1) and (2)	new
1102(1) to (4)	new
1103(1) and (2)	new
1104(1) and (2)	1985 s.710B(1) to (3)
(3)	1985 s.710B(4)
(4)	1985 s.710B(5)
(5)	drafting
1105(1) to (3)	new
1106(1) to (6)	new
1107(1)	drafting
1107(2) and (3)	new
1108(1) to (3)	new
1109(1) and (2)	new
1110(1) to (3)	new
1111(1) to (3)	new
1112(1) and (2)	new
1113(1) to (3)	1985 s.713(1)
(4) and (5)	1985 s.713(2) and (3)
1114(1)	1985 s.715A(1) "document", (2)
(2)	new
1115(1)	new
(2)	1985 s.710A(2)
1116(1) to (6)	new
1117(1) to (3)	new
1118	drafting
1119(1) and (2)	1985 s.704(7) and (8)
(3)	new
1120	new

PART 36 OFFENCES UNDER THE COMPANIES ACTS

Section of 2006 Act	Origin
1121(1)	1985 s.730(5)
(2)	1985 s.744 "officer"
(3)	1985 s.730(5) (changed)
1122(1) to (3)	new
1123(1) to (4)	new
1124 and Sch.3	new (amend 1985 Act)
1125(1)	drafting
(2)	1985 s.730(4)
1126(1)	1985 s.732(1)
(2)	1985 s.732(2) (changed)
(3)	1986 art.680(2) (changed)
1127(1) and (2)	1985 s.731(1)
1128(1)	1985 s.731(2)
(2)	1985 s.731(3)
(3)	1986 art.679(2)
(4)	1985 s.731(4), 1986 art.679(3)
1129	1985 s.732(3) (changed)
1130(1)	1985 s.734(1) (changed)
(2)	1985 s.734(1), (3) and (4)
(3)	1985 s.734(2)
1131(1) and (2)	new
1132(1) and (2)	1985 s.721(1)
(3) to (5)	1985 s.721(2) to (4)
(6)	drafting
1133	new

PART 37 COMPANIES: SUPPLEMENTARY PROVISIONS

1134	1985 s.722(1) (changed)
1135(1)	1985 ss.722(1), 723(1) (changed)
(2)	new
(3) and (4)	new

Section of 2006 Act	Origin
(5)	1985 s.723(2)
1136(1) to (7)	new
1137(1) and (2)	1985 s.723A(1)
(3)	1985 s.723A(2) and (3)
(4)	1985 s.723A(4)
(5) and (6)	1985 s.723A(6) and (7)
1138(1)	1985 s.722(2)
(2) and (3)	1985 s.722(3), Sch.24
(4)	new
1139(1)	1985 s.725(1)
(2)	1985 s.695(1) and (2) (changed)
(3)	new
(4)	1985 s.725(2) and (3)
(5)	drafting
1140(1) to (8)	new
1141(1)	drafting
(2) and (3)	new
1142	new
1143(1) to (4), Schs.4 and 5	new
1144(1) to (3)	new
1145(1) to (5)	new
1146(1) to (4)	new
1147(1) to (6)	new
1148(1) to (3)	new
1149	drafting
1150(1)	1985 s.108(1) (changed)
(2) and (3)	1985 s.108(2) and (3)
(4)	1985 s.108(5)
1151(1) to (4)	new
1152(1) to (6)	new

Section of 2006 Act	Origin
1153(1)	1985 s.110(1)
(2) and (3)	1985 s.110(2) and (3)
(4)	1985 s.110(2), Sch.24
1154(1) to (4)	new
1155(1) and (2)	new
1156(1) to (3)	1985 s.744 "the court", IA 1986 s.117 (changed)
1157(1) to (3)	1985 s.727(1) to (3)
(3) and (4)	
PART 38 COMPANIES: INTERPRETATION	
1158	drafting
1159(1) and (2)	1985 s.736(1) and (2)
(3) and Sch.6	1985 s.736A(1) to (11)
(4)	1985 ss.736(3), 736A(12)
1160(1)	1985 s.736B(1)
(2) to (4)	1985 s.736B(3) to (5)
1161(1) to (5)	1985 s.259(1) to (5)
1162(1) to (5)	1985 s.258(1) to (5)
(6) and Sch.7	1985 s.258(6) and Sch.10A
1163(1) and (2)	1985 s.739(1) and (2)
1164(1) to (3)	1985 s.742B(1) to (3)
(4)	1985 s.255A(4)
(5)	1985 s.255A(5A)
1165(1)	drafting
(2) to (4)	1985 s.742C(1) to (4)
(5)	1985 s.255A(5)
(6)	1985 s.255A(5A)
(7)	1985 s.744 "insurance market activity"
(8)	1985 s.742C(5)
1166	1985 s.743
1167	1985 s.744 "prescribed"

Section of 2006 Act	Origin
1168(1) to (7)	new
1169(1)	1985 s.249AA(4)
(2) and (3)	1985 s.249AA(5) to (7)
(4)	drafting
1170	1985 s.744 "EEA State", drafting
1171 "the former Companies Acts"	1985 s.735(1)(c) (changed)
"the Joint Stock Companies Acts"	1985 s.735(3)
1172	drafting
1173(1) "body corporate" and "corporation"	new
"credit institution"	1985 s.262 "credit institution" (changed)
"financial institution"	1985 s.699A(3) "financial institution"
"firm"	new
"the Gazette"	1985 s.744 "the Gazette"
"hire-purchase agreement"	1985 s.744 "hire purchase agreement"
"officer"	1985 s.744 "officer"
"parent company"	1985 ss.258(1) and 742(1)
"regulated activity"	1985 s.744 "regulated activity"
"regulated market"	1985 *passim* (changed)
"working day"	drafting
(2)	drafting
1174 and Sch.8	drafting

PART 39 COMPANIES: MINOR AMENDMENTS

1175(1) and (2), Sch.9	new (amend 1985 Pt 7 and 1986 Pt 8)
1176(1) to (3)	new (repeals 1985 s.438, amends 1985 ss.439 and 453)
1177	new (repeals 1985 ss.311, 323 and 327, 324 to 326, 328 to 329, Pts 2 to 4 of Sch.13 and ss.343 and 344)
1178	new (repeals 1985 s.720 and Sch.23)
1179	new (repeals 1985 s.729)
1180	new (repeals 1985 Pt 4)
1181(1) to (4)	new (power to amend)

Appendix 2

TABLE OF DESTINATIONS

Companies Act 2006

Destinations

Notes

1.   The table identifies the provisions of the Companies Act 1985 (c. 6) that are repealed and re-enacted (with or without changes) by the Companies Act 2006 and identifies the corresponding provisions in that Act.

2.   The table is based on the table of origins. So it only shows a provision of the Companies Act 2006 as a destination of a provision of the Companies Act 1985 if the latter is cited in that table as an origin for the new provision.

3.   A repealed provision of the Companies Act 1985 may not be listed in this table because the provision is spent or it is otherwise unnecessary to re-enact it, because the new provision is fundamentally different from the existing provision or because as a matter of policy it has been decided to repeal the existing provision without replacing it.

4.   There is no entry for Schedule 24 to the Companies Act 1985 (punishment of offences) in the table. This is cited in the table of origins as the origin for a large number of provisions in the Companies Act 2006.

5.   A section at the end of the table identifies the substantive provisions of the Companies Act 1989 (c. 40) that are repealed and re-enacted by the Companies Act 2006.

COMPANIES ACT 1985

Provision of Companies Act 1985	*Destination in Companies Act 2006*
s.1 Mode of forming incorporated company	
(1)	s.7(1) and (2) (changed)
(2)	s.3(1) to (4)
(3)	s.4(1) to (3)
(4)	s.5(1) and (2)
s.2 Requirements with respect to memorandum	
(1)	s.9(2)
(2)	ss.9(2), 88(2)
(3)	s.9(2) (changed)
(4)	s.11(3) (changed)
s.3 Forms of memorandum	

COMPANIES ACT 1985

Provision of Companies Act 1985	Destination in Companies Act 2006
(1)	s.8(2)

s.7 Articles prescribing regulations for companies

(1)	s.18(2) (changed)
(3)	s.18(3) (changed)

s.8 Tables A, C, D and E

(1)	s.19(1) to (3) (changed)
(2)	s.20(1) and (2) (changed)
(3)	s.19(4)
(4)	s.19(1) to (3) (changed)
(5)	s.19(5)

s.9 Alteration of articles by special resolution

(1) and (2)	s.21(1)

s.10 Documents to be sent to registrar

(1)	s.9(1), (5) and (6) (changed)
(2)	s.12(1) (changed)
(3)	s.12(3)
(4)	s.9(3)
(6)	s.9(5)

s.12 Duty of registrar

(1) and (2)	s.14
(3) and (3A)	s.13(1) and (2) (changed)

s.13 Effect of registration

(1)	s.15(1)
(2)	s.15(3)
(3)	s.16(2) (changed)
(4)	s.16(3)
(5)	s.16(6)
(7)	s.15(4)

s.14 Effect of memorandum and articles

(1)	s.33(1) (changed)

COMPANIES ACT 1985

Provision of Companies Act 1985	Destination in Companies Act 2006
(2)	s.33(2) (changed)

s.15 Memorandum and articles of company limited by guarantee

(1)	s.37
(2)	s.5(3)

s.16 Effect of alteration on company's members

(1)	s.25(1)
(2)	s.25(2)

s.18 Amendments of memorandum or articles to be registered

(1)	s.34(2) (changed)
(2)	ss.26(1), 34(3) (changed)
(3)	ss.26(3) and (4), 34(5) and (6)

s.19 Copies of memorandum and articles to be given to members

(1)	s.32(1) (changed)
(2)	s.32(3) and (4) (changed)

s.22 Definition of "member"

(1)	s.112(1) (changed)
(2)	s.112(2)

s.23 Membership of holding company

(1)	s.136(1)
(2)	s.138(1) and (2)
(3)	s.141(1) and (2)
(3A)	s.141(3)
(3B)	s.141(4)
(3BA)	s.141(5)
(3C)	s.142(1) and (2)
(4) and (5)	s.137(1) and (2)
(6)	s.137(3) and (4)
(7)	s.144
(8)	s.143

s.25 Name as stated in memorandum

COMPANIES ACT 1985

Provision of Companies Act 1985	Destination in Companies Act 2006
(1)	s.58(1) and (2)
(2)	s.59(1), (2) and (3)

s.26 Prohibition on registration of certain names

(1)	ss.53, 65(1) to (5), 66(1)(changed)
(2)	ss.54(1) to (3) and 55(1) (changed)
(3)	s.66(2) and (3) (changed)

s.27 Alternatives of statutory designations

(4)	ss.58(1) and (2), 59(1) and (2)

s.28 Change of name

(1)	s.77(1)
(2)	ss.67(1), 68(2) and (3)
(3)	s.75(1), (2) and (4)
(4)	ss.68(3), 75(3)
(5)	ss.68(5) and (6), 75(5) and (6)
(6)	ss.80(1) to (3), 81(1)
(7)	s.81(2) and (3)

s.29 Regulations about names

(1)	ss.55(1), 56(1)
(2)	s.56(2)
(3)	s.56(3) and (4) (changed)
(6)	s.55(2)

s.30 Exemption from requirement of "limited" as part of the name

(2) and (3)	ss.61(1) to (4), 62(1) to (3) (changed)
(4)	s.60(3)
(5B)	s.60(2)

s.31 Provisions applying to company exempt under s.30

(1)	s.63(1)
(2)	s.64(1) to (4) (changed)
(3)	s.64(7)
(5)	s.63(2) and (3)

COMPANIES ACT 1985

Provision of Companies Act 1985	Destination in Companies Act 2006
(6)	s.64(5) and (6)

s.32 Power to require company to abandon misleading name

(1)	s.76(1)
(2)	s.76(3)
(3)	s.76(4) and (5)
(4)	s.76(6) and (7) (changed)
(5)	ss.80(1) to (3), 81(1)
(6)	s.81(2) and (3)

s.35 A company's capacity not limited by its memorandum

(1)	s.39(1) (changed)
(4)	s.39(2)

s.35A Power of directors to bind the company

(1)	s.40(1)
(2)	s.40(2)
(3)	s.40(3)
(4)	s.40(4)
(5)	s.40(5)
(6)	s.40(6)

s.35B No duty to enquire as to capacity of company or authority of directors

	s.40(2)

s.36 Company contracts: England and Wales

(1) and (2)	s.43(1) and (2)

s.36A Execution of documents: England and Wales

(2)	ss.44(1)
(3)	s.45(1)
(4)	s.44(2), (3) and (4)
(4A)	s.44(6)
(6)	s.44(5)
(7)	s.44(8)
(8)	s.44(7)

COMPANIES ACT 1985

Provision of Companies Act 1985	Destination in Companies Act 2006
s.36AA Execution of deeds: England and Wales	
(1)	s.46(1)
(2)	s.46(2)
s.36B Execution of documents by companies	
(1)	s.48(2)
(2)	s.48(3)
s.36C Pre-incorporation contracts, deeds and obligations	
(1)	s.51(1)
(2)	s.51(2)
s.37 Bills of exchange and promissory notes	
	s.52
s.38 Execution of deeds abroad	
(1)	s.47(1) (changed)
(2)	s.47(2)
(3)	s.47(1)
s.39 Power of company to have official seal for use abroad	
(1)	s.49(1) and (2) (changed)
(2) and (2A)	s.49(3)
(3)	s.49(4)
(4)	s.49(5)
(5)	s.49(6)
s.40 Official seal for share certificates, etc	
(1)	s.50(1) and (2)
s.42 Events affecting a company's status	
(1)	s.1079(1) to (3)
s.43 Re-registration of private company as public	
(1)	s.90(1) and (2) (changed)
(2)	s.90(3)
(3)	ss.92(1) and (2), 94(2) and (3)
(4)	s.92(1)

COMPANIES ACT 1985

Provision of Companies Act 1985	*Destination in Companies Act 2006*
s.44 Consideration for shares recently allotted to be valued	
(1)	s.93(1)
(2)	s.93(2) and (7)
(4) and (5)	s.93(3) to (5)
(6)	s.93(6)
(7)	s.93(6) and (7)
s.45 Additional requirements relating to share capital	
(1) to (4)	s.91(1)
s.46 Meaning of "unqualified report" in s 43(3)	
(2)	s.92(3)
(3)	s.92(4)
(4)	s.92(5) and (6)
s.47 Certificate of re-registration under s 43	
(1)	s.96(1) and (2)
(2)	s.94(4)
(3)	s.91(5) (changed)
(4)	s.96(4)
(5)	s.96(5)
s.48 Modification for unlimited company re-registering	
(1) and (2)	s.90(4)
(5)	s.91(2)
(6)	s.91(3)
(7)	s.91(4)
s.49 Re-registration of limited company as unlimited	
(1)	s.102(1)
(2)	s.102(2)
(4)	s.102(1)
(5) to (7)	s.102(3)
(8)	ss.102(1), 103(2) to (4) (changed)
(8A)	s.103(3) and (4) (changed)

COMPANIES ACT 1985

Provision of Companies Act 1985	Destination in Companies Act 2006
(9)	s.102(4)
s.50 Certificate of re-registration under s 49	
(1)	s.104(1) and (2)
(2)	s.104(4)
(3)	s.104(5)
s.51 Re-registration of unlimited company as limited	
(1)	s.105(1) (changed)
(2)	s.105(2)
(3)	s.105(3) and (4)
(5)	s.106(2)
s.52 Certificate of re-registration under s 51	
(1)	s.107(1) and (2)
(2)	s.107(4)
(3)	s.107(5)
s.53 Re-registration of public company as private	
(1)	ss.97(1), 100(2) (changed)
(2)	s.97(3)
s.54 Litigated objection to resolution under s 53	
(1)	s.98(1)
(2)	ss.98(1), 370(3) (changed)
(3)	s.98(2)
(4)	s.99(1) and (2) (changed)
(5)	s.98(3) and (4)
(6)	s.98(5) and (6)
(7)	s.99(3)
(8)	s.98(6)
(10)	s.99(4) and (5)
s.55 Certificate of re-registration under s 53	
(1)	s.101(1) and (2)
(2)	s.101(4)

COMPANIES ACT 1985

Provision of Companies Act 1985	*Destination in Companies Act 2006*
(3)	s.101(5)

s.58 Document offering shares etc for sale deemed a prospectus

(3)	s.755(2)

s.80 Authority of company required for certain allotments

(1)	s.549(1), s.551(1) (changed)
(2)	ss.549(1) to (3), 551(1), 559
(3)	s.551(2)
(4)	s.551(3) and (4)
(5)	s.551(5)
(6)	s.551(6)
(7)	s.551(7)
(8)	s.551(8)
(9)	s.549(4) and (5)
(10)	s.549(6) (changed)

s.81 Restriction on public offers by private company

(1)	s.755(1)
(3)	s.760

s.84 Allotment where issue not fully subscribed

(1)	s.578(1)
(2)	s.578(2)
(3)	s.578(3) (changed)
(4)	s.578(4) and (5)
(5)	s.578(5)
(6)	s.578(6)

s.85 Effect of irregular allotment

(1)	s.579(1) and (2)
(2)	s.579(3)
(3)	s.579(4)

s.88 Return as to allotments, etc

(1)	s.555(1)

COMPANIES ACT 1985

Provision of Companies Act 1985	*Destination in Companies Act 2006*
(2)	s.555(2) (changed)
(5)	s.557(1) and (2)
(6)	ss.557(3), 597(5) and (6)

s.89 Offers to shareholders to be on pre-emptive basis

(1)	s.561(1)
(2)	s.568(1)
(3)	s.568(1) and (2)
(4)	ss.561(2), 565
(5)	s.566
(6)	s.561(4)

s.90 Communication of pre-emption offers to shareholders

(1)	s.562(1)
(2)	s.568(3)
(5)	s.562(3) (changed)
(6)	s.562(4) and (5) (changed)

s.91 Exclusion of ss 89, 90 by private company

(1)	s.567(1) and (2)
(2)	s.567(3) and (4)

s.92 Consequences of contravening ss 89, 90

(1)	ss.563(1) and (2), 568(4)
(2)	ss.563(3), 568(5)

s.93 Saving for other restrictions as to offers

(1)	s.575(1)
(2)	s.575(2)

s.94 Definitions for ss 89-96

(2)	ss.560(1), 564, 577
(3)	ss.560(2), 561(3)
(3A)	s.560(2)
(5)	s.560(1)
(7)	s.574(1) and (2)

COMPANIES ACT 1985

Provision of Companies Act 1985	*Destination in Companies Act 2006*
s.95 Disapplication of pre-emption rights	
(1)	ss.570(1) and (2), 573(2), (3) and (5)
(2)	ss.571(1) and (2), 573(4)
(2A)	s.573(1) to (5 |)
(3)	ss.570(3), 571(3)
(4)	ss.570(4), 571(4), 573(3) and (5)
(5)	ss.571(5) to (7), 573(5) (changed)
(6)	572(1) to (3)
s.96 Saving for company's pre-emption procedure operative before 1982	
(1) and (2)	s.576(1)
(3)	s.576(2)
(4)	s.576(3)
s.97 Power of company to pay commissions	
(1)	s.553(1)
(2)	s.553(2)
s.98 Apart from s 97, commissions and discounts barred	
(1)	s.552(1)
(2)	s.552(2)
(3)	s.552(3)
(4)	s.553(3)
s.99 General rules as to payment for shares on allotment	
(1)	s.582(1) and (3)
(2)	s.585(1)
(3)	s.585(2)
(4)	s.582(2)
(5)	s.585(3)
s.100 Prohibition on allotment of shares at a discount	
(1)	s.580(1)
(2)	s.580(2)
s.101 Shares to be allotted as at least one-quarter paid-up	

COMPANIES ACT 1985

Provision of Companies Act 1985	Destination in Companies Act 2006
(1)	s.586(1)
(2)	s.586(2)
(3) and (4)	s.586(3)
(5)	s.586(4)

s.102 Restriction on payment by long-term undertaking

(1)	s.587(1)
(2)	s.587(2)
(3) and (4)	s.587(3)
(5) and (6)	s.587(4)
(7)	s.587(5)

s.103 Non-cash consideration to be valued before allotment

(1)	s.593(1)
(2)	s.593(2)
(3)	s.594(1) to (3)
(4)	s.594(4) and (5)
(5)	s.595(1) and (2)
(6)	s.593(3)
(7)	ss.594(6), 595(3)

s. 104 Transfer to public company of non-cash asset in initial period

(1)	s.598(1)
(2)	s.598(2)
(3)	s.603
(4)	ss.599(1) and (3), 601(1) to (3) (changed)
(5)	s.599(2) and (4)
(6)	s.598(4) and (5)

s.105 Agreements contravening s 104

(1)	s.604(1)
(2)	s.604(2)
(3)	s.604(3)

s.106 Shares issued to subscribers of memorandum

COMPANIES ACT 1985

Provision of Companies Act 1985	*Destination in Companies Act 2006*
	s.584
s.107 Meaning of "the appropriate rate"	
	ss.592(1) and (2), 609(1) and (2)
s.108 Valuation and report (s 103)	
(1)	s.1150(1) (changed)
(2)	s.1150(2)
(3)	s.1150(3)
(4)	s.596(2)
(5)	s.1150(4)
(6)	ss.596(3), 600(3)
(7)	s.596(4) and (5)
s.109 Valuation and report (s 104)	
(2)	s.600(2) and (3)
(3)	s.600(4) and (5)
s.110 Entitlement of valuer to full disclosure	
(1)	s.1153(1)
(2)	s.1153(2) and (4)
(3)	s.1153(3)
s.111 Matters to be communicated to registrar	
(1)	s.597(1) and (2)
(2)	s.602(1)
(3)	s.597(3) to (6)
(4)	s.602(2) and (3)
s.111A Right to damages, &c not affected	
	s.655
s.112 Liability of subsequent holders of shares allotted	
(1)	ss.588(1), 605(1)
(2)	s.605(2)
(3)	ss.588(2), 605(3)
(4)	ss.588(3), 605(4)

COMPANIES ACT 1985

Provision of Companies Act 1985	Destination in Companies Act 2006
(5)	s.588(1) and (4)

s.113 Relief in respect of certain liabilities under ss 99 ff

(1)	ss.589(1) and (2), 606(1)
(2)	ss.589(3), 606(2) (changed)
(3)	ss.589(3), 606(2)
(4)	ss.589(4), 606(3)
(5)	ss.589(5), 606(4)
(6) and (7)	ss.589(6), 606(5)
(8)	s.606(6)

s.114 Penalty for contravention

	ss.590(1) and (2), 607(2) and (3)

s.115 Undertakings to do work, etc

(1)	ss.591(1) and (2), 608(1) and (2)

s.117 Public company share capital requirements

(1)	s.761(1)
(2)	s.761(2) (changed)
(3)	s.762(1) (changed)
(4)	s.761(3)
(5)	s.762(3)
(6)	s.761(4) (changed)
(7)	s.767(1) and (2)
(8)	s.767(3)

s.118 The authorised minimum

(1)	ss.763(1), 764(1) (changed)
(2)	s.764(3)
(3)	s.764(4)

s.119 Provision for different amounts to be paid on shares

	s.581

s.121 Alteration of share capital (limited companies)

(1)	s.617(1) (changed)

COMPANIES ACT 1985

Provision of Companies Act 1985	*Destination in Companies Act 2006*
(2)	ss.617(2) and (3), 618(1), 620(1) (changed)
(3)	s.618(2)
(4)	ss.618(3), 620(2) (changed)
s.122 Notice to registrar of alteration	
(1)	ss.619(1) to (3), 621(1), 663(1), 689(1) (changed)
(2)	ss.619(4) and (5), 621(4) and (5), 663(4) and (5), 689(4) and (5)
s.125 Variation of class rights	
(1)	s.630(1)
(2)	s.630(2) to (4) (changed)
(6)	s.334(1) to (4) and (6) (changed)
(7)	ss. 334(7), 630(5)
(8)	s.630(6)
s.126 Saving for court's powers under other provisions	
	s.632
s.127 Shareholders' right to object to variation	
(1)	s.633(1)
(2)	s.633(2) and (3)
(2A)	s.633(2)
(3)	s.633(4)
(4)	s.633(5)
(5)	s.635(1) to (3)
(6)	s.633(6)
s.128 Registration of particulars of special rights	
(1)	s.556(1) to (3) (changed)
(2)	ss.556(1) and (4), 629(2)
(3)	s.637(1) (changed)
(4)	s.636(1) (changed)
(5)	ss.557(1) and (2), 636(2) and (3), 637(2) and (3) (changed)

COMPANIES ACT 1985

Provision of Companies Act 1985	Destination in Companies Act 2006
s.129 Registration of newly created class rights	
(1)	s.638(1) (changed)
(2)	s.640(1) (changed)
(3)	s.639(1) (changed)
(4)	ss.638(2) and (3), 639(2) and (3), 640(2) and (3)
s.130 Application of share premiums	
(1)	s.610(1)
(2)	s.610(2) and (2) (changed)
(3)	s.610(4)
(4)	s.610(5) and (6)
s.131 Merger relief	
(1)	s.612(1) and (4)
(2)	s.612(2)
(3)	s.612(3)
(4)	s.613(2) and (3)
(5)	s.613(4)
(6)	s.613(5)
(7)	s.616(1)
s.132 Relief in respect of group reconstructions	
(1)	s.611(1)
(2)	s.611(2)
(3)	s.611(3)
(4)	s.611(4)
(5)	s.611(5)
(8)	s.612(4)
s.133 Provisions supplementing ss 131, 132	
(1)	s.615
(2)	s.616(2)
(3)	s.616(3)

COMPANIES ACT 1985

Provision of Companies Act 1985	*Destination in Companies Act 2006*
(4)	s.616(1)
s.134 Provision for extending or restricting relief from s 130	
(1)	s.614(1)
(3)	s.614(2)
s.135 Special resolution for reduction of share capital	
(1)	s.641(1) to (3) (changed)
(2)	s.641(4)
s.136 Application to court for order of confirmation	
(1)	s.645(1)
(2)	ss.645(2) and (4), 646(4)
(3)	s.646(1)
(4)	s.646(2) and (3)
(5)	s.646(4) and (5)
(6)	s.645(2) and (3)
s.137 Court order confirming reduction	
(1)	s.648(1) and (2)
(2)	s.648(3) and (4)
(3)	s.648(4)
s.138 Registration of order and minute of reduction	
(1)	s.649(1) (changed)
(2)	s.649(3) (changed)
(3)	s.649(4) (changed)
(4)	s.649(5) and (6) (changed)
s.139 Public company reducing capital below authorised minimum	
(1)	s.650(1)
(2)	s.650(2)
(3)	s.651(1) and (2)
(4)	s.651(3) (changed)
(5)	s.651(4), (6) and (7)
s.140 Liability of members on reduced shares	

COMPANIES ACT 1985

Provision of Companies Act 1985	*Destination in Companies Act 2006*
(1)	s.652(1) (changed)
(2)	s.653(1)
(3)	s.653(2)
(4)	s.653(3)
(5)	s.653(3)

s.141 Penalty for concealing name of creditor, etc

	s.647(1), (2) (changed)

s.142 Duty of directors on serious loss of capital

(1)	s.656(1) to (3)
(2)	s.656(4) and (5) (changed)
(3)	s.656(6)

s.143 General rule against company acquiring own shares

(1)	s.658(1)
(2)	s.658(2) and (3)
(2A)	s.725(4)
(3)	s.659(1) and (2)

s.144 Acquisition of shares by company's nominee

(1)	s.660(1) and (2) (changed)
(2)	s.661(1) and (2) (changed)
(3)	s.661(3)
(4)	s.661(4)

s.145 Exceptions from s 144

(1)	s.660(3)
(2)	ss.660(3), 661(5)
(3)	s.671

s.146 Treatment of shares held by or for public company

(1)	ss.662(1), 671
(2)	s.662(2) and (3)
(3)	s.662(3)
(4)	s.662(5) and (6)

COMPANIES ACT 1985

Provision of Companies Act 1985	*Destination in Companies Act 2006*
s.147 Matters arising out of compliance with s 146(2)	
(2)	s.664(1) and (2)
(3)	s.664(4) (changed)
(4)	s.665(1), (2), (4) and (5) (changed)
s.148 Further provisions supplementing ss 146, 147	
(1)	s.668(1) and (2)
(2)	s.668(3)
(3)	s.671
(4)	s.669(1) and (2)
s.149 Sanctions for non-compliance	
(1)	s.666(1) and (2)
(2)	s.667(1) to (3)
s.150 Charges of public companies on own shares	
(1)	s.670(1)
(2)	s.670(2)
(3)	s.670(3)
(4)	s.670(4)
s.151 Financial assistance generally prohibited	
(1)	ss.678(1), 679(1) (changed)
(2)	ss.678(3), 679(3) (changed)
(3)	s.680(1) and (2)
s.152 Definitions for this Chapter	
(1)	ss.677(1), 683(1)
(2)	s.677(2) and (3)
(3)	s.683(2)
s.153 Transactions not prohibited by s 151	
(1)	ss.678(2), 679(2) (changed)
(2)	ss.678(4), 679(4)
(3)	s.681(1) and (2)
(4)	s.682(1) and (2)

COMPANIES ACT 1985

Provision of Companies Act 1985	Destination in Companies Act 2006
(5)	s.682(5)
s.154 Special restriction for public companies	
(1)	s.682(1)
(2)	ss.682(3) and (4), 840(4) and (5)
s.159 Power to issue redeemable shares	
(1)	s.684(1) and (3) (changed)
(2)	s.684(4)
(3)	ss.686(1) to (3) (changed), 691(1) and (2)
s.160 Financing etc of redemption	
(1)	ss.687(1) to (3) and (6), 692(1), (2) and (5)
(2)	ss.687(4) and (5), 692(3) and (4)
(4)	ss.688, 706 (changed)
s.162 Power of company to purchase own shares	
(1)	s.690(1) (changed)
(2)	ss.691(1) and (2), 692(1) to (5)
(2A)	s.706
(2B)	ss.706, 724(1)
(3)	s.690(2)
(4)	s.724(2)
s.162A Treasury shares	
(1)	s.724(3)
(2)	s.724(4)
(3)	s.724(5)
s.162B Treasury shares: maximum holdings	
(1)	s.725(1)
(2)	s.725(2)
(3)	s.725(4)
s.162C Treasury shares: voting and other rights	
(1)	s.726(1)
(2) and (3)	s.726(2)

COMPANIES ACT 1985

Provision of Companies Act 1985	*Destination in Companies Act 2006*
(4)	s.726(3)
(5)	s.726(4)
(6)	s.726(5)
s.162D Treasury shares: disposal and cancellation	
(1)	ss.727(1), 729(1)
(2)	s.727(2) (changed)
(3)	s.727(3)
(4)	s.729(4)
(5)	s.729(5)
s.162E Treasury shares: mandatory cancellation	
(1)	s.729(2)
(2)	s.729(3)
s.162F Treasury shares: proceeds of sale	
(1)	s.731(1)
(2)	s.731(2)
(3)	s.731(3)
(4) and (5)	s.731(4)
s.162G Treasury shares: penalty for contravention	
	s.732(1) and (2) (changed)
s.163 Definitions of "off-market" and "market" purchase	
(1)	s.693(2)
(2)	s.693(3)
(3)	s.693(4)
(4) and (5)	s.693(5)
s.164 Authority for off-market purchase	
(1)	ss.693(1), 694(1)
(2)	s.694(2) (changed)
(3)	ss.694(4), 697(3), 700(3)
(4)	ss.694(5), 697(4), 700(4)

COMPANIES ACT 1985

Provision of Companies Act 1985	Destination in Companies Act 2006
(5)	ss.694(1), (3) and (4), 698(1), (3) and (4), 700(5)
(6)	ss.696(1) to (5), 699(1) to (6), 700(5) (changed)
(7)	ss.697(1) to (4), 698(1), (3) and (4), 699(1) to (6), 700(3) to (5)
s.165 Authority for contingent purchase contract	
(1)	s.694(3)
(2)	ss.694(2), (4) and (5), 695(1), (3) and (5), 696(1) to (5)
s.166 Authority for market purchase	
(1)	ss.693(1), 701(1)
(2)	s.701(2)
(3)	s.701(3) and (5)
(4)	s.701(4) and (5)
(5)	s.701(6)
(6)	s.701(7)
(7)	s.701(8)
s.167 Assignment or release of company's right to purchase own shares	
(1)	s.704
(2)	s.700(1) to (5)
s.168 Payments apart from purchase price to be made out of distributable profits	
(1)	s.705(1)
(2)	s.705(2)
s.169 Disclosure by company of purchase of own shares	
(1)	ss.707(1) to (3), 708(1) (changed)
(1A)	ss.707(1) to (3), 708(1) (changed)
(1B)	ss.707(1) to (3), 708(1) (changed)
(2)	s.707(4)
(3)	s.707(5)
(4)	s.702(1) to (4) (changed)

COMPANIES ACT 1985

Provision of Companies Act 1985	*Destination in Companies Act 2006*
(5)	s.702(6)
(6)	ss.707(6) and (7), 708(4) and (5)
(7)	s.703(1) and (2) (changed)
(8)	s.703(3)
(9)	s.702(7)
s.169A Disclosure by company of cancellation or disposal of treasury shares	
(1)	ss.728(1), 730(1)
(2)	ss.728(2), 730(2)
(3)	ss.728(3), 730(3)
(4)	ss.728(4) and (5), 730(6) and (7)
s.170 The capital redemption reserve	
(1)	s.733(1), (2) and (4)
(2) and (3)	s.733(3)
(4)	s.733(5) and (6)
s.171 Power of private companies to redeem or purchase own shares out of capital	
(1)	s.709(1) (changed)
(2)	s.709(2)
(3)	s.710(1) and (2)
(4)	s.734(2)
(5)	s.734(3)
(6)	s.734(4)
s.172 Availability of profits for purposes of s 171	
(1)	s.711(1) and (2)
(2)	s.712(2)
(3)	s.712(6)
(4)	s.712(3)
(5)	s.712(4)
(6)	s.712(7)
s.173 Conditions for payment out of capital	
(1)	s.713(1) and (2)

COMPANIES ACT 1985

Provision of Companies Act 1985	Destination in Companies Act 2006
(2)	s.716(1)
(3)	s.714(1) to (3)
(4)	s.714(4) (changed)
(5)	s.714(5) and (6) (changed)
(6)	s.715(1) and (2)
s.174 Procedure for special resolution under s 173	
(1)	ss.716(2), 723(1)
(2)	s.717(3)
(3)	s.717(4)
(4)	s.718(2) and (3) (changed)
(5)	s.717(5)
s.175 Publicity for proposed payment out of capital	
(1)	s.719(1)
(2)	s.719(2)
(3)	s.719(3)
(4)	ss.719(4), 720(1)
(5)	s.719(4)
(6)	s.720(1), (2) and (4) (changed)
(7)	s.720(5) and (6)
(8)	s.720(7)
s.176 Objections by company's members or creditors	
(1)	s.721(1) and (2)
(2)	s.721(2)
(3)	s.722(2) and (3)
(4)	s.722(4) and (5)
s.177 Powers of court on application under s 176	
(1)	s.721(3)
(2)	s.721(4) and (5)
(3)	s.721(6)
(4)	s.721(7)

COMPANIES ACT 1985

Provision of Companies Act 1985	Destination in Companies Act 2006
s.178 Effect of company's failure to redeem or purchase	
(1)	s.735(1)
(2)	s.735(2)
(3)	s.735(2) and (3)
(4)	s.735(4)
(5)	s.735(5)
(6)	s.735(6)
s.181 Definitions for Chapter VII	
	s.736
s.182 Nature, transfer and numbering of shares	
(1)	ss.541, 544(1) and (2)
(2)	s.543(1) and (2)
s.183 Transfer and registration	
(1)	s.770(1)
(2)	s.770(2)
(3)	s.773
(4)	s.772
s.184 Certification of transfers	
(1)	s.775(1) and (2)
(2)	s.775(3)
(3)	s.775(4)
s.185 Duty of company as to issue of certificates	
(1)	ss.769(1) and (2), 776(1) and (3)
(2)	s.776(2)
(3)	s.777(1) and (2)
(4)	ss.769(2), 776(3), 778(1)
(4A)	s.778(1)
(4B) and (4C)	s.778(2)
(4D)	s.778(3)
(5)	ss.769(3) and (4), 776(5) and (6)

COMPANIES ACT 1985

Provision of Companies Act 1985	Destination in Companies Act 2006
(6)	s.782(1)
(7)	s.782(2) and (3)
s.186 Certificate to be evidence of title	
(1)	s.768(1) and (2)
(2)	s.768(2)
s.187 Evidence of grant of probate or confirmation as executor	
	s.774
s.188 Issue and effect of share warrant to bearer	
(1)	s.779(1)
(2)	s.779(2)
(3)	s.779(3)
s.189 Offences in connections with share warrants (Scotland)	
(1)	s.781(1) and (3)
(2)	s.781(2) and (4)
s.190 Register of debenture holders	
(1)	s.743(6)
(5)	s.743(2) and (6) (changed)
(6)	s.743(3)
s.191 Right to inspect register	
(1)	s.744(1)
(2)	s.744(2)
(3)	s.749(1)
(4)	ss.746(1) and (2), 749(2) and (3)
(5)	ss.746(3), 749(4)
(6)	s.744(5)
(7)	s.748(1) and (2) (changed)
s.192 Liability of trustees of debentures	
(1)	s.750(1) and (3)
(2)	s.750(2)
(3)	s.751(1) and (2)

COMPANIES ACT 1985

Provision of Companies Act 1985	Destination in Companies Act 2006
(4)	s.751(3) and (4)
s.193 Perpetual debentures	
	s.739(1) and (2)
s.194 Power to re-issue redeemed debentures	
(1)	s.752(1)
(2)	s.752(2)
(3)	s.753
(4)	s.752(3)
(5)	s.752(4)
s.195 Contract to subscribe for debentures	
	s.740
s.196 Payment of debts out of assets subject to floating charge (England and Wales)	
(1)	s.754(1)
(2)	s.754(2)
(3)	s.754(3)
(4)	s.754(4)
s.197 Debentures to bearer (Scotland)	
	s.742
s.198 Obligation of disclosure: the cases in which it may arise and "the relevant time"	
(2)	s.792(1) and (2) (changed)
s.203 Notification of family and corporate interests	
(1)	s.822(1) and (2)
(2)	s.823(1)
(3)	s.832(2)
(4)	s.823(3)
s.204 Agreement to acquire interests in a particular company	
(1)	s.824(1)
(2)	ss.824(1) and (2), 988(4)
(3)	ss.824(3), 988(6)
(4)	s.824(4)

COMPANIES ACT 1985

Provision of Companies Act 1985	Destination in Companies Act 2006
(5)	ss.824(5), 988(7)
(6)	ss.824(6), 988(5)
s.205 Obligation of disclosure arising under s 204	
(1)	s.825(1)
(2)	s.825(2)
(3)	s.825(3)
(4)	s.825(4)
s.207 Interests in shares by attribution	
(1)	ss.783, 785(1)
(2)	s.785(2)
(3)	s.785(3)
(4)	s.785(4)
(5)	s.785(5)
(6)	s.785(6)
(7)	s.788
(9)	s.784(3)
(10)	s.783
s.208 Interests in shares which are to be notified	
(1)	s.820(1)
(2)	s.820(2)
(3)	s.820(3)
(4)	s.820(4)
(5)	s.820(6)
(6)	s.820(5)
(7)	s.820(7)
(8)	s.820(8)
s.210A Power to make further provision by regulations	
(1)	s.828(1) and (2)
(5)	s.828(3)
s.211 Register of interests in shares	

COMPANIES ACT 1985

Provision of Companies Act 1985	Destination in Companies Act 2006
(3)	s.808(2)
(4)	s.808(7)
(5)	s.808(4)
(6)	s.810(1) to (3)
(7)	s.819(1)
(8)	ss.809(1), 810(4), 811(1) and (2), 813(1) to (3) (changed)
(9)	s.826(1)
(10)	ss.808(5) and (6), 819(2) and (3)
s.212 Company investigations	
(1)	s.793(1) and (2) (changed)
(2)	s.793(3), (4) and (6)
(3)	s.793(5)
(4)	s.793(7)
(5)	ss.820(1) to (8), 822(1) and (2), 823(1) to (3), 824(1) to (6), 825(1) to (4)
(6)	s.821(1) and (2)
s.213 Registration of interests disclosed under s 212	
(1)	s.808(1) to (3) (changed)
(3)	ss.808(2) and (4) to (7), 809(1), 810(1) to (4), 811(1) and (2), 813(1) to (3), 819(1) to (3), 826(1)
s.214 Company investigation on requisition by members	
(1)	s.803(1) and (2) (changed)
(2)	s.803(3) (changed)
(4)	s.804(1)
(5)	s.804(2) and (3) (changed)
s.215 Company report to members	
(1)	s.805(1)
(2)	s.805(2) and (3)
(3)	s.805(1) and (3)

COMPANIES ACT 1985

Provision of Companies Act 1985	*Destination in Companies Act 2006*
(4)	s.826(1) and (2)
(5)	s.805(6)
(6)	s.805(7)
(7)	ss.805(4), 807(1) to (5)
(8)	s.806(3) and (4)

s.216 Penalty for failure to provide information

(1)	s.794(1)
(1A)	s.794(3)
(1B)	s.794(2)
(3)	s.795(1) and (3)
(4)	s.795(2)
(5)	s.796(1) and (2)

s.217 Removal of entries from register

(1)	s.816 (changed)
(2)	s.817(1) (changed)
(3)	s.817(2) and (3)
(4)	s.818(1) and (2)
(5)	ss.817(4), 818(3)

s.218 Otherwise, entries not to be removed

(1)	s.815(1)
(2)	s.815(2)
(3)	s.815(3) and (4)

s.219 Inspection of register and reports

(1)	s.807(1), 811(1)
(2)	s.807(2), 811(2)
(3)	ss.807(3) and (4), 813(1) and (2) (changed)
(4)	ss.807(5), 813(3)

s.220 Definitions for Part VI

(2)	s.827

s.221 Duty to keep accounting records

COMPANIES ACT 1985

Provision of Companies Act 1985	*Destination in Companies Act 2006*
(1)	s.386(1) and (2)
(2) to (4)	s.386(3) to (5)
(5)	s.387(1) and (2)
(6)	s.387(3)
s.222 Where and for how long records to be kept	
(1) to (3)	s.388(1) to (3)
(4)	s.389(1), (2) and (4)
(5)	s.388(4) and (5)
(6)	s.389(3) and (4)
s.223 A company's financial year	
(1) to (5)	s.390(1) to (5)
s.224 Accounting reference periods and accounting reference date	
(1)	s.391(1)
(2) and (3)	s.391(2)
(3A)	s.391(4)
(4) to (6)	s.391(5) to (7)
s.225 Alteration of accounting reference date	
(1)	s.392(1)
(3) to (7)	s.392(2) to (6)
s.226 Duty to prepare individual accounts	
(1)	s.394
(2) to (6)	s.395(1) to (5)
s.226A Companies Act individual accounts	
(1) and (2)	s.396(1) and (2)
(3)	s.396(3) (changed)
(4)	s.396(4)
(5) and (6)	s.396(5)
s.226B IAS individual accounts	
	s.397
s.227 Duty to prepare group accounts	

COMPANIES ACT 1985

Provision of Companies Act 1985	*Destination in Companies Act 2006*
(1)	s.399(2)
(2) to (7)	s.403(1) to (6)
(8)	s.399(2) and (3)
s.227A Companies Act group accounts	
(1) and (2)	s.404(1) and (2)
(3)	s.404(3) (changed)
(4)	s.404(4)
(5) and (6)	s.404(5)
s.227B IAS group accounts	
	s.406
s.227C Consistency of accounts	
(1) to (5)	s.407(1) to (5)
s.228 Exemption for parent companies included in accounts of larger group	
(1) and (2)	s.400(1) and (2)
(3)	s.400(4)
(4)	s.400(5)
(5)	s.400(3)
(6)	s.400(6)
s.228A Exemption for parent companies included in non-EEA group accounts	
(1) and (2)	s.401(1) and (2)
(3)	s.401(4)
(4)	s.401(5)
(5)	s.401(3)
(6)	s.401(6)
s.229 Subsidiary undertakings included in the consolidation	
(1) and (2)	s.405(1) and (2)
(3)	s.405(3) and (4)
(5)	s.402
s.230 Treatment of individual profit and loss account where group accounts prepared	
(1)	s.408(1) (changed)

COMPANIES ACT 1985

Provision of Companies Act 1985	Destination in Companies Act 2006
(2)	s.408(2) (changed)
(3) and (40	s.408(3) and (4)

s.231 Disclosure required in notes to accounts: related undertakings

(1) and (2)	s.409(1) and (2) (changed)
(3)	s.409(3) and (4) (changed)
(4)	s.409(5)
(5)	s.410(1) and (2)
(6)	s.410(3)
(7)	s.410(4) and (5)

s.231A Disclosure required in notes to annual accounts: particulars of staff

(1)	s.411(1)
(2) to (4)	s.411(3) to (5)
(5)	s.411(2)
(6)	s.411(7)
(7)	s.411(6)

s.232 Disclosure required in notes to accounts: emoluments and other benefits of directors and others

(3)	s.412(5)
(4)	s.412(6)

s.233 Approval and signing of accounts

(1) and (2)	ss.414(1) and (2), 450(1) and (2)
(3)	ss.433(1) to (3), 436(1) and (2),
(4)	ss.444(6), 445(5), 446(3), 447(3) (changed)
(5)	ss.414(4) and (5) (changed)
(6)(a)	s.433(4) and (5),

s.234 Duty to prepare directors' report

(1)	ss.415(1), 417(1), 418(2)
(2) and (3)	s.415(2) and (3)
(5)	ss.415(4) and (5), 419(3) and (4)

s.234ZZA Directors' report: general requirements

COMPANIES ACT 1985

Provision of Companies Act 1985	Destination in Companies Act 2006
(1)	s.416(1) and (3)
(2)	s.416(2)
(3) and (4)	s.416(4) (changed)
s.234ZZB Directors' report: business review	
(1) and (2)	s.417(3) and (4)
(3)	s.417(6)
(4)	s.417(8)
(5)	s.417(6)
(6)	s.417(9)
s.234ZA Statement as to disclosure of information to auditors	
(1) to (4)	s.418(1) to (4)
(6)	s.418(5) and (6)
s.234A Approval and signing of directors' report	
(1)	s.419(1)
(2)	ss.433(1) to (3), 436(1) and (2)
(3)	ss.444(6), 445(5), 446(3), 447(3)
(4)	ss.419(3) and (4), 433(4) and (5)
s.234B Duty to prepare directors' remuneration report	
(1)	ss.420(1), 421(1) and (2)
(2)	s.421(1) and (2)
(3) and (4)	s.420(2) and (3)
(5) and (6)	s.421(3) and (4)
s.234C Approval and signing of directors' remuneration report	
(1)	s.422(1)
(2)	ss.433(1) to (3), 436(1) and (2)
(3)	s.447(3)
(4)	s.422(2) and (3)
s. 235 Auditors' report	
(1)	ss.475(1), 495(1)
(1A)	s.495(2)

COMPANIES ACT 1985

Provision of Companies Act 1985	Destination in Companies Act 2006
(1B) and (2)	s.495(3)
(2A)	s.495(4)
(3)	s.496
(4) and (5)	s.497(1) and (2)
s.236 Signature of auditors' report	
(1)	s.503(1) and (2)
(2)	s.505(1) and (2) (changed)
(3)	s.444(7) (changed)
(4)	s.505(3) and (4)
s.237 Duties of auditors	
(1) to (4)	s.498(1) to (4)
(4A)	s.498(5)
s.238 Persons entitled to receive copies of accounts and reports	
(1) and (1A)	ss.423(1), 424(1) to (3) (changed)
(3)	s.423(4)
(4)	s.424(4) (changed)
(5)	s.425(1) and (2)
(6)	s.423(5)
s.239 Right to demand copies of accounts and reports	
(1) and (2)	ss.431(1) and (2), 432(1) and (2)
(3)	ss.431(3) and (4), 432(3) and (4)
s.240 Requirements in connection with publication of accounts	
(1)	s.434(1) (changed)
(2)	s.434(2) (changed)
(3)	s.435(1) and (2) (changed)
(4)	s.436(1) and (2) (changed)
(5)	ss.434(3), 435(3) (changed)
(6)	s.435(5) and (6)
s.241 Accounts and reports to be laid before company in general meeting	
(1)	s.437(1) (changed)

COMPANIES ACT 1985

Provision of Companies Act 1985	*Destination in Companies Act 2006*
(2)	ss.437(2), 438(1) and (4)
(3) and (4)	s.438(2) and (3)

s.241A Members' approval of directors' remuneration report

(1) and (3)	s.439(1)
(4)	s.439(2)
(5)	s.439(3)
(6)	s.439(4)
(7)	s.439(3)
(8)	s.439(5)
(9)	s.440(1) and (4)
(10)	s.440(2) to (4)
(11)	s.440(2) and (3)
(12)	s.439(6)

s.242 Accounts and reports to be delivered to the registrar

(1)	s.441(1), 444(1) and (2), 445(1) and (2), 446(1) and (2), 447(1) and (2) (changed)
(2)	s.451(1)
(3)	s.452(1) and (2)
(4) and (5)	s.451(2) and (3)

s.242A Civil penalty for failure to deliver accounts

(1)	s.453(1)
(2)	s.453(2) (changed)
(3) and (4)	s.453(3) and (4)

s.242B Delivery and publication of accounts in ECUs

(1) to (4)	s.469(1) to (4)

s.244 Period allowed for laying and delivering accounts and reports

(1) and (2)	s.442(2) and (3) (changed)
(4) and (5)	s.442(4) and (5)
(6)	s.442(7)

s.245 Voluntary revision of annual accounts or directors' report

COMPANIES ACT 1985

Provision of Companies Act 1985	Destination in Companies Act 2006
(1) to (3)	s.454(1) to (3)
(4)	s.454(4) (changed)
(5)	s.454(5)

s.245A Secretary of State's notice in respect of annual accounts

(1)	s.455(1) and (2)
(2) to (4)	s.455(3) to (5)

s.245B Application to court in respect of defective accounts

(1) to (3)	s.456(1) to (3)
(3A)	s.456(4)
(4) to (7)	s.456(5) to (8)

s.245C Other persons authorised to apply to court

(1)	s.457(1)
(1A)	s.457(5)
(2) and (3)	s.457(2) and (3)
(4)	s.457(7)
(4A)	s.457(5)
(4B)	s.457(4)
(5)	s.457(6)

s.245D Disclosure of information held by Inland Revenue to persons authorised to apply to court

(1)	s.458(1)
(2)	s.458(2)
(3)	s.458(1)

s.245E Restrictions on use and further disclosure of information disclosed under section 245D

(1) and (2)	s.458(3)
(3)	s.458(4) and (5)
(4)	s.458(4) (changed)
(5)	ss.1126, 1130

s.245F Power of authorised persons to require documents, information and explanations

(1) to (8)	s.459(1) to (8)

COMPANIES ACT 1985

Provision of Companies Act 1985	Destination in Companies Act 2006
s.245G Restrictions on further disclosure of information obtained under section 245F	
(1) and (2)	s.460(1) and (2)
(3)	ss.460(3), 461(1) to (6)
(4) to (6)	s.462(1) to (3)
(7)	s.460(4) and (5)
(8)	s.460(4)
(9)	ss.1126, 1130
(10)	s.460(3)
(11)	s.461(7)
s.246 Special provisions for small companies	
(3)	s.411(1)
(4)	ss.416(3), 417(1)
(5)	s.444(1) and (3) (changed)
(6)	s.444(3) (changed)
(7)	ss.444(6), 450(1) and (2)
(8)	ss.414(3), 419(2), 444(5), 450(3)
s.246A Special provisions for medium-sized companies	
(1)	s.445(1)
(2)	s.445(3) (changed)
(2A)	s.417(7)
(3)	s.445(3) (changed)
(4)	s.450(3)
s.247 Qualification of company as small or medium-sized	
(1)(a)	ss.382(1), 465(1)
(1)(b) and (2)	ss.382(2), 465(2)
(3) and (4)	ss.382(3) and (4), 465(3) and (4)
(5)	ss.382(5), 465(5) (changed)
(6)	ss.382(6), 465(6)
s.247A Cases in which special provisions do not apply	
(1) to (1B)	ss.384(1), 467(1)

COMPANIES ACT 1985

Provision of Companies Act 1985	Destination in Companies Act 2006
(2)	ss.384(2), 467(2) (changed)
(2A)	ss.384(3), 467(3)
(3)	ss.383(1), 466(1)
s.247B Special auditors' report	
(1)	s.449(1)
(2)	ss.444(4), 445(4), 449(2)
(3) to (5)	s.449(3) to (5)
s.248 Exemption for small and medium-sized groups	
(1) and (2)	ss.398, 399(1) and (2) (changed)
s.249 Qualification of group as small or medium-sized	
(1)(a)	s.466(2)
(1)(b) and (2)	s.466(3)
(3)	s.466(4)
(4)	s.466(5) and (6)
(5) and (6)	s.466(7)
s.249A Exemptions from audit	
(1)	s.477(1)
(3)	s.477(2) and (4)
(6)	s.477(3)
(7)	s.477(4)
s.249AA Dormant companies	
(1) and (2)	s.480(1) and (2)
(3)	s.481
(4)	s.1169(1)
(5) to (7)	s.1169(2) and (3)
s.249B Cases where exemptions not available	
(1)	ss.478, 479(1) to (3)
(1A)	s.479(3)
(1B)	s.479(1) to (3)
(1C)	s.479(2), (5) and (6)

COMPANIES ACT 1985

Provision of Companies Act 1985	Destination in Companies Act 2006
(2) and (3)	s.476(1) to (3)
(4)	s.475(2) and (3)
(5)	s.475(4)
s.249E Effect of exemptions	
(1)(b)	ss.444(2), 445(2), 446(2) (changed)
s.251 Provision of summary financial statement to shareholders	
(1)	ss.426(1), 427(1)
(2)	s.426(2) and (3)
(3)	ss.427(2), 428(2)
(3A)	ss.427(3), 428(3)
(4)	ss.427(4), 428(4)
(5)	ss.427(6), 428(6)
(6)	s.429(1) and (2)
(7)	ss.434(6), 435(7)
s.254 Exemption from requirement to deliver accounts and reports	
(1) to (3)	s.448(1) to (3)
(4)	s.448(4)
s.255A Special provisions for banking and insurance groups	
(4)	s.1164(5)
(5)	s.1165(5)
(5A)	ss.1164(5), 1165(6)
s.255D Power to apply provisions to banking partnerships	
(1)	s.470(1)
(2) and (2A)	s.470(2)
(4)	s.470(4)
(5)	s.470(3)
s.256 Accounting standards	
(1) and (2)	s.464(1) and (2)
(4)	s.464(3)
s.257 Power of Secretary of State to alter accounting requirements	

COMPANIES ACT 1985

Provision of Companies Act 1985	Destination in Companies Act 2006
(1)	s.484(1)
(2)	ss.473(1) to (4) (changed), 484(3)
(3)	s.484(4)
(4)(c)	s.484(2)
s.258 Parent and subsidiary undertakings	
(1) to (6)	s.1162(1) to (6)
s.259 Meaning of "undertaking" and related expressions	
(1)	ss.1161(1), 1173 "parent company"
(2) to (5)	s.1161(2) to (5)
s.261 Notes to the accounts	
(1) and (2)	s.472(1) and (2)
s.262 Minor definitions	
(1)	ss.474(1), 539, 835(6), 1173 "credit institution" (changed)
(2)	s.474(2)
(3)	s.853(4) and (5)
s.263 Certain distributions prohibited	
(1)	s.830(1)
(2)	s.829(1) and (2)
(3)	s.830(2) and (3)
(4)	s.849
(5)	s.850(1) to (3)
s.264 Restriction on distribution of assets	
(1)	s.831(1) and (6)
(2)	s.831(2) and (3)
(3)	s.831(4)
(4)	s.831(5)
s.265 Other distributions by investment companies	
(1)	s.832(1) to (3)
(2)	s.832(4)

COMPANIES ACT 1985

Provision of Companies Act 1985	Destination in Companies Act 2006
(3)	s.832(7)
(4)	s.832(5)
(4A)	s.832(6)
(5)	s.832(6)
(6)	s.832(5)
s.266 Meaning of "investment company"	
(1)	s.833(1)
(2)	ss.833(2), 834(1)
(2A)	s.833(3)
(3)	s.833(4) and (5)
(4)	s.834(2) to (5)
s.267 Extension of ss 265, 266 to other companies	
(1)	s.835(1)
(2)	s.835(2)
s.268 Realised profits of insurance company with long term business	
(1)	s.843(1), (2), (4) and (5)
(2)	s.843(3) and (4)
(3)	s.843(6) and (7)
(4)	s.843(7)
s.269 Treatment of development costs	
(1)	s.844(1)
(2)	s.844(2) and (3)
s.270 Distribution to be justified by reference to company's accounts	
(1) and (2)	s.836(1)
(3)	ss.836(2), 837(1)
(4)	ss.836(2), 838(1), 839(1)
(5)	s.836(3) and (4)
s.271 Requirements for last annual accounts	
(2)	s.837(2)
(3)	s.837(3) and (4)

COMPANIES ACT 1985

Provision of Companies Act 1985	*Destination in Companies Act 2006*
(4)	s.837(4)
(5)	s.837(5)
s.272 Requirements for interim accounts	
(1)	s.838(2)
(2)	s.838(3)
(3)	ss.838(4) and (5), 839(4)
(4) and (5)	s.838(6)
s.273 Requirements for initial accounts	
(1)	s.839(2)
(2)	s.839(3)
(3)	s.839(4)
(4)	s.839(5) and (6)
(5)	s.839(6)
(6) and (7)	s.839(7)
s.274 Method of applying s 270 to successive distributions	
(1)	s.840(1)
(2)	s.840(1) and (2)
(3)	s.840(3) to (5)
s.275 Treatment of assets in the relevant accounts	
(1)	s.841(1) and (2)
(1A)	s.841(3)
(2)	s.841(5)
(3)	s.842
(4) to (6)	s.841(4)
s.276 Distributions in kind	
	s.846(1) and (2) (changed)
s.277 Consequences of unlawful distribution	
(1)	s.847(1) and (2)
(2)	s.847(3) and (4)
s.278 Saving for provision in articles operative before Act of 1980	

COMPANIES ACT 1985

Provision of Companies Act 1985	*Destination in Companies Act 2006*
	s.848(1) and (2)
s.280 Definitions for Part VIII	
(1)	s.853(1)
(2)	s.853(2)
(3)	s.853(3)
s.281 Saving for other restraints on distribution	
	ss.851, 852 (changed)
s.282 Directors	
(1)	s.154(2) (changed)
(3)	s.154(1)
s.283 Secretary	
(1)	s.271 (changed)
(3)	ss.270(3), 274 (changed)
s.284 Acts done by person in dual capacity	
	s.280
s.285 Validity of acts of directors	
	s.161(1) and (2) (changed)
s.286 Qualifications of company secretaries	
(1)	s.273(1) and (2) (changed)
(2)	s.273(3)
s.287 Registered office	
(1)	s.86
(3)	s.87(1)
(4)	s.87(2)
(5)	s.87(3)
(6)	s.87(4)
s.288 Register of directors and secretaries	
(1)	ss.162(1) to (3), 275(1) to (3) (changed)
(2)	ss.167(1) and (2), 276(1) and (2)
(3)	ss.162(5), 275(5)

COMPANIES ACT 1985

Provision of Companies Act 1985	Destination in Companies Act 2006
(4)	ss.162(6) and (7), 167(4) and (5), 275(6) and (7), 276(3) and (4)
(5)	ss.162(8), 275(8)
(6)	s.162(6), 167(4), 275(6), 276(3)
s.289 Particulars of directors to be registered under s 288	
(1)	ss.163(1), 164 (changed)
(2)	ss.163(2) and (4), 277(2) and (4) (changed)
s.290 Particulars of secretaries to be registered under s 288	
(1)	ss.277(1), 278(1) (changed)
(2)	s.278(2)
(3)	s.277(2) and (4)
s.292 Appointment of directors to be voted on individually	
(1)	s.160(1)
(2)	s.160(2)
(3)	s.160(3)
(4)	s.160(4)
s.303 Resolution to remove director	
(1)	s.168(1) (changed)
(2)	s.168(2)
(3)	s.168(3)
(4)	s.168(4)
(5)	s.168(5)
s.304 Director's right to protest removal	
(1)	s.169(1) and (2)
(2)	s.169(3)
(3)	s.169(4)
(4)	s.169(5)
(5)	s.169(6)
s.309 Directors to have regard to interests of employees	
(1)	s.172(1)

COMPANIES ACT 1985

Provision of Companies Act 1985	Destination in Companies Act 2006
s.309A Provisions protecting directors from liability	
(1)	s.232(1) and (2)
(2)	s.232(1)
(3)	s.232(2)
(4)	s.234(1)
(5)	s.233
(6)	s.232(3)
s.309B Qualifying third party indemnity provisions	
(1) and (2)	s.234(2)
(3)	s.234(3)
(4)	s.234(3) and (6)
(5)	s.234(4)
(6) and (7)	s.234(5)
s.309C Disclosure of qualifying third party indemnity provisions	
(1)	s.236(1) (changed)
(2)	s.236(2) and (3)
(3)	s.236(4) and (5) (changed)
(4)	s.237(1)
(5)	ss.237(1) to (3) and (5) to (8), 238(1) and (3) to (5)
s.310 Provisions protecting auditors from liability	
(1)	s.532(1) and (3) (changed)
(2)	s.532(2)
(3)	s.533
s.312 Payment to director for loss of office, etc	
	ss215(1), 217(1) and (3) (changed)
s.313 Company approval for property transfer	
(1)	ss.215(1), 218(1) and (3) (changed)
(2)	s.222(2)
s.314 Director's duty of disclosure on takeover, etc	

COMPANIES ACT 1985

Provision of Companies Act 1985	Destination in Companies Act 2006
(1)	ss.215(1), 219(1) (changed)

s.315 Consequences of non-compliance with s 314

(1)	ss.219(1) and (2), 222(3) (changed)
(3)	s.219(5)

s.316 Provisions supplementing ss 312 to 315

(1)	ss.218(5), 219(7)
(2)	s.216(1) and (2) (changed)
(3)	s.220(1)

s.317 Directors to disclose interest in contracts

(1)	s.182(1) (changed)
(2)	s.182(2) (changed)
(3)	s.185(1) and (2) (changed)
(4)	s.185(4)
(5)	s.185(1) (changed)
(7)	s.183(1) and (2)
(8)	s.187(1) to (4)

s.318 Director's service contracts to be open to inspection

(1)	ss.228(1), 237(2)
(2) and (3)	ss.228(2), 237(3) (changed)
(4)	ss.228(4), 237(5)
(6)	s.230
(7)	ss.229(1), 238(1)
(8)	ss.228(5) and (6), 229(3) and (4), 237(6) and (7), 238(3) and (4) (changed)
(9)	ss.229(5), 238(5) (changed)
(10)	ss.228(7), 237(8)

s.319 Director's contract of employment for more than 5 years

(1)	s.188(1) and (3) (changed)
(2)	s.188(4) (changed)
(3)	s.188(2) (changed)

COMPANIES ACT 1985

Provision of Companies Act 1985	Destination in Companies Act 2006
(4)	s.188(6)
(5)	s.188(5)
(6)	s.189
(7)	ss.188(7), 223(1)
s.320 Substantial property transactions involving directors, etc	
(1)	s.190(1) and (2) (changed)
(2)	s.191(1) to (5) (changed)
(3)	s.223(1)
s.321 Exceptions from s 320	
(1)	s.190(4)
(2)	ss.192, 193(1) and (2) (changed)
(3)	s.192
(4)	s.194(1) and (2)
s.322 Liabilities arising from contravention of s 320	
(1)	s.195(1) and (2)
(2)	ss.195(2) and 196
(3)	s.195(1), (3) and (4)
(4)	s.195(3), (5) and (8)
(5)	s.195(6)
(6)	s.195(7)
s.322A Invalidity of certain transactions involving directors, etc	
(1)	s.41(1) and (2)
(2)	s.41(2)
(3)	s.41(3)
(4)	s.41(1)
(5)	s.41(4)
(6)	s.41(5)
(7)	s.41(6)
(8)	s.41(7)
s.322B Contracts with sole members who are directors	

COMPANIES ACT 1985

Provision of Companies Act 1985	Destination in Companies Act 2006
(1)	s.231(1) and (2) (changed)
(2)	s.231(1)
(3)	s.231(5)
(4)	s.231(3) and (4) (changed)
(5)	s.231(7)
(6)	s.231(6)
s.325 Register of directors' interests notified under s 324	
(5)	s.809(2) and (3)
s.330 General restriction on loans etc to directors and persons connected with them	
(2)	s.197(1) (changed)
(3)	ss.198(1) and (2) (changed), 200(1) and (2)
(4)	s.201(1) and (2) (changed)
(5)	s.223(1)
(6)	s.203(1) and (6) (changed)
(7)	s.203(1) (changed)
s.331 Definitions for ss 330 ff	
(3)	s.199(1)
(4)	s.199(2) and (3)
(6)	ss.198(1), 200(1), 201(1)
(7)	s.202(1)
(8)	s.202(3)
(9)	ss.202(2), 212
(10)	s.202(3)
s.333 Inter-company loans in same group	
	s.208(1) (changed)
s.334 Loans of small amounts	
	s.207(1) (changed)
s.335 Minor and business transactions	
(1)	s.207(2) (changed)
(2)	s.207(3)

COMPANIES ACT 1985

Provision of Companies Act 1985	Destination in Companies Act 2006
s.336 Transactions at behest of holding company	
	208(1) and (2) (changed)
s.337 Funding of director's expenditure on duty to company	
(1) and (2)	s.204(1) (changed)
(3)	s.204(2) (changed)
s.337A Funding of director's expenditure on defending proceedings	
(1)	s.205(1) (changed)
(2)	s.205(5)
(3)	s.205(1) (changed)
(4)	s.205(2)
(5)	s.205(3)
(6)	s.205(4)
s.338 Loan or quasi-loan by money-lending company	
(1)	s.209(1)
(2)	s.209(2)
(3)	s.209(1)
(6)	s.209(3) and (4)
s.339 "Relevant amounts" for purposes of ss 334 ff	
(1)	ss.204(2), 207(1) and (2), 210(1)
(2)	ss.204(2), 207(1) and (2), 210(2) to (4)
(3)	s.210(3) and (4)
(5)	s.210(5)
(6)	s.211(1)
s.340 "Value" of transactions and arrangements	
(2)	s.211(2)
(3)	s.211(3)
(4)	s.211(5)
(5)	s.211(6)
(6)	s.211(4)
(7)	s.211(7) (changed)

COMPANIES ACT 1985

Provision of Companies Act 1985	Destination in Companies Act 2006
s.341 Civil remedies for breach of s 330	
(1)	s.213(1) and (2)
(2)	s.213(3) and (4)
(3)	s.213(5) and (8)
(4)	s.213(6)
(5)	s.213(7)
s.345 Power to increase financial limits	
(1)	s.258(1)
(2)	s.258(2)
(3)	s.258(3)
s.346 "Connected persons", etc	
(1)	ss.252(1), 254(1), 255(1)
(2) and (3)	ss.252(2) and (3), 253(2) (changed)
(4)	s.254(2) and (5)
(5)	s.255(2) and (5)
(6)	ss.254(6), 255(6)
(7)	ss.254(3), 255(3)
(8)	ss.254(4), 255(4)
s.347 Transactions under foreign law	
	s.259
s.347A Introductory provisions	
(1)	s.362 (changed)
(3)	s.379(1)
(4)	s.364(2)
(5)	s.365(1) (changed)
(6)	s.363(1) and (2)
(7)	s.363(1) and (2) (changed)
(8)	s.379(1)
(9)	s.363(1)
(10)	ss.366(5), 379(2)

COMPANIES ACT 1985

Provision of Companies Act 1985	Destination in Companies Act 2006
s.347B Exemptions	
(1)	s.375(1)
(2)	s.375(2) (changed)
(3)	s.376(1) and (2)
(4)	s.378(1) (changed)
(5)	s.378(3)
(6) and (7)	s.378(1) (changed)
(8)	s.377(1)
(9)	s.377(3)
(10)	s.377(2)
(11)	s.377(4)
s.347C Prohibition on donations and political expenditure by companies	
(1)	s.366(1), (2) and (5) (changed)
(2)	s.367(3) and (6) (changed)
(3)	s.368(1) and (2)
(4)	s.367(5)
(6)	s.366(6)
s.347D Special rules for subsidiaries	
(1)	s.366(2)
(2)	s.366(2) and (5) (changed)
(3)	s.366(2), (3) and (5) (changed)
(4)	s.367(3) and (6) (changed)
(5)	s.368(1) and (2)
(6)	s.367(5)
(9)	s.366(6)
s.347F Remedies for breach of prohibitions on company donations etc	
(1)	s.369(1)
(2)	s.369(2) and (3) (changed)
(3)	s.369(2) and (5)
(4)	s.369(2)

COMPANIES ACT 1985

Provision of Companies Act 1985	*Destination in Companies Act 2006*
(5)	s.369(6)
(6)	s.369(3) (changed)

s.347I Enforcement of directors' liabilities by shareholder action

(1)	s.370(1) and (2) (changed)
(2)	s.370(3)
(3)	ss.370(4), 371(1)
(4) and (5)	s.371(2)
(6)	s.371(3)
(7)	s.371(4)
(8)	s.371(5)

s.347J Costs of shareholder action

(1)	s.372(1)
(2)	s.372(2)
(3)	s.372(3)
(4) and (5)	s.372(4)
(6)	s.372(5)

s.347K Information for purposes of shareholder action

(1)	s.373(1)
(2)	s.373(2)

s.348 Company name to appear outside place of business

(1)	s.82(1) and (2)
(2)	s.84(1) and (2)

s.349 Company's name to appear in its correspondence, etc

(1)	s.82(1) and (2)
(2) and (3)	s.84(1) and (2)

s.350 Company seal

(1)	s.45(2) and (3) (changed)
(2)	s.45(4) and (5)

s.351 Particulars in correspondence etc

(1) and (2)	s.82(1) and (2)

COMPANIES ACT 1985

Provision of Companies Act 1985	Destination in Companies Act 2006
(5)	s.84(1) and (2)
s.352 Obligation to keep and enter up register	
(1)	s.113(1)
(2)	s.113(2)
(3)	s.113(3) and (4)
(4)	s.113(6)
(5)	s.113(7) and (8)
(6)	s.121 (changed)
(7)	s.128(1) and (2)
s.352A Statement that company has only one member	
(1)	s.123(2) (changed)
(2)	s.123(3) (changed)
(3)	s.123(4) and (5)
(3A)	s.124(1) and (2)
s.353 Location of register	
(1)	s.114(1) (changed)
(2)	s.114(2)
(3)	s.114(3) and (4)
(4)	s.114(5) and (6)
s.354 Index of members	
(1)	s.115(1) and (2)
(2)	s.115(3)
(3)	s.115(4) (changed)
(4)	s.115(5) and (6)
s.355 Entries in register in relation to share warrants	
(1)	s.122(1) (changed)
(2)	s.122(4)
(3)	s.122(5)
(4)	s.122(2) and (6)
(5)	s.122(3)

COMPANIES ACT 1985

Provision of Companies Act 1985	*Destination in Companies Act 2006*
(5)	s.84(1) and (2)

s.352 Obligation to keep and enter up register

(1)	s.113(1)
(2)	s.113(2)
(3)	s.113(3) and (4)
(4)	s.113(6)
(5)	s.113(7) and (8)
(6)	s.121 (changed)
(7)	s.128(1) and (2)

s.352A Statement that company has only one member

(1)	s.123(2) (changed)
(2)	s.123(3) (changed)
(3)	s.123(4) and (5)
(3A)	s.124(1) and (2)

s.353 Location of register

(1)	s.114(1) (changed)
(2)	s.114(2)
(3)	s.114(3) and (4)
(4)	s.114(5) and (6)

s.354 Index of members

(1)	s.115(1) and (2)
(2)	s.115(3)
(3)	s.115(4) (changed)
(4)	s.115(5) and (6)

s.355 Entries in register in relation to share warrants

(1)	s.122(1) (changed)
(2)	s.122(4)
(3)	s.122(5)
(4)	s.122(2) and (6)
(5)	s.122(3)

COMPANIES ACT 1985

Provision of Companies Act 1985	*Destination in Companies Act 2006*
(2)	s.856(2)
(3)	s.856(2) (changed)
(4)	s.856(3)
(5)	s.856(4)
(6)	s.856(5)
(8)	s.856(6)
s.365 Supplementary provisions: regulations and interpretation	
(1)	s.857(1) and (2)
(2)	s.857(3)
(3)	s.859
s.366 Annual general meeting	
(1)	ss.336(1), 337(1)
(4)	s.336(3) and (4)
s.368 Extraordinary general meeting on members' requisition	
(1)	s.303(1) and (2)
(2)	s.303(2) and (3) (changed)
(2A)	s.303(2)
(3)	s.303(4) and (6) (changed)
(4)	ss.304(1), 305(1) and (3)
(5)	s.305(4)
(6)	s.305(6) and (7)
(7)	s.304(4)
(8)	s.304(1)
s.369 Length of notice for calling meetings	
(1) and (2)	s.307(2) and (3) (changed)
(3)	ss.307(4), 337(2) (changed)
(4)	s.307(5) and (6) (changed)
(4A)	s.308 (changed)
(4B)	ss.308, 309(1) and (3) (changed)
(4C)	s.309(2)

COMPANIES ACT 1985

Provision of Companies Act 1985	*Destination in Companies Act 2006*
s.370 General provisions as to meetings and votes	
(1)	ss.284(4), 310(4), 318(2), 319(2)
(2)	s.310(1)
(4)	s.318(2) (changed)
(5)	s.319(1)
(6)	s.284(1) and (3)
s.370A Quorum at meetings of the sole member	
	s.318(1) and (3) (changed)
s.371 Power of court to order meeting	
(1)	s.306(1) and (2)
(2)	s.306(3) and (4)
(3)	s.306(5)
s.372 Proxies	
(1)	s.324(1)
(2)	s.324(2) (changed)
(3)	s.325(1) (changed)
(4)	s.325(3) and (4)
(5)	s.327(1) and (2) (changed)
(6)	s.326(1) to (4) (changed)
s.373 Right to demand a poll	
(1)	s.321(1) and (2) (changed)
(2)	s.329(1) and (2) (changed)
s.374 Voting on a poll	
	s.322
s.375 Representation of corporations at meetings	
(1)	s.323(1)
(2)	s.323(2) and (3) (changed)
s.376 Circulation of members' resolutions	
(1)	ss.314(1) and (4), 315(2), 316(2), 338(1) and (4), 339(2), 340(2)

COMPANIES ACT 1985

Provision of Companies Act 1985	Destination in Companies Act 2006
(2)	ss.314(2) and (3), 338(3)
(3)	ss.315(1), 339(1)
(5)	ss.315(1), 339(1)
(6)	s.339(3)
(7)	ss.315(3) and (4), 339(4) and (5)
s.377 In certain cases, compliance with s 376 not required	
(1)	ss.314(4), 316(2), 338(4), 340(2) (changed)
(3)	s.317(1) and (2) (changed)
s.378 Extraordinary and special resolutions	
(1)	s.283(1), (4) and (5) (changed)
(2)	s.283(1) and (4) to (6) (changed)
(4)	s.320(1) and (3)
(5)	s.283(5) (changed)
(6)	s.301 (changed)
s.379 Resolution requiring special notice	
(1)	s.312(1)
(2)	s.312(2) and (3) (changed)
(3)	s.312(4)
s.380 Registration, etc of resolutions and agreements	
(1)	s.30(1)
(2)	s.36(1) and (2) (changed)
(4)	s.29(1) (changed)
(4A)	s.29(2)
(5)	s.30(2) and (3)
(6)	s.36(3) and (4) (changed)
(7)	ss.30(4), 36(5)
s.381 Resolution passed at adjourned meeting	
	s.332
s.381A Written resolutions of private companies	
(1)	ss.288(1), 289(1) (changed)

COMPANIES ACT 1985

Provision of Companies Act 1985	Destination in Companies Act 2006
(2)	s.296(1) (changed)
(4)	s.288(5)
(7)	s.288(2)

s.381C Written resolutions: supplementary provisions

(1)	s.300

s.382 Minutes of meetings

(1)	ss.248(1), 355(1)
(2)	ss.249(1), 356(4)
(4)	ss.249(2), 356(5)
(5)	ss.248(3) and (4), 355(3) and (4) (changed)

s.382A Recording of written resolutions

(1)	s.355(1) (changed)
(2)	s.356(2) and (3)

s.382B Recording of decisions by the sole member

(1)	s.357(1) and (2)
(2)	s.357(3) and (4)
(3)	s.357(5)

s.383 Inspection of minute books

(1)	s.358(1) and (3) (changed)
(3)	s.358(4) (changed)
(4)	s.358(5) and (6) (changed)
(5)	s.358(7)

s.384 Duty to appoint auditors

(1)	ss.485(1), 489(1) (changed)
(2)	s.489(2)

s.385 Appointment at general meeting at which accounts laid

(2)	ss.489(2) and (4), 491(1) (changed)
(3)	s.489(3) (changed)
(4)	s.489(4) (changed)

s.387 Appointment by Secretary of State in default of appointment by company

COMPANIES ACT 1985

Provision of Companies Act 1985	Destination in Companies Act 2006
(1)	ss.486(1), 490(1)
(2)	ss.486(2) to (4), 490(2) to (4)
s.388 Filling of casual vacancies	
(1)	ss.489(3), 526
s.389A Rights to information	
(1)	s.499(1)
(2)	s.499(2)
(3)	s.500(1)
(4)	s.500(2)
(5)	s.500(3)
(6)	ss.499(3), 500(4)
(7)	ss.499(4) 500(5)
s.389B Offences relating to the provision of information to auditors	
(1)	s501(1) and (2)
(2)	s.501(3)
(3)	s.501(3) (changed)
(4)	s.501(4) and (5)
(5)	s.501(6)
s.390 Right to attend company meetings, &c	
(1)	s.502(2)
(2)	s.502(1)
(3)	s.502(2)
s.390A Remuneration of auditors	
(1)	s.492(1)
(2)	s.492(2) and (3)
(4)	s.492(4)
(5)	s.492(5)
s.390B Disclosure of services provided by auditors or associates and related remuneration	
(1)	ss.494(1), 501(1) and (2)
(2)	s.494(2)

COMPANIES ACT 1985

Provision of Companies Act 1985	Destination in Companies Act 2006
(3)	s.494(3)
(4)	s.494(4)
(5)	s.494(5)
(8)	s.494(1)
(9)	s.494(6)
s.391 Removal of auditors	
(1)	s.510(1) and (2)
(2)	s.512(1) to (3)
(3)	s.510(3)
(4)	s.513(1) and (2)
s.391A Rights of auditors who are removed or not re-appointed	
(1)	ss.511(1), 515(1) and (2) (changed)
(2)	ss.511(2), 515(3)
(3)	ss.511(3), 515(4)
(4)	ss.511(4), 515(5)
(5)	ss.511(5), 515(6)
(6)	ss.511(6), 515(7)
s.392 Resignation of auditors	
(1)	s.516(1) and (2)
(2)	s.516(3)
(3)	s.517(1) to (3)
s.392A Rights of resigning auditors	
(1)	s.518(1)
(2)	s.518(2)
(3)	s.518(3)
(4)	s.518(4)
(5)	s.518(5) to (7)
(6)	s.518(8)
(7)	s.518(9)
(8)	s.518(10)

COMPANIES ACT 1985

Provision of Companies Act 1985	*Destination in Companies Act 2006*
s.394 Statement by person ceasing to hold office as auditor	
(1)	s.519(1) to (3) and (7) (changed)
(2)	s.519(4) (changed)
(3)	s.520(2)
(4)	s.520(3)
(5)	s.521(1)
(6)	s.520(4)
(7)	ss.520(5), 521(2) (changed)
s.394A Offences of failing to comply with s 394	
(1)	ss.519(5), 521(3) to (5)
(2)	ss.519(6), 521(4)
(4)	s.520(6) and (8) (changed)
s.395 Certain charges void if not registered	
(1)	ss.860(1), 861(5), 870(1). 874(1) and (2)
(2)	s.874(3)
s.396 Charges which have to be registered	
(1)	ss.860(7), 861(2)
(2)	s.861(3)
(3)	s.861(1)
(3A)	s.861(4)
(4)	s.861(5)
s.397 Formalities of registration (debentures)	
(1)	ss.863(1) to (4), 870(3)
(2)	s.864(1) and (3)
(3)	s.864(2)
s.398 Verification of charge on property outside United Kingdom	
(1)	s.866(1)
(2)	s.870(1)
(3)	s.866(2)

COMPANIES ACT 1985

Provision of Companies Act 1985	*Destination in Companies Act 2006*
(4)	s.867(1) and (2)
s.399 Company's duty to register charges it creates	
(1)	ss.860(1) and (2), 863(5)
(2)	ss.860(3), 863(5)
(3)	ss.860(4) to (6), s.863(5)
s.400 Charges existing on property acquired	
(1)	ss.861(5), 862(1)
(2)	ss.862(2) and (3), 870(2)
(3)	s.870(2)
(4)	s.862(4) and (5) (changed)
s.401 Register of charges to be kept by registrar of companies	
(1)	s.869(1), (2) and (4)
(2)	s.869(5) and (6)
(3)	s.869(7)
s.402 Endorsement of certificate on debentures	
(1)	s.865(1)
(2)	s.865(2)
(3)	s.865(3) and (4)
s.403 Entries of satisfaction and release	
(1)	s.872(1) and (2) (changed)
(2)	s.872(3)
s.404 Rectification of register of charges	
(1)	s.873(1)
(2)	s.873(2)
s.405 Registration of enforcement of security	
(1)	s.871(1) and (3)
(2)	s.871(2) and (3)
(4)	s.871(4) and (5)
s.406 Companies to keep copies of instrument creating charges	
(1)	ss.875(1), 877(2) (changed)

COMPANIES ACT 1985

Provision of Companies Act 1985	Destination in Companies Act 2006
(2)	s.875(2)
s.407 Company's register of charges	
(1)	ss.876(1), 877(2) (changed)
(2)	s.876(2)
(3)	s.876(3) and (4)
s.408 Right to inspect instruments which create charges, etc	
(1)	s.877(1), (2) and (4) (changed)
(2)	s.877(2) (changed)
(3)	s.877(5) and (6)
(4)	s.877(7)
s.410 Charges void unless registered	
(1)	s.878(1)
(2)	ss.886(1), 889(1)
(3)	s.889(2)
(4)	ss.878(7), 879(1) and (3)
(5)	s.879(5) and (6)
s.411 Charges on property outside United Kingdom	
(1)	s.886(1)
(2)	s.884
s.412 Negotiable instrument to secure book debts	
	s.879(4)
s.413 Charges associated with debentures	
(1)	s.879(2)
(2)	ss.882(1) to (4), 886(3)
(3)	s.883(1) to (3)
s.414 Charge by way of ex facie absolute disposition, etc	
(1)	s.881(1)
(2)	s.881(2) and (3)
s.415 Company's duty to register charges created by it	
(1)	ss.878(1) and (2), 882(5)

COMPANIES ACT 1985

Provision of Companies Act 1985	*Destination in Companies Act 2006*
(2)	s.878(3), 882(5)
(3)	s.878(4) to (6), 882(5)
s.416 Duty to register charges existing on property acquired	
(1)	ss.880(1) and (2), 886(2)
(2)	s.886(2)
(3)	s.880(3) and (4) (changed)
s.417 Register of charges to be kept by registrar of companies	
(1)	s.885(1)
(2)	s.885(2)
(3)	s.885(3)
(4)	s.886(6)
s.418 Certificate of registration to be issued	
(1)	s.885(4)
(2)	s.885(4) and (5)
s.419 Entries of satisfaction and release	
(1)	s.887(1) and (3) (changed)
(1B)	s.887(2)
(2)	s.887(4)
(3)	s.887(2)(changed)
(4)	s.887(5)
s.420 Rectification of register	
	s.888(1) and (2)
s.421 Copies of instruments creating charges to be kept by company	
(1)	ss.890(1), 892(2) (changed)
(2)	s.890(2)
s.422 Company's register of charges	
(1)	ss.891(1), 892(2) (changed)
(2)	s.891(2)
(3)	s.891(3) and (4)
s.423 Right to inspect copies of instruments, and company's register	

COMPANIES ACT 1985

Provision of Companies Act 1985	Destination in Companies Act 2006
(1)	s.892(1), (2) and (4) (changed)
(2)	s.892(4) (changed)
(3)	s.892(5) and (6)
(4)	s.892(7)

s.425 Power of company to compromise with creditors and members

(1)	ss.895(1), 896(1) and (2)
(2)	ss.899(1) and (3), 907(1), 922(1)
(3)	s.899(4), 901(3) and (4) (changed)
(4)	s.901(5) and 96)
(6)	s.895(2)

s.426 Information as to compromise to be circulated

(1)	s.897(1)
(2)	s.897(1) and (2)
(3)	s.897(1)
(4)	s.897(3)
(5)	s.897(4)
(6)	ss.895(1), 897(5) to (8)
(7)	s.898(1) to (3)

s.427 Provisions for facilitating company reconstruction or amalgamation

(1)	s.900(1)
(2)	s.900(1) and (2)
(3)	s.900(2)
(4)	s.900(3) and (4)
(5)	s.900(6) to (8)
(6)	ss.900(5), 941

s.427A Application of ss 425-427 to mergers and divisions of public companies

(1)	ss.902(1), 903(1), 907(2), 922(2)
(2)	ss.904(1), 919(1)
(3)	s.938(1) and (2)
(4)	s.902(3)

COMPANIES ACT 1985

Provision of Companies Act 1985	*Destination in Companies Act 2006*
(8)	s.941
s.428 Takeover offers	
(1)	s.974(1) to (3)
(2)	s.974(4) and (5)
(2A)	s.974(6)
(3)	s.976(1)
(4)	s.976(3)
(5)	s.975(1) and (2) (changed)
(6)	s.975(3) (changed)
(7)	s.974(7)
(8)	s.991(1)
s.429 Right of offeror to buy out minority shareholders	
(1)	s.979(1) and (2) (changed)
(2)	s.979(3) and (4) (changed)
(3)	s.980(2) (changed)
(4)	s.980(1) and (4)
(5)	s.980(5)
(6)	s.980(6) and (8)
(7)	s.980(7)
(8)	ss.977(1), 979(8) to (10) (changed)
s.430 Effect of notice under s 429	
(1)	s.981(1)
(2)	s.981(2)
(3)	s.981(3)
(4)	s.981(4) and (5) (changed)
(5)	s.981(6)
(6)	s.981(7)
(7)	s.981(8(
(8)	s.981(6)
(9)	s.981(9)

COMPANIES ACT 1985

Provision of Companies Act 1985	Destination in Companies Act 2006
(10)	s.982(2) and (3)
(11)	s.982(4) and (5)
(12)	s.982(6)
(13)	s.982(7)
(14)	s.982(8)
(15)	s.982(9)
s.430A Right of minority shareholder to be bought out by offeror	
(1)	ss.983(1) to (3), 984(1)
(1A)	s.983(1)
(2)	s.983(4)
(2A)	s.983(5)
(3)	s.984(3)
(4)	s.984(2)
(5)	s.984(4)
(6)	s.984(5) and (7)
(7)	s.984(6)
s.430B Effect of requirement under s 430A	
(1)	s.985(1)
(2)	s.985(2)
(3)	s.985(3)
(4)	s.985(4) and (5) (changed)
s.430C Applications to the court	
(1)	s.986(1) and (2)
(2)	s.986(2)
(3)	s.986(3)
(4)	s.986(5)
(5)	s.986(9) and (10)
s.430D Joint offers	
(1)	s.987(1)
(2)	s.987(2) and (3) (changed)

COMPANIES ACT 1985

Provision of Companies Act 1985	Destination in Companies Act 2006
(3)	s.987(5) and (6)
(4)	s.987(4) and (7)
(5)	s.987(8)
(6)	s.987(9)
(7)	s.987(10)
s.430E Associates	
(1)	ss.975(4), 977(2) (changed)
(2)	s.979(9)
(3)	s.983(8)
(4)	s.988(1) and (4)
(5)	s.988(2)
(6)	s.988(3)
(7)	s.988(3), (5) and (7)
(8)	s.988(1)
s.430F Convertible securities	
(1)	s.989(1)
(2)	s.989(2)
s.458 Punishment for fraudulent trading	
	s.993(1) to (3)
s.459 Order on application of company member	
(1)	s.994(1)
(2)	s.994(2)
(3)	s.994(3)
s.460 Order on application of Secretary of State	
(1)	s.995(2) and (3)
(1A)	s.995(1)
(2)	s.995(4)
s.461 Provisions as to petitions and orders under this Part	
(1)	s.996(1)
(2)	s.996(2)

COMPANIES ACT 1985

Provision of Companies Act 1985	*Destination in Companies Act 2006*
(3)	s.996(2)
(5)	s.998(1) to (4)
(6)	s.997

s.652 Registrar may strike defunct company off register

(1)	s.1000(1)
(2)	s.1000(2)
(3)	s.1000(3)
(4)	s.1001(1)
(5)	ss.1000(4) to (6), 1001(2) to (4)
(6)	ss.1000(7), 1001(5)
(7)	s.1002(1) to (3)

s.652A Registrar may strike private company off register on application

(1)	s.1003(1) (changed)
(2)	s.1003(2) (changed)
(3)	s.1003(3)
(4)	s.1003(4)
(5)	s.1003(5)
(6)	s.1003(6)
(7)	s.1003(6)

s.652B Duties in connection with making application under section 652A

(1)	s.1004(1)
(2)	s.1004(2)
(3)	s.1005(1)
(4)	s.1005(2)
(5)	s.1005(3)
(6)	s.1006(1)
(7)	s.1006(2)
(8)	s.1006(3)
(9)	s.1004(3)

s.652C Directors' duties following application under section 652A

COMPANIES ACT 1985

Provision of Companies Act 1985	*Destination in Companies Act 2006*
(1)	s.1007(1)
(2)	s.1007(2)
(3)	s.1007(3)
(4)	s.1009(1)
(5)	s.1009(2)
(6)	s.1009(4)
(7)	s.1009(3)
s.652D Sections 652B and 652C: supplementary provisions	
(1)	s.1008(1) and (2)
(2)	s.1008(3)
(3)	s.1008(3)
(4)	s.1008(4)
(5)(c)	ss.1004(4), 1006(1), 1007(2), 1009(4)
(6)	s.1010
(8)	s.1011
s.652E Sections 652B and 652C: enforcement	
(1)	ss.1004(5) and (7), 1005(4) and (6), 1006(4) and (6), 1007(4) and (6), 1009(5) and (7)
(2)	ss.1006(4) and (7), 1007(4) and (7)
(3)	ss.1004(6), 1005(5)
(4)	s1006(5)
(5)	ss 1007(5), 1009(6)
s654 Property of dissolved company to be bona vacantia	
(1)	s.1012(1)
(2)	s.1012(2)
s.655 Effect on s.654 of company's revival after dissolution	
(1)	s.1034(1)
(2)	s.1034(2)
(3)	s.1034(4)
(4)	s.1034(5)

COMPANIES ACT 1985

Provision of Companies Act 1985	Destination in Companies Act 2006
s.656 Crown disclaimer of property vesting as bona vacantia	
(1)	s.1013(1)
(2)	s.1013(2) (changed)
(3)	s.1013(3) to (5) (changed)
(5)	s.1013(6) and (7)
(6)	s.1013(8)
s.657 Effect of Crown disclaimer under s 656	
(1)	s.1014(1)
(2)	ss.1015(1) and (2), 1016(1) and (2), 1017(1) to (5), 1018(1) to (5), 1019
(4)	s.1020(1) and (2)
(5)	s.1021(1) and (2)
(6)	s.1021(3)
s. 658 Liability for rentcharge on company's land after dissolution	
(1)	s.1023(1) and (2)
(2)	s.1023(3)
s.680 Companies capable of being registered under this Chapter	
(1)(a) and (b)	s.1040(1)
(1) (closing words)	s.1040(2), (3) and (6)
(1A)	s.1040(1)
(2)	s.1040(1)
(3)	s.1040(4)
(4)	s.1040(4)
(5)	s.1040(5)
s.683 Definition of "joint stock company"	
(1)	s.1041(1)
(2)	s.1041(2)
s.694 Regulation of oversea companies in respect of their names	
(4)	s.1048(1) and (2) (changed)
(5)	s.1048(3) to (5)

COMPANIES ACT 1985

Provision of Companies Act 1985	Destination in Companies Act 2006
s.695 Service of documents on oversea company	
(1) and (2)	s.1139(2) (changed)
s.695A Registrar to whom documents to be delivered: companies to which section 690A applies	
(4)	s.1059
s.699A Credit and financial institutions to which the Bank Branches Directive (89/117/EEC) applies	
(3) ("financial institution")	s.1173(1)
s.704 Registration offices	
(2)	s.1060(1) and (2)
(4)	s.1062 (changed)
(7) and (8)	s.1119(1) and (2)
s.705 Companies' registered numbers	
(1) to (3)	s.1066(1) to (3)
(4)	s.1066(4) and (5)
(5)(za)	s.1066(6)
s.705A Registration of branches of oversea companies	
(1)	s.1067(1) (changed)
(2)	s.1067(1)
(3)	s.1067(2)
(4)	s.1067(3)
(5)	s.1067(4) and (5)
s.707A The keeping of company records by the registrar	
(1)	s.1080(4)
(2)	s.1083(1) (changed)
(3)	s.1084(1) to (3) (changed) and (5)
(4)	s.1084(4)
s.708 Fees payable to registrar	
(1)	s.1063(1) to (3) (changed)
(2) and (3)	s.1063(4) (changed)
(4)	s.1063(6)

COMPANIES ACT 1985

Provision of Companies Act 1985	Destination in Companies Act 2006
(5)	s.1063(5) (changed)

s.709 Inspection, &c. of records kept by the registrar

(1) opening words	s.1085(1) and s.1100
(1)(a) and (b)	s.1086(1)
(2)	s.1085(2) (changed)
(3)	s.1091(3)
(4)	s.1091(5)
(5)	s.1092(1) and (2)

s.710 Certificate of incorporation

	s.1065

s.710A Provision and authentication by registrar of documents in non-legible form

(2)	s.1115(2)

s.710B Documents relating to Welsh companies

(1) to (3)	s.1104(1) and (2)
(4)	s.1104(3)
(5)	s.1104(4)

s.711 Public notice by registrar of receipt and issue of certain documents

(1)	ss.1064(1) to (3), 1077(1) to (3), 1078(2) and (3) (changed)
(2)	s.1079(4) (changed)

s.713 Enforcement of company's duty to make returns

(1)	s.1113(1) to (3)
(2) and (3)	s.1113(4) and (5)

s.714 Registrar's index of company and corporate names

(1)	s.1099(1) to (3) (changed)
(2)	s.1099(4) and (5)

s.715A Interpretation

(1) ("document") and (2)	s.1114(1)

s.718 Unregistered companies

(1)	s.1043(1), (3) and (5) (changed)

COMPANIES ACT 1985

Provision of Companies Act 1985	Destination in Companies Act 2006
(2)	s.1043(1)
(3)	s.1043(2) and (5) (changed)
(5)	s.1043(4)
(6)	s.1043(6)

s.719 Power of company to provide for employees on cessation or transfer of business

(1)	s.247(1)
(2)	s.247(2) (changed)
(3)	s.247(4) to (6) (changed)
(4)	s.247(7) (changed)

s.721 Production and inspection of books where offence suspected

(1)	s.1132(1) and (2)
(2) to (4)	s.1132(3) to (5)

s.722 Form of company registers, etc

(1)	ss.1134 and 1135(1) (changed)
(2)	s.1138(1)
(3)	s.1138(2) and (3)

s.723 Use of computers for company records

(1)	s.1135(1) (changed)
(2)	s.1135(5)

s.723A Obligations of company as to inspections of registers, &c.

(1)	s.1137(1) and (2)
(2)	s.1137(3)
(3)	s.1137(3)
(4)	s.1137(4)
(6) and (7)	s.1137(5) and (6)

s.725 Service of documents

(1)	s.1139(1)
(2)	s.1139(4)
(3)	s.1139(4)

s.727 Power of court to grant relief in certain cases

COMPANIES ACT 1985

Provision of Companies Act 1985	Destination in Companies Act 2006
(1) to (3)	s.1157(1) to (3)
s.730 Punishment of offences	
(4)	s.1125(2)
(5)	ss.1121(1) and (3) (changed)
s.731 Summary proceedings	
(1)	s.1127(1) and (2)
(2)	s.1128(1)
(3)	s.1128(2)
(4)	s.1128(4)
s.732 Prosecution by public authorities	
(1)	s.1126(1)
(2)	s.1126(2) (changed)
(3)	s.1129 (changed)
s.734 Criminal proceedings against unincorporated bodies	
(1)	s.1130(1) and (2) (changed)
(2)	s.1130(3)
(3)	s.1130(2)
(4)	s.1130(2)
s.735 "Company", etc	
(1)(a) and (b)	s.1(1)
(1)(c)	s.1171 (changed)
(3)	s.1171
s.736 "Subsidiary"; "holding company" and "wholly-owned subsidiary"	
(1) and (2)	s.1159(1) and (2)
(3)	s.1159(4)
s.736A Provisions supplementing s 736	
(1) to (11)	s.1159(3), Sch.6
s.736B Power to amend ss 736 and 736A	
(1)	s.1160(1)
(3) to (5)	s.1160(2) to (4)

COMPANIES ACT 1985

Provision of Companies Act 1985	*Destination in Companies Act 2006*
s.737 "Called-up share capital"	
(1) and (2)	s.547
s.738 "Allotment" and "paid up"	
(1)	s.558
(2)	s.583(2) to (3)(d)
(3)	s.583(5)
(4)	s.583(6)
s.739 "Non-cash asset"	
(1) and (2)	s.1163(1) and (2)
s.741 "Director" and "shadow director"	
(1)	s.250
(2)	s.251(1) and (2)
(3)	s.251(3)
s.742 Expressions used in connection with accounts	
(1) ("fixed assets")	s.853(6)
(1) ("parent company")	s.1173(1)
(2)	s.853(4) and (5)
s.742A Meaning of "offer to the public"	
(1)	s.756(1) and (2)
(2)	s.756(3)
(3)	s.756(4) and (5)(a) to (d) (changed)
(4)	s.756(4)
(5)	s.756(4)
(6)	s.756(5)(e) and (6)
s.742B Meaning of "banking company"	
(1) to (3)	s.1164(1) to (3)
s. 742C Meaning of "insurance company" and "authorised insurance company"	
(1) to (4)	s.1165(2) to (4)
(5)	s.1165(8)
s.743 "Employees' share scheme"	

COMPANIES ACT 1985

Provision of Companies Act 1985	Destination in Companies Act 2006
	s.1166

s.744 Expressions used generally in this Act

"articles"	s.18(4)
"the Companies Acts"	s.2(1) and (2) (changed)
"the court"	s.1156(1) to (3) (changed)
"debenture"	s.738
"EEA State"	s.1170
"equity share capital"	s.548
"the Gazette"	s.1173(1)
"hire-purchase agreement"	s.1173(1)
"insurance market activity"	s.1165(7)
"officer"	ss.1121(2), 1173(1)
"oversea company"	s.1044 (changed)
"prescribed"	s.1167
"the registrar of companies" and "the registrar"	s.1060(3)
"regulated activity"	s.1173(1)
"share"	s.540(1) and (4)

s.744A Index of defined expressions

	Sch.8

Sch.2 Interpretation of references to "beneficial interest"

Part 1 References in sections 23, 145, 146 and 148

para.1(1)	ss.139(1), 672(1)
para.1(2)	ss.139(2), 672(2)
para.1(3)	ss.139(3), 672(3)
para.1(4)	ss.139(4), 672(4)
para.2(3)	s.672(5)
para.2(4)	s.672(6)
para.3(1) and (2)	ss.140(1) and (2), 673(1) and (2)
para.4(1)	ss.138(1) and (2), 674

COMPANIES ACT 1985

Provision of Companies Act 1985	*Destination in Companies Act 2006*
para.4(2)	s.138(1)
para.4(3)	s.674
para.5(1)	ss.675(1) and (2), 676
para.5(2)	ss.139(5) and (6), 140(3), 675(1) and (2)
para.5(3)	ss.139(6), 140(4), 676

Sch.4 Form and content of company accounts

Part 3 Notes to the accounts

para.56(2) and (3)	ss.382(6), 465(6)

Part 7 Interpretation of Schedule

para.94(1) and (2)	s.411(6)

Sch.7B Specified persons, descriptions of disclosures etc for the purposes of section 245G

Part 1 Specified persons

	s.461(1)

Part 2 Specified descriptions of disclosures

	s.461(4)

Part 3 Overseas regulatory bodies

	s.461(5) and (6)

Sch.10A Parent and subsidiary undertakings: supplementary provisions

para.1	Sch.7 para.1
para.2(1)	Sch.7 para.2(1)
para.2(2)	Sch.7 para.2(2)
para.3(1)	Sch.7 para.3(1)
para.3(2)	Sch.7 para.3(2)
para.3(2)	Sch.7 para.3(3)
para.4(1)	Sch.7 para.4(1)
para.4(2)	Sch.7 para.4(2)
para.4(3)	Sch.7 para.4(3)
para.5(1)	Sch.7 para.5(1)
para.5(2)	Sch.7 para.5(2)
para.6	Sch.7 para.6

COMPANIES ACT 1985

Provision of Companies Act 1985	Destination in Companies Act 2006
para.7(1)	Sch.7 para.7(1)
para7(2)	Sch.7 para.7(2)
para.8	Sch.7 para.8
para.9(1)	Sch.7 para.9(1)
para.9(2)	Sch.7 para.9(2)
para.9(3)	Sch.7 para.9(3)
para.10	Sch.7 para.10
para.11	Sch.7 para.11

Sch.13 Provisions supplementing and interpreting sections 324 to 328

Part 4 Provisions with respect to register of directors' interests to be kept under section 325

para.27	s.809(2) and (3)

Sch.14 Overseas branch registers

Part 1 Countries and territories in which overseas branch register may be kept

	s.129(2)

Part 2 General provisions with respect to overseas branch registers

para.1(1) and (2)	ss.130(1), 135(3)
para.1(3)	ss.130(2) and (3), 135(4) and (5)
para.2(1)	s.131(1)
para.3(1)	s.134(1) and (2) (changed)
para.3(2)	s.134(3)
para.4(1)	s.132(1) and (2) (changed)
para.4(2)	s.132(3) and (4)
para.5	s.133(1) and (2)
para.6	s.135(1) and (2)
para.7	s.131(4)

Sch.15A Written resolutions of private companies

Part 1 Exceptions

para.1	s.288(2)

Part 2 Adaptation of procedural requirements

COMPANIES ACT 1985

Provision of Companies Act 1985	*Destination in Companies Act 2006*
para.3(1) and (2)	ss.571(7), 573(5)
para.5(1) and (2)	ss.695(2), 698(2)
para.5(3) and (4)	ss.696(2), 699(2)
para.6(1)	ss.717(2), 718(2)
para.6(2)	s.717(2)
para.6(3)	s.718(2)
para.7	s.188(5)

Sch.15B Provisions subject to which ss 425-427 have effect in their application to mergers and divisions of public companies

para.1	ss.907(1) and (2), 922(1) and (2)
para.2(1)	ss.905(1), 906(1) to (3), 920(1), 921(1) to (4)
para.2(2)	ss.905(2) and (3), 920(2)
para.2(3)	s.920(3)
para.3	ss.908(1) and (3), 909(1) and (7), 911(1), (2) and (4), 912, 923(1) and (4), 924(1) and (7), 925(5), 926(1), (2) and (4), 927(1) to (3), 928
para.4(1)	ss.908(2), 923(2)
para.4(2)	s.923(3)
para.5(1)	ss.909(2) and (3), 924(2) and (3)
para.5(2)	ss.909(3), 924(3)
para.5(3)	ss.909(4), 924(4)
para.5(4)	s.935(1) (changed)
para.5(6)	s.935(2)
para.5(7)	ss.909(5), 924(5)
para.5(8)	ss.909(6), 924(6)
para.6(1)	ss.910(1), 911(3), 925(1), 926(3)
para.6(2)	ss.910(2), 925(2)
para.6(3)	ss.910(3), 925(3) (changed)
para.6(4)	ss.910(4), 925(4),
para.7	ss.914, 930
para.8(1)	ss.913(1), 929(1)

COMPANIES ACT 1985

Provision of Companies Act 1985	Destination in Companies Act 2006
para.8(2)	ss.913(2), 929(2)
para.9(1)	s.939(1)
para.9(2)	s.939(1) and (2)
para.9(3)	s.939(3) and (4)
para.9(4)	s.939(5)
para.10(1)	ss.918(1), 932(1)
para.10(2)	ss.916(3) to (5), 918(2) to (4), 932(2) to (5)
para.11(1)	s.933(1) to (3), 934(1)
para.11(2)	s.933(1) to (3)
para.11(3)	s.934(1)
para.11(4)	s.934(2) to (4)
para.12(1)	ss.915(1) and (6), 917(1) and (6)
para.12(2)	s.915(2)
para.12(3)	s.915(3) to (5)
para.12(4)	s.917(2)
para.12(5)	ss.917(3) to 95), 931(3) and (5)
para.13(1)	s.931(1)
para.13(2)	s.931(2)
para.13(3)	s.931(3), (4) and (6)
para.14(1)	s.916(1)
para.14(2)	s.916(2)
para.14(3)	s.916(3) to (5)
para.15(1)	s.940(1)
para.15(2)	s.940(2)
para.15(3)	s.940(3)

Sch.20 Vesting of disclaimed property; protection of third parties

Part 2 Crown disclaimer under section 656 (Scotland only)

para.5	s.1022(1)
para.6	s.1022(2)

COMPANIES ACT 1985

Provision of Companies Act 1985	*Destination in Companies Act 2006*
para.7	s.1022(3)
para.8	s.1022(4) and (5)
para.9	s.1022(6)

COMPANIES ACT 1989

1.   Section 130(6) of the Companies Act 1989 (power by regulations to apply provisions relating to company contracts and execution of documents by companies to overseas companies) is re-enacted in section 1045 of the Companies Act 2006.

2.   Section 207 of the Companies Act 1989 (transfer of securities) is re-enacted in sections 783, 784(3), 785 and 788 of the Companies Act 2006.

Appendix 3

COMPANIES ACT 2006 – COMMENCEMENT TABLE – SUMMARY

(as known on 30 September 2008)

In this Table:

'**CA 1985**' means the Companies Act 1985

'**the NI Order**' means the Companies (Northern Ireland) Order 1986

'**Act**' means the Companies Act 2006

'**SI 2006/3428**' means The Companies Act (Commencement No. 1, Transitional Provisions and Savings) Order 2006

'**SI 2007/1093**' means The Companies Act 2006 (Commencement No. 2, Consequential Amendments, Transitional Provisions and Savings) Order 2007

'**SI 2007/2194**' means The Companies Act 2006 (Commencement No. 3, Consequential Amendments, Transitional Provisions and Savings) Order 2007

'**SI 2007/2607**' means The Companies Act 2006 (Commencement No. 4 and Commencement No. 3 (Amendment) Order 2007

'**SI 2007/3495**' means The Companies Act 2006 (Commencement No. 5, Transitional Provisions and Savings) Order 2007

'**SI 2008/674**' means The Companies Act 2006 (Commencement No. 6, Saving and Commencement No. 3 and No. 5 (Amendment) Order 2008

'**SI 2008/1886**' means The Companies Act 2006 (Commencement No. 7, Transitional Provisions and Savings) Order 2008

'**SI 2008/2860**' means The Companies Act 2006 (Commencement No. 8, Transitional Provisions and Savings) Order 2008

This Table is for general reference only. It does not contain full details regarding transitional provisions. For transitional provisions refer to Chapter 12 and the statutory instruments.

Provision	*Date of Commencement*	*SI No.*
s 1 – companies	1 October 2009	SI 2008/2860
s 2 – Companies Acts	6 April 2007	SI 2007/1093
ss 3–6 – types of company	1 October 2009	SI 2008/2860
ss 7–16 – company formation	1 October 2009	SI 2008/2860
ss 17–28 – company's constitution	1 October 2009	SI 2008/2860
ss 29/30 – resolutions etc to be filed	1 October 2007	SI 2007/2194
ss 31–38 – company's constitution	1 October 2009	SI 2008/2860
ss 39–43 – company capacity etc	1 October 2009	SI 2008/2860
s 44 – execution of documents	6 April 2008	SI 2007/3495
ss 45–52 – company capacity	1 October 2009	SI 2008/2860
ss 53–68 – company names	1 October 2009	SI 2008/2860
ss 69–74 – objection to company name	1 October 2008	SI 2007/3495
ss 75–81 – company names	1 October 2009	SI 2008/2860
ss 82–85 – trading disclosures	1 October 2008	SI 2007/3495
ss 86–88 – registered office	1 October 2009	SI 2008/2860
ss 89–111 – re–registration	1 October 2009	SI 2008/2860
ss 112–115, 120 & 122–127 – register of members	1 October 2009	SI 2008/2860
ss 116–119 – inspection of register	1 October 2007	SI 2007/2194
ss 121 & 128 – removal of entries in register	6 April 2008	SI 2007/3495
ss 129–135 – overseas branch register	1 October 2009	SI 2008/2860
ss 136–144 – Prohibition on subsidiary being a member of holding company	1 October 2009	SI 2008/2860
ss 145–153 – Exercise of members' rights	1 October 2007	SI 2007/2194

s 154 – minimum number of directors	1 October 2007	SI 2007/2194
ss 155–159 – requirements for appointment as a director	1 October 2008	SI 2007/3495
ss 160 & 161 – directors	1 October 2007	SI 2007/2194
ss 162–167 – register of directors	1 October 2009	SI 2008/2860
ss 168 & 169 – removal of a director	1 October 2007	SI 2007/2194
ss 170–174 & 178–181 – directors' duties	1 October 2007	SI 2007/2194
ss 175–177 & 182–187 – directors' duties declarations of interest	1 October 2008	SI 2007/3495
ss 188–239 – transactions with directors and directors liabilities	1 October 2007	SI 2007/2194
ss 240–246 – directors' residential addresses	1 October 2008	SI 2008/2860
s 247 – power to make provision for employees	1 October 2008	SI 2008/2860
ss 248–269 & Sch 1 – directors minutes, shadow director, connected persons, derivative claims	1 October 2007	SI 2007/2194
ss 270–274 & 280 – company secretary	6 April 2008	SI 2007/3495
ss 275–279 – register of secretaries	1 October 2008	SI 2008/2860
ss 281–307, 310–326,327(1),(2)(a) and (b) and (3), 328 and 329, 330(1)–(5), (6)(a) and (b) and (7), 331 and 332, and 334–361 – resolutions and meetings	1 October 2007	SI 2007/2194
ss 308,309 and 333	20 January 2007	SI 2006/3428
ss 362–379 – control of political donations and expenditure (in respect of England, Wales & Scotland) (with exceptions for independent candidates)	1 October 2007	SI 2007/2194

ss 362–379 – control of political donations and expenditure (in respect of Northern Irelend) , with exceptions for independent candidates)	1 November 2007	SI 2007/2194
ss 362–367 and 378 – control of political donations and expenditure (in so far as not already in force)	1 October 2008	SI 2007/2194
ss 380–416, 418–462 and 464–474 – accounts and reports	6 April 2008 (generally for financial years starting on or after that date)	SI 2007/3495
s 417 – directors' report business review	1 October 2007 (for financial years beginning on or after that date)	SI 2007/2194
s 463 – directors' liability for false or misleading statements in narrative reports	20 January 2007	SI 2006/3428
ss 475–484 and 489–539 – audit and auditors	6 April 2008	SI 2007/3495
ss 485–488 – appointment of auditors of private companies	1 October 2007	SI 2007/2194
ss 540–543 and 545–640, 641(1)(b), 645–651 and 653 and 655–657 – share capital etc.	1 October 2009	SI 2008/2860
s 544 – transferability of shares	6 April 2008	SI 2007/3495
ss 641(1)(a) and (2)–(6) and 642–644, 654 – reduction of share capital supported by solvency statement	1 October 2008	SI 2008/1886
ss 610(2)–(4), 652(1) and (3) and 733(5) and (6) – so far as relating to a reduction in capital under the sections in the row above	1 October 2008	SI 2008/1886

ss 658–737 (except as noted in the row above) – acquisition by a limited company of its own shares	1 October 2009	SI 2008/2860
ss 738–754 – debentures	6 April 2008	SI 2007/3495
ss 755–760 – prohibition on public offers by private companies	6 April 2008	SI 2007/3495
ss 761–767 – minimum share capital for public companies	6 April 2008	SI 2007/3495
ss 768–790 – certification & transfer of securities	6 April 2008	SI 2007/3495
ss 791–810, 811 (1)–(3), 813 and 815–828 – Information about interests in a public company's shares	20 January 2007	SI 2006/3428
ss 811(4), 812, and 814 – inspection of interests disclosed	6 April 2008	SI 2007/3495
ss 829–853 – distributions	6 April 2008	SI 2007/3495
ss 854–859 – annual return	1 October 2009	SI 2008/2860
ss 860–894 – company charges	1 October 2009	SI 2008/2860
ss 895–941 – Arrangements and reconstructions	6 April 2008	SI 2007/3495
ss 942–992 & Sch 2 – takeovers	6 April 2007	SI 2007/1093
ss 993–999 – fraudulent trading & unfair prejudice	1 October 2007	SI 2007/2194
ss 1000–1034 – dissolution & restoration to the register	1 October 2009	SI 2008/2860
ss 1035–1039 – company investigations	1 October 2007	SI 2007/2194
ss 1040–1042 – UK companies not formed under companies legislation	1 October 2009	SI 2008/2860
s 1043 – unregistered companies	6 April 2007	SI 2007/1093
ss 1044–1059 – overseas companies	1 October 2009	SI 2008/2860

ss 1060–1062, 1063 so far as not already in force, 1064–1067, 1068(1)–(4), (6) and (7) and 1069–1076, 1081–1084, 1093–1101, 1108–1110 and 1112–1120 – registrar of companies etc.	1 October 2009	SI 2008/2860
s 1063 (in respect of England, Wales & Scotland) – registrar's fees	6 April 2007	SI 2006/3428
s 1068 (except subsection (5)) for limited purposes – registrar's requirements	15 December 2007	SI 2007/2194
s 1068(5), 1077–1080, 1085–1092, 1102–1107 and 1111 – delivery to registrar by electronic means, public notice of receipt of documents & the register, inspection of the register, language/translation & certification requirements	1 January 2007	SI 2006/3428
s 1117 (for the purpose of enabling the exercise the registrar to make rules)	6 April 2008	SI 2007/3495
ss 1121–1123 (as they apply to offences under Part 14 or 15 of the Companies Act 1985)	1 October 2007	SI 2007/2194
ss 1121–1123, 1125 and 1127–1133 – offences under the Companies Acts	1 October 2009	SI 2008/2860
s 1124 & Sch 3 – amendments to the Companies Act 1985 relating to certain offences	1 October 2007	SI 2007/2194
ss 1125–1133 (as they apply to certain offences under Part 14 or 15 of the Companies Act 1985)	1 October 2007	SI 2007/2194
s 1126 – consents for certain prosecutions	6 April 2008	SI 2007/3495
ss 1134–1136, 1137(2), (3), (5)(a), 1139–1142, 1149–1156, 1158–1160 and Sch 6, 1163, 1166, 1168, 1171, 1173, 1174 & Sch 8 – interpretation etc	1 October 2009	SI 2008/2860

s 1137(1), (4), (5)(b) and (6) – regulations about inspection of records	30 September 2007	SI 2007/2607
ss 1143–1148 & Schs 4 & 5 – supplying documents or information & electronic communications	20 January 2007	SI 2006/3428
s 1149–1156 – supplementary provisions	1 October 2009	SI 2008/2860
s 1157 – power of court to give relief	1 October 2008	SI 2007/3494
ss 1159 and1160 and Sch 6 so far as necessary for the purposes of ss 1209–1241 and 1245–1264 and Schs 10, 11 13 and 14 – meaning of 'subsidiary' for purposes of statutory auditor provisions	6 April 2008	SI 2007/3495
ss 1161 and 1162 and Sch 7, 1164 and 1165 – parent & subsidiary undertakings & banking & insurance company definitions	6 April 2008	SI 2007/3495
s 1167 – meaning of 'prescribed'	30 September 2007	SI 2007/2607
s 1169 – meaning of dormant company	6 April 2008	SI 2007/3495
s 1170 – meaning of 'EEA State'	6 April 2007	SI 2007/1093
s 1172 – references to requirements of Act	6 April 2008	SI 2007/3495
s 1173 (partially) – minor definitions	6 April 2008	SI 2007/3495
s 1175 (removal of special provisions about accounts & audit of charitable companies) so far as it relates to Part 7 of the Companies Act 1985 and Sch 9, Part 1	1 April 2009	SI 2008/674
ss 1176–1179 – minor amendments	6 April 2007	SI 2006/3428
ss 1180 and 1181 – minor amendments	1 October 2009	SI 2008/2860

ss 1181–1191 – company directors: foreign disqualification	1 October 2009	SI 2008/2860
ss 1192–1208 – business names	1 October 2009	SI 2008/2860
ss 1209–1241 and Schs 10 and 11 – statutory auditors	6 April 2008	SI 2007/3495
ss 1242–1244 and Sch 12 – third country auditors	29 June 2008	SI 2007/3495
ss 1245–1264 and Schs 13 and 14 – auditors provisions	6 April 2008	SI 2007/3495
ss 1265–1273 (with an exception, see s 1300) – transparency obligations etc.	8 November 2006	s 1300 of the Act
ss 1274 and 1276 – grants to bodies concerned with actuarial standards and application of the Act to Scotland & Northern Ireland	8 November 2006	s 1300 of the Act
s 1275 – levy to pay expenses of bodies concerned with actuarial standards etc.	1 October 2009	SI 2008/2860
ss 1277–1280 – various	1 October 2008	SI 2007/3495
s 1281 – disclosure of information under the Enterprise Act 2002	6 April 2007	SI 2006/3428
s 1282 – expenses of winding up	6 April 2008	SI 2007/3495
s 1283 – commonhold associations	1 October 2009	SI 2008/2860
s 1284 so far as it relates to Part 2 of the Companies (Audit, Investigations and Community Enterprise) Act 2004 – extension of Companies Acts to Northern Ireland	6 April 2007	SI 2007/1093
s 1284(2) (partially) – extension of Companies Acts to Northern Ireland	1 October 2008	SI 2007/3495
ss 1284–1287 – (Northern Ireland)	1 October 2009	SI 2008/2860
ss 1288–1297 except s 1295 and Sch 16 (repeals) – general supplementary provisions	8 November 2006	s 1300 of the Act

s 1295 and Sch 16 (partially) – repeals	1 and 20 January 2007, 6 April & 1 October 2007	SI 2006/3428
		SI 2007/1093
	1 & 6 April & 1 October 2008	SI 2007/2194
		SI 2007/3495
	1 October 2009	SI 2008/674
		SI 2008/2860
ss 1298–1300 – title, extent & commencement	8 November 2006	s 1300 of the Act
ss 1298–1300 – title, extent & commencement	8 November 2006	s 1300 of the Act
ss 2, 1068(1)–(4), (6) and (7), 1114, 1117, 1120, 1168, 1173 and 1284 so far as necessary for the purposes of the provisions brought into force on 1 January 2007	1 January 2007	SI 2006/3428
ss 2, 1121 and 1122, 1125,–1131, 1133,1168, 1173 and 1284 so far as necessary for the purposes of the provisions brought into force on 20 January 2007	20 January 2007	SI 2006/3428
ss 546, 558, 1060 and 1061, 1121–1123, 1125–1135, 1138–1140, 1168, 1173 and 1284 so far as necessary for the purposes of the provisions brought into force on 6 April 2007	6 April 2007	SI 2006/3428
		SI 2007/1093
ss 17, 385, 540(1) and (4), 545, 546, 548, 629, 1121, 1122, 1125, 1127–1133, 1158, 1168, 1173 and 1284 so far as necessary for the purposes of the provisions brought into force on 1 October 2007	1 October 2007	SI 2007/2194
ss 546, 1158,1173 and 1284 so far as necessary for the purposes of the provisions brought into force on 1 November 2007	1 November 2007	SI 2007/2194

ss 1168 and 1284 so far as necessary for the purposes of the provisions brought into force on 15 December 2007	15 December 2007	SI 2007/2194
ss 17, 540(1) and (4), 545, 546, 548, 629, 1121–1123, 1125, 1127–1133, 1139, 1140, 1168 and 1173 (partially) so far as necessary for the purposes of the provisions brought into force on 6 April 2008	6 April 2008	SI 2007/3495
s 1284 so far as necessary for the purposes of the provisions brought into force on 6 April 2008 except ss 1209–1241 and 1245–1264 and Schs 10, 11, 13 and 14	6 April 2008	SI 2007/3495
s 1284 so far as necessary for the purposes of the provisions brought into force on 1 October 2008	1 October 2008	SI 2007/2194 SI 2007/3495
ss 1121–1123, 1125, 1127–1133, 1168 and 1173 (partially) so far as necessary for the purposes of the provisions brought into force on 1 October 2008 except ss 1277–1280	1 October 2008	SI 2007/3495
The provisions of the Act , so far as not brought into force by s 1300(1) of the Act, or by arts 2 and 3(1) and (2) of SI 2006/3428, for the purpose of enabling the exercise of powers to make orders or regulations by statutory instrument	20 January 2007	SI 2006/3428

Appendix 4

TABLE OF MAIN CHANGES TO ANNUAL AND EVENT DRIVEN COMPLIANCE FOR PRIVATE COMPANIES

Annual compliance

Provision under previous legislation	*New provisions*	*Sections in Act*
Requirement for company secretary	Company secretary now an optional appointment for a private company – if appointed, requirements apply re notification to Registrar and register of secretaries. Secretary can have a service address	ss 270 and 274–280
Annual General Meeting	Not required for a private company (but is required for a public company)	ss 1295 and Sch 16 and ss 336–354
Presentation of annual accounts to a meeting	Not required for a private company, but accounts (or a summary financial statement) must still be circulated within time limits (but presentation of annual accounts etc is still required for a public company)	ss 423–440, 1295 and Sch 16
Annual re-appointment of auditors	If auditors are not to be appointed for any financial year, the directors must reasonably resolve otherwise on the ground that audited accounts are unlikely to be required Auditors may need to be re-appointed by the members in some circumstances (eg if appointed by the directors)	ss 485–488

Provision under previous legislation	*New provisions*	*Sections in Act*
Elective resolutions	Abolished	s 1295 and Sch 16
Annual accounts to be delivered to the Registrar within 10 months	Annual accounts to be delivered to the Registrar within 9 months (also modifications to 'same day rule')	ss 441–453
Keep Register of directors and notify changes to the Registrar	Service addresses for directors Changed content (service addresses, usual country of residence and details of former names) Every company must have at least one director who is a natural person No director under 16	ss 154–167
Register of directors	Keep additional register of directors usual residential addresses, to which there is restricted access and notify changes to the Registrar	ss 165, 167 and 240–246
Keep a register of directors' interests in shares	No longer required	s 1177
Keep registers at registered office	Keep registers at registered office or at a place specified in regulations	Various
Right to inspect and have copies of register of members	Person making request must provide required information (subject to criminal penalty for false information) and company can apply to court to prevent inspection etc	ss 116–120
Keep register of members, records of resolutions and minutes of members and directors meetings etc	Entries in register of members can be removed after 10 years and records of resolutions, minutes etc to be kept for 10 years	ss 121, 248 and 355

Provision under previous legislation	New provisions	Sections in Act
	Limitation of directors' liability in relation to directors' report etc	s 463
Signature of audit report	Signature of audit report by senior statutory auditor on behalf of the firm	ss 503–506
	Provision for liability limitation agreement with the auditor	ss 532–538

Event related compliance

Provision under previous legislation	New provisions	Sections in Act
Company formation	Any company may be formed by one subscriber	ss 7–16, 31, 154-159, 162-166 and 270
	Memorandum reduced to prescribed form	
	Model articles apply for limited companies unless company delivers articles that exclude or modify	
	Company secretary optional	
	At least one director must be a natural person	
	No director under 16	
	Directors' service addresses	
	Abolition of statutory authorised share capital	
	Statement of capital and initial shareholdings	
	Statement of compliance replaces statutory declaration	
	New companies have unrestricted objects unless the articles specifically restrict them	
	Notify to Registrar details of any change to particulars contained in register of directors' residential addresses within 14 days	s 167

Provision under previous legislation	New provisions	Sections in Act
Change of name by special resolution	Change of name by special resolution or as provided by company's articles. In either case, an additional notice is now required for the Registrar. Provision for conditional resolutions	ss 77–81
	Possibility of objection to company names adjudicators etc in respect of company name infringing goodwill	ss 69–74
Registrar to be sent copy of amended memorandum and articles	If failure to send copy of amended articles, Registrar can require by notice, failure to comply within 28 days results in automatic £200 civil penalty	ss 26 and 27
Document signed by two directors (or by director and company secretary) is executed by the company	A document can be executed by a company if it is signed on behalf of the company by a director in the presence of a witness who attests the signature (or by two authorised signatories, who are directors and secretary)	s 44
	Provision may be made in articles allowing a member to nominate another person to enjoy or exercise membership rights	s 145
Common law provisions	Codification of directors duties and related items must be considered (especially s 172 duty to promote success of the company and s 175 duty to avoid conflicts of interest)	ss 170–187
Common law provisions	Note codification of derivative claims procedures	ss 260–269

Provision under previous legislation	*New provisions*	*Sections in Act*
Provisions intended to deal with situations where a director has a conflict of interest	Replacement provisions contain a number of changes. Loans to directors permitted subject to members' approval	ss 188–226
	New definition of director's service contract that must be kept available for inspection	s 227
Unanimous written resolutions of the members	New provisions regarding written resolutions – by majority but additional requirements including time limit, circulation etc; new possibilities regarding assent	ss 288–300 and 1146
Special resolutions require 21 days notice	All meetings of private companies (including those at which special resolutions are to be proposed) require 14 days notice (unless 'special notice' is required in accordance with s 312)	ss 307, 360 and 312
Extraordinary resolutions	Extraordinary resolutions are abolished	
Meetings of shareholders	Statutory provisions regarding meetings of shareholders, proxies etc – some can be modified by articles, but not all	ss 318–335
Communication with shareholders and to the company	New provisions regarding electronic communication with shareholders etc and deemed consent to such communication	ss 308, 333, 1143–1148 and Schs 4 & 5

Provision under previous legislation	New provisions	Sections in Act
Authorised share capital	Statutory concept of authorised share capital is abolished but may be retained in the articles (and will be so retained for existing companies unless resolved otherwise by the members)	
	New provisions requiring delivery of a statement of capital to the Registrar if the share capital changes	Various
Prohibition on reduction of issued share capital unless a court order was obtained	Additional possibility of reduction of issued share capital by special resolution and solvency statement	ss 641–644
Requirement for directors to be given authority to allot shares	Directors of a private company having one class of shares given authority by statute (subject to articles)	ss 549–551
Prohibition on a private company giving financial assistance for the purchase of its shares – subject to a 'whitewash' procedure that allowed it if the procedure was followed	Abolition of the statutory prohibition of a private company giving financial assistance for the purchase of its shares, but provisions still apply to public companies	ss 677–683
Subdivision and consolidation of share capital	Changed provisions regarding the subdivisions and consolidation of share capital	ss 617–619
	New provisions enabling a company to redenominate its shares into a different currency	ss 622–628

Provision under previous legislation	New provisions	Sections in Act
Issue of redeemable shares	New provisions for determining the terms, conditions and manner of redemption of redeemable shares	ss 684 and 685
	If a company refuses to register a transfer, it must provide the transferee with such further information about the reasons for the refusal as the transferee may reasonably request	s 771
	Statutory confirmation that if a company has profits available for distribution, it may transfer assets at book value without making an unlawful distribution	ss 845 and 846
	New additional procedure for administrative restoration of a company that has been struck off that may be used if the strike off was instigated by the Registrar	ss 1024-1028
Possibility of applying to restore a company to the register for 20 years after striking off	The period to apply to the court for restoration of a company has been standardised at 6 years (or at any time for the purpose of bringing proceedings against the company for damages for personal injury) for both liquidation and striking off	s 1030

Appendix 5

USEFUL CONTACT DETAILS AND WEB ADDRESSES

Organisation	Address	Website(s) and telephone no's
Companies House Cardiff	Companies House Crown Way Maindy Cardiff CF14 3UZ	www.companieshouse.gov.uk/ London Information Centre opening hours – Monday to Friday 8.30am – 5.00pm
Companies House Edinburgh	Companies House 37 Castle Terrace Edinburgh EH1 2EB	You can get in touch with the Companies House Contact Centre on 0303 1234 500, Minicom – 02920 381245 or by email at enquiries@companies-house.gov.uk Lines are open 08:30 – 18:00 UK time Monday to Friday, except national holidays
Companies House London	Companies House Executive Agency 21 Bloomsbury Street London WC1B 3XD	
Companies Registry Northern Ireland (part of the Department of Enterprise, Trade and Investment)	Customer Counter 1st Floor, Waterfront Plaza, 8 Laganbank Road, Belfast BT1 3BS	http://www.detini.gov.uk Open to personal callers from 10.00 am to 4.00 pm Monday to Friday excluding Public and Bank Holidays Tel: Contact Centre 0845 604 8888

Organisation	Address	Website(s) and telephone no's
Department for Business, Enterprise & Regulatory Reform (BERR)	Department for Business, Enterprise & Regulatory Reform 1 Victoria Street London SW1H 0ET	www.berr.gov.uk There is a specific page relating to the Companies Act 2006 at www.berr.gov.uk/whatwedo/ businesslaw/co-act-2006/index.html You can call the DTI on: 020 7215 5000 Minicom: 020 7215 6740 or by email at enquiries@berr.gsi.gov.uk
HM Revenue & Customs	See website	www.hmrc.gov.uk
United Kingdom Legislation		http://www.opsi.gov.uk/legislation/ uk.htm
Institute of Chartered Secretaries and Administra-tors (ICSA)	16 Park Crescent London W1B 1AH UK	http://www.icsa.org.uk/ Tel: (+44) 020 7580 4741 Fax: (+44) 020 7323 1132 E-mail: info@icsa.co.uk
Charity Commission	Charity Commission Direct PO Box 1227 Liverpool L69 3UG	www.charitycommission.gov.uk To speak to an advisor call Charity Commission Direct on 0845 3000218 Staff are available to take your calls between 0800-2000hrs from Monday to Friday and 0900-1300hrs on Saturdays (except national holidays) Minicom service on 0845 300 0219
Treasury Solicitor (Restora-tions)	The Treasury Solicitor One Kemble Street London WC2B 4TS	General: www.tsol.gov.uk *Guide to company restoration (including tel no)* www.tsol.gov.uk/Publications/ companyrest.pdf *Bona vacantia division* www.bonavacantia.gov.uk

Organisation	Address	Website(s) and telephone no's
The CIC Regulator	The CIC Regulator CIC Team Room 3.68 Companies House Crown Way Maindy Cardiff CF14 3UZ	http://www.cicregulator.gov.uk/ Email: cicregulator@companieshouse. gov.uk Telephone: 029 20346228. This is a 24-hour voicemail service.
The Intellectual Property Office	Concept House Cardiff Road Newport South Wales NP10 8QQ	http://www.ipo.gov.uk/ 0845 9500 505

INDEX

References are to paragraph numbers.